CLASSIC CHINESE CUISINE

CLASSIC CHINESE CUISINE

NINA SIMONDS

Houghton Mifflin Company Boston

Illustrations Carol Winstead Wood

Calligraphy Ifan Chiu

Library of Congress Cataloging in Publication Data
Simonds, Nina.
    Classic Chinese cuisine.
    Includes index.
    1. Cookery, Chinese. I. Title.
TX724.5.C5S59 641.5951 82-6037
AACR2
ISBN 0-395-32218-9
ISBN 0-395-36645-3 (pbk.)

M 10 9 8 7 6 5 4 3

Some of the material in this book appeared in a different form in *Gourmet* magazine.

ACKNOWLEDGMENTS

This book is the product of more than ten years of study, research, and experience. So many people have contributed by sharing their knowledge, expertise, and encouragement. I greatly regret that only a few can be mentioned by name.

My sincere thanks go to Huang Su Huei and the Chinese master chefs at the Wei-Chuan school in Taipei who all taught me so much during my years in Taiwan.

I am deeply grateful to *Gourmet* magazine for publishing my articles on Chinese cuisine, thereby providing the roots for this book. In particular, Zanne Zakroff, Kemp Miles, Gail Zweigenthal, Pat Bell, and Jane Montant deserve special mention.

I also must thank Debby Richards, my tireless assistant recipe tester; Linda Glick, my editor; Sarah Flynn, my meticulous copy editor; Judy Chiu of Chiu's Garden restaurant, Boston; Stella and Pickering Lee; Andrea Lee; Laurie Murphy; and Bob Somma.

On a more personal note, recognition should be given to Don Rose and the rest of my family for providing immeasurable help and support over the years. And, of course, I am grateful to *many* friends and students for their unflagging enthusiasm, which fueled my commitment to this project.

Lastly, I must express my deepest thanks to Ifan Chiu for his beautiful calligraphy and Carol Wood for her exquisite illustrations that grace this book.

A NOTE ABOUT ROMANIZATION

There are three main systems of romanization used for translating Chinese characters into English words: Pinyin, Yale, and Wade-Giles. The Pinyin system, which was officially adopted by the People's Republic of China in 1979, has been used for most of the Chinese words in this book, including the recipe titles. In some cases (such as with the names of the dynasties and other notable proper nouns), the more familiar Wade-Giles spellings have been used.

CONTENTS

INTRODUCTION

For a foreigner in Taiwan whose basic Chinese vocabulary consisted of the words "hello," "good-bye," "thank you," and "no MSG," the phrase *Ni chi bao le mei you?* was extremely useful. This salutation is uttered when greeting a relative or friend; it often begins a telephone conversation; and it is frequently blurted out at acquaintances when further conversation is impossible. Although the phrase symbolizes a wish of well-being, translated literally it means "Have you eaten yet?" For a nineteen-year-old woman who had grown up fascinated by all aspects of food and who had traveled to the Orient to study Chinese cuisine, this sentence was a revelation. Clearly, I had come to the right place.

I grew up in New England in a family for whom food had always held a special importance. While most parents are content to read fairy tales to their children at bedtime, my father would bundle the four of us, pajama-clad and squeaky clean from our evening baths, into our beds and then describe, in mouth-watering detail, the various delicacies sampled on his latest business trips. By the age of five, we were all well versed in the subtleties of cold stone crab with mustard sauce and familiar with the heady fragrance of fried *saganaki*.

It was hardly surprising that after one uninspiring year in college, I decided to reassess my goals and steer myself toward a food-oriented career. An introductory course in Mandarin and a growing fascination with Chinese cuisine led me to Taiwan, where for three and a half years I apprenticed in restaurant kitchens with some of Taipei's foremost chefs. Many of these professionals were the finest of the Chinese master chefs who had fled from China after the revolution. I was overjoyed to discover that in Taiwan all of the various regional flavors of China had been preserved and the excellent standards of expertise and quality had been admirably maintained. The restaurants of Taipei were an ideal training ground for studying authentic Chinese cuisine.

During that time, I translated several cookbooks with Huang Su Huei, a renowned authority on Chinese food. I lived with a Chinese family and for the first time in my life was surrounded by a nation of people whose preoccupation with food outdid my own.

The Chinese fascination with food dates back to the beginning of an established culture. Ancient Chinese society held men with a refined knowledge of food and drink in high esteem. In *Food in Chinese Culture*, K. C. Chang relates that I Yin, a prime minister of the Shang dynasty (eighteenth century B.C. to twelfth century B.C.) and once a chef, apparently initiated his political career on the strength of his cooking prowess.

At a time when most other cultures regarded food solely in terms of basic survival, Chinese cuisine was well developed, and correct preparation, service, and consumption were an essential part of social behavior. In his writings, Confucius placed great emphasis on food and helped to establish the refined standards of Chinese cuisine that have endured to this day. By the Han dynasty (206 B.C. to A.D. 220), the *Li chi*, the most extensive handbook of ritual and social behavior ever compiled, was widely in use. Some of the earliest written recipes and rules of conduct for meals appear in this volume. A section titled "Five Points to Ponder at Meals for Scholarly Gentlemen" gives guidelines for "Taking Food as a Means of Attaining Tao":

> The superior person does not for one moment act contrary to virtue, not even for the space of a single meal. He first adopts the right posture, makes the proper table arrangements and reflects on his own adequacy before he takes any food.

Through the centuries, food has been the inspiration for innumerable Chinese scholars, artists, and poets. One of the earliest examples is a poem written in 200 B.C. by Chü Yuan as an appeal to the departing soul of a beloved king. Culinary delicacies, in appetizing detail, are mentioned in an attempt to lure him back to life.

A modern poem, written in the nineteenth century, shows the same lusty appreciation of good food:

Suzhou, the good place. In summer
Plump fish dart about the river
Avoiding the fisherman's boat
Purple crabs and red wine dregs
Make the autumn pass.
When waxy meats and sturgeon appear
Carp and bream leap into the pot.

Food is an international language that can provide valuable clues to the history and culture of any country. This is particularly true of China, and it is my belief that insight into the history and philosophy of food in ancient China contributes to the understanding of modern Chinese cuisine and culture. Accordingly, I have tried to acquaint the reader with the stories behind the food, relating the origin of the dishes, their symbolic importance, and their significance in the contemporary Chinese diet. The recipes have been carefully selected from the repertory of classic Chinese dishes to represent a sampling of traditional specialties from all parts of China. Although refined by chefs throughout the centuries and slightly adapted to modern methods, many of these dishes were originally conceived and developed in ancient China.

In China, more than in any other culture, food and civilization are synonymous. I hope this book will contribute to an understanding of both.

Nina Simonds

CLASSIC CHINESE CUISINE

THE PEOPLE'S REPUBLIC OF CHINA

Heilongjiang

Jilin

Liaoning

Inner Mongolia

BEIJING

TIANJIN

Hebei

Xinjiang

Gansu

Ningxia

Shanxi

Shandong

Qinghai

Gansu

Shaanxi

Henan

Jiangsu

SHANGHAI

Anhui

Zhejiang

Tibet

Hubei

Sichuan

Hunan

Jiangxi

Fujian

Guizhou

Yunnan

Guangxi

Guangdong

Taiwan

The Northern School   The Eastern School   The Western School   The Southern School

Base map courtesy Eurasia Press

THE BASICS

THE REGIONAL FLAVORS

China is a vast country and each region has developed its own distinct culinary style. Geography, climate, and the availability of ingredients are just a few of the factors that influence and shape each area's cuisine.

Generally speaking, China is divided into four main culinary schools: the northern school, encompassing Peking, the northern provinces (including Shandong, Hebei, and Shanxi, among others), and Mongolia; the western school, comprising Sichuan, Hunan, Guizhou, and Yunnan; the eastern school, made up of Shanghai, Zhejiang, Jiangsu, and Fujian (sometimes this school is divided in two, with Fujian counted as another regional school); and the southern school of Guangdong and Guangxi.

THE NORTHERN SCHOOL
This is probably the most eclectic regional cuisine; it incorporates provincial dishes of the northern provinces, Imperial Palace and Peking delicacies, and Mongolian and Moslem dishes.

The vast plains that cover most of this area do little to protect it from the frigid Siberian winter winds and the arid breezes from the Gobi Desert in the summer. Accordingly, the climate for most of this region is one of extremes. Shandong, a relatively sheltered province bordering the sea, enjoys a more temperate climate. This, in addition to its fertile terrain, makes it a major agricultural area: Wheat, barley, millet, corn, and soybeans are staple crops. A number of vegetables, particularly of the cabbage and gourd families, and fruits (such as pears, apples, grapes, and persimmons) thrive, and meat and poultry are plentiful. The long coastline of Shandong provides the area with a wealth of seafood. Because of the somewhat cool climate, wheat rather than rice is the primary staple crop and flour-based products such as steamed breads, pancakes, and noodles grace the tables for everyday meals.

1

The repertory of Palace dishes (which all figure notably in the northern school) is extensive and extremely varied. These dishes are the creations of the Palace chefs who came from all parts of China to serve the Imperial rulers. The chefs introduced ingredients and techniques from their respective regions, refining them still further for their illustrious audience. Some Palace dishes were created to suit the palates of the different ruling monarchs, and these dishes reflect the tastes and personalities of the individual emperors. Many of these recipes have survived intact and are served as they were many years ago.

Since the largest concentration of Moslems is situated in the north, the culinary style of this area has been greatly influenced by their tastes and habits. Moslems shun pork for religious reasons; as a result, there are a number of beef and lamb dishes in this cuisine. According to Kenneth Lo, an eminent authority on Chinese cooking, Peking often was called Mutton City because of the prevalence of lamb there. Mongolian influence, too, was a factor in shaping the regional style; the northern nomads introduced and popularized boiling, roasting, and barbecuing. Mongolian fire pot and Mongolian barbecue are two dishes that utilize these methods.

While northern cooking is often described as being light and delicate in contrast to the other cuisines, northerners relish such pungent seasonings as garlic, chives, scallions, leeks, star anise, and sweet bean sauce. Stir-frying, pan-frying, stewing, and braising, in addition to barbecuing and roasting, are the most popular cooking methods.

THE WESTERN SCHOOL

Moving in a southwesterly direction to the provinces of Sichuan and Hunan, one notices that the geography changes dramatically. The northern plains give way to majestic peaks and the arid climate is replaced by a sultry humidity. The meteorological calendar is characterized by steamy summers and mild winters. In this Land of Abundance, as it is sometimes called, subtropical fruits such as oranges, tangerines, and kumquats thrive. This is one of the major rice bowls of China. Sichuan province is the home of the panda, which lives in the thick bamboo groves, and the people here are partial to the tender bamboo shoots. Black mushrooms, wood ears, and silver tree ears are popular dried ingredients. The red chili pepper, by itself, in pastes, and infused in chili oil, provides the spice for a number of fiery dishes. Other pungent seasonings include Sichuan peppercorns, garlic, onions, dried tangerine peel, and gingerroot. Some theorize that the spicy cuisine developed as a result of the climate: The fiery seasonings create a natural air-conditioning effect. Others uncharitably conclude that the strong flavorings were used initially by the ancient Chinese to cover up the "off" flavors of food that had spoiled in the muggy heat. These same fiery seasonings — so the Sichuanese chefs maintain — sensitize the palate to the subtle nuances of flavor in the sauces. Flavorings and condiments are combined to create intricate blendings of hot, sour, sweet, and salty in one mouthful.

Although the western school is renowned for its hot and spicy specialties, there are a number of delicately flavored dishes. These platters are mostly banquet dishes that were introduced long ago by the Imperial Palace chefs who came from other provinces; they are generally reserved for special occasions and banquets.

While all cooking methods are used in this region, stir-frying and steaming seem to be especially popular.

THE EASTERN SCHOOL

The nicknames Heaven on Earth and The Land of Fish and Rice hint at the bounty and affluence of eastern China. The climate is basically subtropical, with warm, wet summers and cool winters, allowing a year-round growing season. Wheat, barley, rice, corn, sweet potatoes, and soybeans are the major staple crops. Numerous varieties of bamboo shoots, beans, melons, gourds, squashes, and leafy vegetables are found here, and peaches, plums, and grapes flourish. It was in this region that Chinese vegetarian cuisine was elevated to sophisticated heights, as a result of the wealth of ingredients and the expertise of the regional chefs.

The Yangtse River threads its way inland through the eastern provinces, and innumerable streams, ponds, and lakes provide the area with a host of freshwater species (crabs, shrimp, carp, and shad) in addition to creating a fertile breeding ground for geese, duck, and chicken. Because these provinces border the sea, salt-water products are also abundant.

Some notable ingredients and popular condiments from this region include Shaohsing wine, a high-quality yellow grain wine; soy sauce (the area is reputed to produce the best soy sauce in China); Chinkiang vinegar, a Chinese black vinegar used as a dipping sauce and as a condiment in numerous seafood dishes; and Jinhua ham, a type of cured ham known for its smoky flavor and scarlet color.

The seasonings of this regional style are unusually light and delicate to accentuate the natural flavors of the superior ingredients. For the same reason, eastern chefs are partial to stir-frying, steaming, red-cooking, and quick-simmering (blanching). Curing and pickling are used to preserve and flavor meat, chicken, and vegetables.

THE SOUTHERN SCHOOL

Touted by some as the haute cuisine of China, Cantonese cuisine is a subtle blending of delicate seasonings and ingenious technique. Canton, the capital of Guangdong province, has long been proclaimed a culinary mecca of China. An ancient Chinese proverb states: "If you like good food, go to Canton." Canton was an ancient trading port where wealthy Chinese merchants and foreigners resided in comfort, catering to their culinary whims. The city was said to breed gourmands with tastes for unusual foods: Frogs' legs, snakes, turtles, dogs, and game were popular. Ingredients and techniques from the West were incorporated into the regional cuisine.

The area is subtropical, with a lush, humid climate. The growing season extends year-round, as it does in the east, making it a major agricultural region. Vegetables grow abundantly and fruits such as bananas, pineapples, oranges, and lychees are readily available. The proximity of the sea provides a variety of fish and shellfish.

Cantonese chefs excel at a number of cooking methods: Steaming, blanching, barbecuing, roasting, and simmering are used in the preparation of various dishes. These chefs have an especially light touch with fresh, top-quality ingredients, and the foods are often slightly undercooked so as to accentuate the natural flavors.

Although *dim sum* are prepared all over China, the Cantonese are acknowledged as the true masters of this food form. These "dot the heart" treats include sweet and savory pastries, dumplings, soups, breads, cakes, and noodle dishes. *Dim sum* are featured in teahouses between eleven in the morning and two in the afternoon, but they may be eaten as snacks at any time of day.

CONDIMENTS, SEASONINGS, AND SPECIAL INGREDIENTS

A familiarity with the basic condiments and seasonings used in Chinese cuisine is essential. Gingerroot, scallions, garlic, star anise, and red pepper are just a few of the prominent flavorings. Many of these seasonings were first utilized by the ancient Chinese for their medicinal properties. According to ancient pharmacology, certain herbs and spices were believed to help prolong youth, restore waning sexual powers, and lengthen life.

The Chinese believe in harmony and balance in every aspect of life: Hot must complement cold and yin balance with yang. This philosophy applies to food as well, and seasonings play a prominent role in establishing this balance. Each food is classified as being hot (yang), meaning that the food has a stimulating effect on the body, or as cold (yin), implying a cooling or quieting effect. Chili peppers, beef, and pork, for instance, are considered to be hot foods, whereas duck and most seafoods are classified as cold. Many seasonings were originally paired with foods to neutralize the effects on the body. Hence, a "hot" flavoring was cooked or served with a "cold" food to create an overall balanced effect. Of course, there's no minimizing the importance of seasonings just for the flavor they impart to foods. Following is a glossary of some of the more prominent condiments, seasonings, and special ingredients used in Chinese cuisine. They have been divided into three major groups: Sauces, Spirits, Oils, and Pastes; Seasonings and Spices; and Selected Fresh and Pickled Vegetables.

SAUCES, SPIRITS, OILS, AND PASTES

CHILI PASTE AND HOT BEAN PASTE Chili paste (or sauce, depending on the manufacturer), made with mashed chili peppers, vinegar, and seasonings, and hot bean paste (a variation made with whole beans) both impart a fiery taste and a vibrant red color to dishes. A number of canned bean pastes tend to be salty; therefore, chili paste is recommended. It will keep indefinitely if refrigerated in a covered jar, but it is apt to lose its fiery intensity with age.

5

CHINESE RICE VINEGAR   The Chinese are partial to grain vinegars, which tend to be lighter and sweeter than Western vinegars. American and European vinegars are not acceptable substitutes. There are three main types of Chinese vinegar: white (clear), red, and black. Clear rice vinegar is used most frequently in sauces, pickling mixtures, and dressings; red vinegar is used mainly as a dipping sauce (especially for steamed crab); and Chinese black vinegar (the flavor of which resembles Worcestershire sauce) is commonly used as a dipping sauce and as an ingredient in the sauces of many seafood dishes. Although black vinegar is imported from Hong Kong, the mainland Chinese brand from Chinkiang is considered to have the best flavor.

DUCK (OR PLUM) SAUCE   A fruity, thick sauce with a sweet and tart flavor made from plums, apricots, vinegar, and sugar. In traditional Chinese cooking, duck sauce is primarily used as a dipping sauce in Cantonese cuisine — most notably with duck or goose. Refrigerated in a covered jar, it will keep indefinitely.

HOISIN SAUCE   This is the southern (Cantonese) variation of sweet bean sauce. It is made with fermented, mashed beans, salt, sugar, garlic, and, occasionally, pumpkin. The ingredients and flavor vary slightly with each manufacturer. Like its northern cousin, hoisin sauce is a thick, rich paste used as a flavoring in sauces, in marinades for roasted and barbecued meats, and as a dipping sauce. It will keep indefinitely if refrigerated in a covered jar.

OYSTER SAUCE   A pungently rich concentrate made from oysters, salt, soy sauce, and assorted seasonings. Once reduced to a thick paste, the sauce is cured. Oyster sauce is used primarily in Cantonese seafood dishes, where its unctuous consistency provides a richness and a delicate flavor. Oyster sauce will keep indefinitely in the refrigerator.

RICE WINE   Rice wine is a yellow grain wine that is used in all Chinese cooking. Shaohsing, a high-quality rice wine imported from Taiwan and China, is particularly flavorful. Many Oriental stores sell several types of rice wine for cooking, including *mirin*, a sweetened Japanese cooking wine. These are also acceptable. If

Chinese rice wine is unavailable, substitute a Japanese *sake,* Scotch, or a dry, white vermouth.

SESAME OIL   This amber-colored oil is extracted from roasted sesame seeds. Unlike the light-colored sesame oil found in many specialty shops and health-food stores, Chinese sesame oil has a strong, pungent flavor. It is used primarily as a seasoning in marinades, sauces, and dressings. Because of its overpowering taste and tendency to smoke when heated, sesame oil generally is not used as a cooking oil, except in certain vegetarian, beef, and lamb dishes.

SESAME PASTE   A thick, pungent nut butter made from roasted sesame seeds, sesame paste is primarily used in dressings in cold salads and noodle dishes. Peanut butter may be substituted. It will keep indefinitely in the refrigerator.

SOY SAUCE   Chinese soy sauce is available is three grades: light, medium, and heavy. Light soy sauce is delicate and slightly more subtle in flavor than the other varieties. Consequently, it is served as a dipping sauce and used in light-colored dishes and soups — such as with seafood and chicken. Medium, or thin, soy is darker and slightly thicker than light soy. This is an all-purpose soy sauce that is used for most cooking. Heavy, or thick, soy sauce is colored with molasses and used in rich, hearty dishes, such as stews, and with barbecued and roasted meats. If Japanese soy sauce is substituted, the quantity should be increased to taste, since it tends to be lighter and sweeter than most Chinese brands.

SWEET BEAN SAUCE   A thick paste with a salty-sweet flavor made from a fermentation of beans, salt, flour, and water. Northern Chinese are particularly partial to this condiment; they use it in sauces and meat marinades, and as a dipping sauce, particularly with Peking duck. There are a number of bean pastes made by the Chinese, including brown bean paste and yellow bean paste. The pastes may be smooth purées or contain whole beans. The various bean pastes differ in texture and flavor, but they may be used interchangeably. All will keep indefinitely stored in an airtight container in the refrigerator.

SEASONINGS AND SPICES

CHILI PEPPERS   Chili peppers are grown in several parts of China, but the hottest varieties and the thickest concentration are found in the provinces of Sichuan and Hunan. In both fresh and dried form, as well as in a paste, chili peppers are used to infuse dishes with a fiery seasoning. Chili oil, made from chili peppers, is added to dressings and used as a dipping sauce. It is sold in Chinese grocery stores, but a more flavorful version can be made at home: Heat 1 cup of sesame oil in a wok until smoking. Add 1 tablespoon Sichuan peppercorns, 6 stalks smashed scallions, 6 slices smashed ginger-root, and ½ cup ½-inch pieces of dried chili peppers. Turn off the heat, cover the mixture, and let it sit for 30 minutes. Strain out the seasonings and transfer the oil to a jar. Chili oil will keep indefinitely in a cool, dry place.

CHINESE CINNAMON BARK   Westerners are familiar with rolled cinnamon sticks (a good substitute for cinnamon bark), but the Chinese prefer to use thin slices of bark from the cassia tree for seasoning, braising, and stewing. Cinnamon bark is also ground and used in five-spice powder.

CHINESE HAM   The Chinese cure ham in a manner similar to that used for Smithfield hams. The flavors are similar and Smithfield ham may be used as a substitute. Chinese ham, with its salty, smoky flavor, is a popular seasoning in soups, as well as seafood, vegetable, and poultry dishes. Minced ham is also sprinkled on top of dishes as a garnish. When Chinese or Smithfield ham is unavailable, use an imported prosciutto.

CHINESE PARSLEY (CORIANDER)   A pungent, flat-leaf parsley that is used as a seasoning and garnish in soups, cold platters, and hot dishes, Chinese parsley is found in most Oriental markets and in some ethnic food stores. It will keep for up to five days, refrigerated, with the stems resting in water.

CHINESE SAUSAGE   Two types of Chinese sausage are available in Oriental grocery stores — pork and liver. Pork sausage is a red color, with a sweet, pungent flavor. (A recipe for homemade pork sausage appears on page 235.) Liver sausage, made of pork or duck liver, tends to be a brown color, is slightly sweeter than pork sausage, and has an unusual texture. Both varieties will keep indefinitely, wrapped in plastic, in the refrigerator or freezer.

DRIED CHINESE BLACK MUSHROOMS Dried mushrooms provide a strong, smoky flavor in Chinese dishes. They are available in several grades, and prices vary accordingly. The more expensive black mushrooms, with thick caps and a full, rich flavor, are usually "winter" black mushrooms. These are reserved for banquet dishes or recipes calling for whole caps. The thinner, less expensive mushrooms are used in dishes in which the caps are cut up. Fresh mushrooms are not an adequate substitute for dried Chinese black mushrooms. Store dried mushrooms in a cool, dry place in an airtight plastic bag with a dried chili pepper (to prevent worms).

DRIED TANGERINE OR ORANGE PEEL This is a pungent flavoring used as a seasoning in stir-fried and braised dishes. Usually the peel is reconstituted in hot water before being used in stir-fried dishes. The older the skin, the more prized the flavor. Homemade peel may be made by air-drying tangerine or clementine peels for several days. Store the peels indefinitely in a cool, dry place.

DRIED OYSTERS AND SCALLOPS Both oysters and scallops are dried and used as seasonings in soups, vegetable dishes, and stews. Dried scallops, in particular, are considered a delicacy. Both are sold by weight in Chinese grocery stores. Dried oysters should be soaked overnight in hot water to cover and rinsed thoroughly to remove any shells. Dried scallops should be rinsed, steamed for 30 minutes over high heat in ¼ cup water with 2 tablespoons of rice wine, and then shredded by hand. Both dried oysters and dried scallops will keep indefinitely if refrigerated in a plastic bag.

DRIED SHRIMP Miniature shrimp are preserved in a salty brine, dried, and used as a seasoning in soups and vegetable dishes. The shrimp are extremely pungent and should be used sparingly. Dried shrimp will keep indefinitely in a plastic bag in the refrigerator.

FENNEL SEED This is a licoricelike seasoning used in braised dishes and stews, and to lend a fragrance to tea-smoked dishes. Chinese herbalists also recommend fennel seed for stomach maladies.

9

FIVE-SPICE POWDER   A fragrant powder made with a number of spices that may include star anise, cinnamon, fennel, Sichuan peppercorns, cloves, and nutmeg, five-spice powder is used in marinades for meat and poultry, and, when combined with salt, as a dipping powder for deep-fried foods.

FERMENTED BLACK BEANS   A popular condiment made from black beans preserved in a salty brine and then dried, fermented black beans are available in plastic bags and in cans. While the beans themselves are quite salty and pungent, black bean sauce, made with fermented black beans and other seasonings, tends to be quite delicate and is used in seafood, poultry, meat, and vegetable dishes, where it accentuates the natural flavors of the foods. Packed in an airtight container and refrigerated, the beans will keep indefinitely.

GINGERROOT   A knobby stem (tuber rhizome) that grows underground, developing knuckles or "lobes," gingerroot is usually available in two forms: spring and mature. Spring gingerroot, which is available seasonally, has a papery skin, a delicate flavor, and pink tips. It is served in soups, pickled in a sweet-and-sour dressing, and sprinkled on top of dishes as a garnish. Mature gingerroot, which has a thick skin and a much stronger flavor, is used mainly as a seasoning to flavor and remove strong tastes, particularly in seafood. Gingerroot is also regarded for its medicinal properties and is said to cure colds, aid digestion, and revitalize the body. To store gingerroot, bury the unpeeled root in a pot of sand, or place it, peeled, in a jar of rice wine in the refrigerator. When a slice of gingerroot is called for, it should be about the size of a quarter.

GARLIC   One finds a liberal use of garlic in many Chinese dishes. Garlic cloves and the fresh green stalks are equally popular. Garlic is also credited with prolonging life and strengthening the body.

SCALLIONS   Scallions are a prime seasoning in Chinese cooking. The white part is usually reserved for flavoring, and the greens are used as a garnish. Thus, when you are directed to smash a scallion with the flat side of a cleaver, use only the white part, reserving the greens for other uses.

STAR ANISE   An eight-pointed star with a licoricelike flavor, this seasoning is used in marinades and in braised dishes and stews. Unlike European anise, which is from a bush, star anise is from a tree of the magnolia family. Some Chinese use star anise as a breath freshener or a digestive aid.

SICHUAN (SZECHWAN) PEPPERCORNS   Reddish-brown, open-husked peppercorns with a sharp, slightly numbing flavor, Sichuan peppercorns are used as a seasoning in marinades and sauces. Toasted lightly, pulverized, and added to salt, they become a dipping powder for deep-fried foods. Sichuan peppercorns will keep indefinitely in a cool, dry place.

SELECTED FRESH AND PICKLED VEGETABLES

BAMBOO SHOOTS   Few Americans are aware of the delightful flavor and variety of fresh bamboo shoots. In the Far East one has a choice of spring, summer, and winter shoots, whereas in the United States the selection is restricted to canned summer and winter shoots. Winter bamboo shoots are preferable, since the shoots are at their peak during that season. Because canned bamboo shoots have a very strong flavor, they should be plunged in boiling water and refreshed in cold water before being used. Store the shoots in cold water, refrigerated in a covered jar. If the water is changed once a week, they will keep for several weeks.

BEAN SPROUTS   There are two main types of bean sprouts used in Chinese cuisine: those made from mung beans (which are green) and those sprouted from soybeans (which are yellow). Mung bean sprouts are thinner, more delicate in flavor, and they require little or no cooking. They are used primarily in salads and stir-fried dishes. Soybean sprouts have a yellow tip (from the soybean), a stronger flavor, and they require a lengthier cooking time. These sprouts are used in braised dishes and soups. Canned bean sprouts are mushy and unacceptable. Unless directed otherwise, use mung bean sprouts when bean sprouts are called for. Store bean sprouts refrigerated in plastic bags. They will keep for five days to a week.

CHINESE CABBAGE   The Chinese cabbage family is extensive, and most Oriental markets carry a number of different varieties. Napa, with an oval head and full leaves, is used in a number of dishes, but it is especially fine for dumpling fillings, soups, and casseroles. Another type is celery cabbage, with an elongated head and a great deal of stem, which is appropriate for stir-fried dishes and salads. *Bok choy,* with fat stems and flowing green leaves that look somewhat like Swiss chard, is recommended for stir-fried dishes and soups. The small tender hearts of cabbages that are sold in most Oriental markets are excellent for braised dishes and as a decorative, edible vegetable garnish. All Chinese cabbages should be wrapped in plastic and refrigerated. They will keep for up to one week.

CHINESE GARLIC CHIVES   Chinese garlic chives, with flat stalks and a pronounced garlicky flavor, are used in soups, stir-fried dishes, noodles, and dumplings. There are two main types: yellow and green. Green garlic chives are available seasonally at most Oriental markets (if they are unavailable, an equal amount of scallion greens and some minced garlic may be substituted). Yellow garlic chives (which may be used interchangeably with green chives in soups, stir-fried dishes, and noodles) are found seasonally at selected markets.

CHINESE TURNIP (DAIKON RADISH)   While Chinese turnips are similar in texture to the Western radish, they tend to have a stronger taste and they are much bigger. The size of Chinese turnips varies. They are a popular vegetable in Chinese cooking and are used in salads, soups, stir-fried dishes, stews, and savory pastries. They will keep for up to two weeks if refrigerated in plastic wrap. Salted and dried in strips, Chinese turnip is used as a seasoning in stir-fried dishes and soups.

NORI (PURPLE LAVER)   Nori are thin, paperlike sheets of dried seaweed used in soups and rice dishes, and for wrapping foods. The color may be purple or deep green, depending on the manufacturer. It is available at most Oriental markets in packages of ten. Nori will keep indefinitely if wrapped tightly in plastic and refrigerated.

PICKLED CUCUMBERS Pickled cucumbers are ones that have been seeded, cut into strips, and preserved in a soy sauce brine. They are crisp, slightly salty, and refreshing. They are used as a seasoning in soups, stir-fried dishes, and salads. They are also served by themselves as a condiment. They are available in cans and will keep indefinitely if transferred to a jar and refrigerated.

RED-IN-SNOW This is a spinachlike vegetable that has been preserved in salt, giving it a pungent sour taste. Although preserved, the vegetable retains its original pleasing, crisp texture. Whole or minced, it is used as a flavoring in stir-fried dishes, soups, and steamed dumplings and buns. In some Chinese grocery stores red-in-snow is available fresh; in others it is available in cans. Packed in a tightly covered jar in the refrigerator, it will keep indefinitely.

SICHUAN (SZECHWAN) PRESERVED MUSTARD GREENS The Sichuanese preserve the central heart of a variety of cabbage green in salt, chili pepper, and assorted seasonings. Left to sit for several months, the knobby stems retain their crisp texture but acquire a hot, spicy flavor. This pickle is then used in soups and stir-fried dishes, or sprinkled on top of cold platters. Sichuan preserved mustard greens are sold in cans or by weight from huge, earthenware pickling crocks in Chinese grocery stores. They will keep indefinitely if refrigerated in a closed container.

STRAW MUSHROOMS Straw mushrooms, with their pointed caps and brownish-yellow body, have a flavor and texture unlike any other mushroom. They are available in cans — peeled and unpeeled. (I prefer the unpeeled because of their unusual bulblike shape.) The mushrooms will keep for about a week, refrigerated in jars with water to cover. Dried straw mushrooms, which have a mild flavor, are also available. They can be stored in the same manner as dried black mushrooms.

WATER CHESTNUTS The edible portion of the water chestnut is the starchy fruit of a water plant found in the tropics. The sweet, crunchy meat is covered with a tough, outer skin. Fresh water chestnuts, found in most Chinese markets, are eaten raw, candied, in sweet confections, and cooked in numerous savory dishes. For savory dishes, fresh water chestnuts should be peeled and cooked for 20 minutes in boiling water. Canned water chestnuts should always be plunged into boiling water and refreshed in cold water to remove the tinny flavor. Unpeeled fresh water chestnuts will keep (refrigerated, wrapped in plastic) for two weeks, whereas the peeled, tinned ones should be stored in water. These will keep a bit longer.

YARD-LONG STRING BEANS Although they hardly measure a yard in length, yard-long string beans tend to be about three times as long as their Western cousins. Some say that the flavor and texture of this bean is reminiscent of the French *haricot vert*. Yard-long string beans are available year-round at most Chinese markets. They will keep for up to a week wrapped in plastic in the refrigerator.

COOKING METHODS

Chinese cooking technique has been refined through the centuries to a high art form. Even in its earliest stages, the system of elaborately conceived cooking methods used in Chinese dishes suggested a level of sophistication that other cuisines lacked. The ancient Chinese chefs developed more than fifty different cooking processes with subtle variations in heat and technique. Obviously, it would be impossible to describe all of these methods; an explanation of those used most frequently in Chinese cooking is given below. These basic techniques serve as a foundation for all cooking, not just Chinese.

STIR-FRYING
CHAO

This is one of the fundamental methods used by Chinese chefs. Intensely high heat, organization, and expedience are key factors. All the preparations, including steps 1, 2, and 3, should be completed before the cooking begins.

1 The ingredients (that is, the meat, poultry, fish, seafood, vegetables) are cut to the desired size. Uniformity is stressed so that the food will cook evenly. Cut meat, poultry, or seafood usually is then

mixed with a marinade containing rice wine, cornstarch, and other ingredients, and left to marinate. This tenderizes and flavors the food. The cornstarch (potato starch, water chestnut flour, or arrowroot may be substituted) coats the food, sealing in the natural juices so that the cooked product will be tender and juicy.

2 The seasonings, such as garlic, scallions, and gingerroot, are cut and the sauce is assembled. Homemade chicken broth (see Chinese chicken broth on page 299) is often used as a base for sauces, but water or a good-quality canned broth may be used.

3 Any vegetables requiring partial cooking, such as broccoli, carrots, and snow peas, are parboiled or steamed, and immediately immersed in cold water to prevent them from overcooking and to keep their colors bright.

4 The wok is heated until very hot. This step is extremely important, as the food will stick to the pan if it has not been heated properly. The hot wok will transmit heat directly to the oil added to the pan, speeding up the process and thereby saving heat. To test the heat of the wok, a few drops of water are sprinkled on the surface. If they evaporate immediately, the wok is ready.

5 The proper amount of oil is added to the wok and heated until very hot; the oil should be swirled around the pan to lubricate the surface. Vegetable oils such as peanut, safflower, or corn oil are recommended, since they reach a very high temperature before smoking and the flavor of the cooked oil is good. (Chinese chefs usually use quite a bit of oil in this step, but the quantity is usually reduced for home use. Also, they use the oil over and over again, until it is all gone.)

6 The meat, poultry, or seafood (no more than a pound at a time) is turned in the hot oil, using the shovel to separate the pieces and keep them constantly in motion. Once the pieces of food turn color and separate, they are removed with the shovel and handled strainer, and drained. For beef, lamb, and pork, the oil should be extremely hot, about 400°, to tenderize, whereas for chicken, fish, and shellfish, a moderately hot (350°) oil is recommended.

7 A little oil is added to the hot pan and heated until very hot. The seasonings are added and stirred over high heat, mixing constantly until fragrant, so that the oil will be flavored by the seasonings.

8 The cooked meat, seafood, or poultry, the cooked vegetables, and the sauce are all added to the wok and tossed over high heat

until the ingredients are heated through and the sauce is boiling. (If the sauce does not already contain a thickener, it is added at this point.) Once the sauce has thickened, the dish is transferred to a platter and served immediately.

DEEP-FRYING
JIA

Most Westerners are surprised at the prevalence of oil and deep-frying in Chinese cooking. Deep-fried foods are popular because they are attractive and have a pleasing texture and taste. Their dry, crisp consistency complements wine and beer.

The green end of a scallion, or a chopstick, is often used to test the temperature of hot oil in deep-frying. Though this is not the most accurate method, the following signs give a fairly reliable reading: At 350°, the bubbles emerging from the scallion green or chopstick are quite small and slow-moving. There is no sound. At 375°, the bubbles are bigger, they appear more quickly, and there is a slight sizzling noise. At 400° to 425°, the bubbles are still bigger, they emerge at a furious pace, there is a distinctive sizzling noise, and the scallion tip turns golden brown. Of course, for greater accuracy a thermometer can be used.

Following are the steps used in deep-frying.

1   The food is cut to the desired shape and size, and usually marinated to tenderize and flavor.
2   For "dry-frying," the food is cooked without a coating. In "wet-frying," the food is dipped in a batter or coating made of cornstarch, egg whites, egg yolks, whole eggs, flour, or a combination of these ingredients.
3   The wok is heated until very hot; oil is added to the pan and heated to the proper temperature. Chinese deep-frying is usually done in two stages. The oil is heated to 350° and the food is placed in the hot oil by carefully rolling it down the sloping sides of the pan, in order to prevent the oil from splashing. The food is deep-fried until pale golden, then removed and drained on absorbent paper. (Other batches of the food are given the first frying at this point, then removed and drained. This step may be completed early in the day.)

4 The oil is reheated to a very hot temperature, about 425° or until smoking, and all the food is added a second time. In this stage, it is cooked until crisp and golden brown. This second frying removes any excess oil, sealing in the natural juices and leaving the food tender and juicy. The food is removed from the oil, drained on absorbent paper, arranged on a platter, and served immediately.

STEAMING
JENG

Steaming is a process used to cook a number of foods, including meat, poultry, seafood, vegetables, soups, buns, dumplings, and sweet and savory pastries. The ingredients should be of the finest quality and as fresh as possible, since the seasonings are usually light. Steaming tends to accentuate and complement the natural flavors of foods. There are two main methods of steaming: "open steaming" and "closed steaming." In closed steaming, the food is placed in a closed, heat-proof container, such as an earthenware pot, the edges are sometimes sealed with paper or a flour-and-water paste, the container is placed in a steamer made of either bamboo or metal, placed over boiling water, and steamed over high heat. Soups are often prepared in this manner, creating an intense flavor and unusually clear broth. In open steaming:

1 The food is cut, scored, or marinated, as directed in the recipe, and placed on a heat-proof plate, in a bowl, or directly on the steamer tray, which has been lined with moistened cheesecloth, muslin, or parchment paper. (The food may be placed in several steamer trays, which are stacked, and steamed simultaneously.)
2 A wok is filled with water level with the bottom edge of the steamer tray and heated until boiling.
3 The steamer tray is placed over the boiling water in the wok, the lid is placed over the steamer tray, and the food is steamed over high heat. The water should be boiling vigorously at all times. The water level should be checked periodically to make certain that it doesn't boil away. When food is steaming for a long time, a boiling kettle of water should be kept on the stove and extra water added when necessary. When more than one steamer tray is used, the order of the trays is reversed periodically to ensure even cooking.

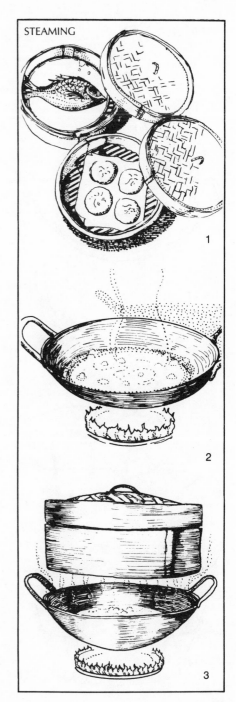

STEAMING

1

2

3

17

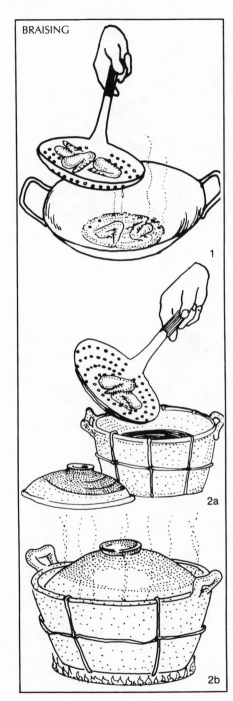

BRAISING

1

2a

2b

4 The food is steamed for the prescribed period, or until slightly underdone (it will continue to cook after it is taken from the steamer), removed to a platter and served, or served directly from the steamer.

COOKING IN LIQUID: BLANCHING, BRAISING, AND SIMMERING

Chinese cooks often divide their cooking methods into two major categories: cooking in oil and cooking in liquid. The "cooking in oil" methods include stir-frying, deep-frying, and the like, while the "cooking in liquid" category is more extensive and varied. Poaching, braising, simmering, and stewing are some of the methods. The liquid may be water, chicken broth, a salty brine, or a soy sauce—based mixture. There are a number of variations. An explanation of the more prominent "cooking in liquid" methods is given below.

Blanching
TANG

This process is similar to scalding; the food is cut as directed, then immersed briefly in boiling stock or water.

Braising
SHAO

1 The food is cut up, marinated (if necessary), and seared in hot oil. This step seals in the natural juices, colors the food to a deep golden brown, and gives the dish a rich flavor. The ingredients of the braising liquid are assembled and mixed.

2 The food is placed in a heavy pot or casserole with the braising liquid and prescribed seasonings (a). The liquid is heated until boiling and the heat is reduced to low, allowing the mixture to simmer slowly (b). The food is cooked until tender and the sauce is reduced until thick. The braising liquid may be dark, made with soy sauce, sugar, star anise, water, and other seasonings, or light, made with salt, seasonings, and water or chicken broth. (The term *red-cooked* refers to foods that are cooked slowly in a soy-based liquid or braising mixture. The soy sauce colors the food a rich, reddish brown — hence the name.)

3 The cooked food is transferred to a platter and served hot with the reduced sauce spooned over the top.

The same steps are followed in two variations of this method. In the first (*men*), a longer braising period is used and more sauce is added. In the second (*wen*), a thickener is added toward the end of the braising period.

Simmering
LU

This method differs slightly from braising in that the meat, poultry, or seafood most often is not seared prior to stewing.

1 The ingredients of the *lu*, or cooking marinade, are assembled and placed in a pot or casserole. The mixture may consist of soy sauce or salt, rice wine, sugar, star anise, fennel seed, tangerine peel, and Chinese cinnamon bark. The *lu* is cooked for a period to allow the flavors to intensify and marry.

2 The food (whole or in large pieces) is then added to the *lu* and simmered over low heat until tender. The food picks up the pungent flavors of the marinade. Food simmered in a *lu* is also sometimes said to be red-cooked. Such dishes are often served cold or at room temperature. When the food is served hot, some of the marinade is spooned over the top. The *lu* is saved and reused, and the seasonings and liquids are replenished periodically. It is believed that the flavor of the *lu* is enhanced with each use.

SMOKING
XUN

Smoking is not actually a cooking process; it is more a means for flavoring and coloring foods. The food is generally cooked prior to smoking (except for seafood and fish, which require little cooking) by boiling or steaming. Chinese chefs use two methods of smoking: tea-smoking (*xiong*), using tea leaves in the smoking mixture, and wood-smoking (*yen*), using wood chips. The smoking mixture may also include brown sugar, rice, and anise or fennel seed.

1   The food is marinated in a light mixture consisting of salt, rice wine, and seasonings, or a dark one, made of soy sauce, rice wine, sugar, and seasonings.

2   The food is cooked by boiling or steaming, and left to cool.

3   The wok and dome lid are covered with several layers of aluminum foil (a) and the smoking mixture is placed in the bottom of the wok. A smoking rack (or crisscrossed chopsticks) is placed at least 2 inches above the smoking mixture (b). The food is then arranged on the rack (c) and the wok is covered securely with the lid.

4   The wok is placed over high heat, and when the fragrance of smoke is detected, the timing begins and the food is smoked for the prescribed period. The wok is then removed from the heat and left undisturbed for 5 minutes. The food is removed (it should be golden brown), brushed with sesame oil, cut as directed, arranged on a platter, and served.

BARBECUING AND ROASTING
KAO AND SHAO

Chinese cooks do not use these methods as much as Western chefs because the necessary equipment and fuel are not always readily available. These two techniques are more popular in northern China and in Canton.

In barbecuing, the food is generally marinated (to tenderize, flavor, and provide a coating), skewered or put on a spit, and cooked over an open fire. The intense heat seals in the natural juices and cooks the outside to a crusty, charcoal brown. The food is then removed, sliced, and served.

In roasting, the food is usually marinated, then placed or hung in some type of oven or closed, heated container. All surfaces of the food are exposed to the heat so that it cooks evenly. Once cooked, the food is removed, cut, and served.

SMOKING

3a

3b

3c

4

CUTTING TECHNIQUES

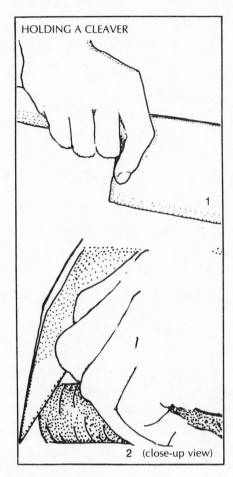

HOLDING A CLEAVER

1

2 (close-up view)

HOLDING A CLEAVER
Grasp the cleaver firmly by the handle with the thumb and index finger of your hand on the blade (1). This position will improve control and manipulation of the knife. Curl the fingers of the opposite hand so that the tips will not be exposed to the blade. Lightly lean the cleaver against your knuckles and the middle joints of the curled fingers. Cut, pushing forward with a decisive motion (2).

SCORING
This technique is used to tenderize foods, to create attractive shapes, and to even out the thickness, ensuring uniform cooking.

Grasp the cleaver firmly by the handle and lightly cut across the food, being careful not to cut completely through it.

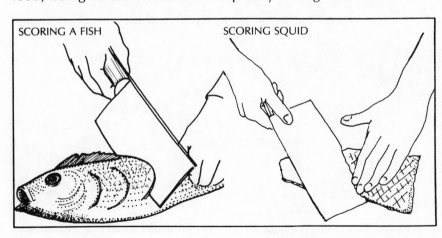

SCORING A FISH   SCORING SQUID

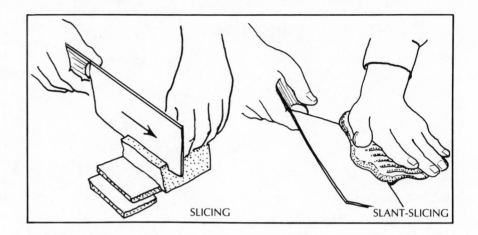

SLICING   SLANT-SLICING

SLICING

Foods such as meat and chicken are partially frozen before being cut into paper-thin slices to make cutting easier. Foods may be cut directly across the grain for tenderizing meats or on the diagonal (slant-slicing) to extend the cooking surface and create decorative shapes.

Holding the food firmly in one hand, push the blade forward straight across the grain or on the diagonal. Let the slice fall naturally as it is cut.

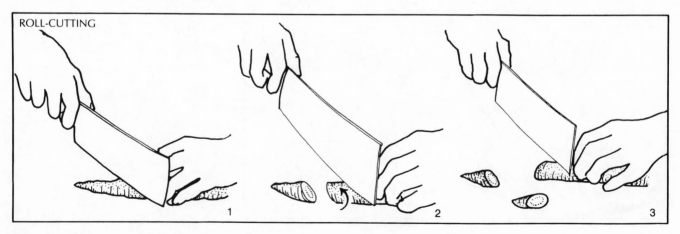

ROLL-CUTTING

1

2

3

ROLL-CUTTING

This technique is used primarily for root vegetables (carrots, turnips, radishes, and cucumbers) to extend the cooking surface and to create decorative shapes.

Holding the food firmly with one hand, push the cleaver across the food with a decisive motion, cutting on the diagonal (1). Give the food a quarter turn (2) and slice again on the diagonal (3).

SHREDDING

Shreds evolve from slices. Sizes vary from a large julienne (the size of a matchstick) to as fine as a toothpick.

Holding the food firmly, slice, across the grain, cutting with a decisive motion. Let the slices fall naturally as they are cut; they should be stacked in an orderly fashion, domino-style. Cut several stacked slices at a time into long, thin, uniform strips.

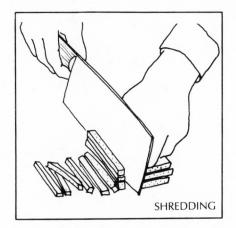

SHREDDING

DICING

Dices evolve from strips. The size may vary, but it is generally about ¼ to ½ inch square. Whatever the size, uniformity is crucial.

Holding the food firmly, cut, across the grain, into thick slices. The slices should fall naturally so that they are stacked in an orderly fashion, domino-style. Cut the slices into long, uniform strips. Gather the strips together neatly and cut them crosswise into cubes or dice.

DICING

MINCING

Minces evolve from shreds. Usually two cleavers are used in the final step to speed up the process.

Holding the food firmly, cut, across the grain, into paper-thin slices, cutting forward with a decisive motion. Let the slices fall naturally so that they are stacked in an orderly fashion, domino-style. Cut the food into thin, uniform strips, then into tiny dices. Chop the dices repeatedly until the food is in tiny pieces.

MINCING

A WORD ABOUT EQUIPMENT

Chinese food can be prepared with the most rudimentary tools. With a bit of imagination and ingenuity, you can substitute a frying pan for a wok, and a spaghetti pot and pie plate can become a makeshift steamer. Following are brief descriptions and some suggestions concerning the more traditional tools.

WOK AND DOME LID

This all-purpose cooking vessel is used for stir-frying, steaming, smoking, deep-frying, braising, and poaching. The pan is designed with long, sloping sides to create an extended cooking surface and for easy tossing of ingredients. The dome lid is used for steaming, braising, and as a shield to protect the cook from splashing oil when first placing the food in hot oil.

Woks are available in a number of sizes and are made from various metals. Light iron woks, manufactured in the Orient and available in some Oriental specialty shops, conduct heat most efficiently. Rolled steel woks, the most common type found in shops, are a very suitable substitute. These heavier pans are preferable because they conduct heat most efficiently and evenly. Stainless steel and light aluminum woks are to be avoided because both conduct heat unevenly. For most cooking, a 14- or 16-inch wok is recommended; with anything smaller, the surface area is too limited. Gas is the best kind of heat (the more powerful the fire, the better). An electric stove can be used, but a flat-bottomed wok is recommended in this case, since it hugs the burner, preventing loss of heat.

Electric woks are available, but they are best reserved for tabletop cooking. For the most part, they do not get hot enough for proper stir-frying and deep-frying. They can be used somewhat satisfactorily for steaming and braising, however, since they maintain an even, constant temperature.

TO SEASON A NEW WOK:

1   Scrub the pan thoroughly to remove any lacquer or protective coating that may have been put on the pan by the manufacturer to prevent it from rusting in the store. Dry the pan thoroughly.

2   Pour a generous amount of peanut, safflower, or corn oil (about 2 cups) into the wok and swirl it around to make sure the entire pan is thoroughly coated with the oil.

3   Place the pan over medium heat and heat until the oil begins to smoke, swirling occasionally to lubricate the surface with the oil. Turn off the heat and let the pan sit until cool.

4   Swirl the oil again to coat the surface of the wok. Heat it over medium heat until the oil begins to smoke, swirling occasionally. Turn off the heat and let the pan cool. Repeat this step two or three times.

TO CLEAN A WOK:

1   Wash the pan with a bamboo cleaner or a dishwashing brush, using hot water and a mild dishwashing liquid. Rinse thoroughly.

2   Place the pan over high heat until completely dry.

3   If the pan rusts, wipe the surface with an oil-soaked paper towel before storing.

STEAMERS

There are a number of layered steamers available — made of stainless steel, aluminum, or bamboo. The traditional Chinese bamboo steamer, with two layers and lid, is recommended over the other types. Bamboo absorbs the steam so that it doesn't condense on the lid and drip back into the food, resulting in soggy cakes and steamed breads. The efficient absorption of the steam also creates an intensely hot container, so the food cooks quickly and stays hot. Because the bamboo steamer is attractive, food may be served directly from it. If the bamboo steamer is new, it may release impurities into the water, turning the water an unattractive green. To prevent this, season the steamer before the first use by soaking it for 1 hour in cold water to cover. (A bathtub is the easiest place to do this.) If you use a 14-inch wok, a 12-inch steamer is recommended; for a 16-inch wok, use a 14-inch steamer.

An aluminum steaming tray may also be used to steam foods. The tray is placed in a wok that has been filled with boiling water. The food to be steamed is placed directly on the tray or in a heat-proof bowl or plate on the tray. A dome lid is used to cover the tray, creating an airtight steamer.

SHOVEL, LADLE, AND HANDLED STRAINER

There are three basic hand utensils used in Chinese cooking. The *shovel* is a wide spatula designed to conform to the slanted sides of the wok, allowing greater control in handling food. The *ladle* is used by professional Chinese chefs to toss food and add seasonings. In the home, it is more commonly used to add or remove hot oil or water from the pan, and to ladle hot oil or water over foods to ensure even cooking. Stainless steel ladles and shovels with wooden handles are recommended. The *handled strainer* is another multipurpose utensil used to remove foods from hot oil and water. It also works well as a colander for draining foods and as a mold for fashioning deep-fried bird's nests with shredded potatoes and noodles. In the Orient, a sturdy strainer is made with a wide, steel, perforated body and a hardwood handle. In the United States, a slightly flimsier version is generally available with a woven, wire-mesh basket and a handle. Both work quite well.

CHINESE CLEAVER

A cleaver is the all-purpose cutting utensil used by Chinese chefs; it is an extremely versatile tool. The sharp edge is used for all types of cutting, the blunt edge is used for tenderizing, and the flat side is used for flattening. Cleavers are available in three sizes: light, medium, and heavy. The light cleaver is used for chopping vegetables and seasonings. The medium one is used for cutting all kinds of ingredients. Its weight makes it heavy enough to cut through chicken bones yet light enough to handle most foods. The heavy-weight cleaver is reserved for heavy-duty cutting, such as chopping hefty bones and tough meat.

Cleavers are usually made of carbon steel or stainless steel. Because carbon steel is a soft metal, it is easier to sharpen and holds its cutting edge better. Its one disadvantage is that is discolors when exposed to certain foods. Stainless steel, on the other hand, will not discolor, but since it is a more brittle metal, it is more difficult to sharpen and dulls easily. Some companies now manufacture high-carbon stainless steel cleavers, which contain the best properties of both metals. These cleavers are higher priced, but generally worth the additional expense.

SANDY POT

For braising, stewing, and casserole cooking, a sandy pot is traditionally used. This heavy earthenware pot is made from a mixture of clay and sand, and fired at an extremely high temperature. It withstands direct heat and distributes heat efficiently and evenly, making it ideal for slow cooking. Most sandy pots are glazed on the outside and unglazed inside for better heat absorption. They are available in several sizes and shapes.

SANDY POTS

MONGOLIAN FIRE POT (OR HOT POT)

This specialty pot is used exclusively for Mongolian fire pot or rinsed lamb pot — dishes that are something like fondue in that each diner cooks his own food in the pot. Fire pots come in a variety of metals, most notably brass, copper, and steel. There are two major types: One is shaped like a chafing dish with a small stand underneath for Sterno or an alcohol lamp. The other, more popular, variety is a much larger, more impressive-looking affair with a tall chimney to hold charcoal attached to a round, tubular pan that holds the boiling broth.

MONGOLIAN FIRE POT

A WORD ABOUT MENU PLANNING

A traditional Chinese family meal consists of four dishes — meat or poultry, fish or seafood, a vegetable, and soup. The menu always includes a staple, such as rice, steamed breads, pancakes, or noodles. In a family-style situation, all the dishes are served simultaneously, with the diners helping themselves to each. The soup is served as a beverage and diners frequently dip their spoons into the broth to flavor their rice and quench their thirst. The main dishes are prepared in small quantities, since their purpose is to garnish the staple food — usually rice — rather than be the main filler. Once the rice bowls are emptied, they are filled with soup, signifying the end of the meal.

In a more formal situation (at a restaurant or banquet), the meal is a much lengthier affair with anywhere from ten to fourteen courses. The courses follow a specific order, usually starting with a cold platter, followed by "wine-accompanying" dishes, which are often dry and crisp to complement the flavor of spirits. Most of the drinking and toasting takes place during this part of the meal. The main dishes (*da cai*) follow, and may include Peking duck, roast suckling pig, or a whole fish. This is the focal point of the meal. Finally, the simpler, "rice-accompanying" dishes are served — vegetable, bean curd, and egg platters. In a traditional banquet, the courses are punctuated with sweet and savory soups or pastries, which serve to cleanse the palate and clear the stage for another type of dish.

When you plan a Chinese meal for guests, I recommend preparing a reasonably simple one. Start with a cold platter, continue with a fish (possibly steamed), meat or poultry (braised, deep-fried, stir-fried, or smoked), a vegetable (steamed or stir-fried), a staple (rice, noodles, pancakes, or steamed breads), a soup, and sliced fruits or a fruit salad. The dishes should be selected with an eye to contrasting and complementing flavors (sweet versus salty, sour versus sweet, and delicate versus spicy), textures, colors, and cooking methods. The last consideration is particularly important, so that you do not spend the entire evening in the kitchen.

With entertaining in mind, I have made sure that all the recipes in this book serve six people. In Chinese cooking it is especially important to read each recipe completely before proceeding with any of the preparation, and I urge you to do that. The ingredients are organized into small groups (for example, meat marinade, sauce, braising mixture, thickener). Before beginning to cook, you should prepare these mixtures and place them near the cooking area. In some cases, instructions for preparing the mixtures appear in the recipes. Most of the dishes, unless otherwise directed, should be served as soon as they are cooked. The Chinese believe that the guests may wait for the food, but the food must never wait for the guests.

RICE 飯類

Every Sunday night from the time I was old enough to gnaw on a sparerib, my family and I would dine at a local Chinese restaurant. We prided ourselves on knowing authentic Chinese cuisine, choosing such sophisticated entrées as *mu shu* pork and sweet-and-sour yellow fish, and shunning the chop suey–chow mein items on the menu. Anyone who ordered these "pseudo-Chinese" platters and was unfortunate enough to sit near our table was the target of disdainful glances cast in his direction. We felt very smug to be eating just like the native Chinese.

Once I had traveled to the Orient and become familiar with the eating habits of the Chinese, I realized how Western we really were. We never ordered rice or any staple food to accompany the meat, fish, and vegetable entrées; instead, we filled ourselves on those dishes and experienced the syndrome known to countless Americans who eat in the same manner. We too were hungry an hour later.

For most Chinese formal banquets in celebration of a special holiday or event, the custom is to fill oneself up on the numerous entrées or courses. Even so, at least one type of rice, noodle, or steamed bread is always served — if for no other reason than for the sake of appearance. For an everyday, home-style meal, the situation is very different; rice, noodles, steamed bread, or some other staple are the main filler and the assorted meat, vegetable, and fish entrées act as garnishes. Soup is served as a beverage, and also as a flavoring to be spooned over rice. In addition to being a filler, rice provides an excellent foil for the pungent seasonings, rich sauces, and varied textures of the entrées. Having been weaned on processed "minute" rices, I was surprised at the delicate sweetness and pleasant texture of the cooked natural rice served to me in the Orient.

Rice as a filler is a custom that has evolved from ancient times; in the *Shih ching* (*Book of Songs*), the earliest written text, this precedent was clearly set forth: "The meat that he eats must at the very most, not be enough to make his breath smell of meat rather than rice."

It is believed that rice was introduced to China from the Indus Valley before 2800 B.C. Other grains, such as millet, wheat, barley, hemp, and sorghum, also were cultivated and were highly regarded for their nutritional value and level of productivity. Symbolically, rice played a special role in epitomizing fertility and life.

The ancient Chinese farmers quickly learned that rice demanded a warm, moist climate and thrived in the areas where these conditions prevailed. In regions where the ideal conditions were not prevalent, experimentation in cross pollination and the natural selection process produced hundreds of variant strains: shorter-grain rices for longer days and shorter growing seasons; lower-yield, higher-protein rices in dry areas; and salt-tolerant rices in marshy areas. Other unique varieties included rices that were yellow, pink, white, red, black, oval-grain, or glutinous. Each strain had its own individual flavor and texture. So varied was this staple food in ancient China that it was treated as a delicacy; in the city of Hangzhou, reputed to be the hotbed of Chinese haute cuisine in its day, well-to-do families were known to import special, selected varieties of rice daily to their homes.

Today, the number of strains generally used for Chinese cooking is restricted to four or five: Extra-long-grain and long-grain, both used for everyday dishes, are two of the most popular, because both types yield more cooked rice per cup of raw rice and the texture of the cooked rice is very fluffy. Short-grain, or Japanese, rice is very sticky once it is cooked, making it ideal for *sushi* and other dishes requiring a sticky texture. The Japanese and many Chinese from Taiwan prefer these shorter strains for everyday eating. Glutinous, or sweet, rice is an oval-grain variety with an extremely sticky consistency. It is used primarily for sweet and savory fillings, sweet pastries, and coatings for food.

A large portion of the agricultural population in China consumes brown rice, and for good reason. While perhaps not as aesthetically pleasing as white rice, brown rice contains much more protein, starch, fat, minerals, and vitamins. Most of these nutrients are lost in the milling process, though white rice is usually enriched after it is milled, to replace some of the lost nutrients and vitamins.

In addition to its role as a staple, rice is ground into powder and used in cakes and puddings, and as a coating for meats and poultry. Rice powder also is used to make rice stick noodles (rice vermicelli).

Before cooking rice, it is important to rinse it thoroughly. This is done for three reasons: to remove any talc remaining from the polishing; to remove any impurities and excess starch; and to allow the grains to separate during cooking, creating a fluffier product.

The Chinese use two main methods for cooking rice, boiling and steaming. Boiling, which is somewhat more convenient, produces a slightly sticky rice. (We always used a pressure cooker in our Chinese household.) Steaming, the lengthier method, produces a fluffier cooked rice. Electric rice cookers are often used for steaming; they are simple to use and shut off automatically when the rice is cooked. Either of the following methods will yield perfectly cooked grains of rice.

BOILED RICE
Using your fingers as a rake, rinse the rice thoroughly under cold running water until the water runs clear. Drain, and place the rice and the appropriate amount of water in a heavy saucepan. Cook over high heat until the water begins to boil. Cover, turn the heat to low, and simmer for 20 minutes, until the water has evaporated and craters have formed on the surface of the rice. Turn off the heat and let the rice rest, covered, for 10 minutes. Fluff the rice with a fork or chopsticks, and serve.

STEAMED RICE
Using your fingers as a rake, rinse the rice thoroughly under cold running water until the water runs clear. Drain, and place the rice and water to cover in a heavy saucepan. Heat uncovered until boiling; boil for 5 minutes. Drain the rice and place it in a steamer tray lined with moistened cheesecloth. Fill a wok with water level with the bottom edge of the steamer tray and bring the water to a boil. Cover the tray and place the steamer over the boiling water. Steam for 30 minutes over high heat. Let the rice rest, covered, for 10 minutes. Fluff with a fork or chopsticks, and serve.

In cooking rice, the proportion of water used varies in accordance with personal taste, the type of rice, and regional customs. The chart on the next page lists the necessary amount of water and raw rice for the various strains in relation to yield per cup.

FOUR TYPES OF RICE (ACTUAL SIZE)

LONG-GRAIN RICE

SHORT-GRAIN (JAPANESE) RICE

GLUTINOUS (SWEET) RICE

TYPE OF RAW RICE	WATER	YIELD
1 cup long-grain or extra-long-grain rice	1½ cups	3 cups
1 cup short-grain, or Japanese, rice	1 cup	2 to 2½ cups
1 cup glutinous, or sweet, rice	1 cup	2 cups
1 cup brown rice	1¾ cups	2½ cups

BROWN RICE

In cooking more than 2 cups of long-grain or extra-long-grain rice, the quantity of water decreases proportionally as the quantity of rice increases. Hence:

3 cups raw long-grain rice	4 cups water	9 cups cooked rice
4 cups raw long-grain rice	5 cups water	12 cups cooked rice
5 cups raw long-grain rice	6 cups water	15 cups cooked rice

RAINBOW CONGEE

XIAN ZHOU

To the Chinese, congee (rice gruel) is a dish for many occasions. It is served as a breakfast cereal with side dishes of pickled vegetables, dried and salted fish, or leftovers from the previous evening's meal; it is often prepared for convalescents, since it is soothing and easy to digest; and it is excellent as a filling, flavorful snack. Glutinous and short-grain rice are both suitable substitutes for long-grain rice in this recipe.

1   Using your fingers as a rake, rinse the rice in cold running water until the water runs clear. Drain and set aside. Soften the dried mushrooms in hot water to cover for 20 minutes, or until spongy. Remove and discard the stems. Cut the caps into ¼-inch dice.
2   Heat a wok, add the oil, and heat the oil until very hot. Add the minced shallots and stir-fry over high heat, stirring constantly until the shallots are soft and transparent. Add the mushrooms, carrots, and sausage and stir-fry for about 1 minute, until fragrant. Add the **rice seasonings** and heat until boiling. Add the rice and heat until boiling. Cook for about 2 minutes over high heat, stirring occasionally. Reduce the heat to low, cover, and simmer for about 1 hour. The mixture should be the consistency of porridge. Add the peas, toss lightly to mix, cover, and let sit for 10 minutes. Serve immediately.

SIX SERVINGS

3 cups long-grain rice
5 dried Chinese black
  mushrooms
2 tablespoons peanut,
  safflower, or corn oil
¼ cup minced shallots
3 carrots, cut into ¼-inch
  dice
4 Chinese pork sausages, cut
  into ¼-inch dice

Rice Seasonings
12 cups chicken broth
1 teaspoon salt
2 tablespoons soy sauce

2 cups fresh peas, cooked
  for 1 minute in boiling
  water (or thawed frozen
  peas)

6 dried Chinese black
   mushrooms
½ teaspoon dried shrimp
3 tablespoons peanut,
   safflower, or corn oil
1 cup diced cooked ham
¼ cup 1-inch pieces of
   scallion greens
3 cups cold cooked
   long-grain rice

Rice Sauce

2 tablespoons chicken broth
1 tablespoon rice wine
½ tablespoon soy sauce
1 teaspoon salt

Egg Mixture

4 eggs
2 tablespoons water
½ teaspoon salt

SLICED CHINESE RICE OMELET

ZHONG SHI DAN BAO FAN 中式蛋包飯

Long-grain rice generally is used in this omelet, but glutinous (sweet) rice may be substituted, producing a slightly heavier version. I usually serve the omelet as a staple, instead of rice, or as a snack. It is also excellent with soup for a light yet filling meal.

1　Soften the dried mushrooms for 20 minutes in hot water to cover. Drain, remove and discard the stems, and dice the caps. Soften the dried shrimp in hot water to cover for 1 hour. Drain and mince them.

2　Heat a wok, add the oil, and heat until very hot. Add the mushrooms and shrimp, and stir-fry over high heat for 10 seconds, until fragrant. Add the diced ham, the scallion greens, and the cooked rice. Stir the mixture well, to separate the grains of rice and combine the ingredients. Add the **rice sauce** and toss to combine evenly. When the ingredients are heated through, remove the mixture to a plate.

3　Heat a nonstick skillet or a well-seasoned wok until hot. Rub the surface with an oil-soaked cloth or paper towel, and let the pan cool slightly. Lightly beat the **egg mixture** and pour half of it into the pan. With the pan still off the heat, tilt it so that the egg spreads to form a thin pancake, about 8 inches in diameter. Cook over medium heat until set. Spoon half the rice mixture lengthwise into the center of the pancake. Fold in the opposite edges of the circle to enclose the rice filling and to form a roll. Fry the roll until it is lightly golden; then invert it, joined edges down, onto a platter. Place in a warm oven. Prepare another egg omelet in exactly the same way. Cut each roll into 1-inch-thick slices and serve immediately..

STIR-FRIED BEEF WITH VEGETABLES OVER RICE

NIU ROU HUI FAN

牛肉燴飯

The delicate, sweet flavor of rice provides a perfect complement to any pungent dish — be it sweet, sour, salty, or hot. This is a fine example of the meal-in-one-dish platters, which are combinations of meat, seafood, poultry, or vegetables served over rice.

1   Remove any fat or gristle from the beef and discard. Cut the meat, across the grain, into slices that are 1/8 inch thick. Cut the slices into pieces about 1½ inches square and place them in a bowl with the **beef marinade.** Toss lightly and let the beef marinate for at least 20 minutes. Blanch the snow peas in boiling water for 5 seconds. Refresh them immediately in cold water and drain thoroughly.

2   Heat a wok, add the oil, and heat the oil to 400°. Drain the beef and add half the slices to the hot oil. Deep-fry them until the color changes and the meat is cooked. Remove and drain. Reheat the oil, add the remaining beef slices, and deep-fry them in the same manner. Remove with a handled strainer and drain. Remove the oil from the pan, reserving 3 tablespoons.

3   Reheat the wok, add the 3 tablespoons of oil, and heat until very hot. Add the diced onion and stir-fry over high heat until soft and transparent. Add the green peppers, tomatoes, and mushrooms. Stir-fry for 1½ minutes over high heat, stirring constantly. Add the **beef sauce** and heat until boiling. Add the **thickener,** stirring constantly to prevent lumps. When the sauce has thickened, add the cooked meat slices, the snow peas, and the sesame oil. Toss lightly to combine the ingredients and spoon over the hot rice. Serve immediately.

SIX SERVINGS

1½ pounds eye of the round roast or top sirloin roast

Beef Marinade

2 tablespoons soy sauce
1 tablespoon rice wine
1 teaspoon sesame oil
1 tablespoon water
1 tablespoon cornstarch

1 cup snow peas, ends snapped and veiny strings removed
1 cup peanut, corn, or safflower oil
1 medium-sized onion, diced
2 green peppers, diced
2 tomatoes, seeded and diced
1 cup fresh mushrooms, rinsed lightly and quartered

Beef Sauce

4 tablespoons soy sauce
2 tablespoons rice wine
1 teaspoon salt
3 tablespoons sugar
2 tablespoons ketchup
1½ tablespoons Chinese black vinegar
3 cups chicken broth

Thickener

3 tablespoons cornstarch
5 tablespoons water

1½ teaspoons sesame oil
6 cups hot cooked rice

1 pound medium-sized raw
shrimp, shelled

Shrimp Marinade

1½ tablespoons rice wine
½ teaspoon salt
2 slices gingerroot, smashed
with the flat side of a
cleaver
2 teaspoons cornstarch

4 cups peanut, safflower, or
corn oil

Minced Seasonings

2 tablespoons minced
scallions
1 tablespoon minced
gingerroot

Shrimp Sauce

4 cups chicken broth
2½ tablespoons rice wine
2½ teaspoons salt
2½ tablespoons sugar
3½ tablespoons ketchup

Thickener

2 tablespoons cornstarch
3 tablespoons water

2 cups snow peas, ends
snapped and veiny strings
removed
12 sizzling rice cakes

SHRIMP WITH SIZZLING RICE

GUO BA XIA JEN   鍋巴蝦仁

It has been suggested that a resourceful Chinese chef, ever mindful of eliminating waste of any type, invented the concept of sizzling rice so that the layer of cooked rice that often sticks to the pot would be put to good use. Once deep-fried, these cakes supply a crisp garnish similar to croutons, and in this dish the hot oil (from the cakes) combines with the sweet-and-sour sauce to create the "sizzling" effect.

1   Score each shrimp along the length of the back and remove the vein; the scoring will allow the shrimp to "butterfly" when it is cooked. Rinse all the shrimp and drain thoroughly. Place the shrimp in a bowl. Pinch the gingerroot slices in the **shrimp marinade** repeatedly for several minutes to impart their flavor. Discard the gingerroot. Add the marinade to the shrimp, toss lightly, and let sit for 20 minutes.
2   Heat a wok, add 4 tablespoons of the oil, and heat until very hot. Add the shrimp and stir-fry over high heat until they change color, about 1 minute. Remove and drain. Reheat the pan, add 2 tablespoons of the oil, and heat until very hot. Add the **minced seasonings** and stir-fry for about 10 seconds, until fragrant. Add the **shrimp sauce** and heat until boiling. Slowly add the **thickener,** stirring constantly to prevent lumps. Add the shrimp and the snow peas. Turn the heat to very low to keep hot.
3   Heat another wok, add the remaining oil, and heat to 425°, or until almost smoking. Add the sizzling rice cakes and deep-fry, turning constantly until puffed and golden. Remove with a handled strainer and place in a serving bowl. Pour the shrimp mixture over the rice cakes immediately to create the sizzling sound. Serve immediately.

SIZZLING RICE CAKES

To prepare the sizzling rice cakes, rinse 1½ cups long-grain rice until the water runs clear. Drain and place in the bottom of a lasagna pan (9 by 12 inches) and add 2 cups of cold water. Spread the rice evenly over the bottom of the pan. Cover the pan with aluminum foil and let it sit for 30 minutes. Preheat the oven to 350° and bake the rice, still covered, for 30 minutes. Remove the foil, flatten the rice with a spatula, and return it to the oven, uncovered. Turn the heat to the lowest setting and bake for 8 to 10 hours, or until the rice is completely dry. Take the rice out of the pan and break it into squares roughly 2 inches on each side. Sizzling rice cakes will keep indefinitely in an airtight container.

CURRIED FRIED RICE

JIA LI FAN   咖喱飯

The ancient Cantonese were known for their adventurous palates, utilizing foreign spices and ingredients that their countrymen shunned. Gradually these seasonings were introduced and adapted to the other regional cuisines, and by now they have become quite popular. This is the case with curry powder; curries, once unique to southern China, are now enjoyed throughout the country. Fried rice dishes, such as the one below, are often served as a staple accompanying the entrées in American Chinese restaurants. In truth, they are more correctly served as a snack, or with a light soup for a meal in itself.

1   Heat a wok, add the oil, and heat the oil until very hot. Add the diced onion and stir-fry over high heat, stirring constantly until soft and transparent. Add the curry powder and stir-fry for about 5 seconds, until fragrant. Add the carrots, chicken, and peas. Toss lightly over the heat; then add the rice. Mix thoroughly to break up the rice and combine the ingredients well. Add the **rice sauce** and quickly toss the mixture to coat evenly. Transfer the rice to a platter and serve immediately.

SIX SERVINGS

4 tablespoons peanut, safflower, or corn oil
1 cup diced onion
1½ tablespoons curry powder
1 cup diced carrot, cooked for 1 minute in boiling water
1 cup diced cooked chicken meat
1 cup fresh peas, cooked for 1 minute in boiling water (or thawed frozen peas)
6 cups cold cooked rice

Rice Sauce
2 teaspoons salt
½ teaspoon freshly ground black pepper
3 tablespoons chicken broth

37

1½ pounds flank steak or
London broil

Beef Marinade
3 tablespoons soy sauce
3 tablespoons rice wine
2 tablespoons sesame oil
2 tablespoons minced
scallions
1 tablespoon minced garlic
1 tablespoon minced
gingerroot
1½ tablespoons sweet bean
sauce
1½ tablespoons sugar
1½ teaspoons chili paste

2 cups glutinous (sweet) rice,
rinsed, soaked for 4 hours
in hot water to cover, and
drained
2 teaspoons five-spice
powder
2 tablespoons minced
scallion greens

STEAMED BEEF WITH SPICY RICE POWDER

FEN ZHENG NIU ROU　　　　　粉蒸牛肉

Spicy rice powder is a seasoned coating used frequently in chicken, duck, pork, and beef dishes. The seasoned rice bits coat the meat pieces, sealing in the natural juices and producing a succulently tender and flavorful result. Seasoned rice powder is available in packages in grocery stores all over the Far East, but it seems to be very scarce in the West. Preparing spicy rice powder is quite simple, and the homemade variety is far more tasty.

1　Remove any fat or gristle from the meat and discard. Cut the meat, across the grain, into thin slices about ¼ inch thick and 1½ inches long. Place the beef slices in a bowl, add the **beef marinade,** toss lightly, and let marinate for at least 1 hour.
2　Place the soaked rice in a heavy pan (with no oil) and stir-fry over medium-low heat, stirring constantly until the rice is very dry and lightly golden brown, 10 to 15 minutes. Remove and pulverize to a coarse powder in a blender or in a food processor fitted with the steel blade. Mix the rice powder with the five-spice powder.
3　Dredge the beef slices in the rice powder so that they are completely coated. Arrange the coated meat pieces in one layer on a steamer tray lined with a sheet of parchment paper that has been punched with holes.
4　Fill a wok with water level with the bottom edge of the steamer tray and heat until boiling. Place the steamer tray containing the beef directly over the boiling water, cover, and steam for 20 minutes over high heat, or until the meat is cooked and the rice is tender. Sprinkle the minced scallion greens on top and serve immediately.

STEAMED RICE CASSEROLE

LA WEI FAN 腊味饭

Many Americans marvel at the fluffy consistency of rice served in Chinese restaurants. (I know a student who always buys cooked rice at a nearby Chinese restaurant, rather than make it herself.) The secret behind this texture may be the fact that often the rice is steamed rather than boiled. Steaming allows each grain to cook separately, resulting in a fluffy, full texture. This tasty dish is simple, attractive, and a filling meal in itself.

1   Cut the sausages into diagonal slices about ⅛ inch thick. Soften the dried mushrooms for 20 minutes in hot water to cover. Remove and discard the stems, and cut the caps in half. Peel the carrots and roll-cut into ½-inch pieces. Blanch the snow peas for 5 seconds in boiling water. Refresh them in cold water immediately. Drain and reserve.

2   Using your fingers as a rake, rinse the rice in cold running water until the water runs clear. Drain. Place the rice in a 4-quart casserole or Dutch oven and add the water and the salt. Cook over high heat until the water reaches a boil. Stir the rice and arrange the sausage slices, mushrooms, and carrots in separate mounds on top of the rice. Cover, reduce the heat to low, and simmer for 20 minutes.

3   Heat a wok, add the oil, and heat the oil until very hot. Add the minced garlic. Stir-fry the garlic very briefly over high heat and add the cabbage squares. Stir-fry until the cabbage is slightly limp, about 3 minutes; then add the **cabbage seasonings**. Continue cooking for another 5 minutes, until the cabbage is tender. Spoon the cabbage over the rice and arrange the snow peas next to the cabbage. Pour the **rice seasonings** over the rice. Cover the casserole.

4   Preheat the oven to 350° and bake the casserole for 15 minutes. Serve immediately.

SIX SERVINGS

4 Chinese pork sausages
8 dried Chinese black mushrooms
2 carrots
¼ pound fresh snow peas, ends snapped and veiny strings removed
2½ cups long-grain rice
2½ cups water
½ teaspoon salt
1 tablespoon peanut, safflower, or corn oil
1 teaspoon minced garlic
2 cups Chinese cabbage (Napa), cut into 2-inch squares

Cabbage Seasonings
2 tablespoons rice wine
1 teaspoon salt
½ teaspoon sugar

Rice Seasonings
1 cup chicken broth
5 tablespoons soy sauce
¼ cup rice wine
2 teaspoons sesame oil

1 cup glutinous (sweet) rice
2 tablespoons peanut,
    safflower, or corn oil

Shao mai Garnishes
½ cup dried Chinese black
    mushrooms, softened and
    diced
1½ cups diced cooked pork
    loin
½ cup diced cooked shrimp
¼ cup minced scallion
    greens

Shao mai Sauce
3 tablespoons soy sauce
2 tablespoons rice wine
1 teaspoon sesame oil
1 teaspoon sugar
¼ teaspoon black pepper
2 tablespoons chicken broth

36 dumpling skins (page 91)
    or *shao mai* skins (page
    100)

GLUTINOUS SHAO MAI

LUO MI SHAO MAI 糯米燒賣

Shao mai are a well-known Cantonese *dim sum* or open-faced dumpling, characterized by their unique shape. Though the more popular version has a filling of pork, water chestnuts, and shrimp, the addition of glutinous rice, as below, creates a flavorful, more substantial pastry. Serve these steamed dumplings with soup as a filling lunch or supper.

1   Using your fingers as a rake, rinse the rice in cold water until the water runs clear. Place the rice in cold water to cover and let soften for 1 hour. Drain and place in a saucepan with 1 cup water. Place the saucepan over high heat and heat until the liquid boils. Turn the heat to low, cover, and cook for 20 minutes. Turn off the heat and let sit for 10 minutes. Uncover and let cool to room temperature.
2   Heat a wok, add the oil, and heat until very hot. Add the diced mushrooms and stir-fry for about 15 seconds over high heat. Then add the remaining **shao mai garnishes.** Toss lightly and add the cooked rice. Toss the mixture repeatedly over the heat to mix the ingredients evenly. Add the **shao mai sauce** and mix. Roughly divide the rice mixture into thirty-six portions.
3   Line a steamer tray with cheesecloth or muslin that has been moistened with water, or with parchment paper that has been punched with holes. Place a portion of the rice mixture in the center of each dumpling skin. Gather up the edges of the skin around the filling. Holding the dumpling between your thumb and index finger, lightly squeeze it to form a "waist"; at the same time, push up the filling from the bottom with the other hand, creating a flat bottom. Smooth the surface of the filling with the underside of a spoon dipped in water. (See the recipe for *shao mai* on page 101 for step-by-step illustrations.) Arrange the *shao mai* in the steamer tray about ¼ inch apart.
4   Fill a wok with water level with the bottom of the steamer tray and heat until boiling. Place the steamer tray over the boiling water, cover, and steam the dumplings for 15 minutes over high heat. Serve with soy sauce.

PEARL BALLS

ZHEN ZHU WAN ZI 珍珠丸子

Pearl balls are so named because once they are steamed, the glutinous rice blooms into pearllike grains. Glutinous (sweet) rice is essential to this dish since its sticky quality allows the grains to adhere firmly to the meatballs. This famous dish originated in the province of Hunan, one of China's major rice basins.

1　Using your fingers as a rake, rinse the rice in cold water until the water runs clear. Drain the rice and place it in cold water to cover. Let it sit for 1 hour. Drain the rice and transfer it to a tray.
2　Soften the dried mushrooms for 20 minutes in hot water to cover. Remove and discard the stems. Chop the caps coarsely. Plunge the water chestnuts into boiling water for a few seconds to remove the tinny flavor. Refresh them in cold water and chop coarsely. Chop the ground meat for a few minutes until fluffy. Place the meat in a bowl, add the chopped mushrooms, the shredded carrots, the chopped water chestnuts, and the **seasonings.** Stir the mixture vigorously in one direction to combine evenly. Roll the mixture into balls about 1 inch in diameter. Roll each meatball in the glutinous rice so that it is completely coated; lightly press the rice to make it adhere to the meatball. Line a steamer tray with cheesecloth or muslin that has been moistened with water, or with parchment paper that has been punched with holes. Arrange the pearl balls on the steamer tray about ½ inch apart.
3　Fill a wok with water that is level with the bottom edge of the steamer tray and heat until boiling. Place the steamer tray over the boiling water and cover. Steam for 25 minutes over high heat. Remove the pearl balls and serve immediately, with soy sauce if desired.

SIX SERVINGS

1½ cups glutinous (sweet) rice
6 dried Chinese black mushrooms
1 cup water chestnuts
1 pound ground beef or pork
½ cup shredded raw carrot

Seasonings
1 tablespoon minced scallions
1 tablespoon minced gingerroot
2 tablespoons soy sauce
1 tablespoon rice wine
1½ teaspoons sesame oil
2½ tablespoons cornstarch

1 whole roasting chicken, 4½
   to 5 pounds
1½ tablespoons soy sauce
¾ cup glutinous (sweet) rice,
   rinsed thoroughly and
   soaked in water to cover
   for 1 hour
2 tablespoons peanut,
   safflower, or corn oil

Stuffing Garnishes
⅓ cup dried Chinese black
   mushrooms, softened,
   stems removed, and caps
   diced
½ cup diced carrot
½ cup diced Chinese pork
   sausage, fried in oil until
   golden brown
½ cup water chestnuts,
   plunged briefly into
   boiling water, refreshed,
   and diced
½ cup fresh peas (or thawed
   frozen peas)

Stuffing Sauce
1 tablespoon soy sauce
1 tablespoon rice wine
1 teaspoon sesame oil
1½ cups water or chicken
   broth

RED-COOKED EIGHT-TREASURE CHICKEN

LUO MI JI

Eight-treasure chicken is a sumptuous dish inspired by the equally notable eastern classic of eight-treasure duckling. In both these dishes, the sticky rice provides a superb foil for the red-cooked sauce and a delicate filler for the garnishes of sausage and black mushrooms.

Although a bit more time and effort is involved, the chicken may be boned before being stuffed, which simplifies cutting and eating the cooked chicken.

1   Remove the fat pockets from the cavity of the chicken and discard. Rinse the chicken, drain it thoroughly, and rub the soy sauce inside the cavity and all over the skin. Let the chicken sit for 15 minutes. Drain the rice.

2   Heat a wok, add the 2 tablespoons of oil, and heat until very hot. Add the **stuffing garnishes** and stir-fry over high heat, stirring constantly for 1 minute. Add the rice and the **stuffing sauce.** Heat until the liquid boils, stirring constantly; then reduce the heat to medium and cook until the liquid is almost evaporated, stirring occasionally. Remove the stuffing and let cool to room temperature. Clean the wok. Drain the chicken, adding the soy sauce to the

Chicken Braising Liquid
3 scallions, smashed with the
   flat side of a cleaver
3 slices gingerroot, smashed
   with the flat side of a
   cleaver
4 tablespoons soy sauce
2 tablespoons rice wine
1 tablespoon sugar
1 whole star anise
3½ cups water

8 cups peanut, safflower, or
   corn oil

Thickener
1 teaspoon cornstarch
1½ tablespoons water

chicken braising liquid. Stuff the cavity of the chicken with the cooled stuffing and sew up the opening with twine.

3   Reheat the wok, add the 8 cups of oil, and heat it to 400°. Carefully lower the chicken into the oil, breast side down, and ladle the hot oil over the chicken. Deep-fry it briefly until golden brown. Remove and drain.

4   Preheat the oven to 350°. Pour the chicken braising liquid into a heavy pot or Dutch oven and add the chicken, breast side up. Cover and cook for 1½ hours, until the chicken is cooked and golden brown. Remove the chicken, remove the twine, and spoon the filling into a serving bowl. Carve the chicken meat into slices; or cut the chicken, through the bones, into bite-size serving pieces, as for red-cooked chicken (page 151). Arrange the chicken on a platter. Skim off any fat from the braising liquid and strain out the seasonings. Heat the liquid until boiling and add the **thickener,** stirring constantly. Pour over the chicken and serve immediately with the stuffing.

1½ pounds boneless chicken meat

Chicken Marinade
1 tablespoon soy sauce
1 tablespoon rice wine
1 teaspoon sesame oil
2 tablespoons water or 1 lightly beaten egg white
2 teaspoons cornstarch

1 cup snow peas, ends snapped and veiny strings removed
4 cups peanut, safflower, or corn oil
2 ounces rice stick noodles

Minced Seasonings
2 tablespoons minced scallions
1½ tablespoons minced garlic
1 tablespoon minced gingerroot

2 green peppers, cored, seeded, and roll-cut into bite-size pieces
½ pound fresh mushrooms, rinsed and quartered
1 cup water chestnuts, plunged briefly into boiling water, refreshed, and cut in half crosswise

STIR-FRIED CHICKEN IN BIRD'S NEST

QUE CAO JI DING · 雀巢雞丁

This colorful Cantonese platter illustrates well another use of rice stick noodles. When deep-fried in hot oil, they puff up and become golden and crisp, resembling a bird's nest. In this form, they provide a delightfully crisp bed for stir-fried dishes.

A more complicated bird's nest is made with shredded potatoes or taro, mixed with a little cornstarch and molded in a strainer to a shape reminiscent of a bird's nest. The nest is deep-fried until crisp. Both versions form an edible garnish-staple, eliminating the need to serve rice.

1 Remove the skin from the chicken meat and discard. Cut the meat into dices approximately 1 inch square. Place the pieces in a bowl, add the **chicken marinade,** toss lightly, and let marinate for 20 minutes. Blanch the snow peas in boiling water for 5 seconds. Remove and refresh in cold water. Drain and reserve.
2 Heat a wok, add the oil, and heat the oil to 425°, or until smoking. Drop the rice noodles into the hot oil and deep-fry very briefly until they are puffed and lightly golden. (This should take no longer than 5 seconds.) Turn the noodles over and fry for a few seconds more. Remove them and drain on absorbent paper. When they are cool, transfer the noodles to a large platter and lightly break

3 carrots, parboiled for 2 minutes and roll-cut into bite-size pieces
1 cup baby corn ears, parboiled briefly and drained

Chicken Sauce
2 tablespoons soy sauce
2 tablespoons rice wine
2 teaspoons sugar
1½ teaspoons salt
1 teaspoon sesame oil
½ cup chicken broth
1 tablespoon cornstarch

them up with your fingertips. Drain the oil from the wok, reserving
½ cup.

3 Reheat the wok, add the ½ cup of oil, and heat the oil to 375°.
Add half the chicken pieces and stir-fry over high heat until the
color is changed and the pieces are cooked. Remove the chicken
with a handled strainer, drain, and reheat the oil. Cook the remaining chicken pieces in the same manner. Remove all but 3 tablespoons of oil from the wok and heat until very hot. Add the **minced
seasonings** and stir-fry for about 10 seconds over high heat. Add the
green peppers and the mushrooms. Stir-fry, tossing constantly, for
about 15 seconds; then add the water chestnuts, carrots, and baby
corn ears, and continue mixing until all the ingredients are heated
through. Add the **chicken sauce** and mix until it starts to thicken.
Add the chicken meat and the snow peas. Toss lightly to coat with
the sauce. Spoon the mixture into the center of the fried rice noodles
and serve immediately.

1 pound boneless center-cut
pork loin

Pork Marinade
2 tablespoons soy sauce
1 tablespoon rice wine
1 teaspoon sesame oil
2 teaspoons cornstarch
1 tablespoon water

1 pound rice stick noodles
½ cup peanut, safflower, or
corn oil

Minced Seasonings
2 tablespoons minced
scallions
2 tablespoons minced garlic
1 tablespoon minced
gingerroot

2 cups shredded Chinese
cabbage (Napa)
1½ cups shredded carrot
2 cups 1-inch pieces of
scallion greens
2 cups fresh bean sprouts,
lightly rinsed

Noodle Sauce
4½ tablespoons soy sauce
1 teaspoon salt
2 tablespoons rice wine
1½ teaspoons sugar
1 teaspoon sesame oil
1½ cups chicken broth

STIR-FRIED PORK WITH RICE NOODLES

ROU SI CHAO MI FEN　　肉絲炒米粉

Whole grains of rice are often ground to a fine powder and used in making very delicate noodles called *mi fen* — rice stick noodles, or sometimes rice vermicelli. They are extremely versatile and may be deep-fried, served in soups, or stir-fried, as in this dish. They come in dry form and will keep indefinitely stored in an airtight container. To condition them for use in soups and stir-fried dishes, soften them in warm water for 10 minutes, drain, and use as directed in the recipe. Because they are very thin, they cook very quickly.

1　Remove any fat or gristle from the pork loin and discard. Cut the meat, across the grain, into slices about ¼ inch thick. Cut the slices into matchstick-size shreds about 1½ inches long. Place the meat shreds in a bowl, add the **pork marinade,** toss lightly, and let marinate for 20 minutes. Soften the rice noodles for 10 minutes in hot water to cover. Drain them.
2　Heat a wok, add the oil, and heat the oil to 375°. Add the pork shreds and stir-fry over high heat until the meat changes color. Remove the meat with a handled strainer and drain. Remove all but 4 tablespoons of oil from the pan and reheat until very hot. Add the **minced seasonings** and stir-fry for about 10 seconds, until fragrant. Add the cabbage and carrot shreds and stir-fry over high heat for about 1 minute, or until the cabbage is limp. Add the cooked meat, the scallion pieces, and the bean sprouts. Toss lightly and add the **noodle sauce.** Add the rice noodles. Cook for about 1½ minutes over high heat. Transfer the mixture to a platter and serve immediately.

BREADS 中式麵點類

My mentor in Taiwan, Huang Su Huei, a noted authority on Chinese cooking in the Orient, had some definite ideas about my approach to the study of Chinese cuisine. First, it was decided that I should receive a thorough introduction to the basic cooking techniques and the main regional schools. So, every day I was dispatched to her cooking school in Taipei, where I studied Cantonese, Sichuanese, Fujianese, northern, and eastern dishes with some of the foremost master chefs of the city. After one and a half years, another conference was called and it was agreed that I was now ready to select one or two regional styles and explore them in depth working as an apprentice in a restaurant kitchen. "Never spread yourself too thin," my mentor admonished. "It is far better to excel in one cuisine than to be mediocre in three."

I decided to study Hunanese cooking, a cousin to the Sichuanese style but with even spicier seasonings and hotter peppers. After some persistent pleading, I convinced the Hunanese teacher to allow me to work in his restaurant kitchen as an apprentice without pay.

Once the initial uproar caused by a young Caucasian woman in an all-male Chinese restaurant kitchen had subsided and order was restored, I was able to observe firsthand the organization and routine of a professional Chinese kitchen, in addition to learning some valuable culinary skills.

The kitchen was divided into six main areas of preparation, or "stations." One station was devoted to cleaning the ingredients, with the area next to it set aside for cutting, slicing, and all the other preparation work. Four or five huge woks sat in a row next to one wall on powerful gas jets that emitted heat equal to the intensity of an oxyacetylene torch. This was where most of the cooking was done and all the cooks in this area were considered to be master chefs, a position at the highest level of the kitchen hierarchy. To one side, a smaller station was devoted to casserole cooking and braising, with several *sha guo*, clay pots, standing at the ready. To the other side, three rows of bamboo steamer trays were stacked up ten

LOTUS BUNS

SESAME FLAT BREADS

FLOWER ROLLS

SILVER-THREAD LOAVES

47

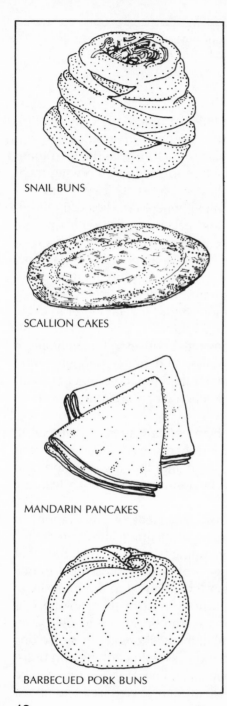

SNAIL BUNS

SCALLION CAKES

MANDARIN PANCAKES

BARBECUED PORK BUNS

or fifteen layers high. Away from the heat, near the sinks, was the pastry and bread corner, where the sweet pastries and savory snacks were prepared.

I spent quite some time in this corner working with a fifteen-year-old chef whose hands were remarkably dexterous. He would take blobs of dough and transform them into butterflies, lotus buns, snail buns, silver-thread loaves, and peach buns. He would stuff dough circles with a pungent meat filling for a savory pastry and with sweet bean paste and date paste for a sweet confection. Once shaped, these pastries would be arranged in bamboo steamer trays and sent over to the next station to be cooked.

All of these pastries, both sweet and savory, are made from the same yeast dough and steamed. These foods, along with pancakes, are in the broad category of breads, and they figure prominently in the grand order of Chinese dishes. Like noodles, Chinese breads may be served as a staple substitute for rice — particularly in northern China, where wheat reigns supreme as a staple crop — or, as a *dim sum* (snack), or occasionally as a meal in themselves. Examples of these breads include Mandarin pancakes, which are served with Peking duck and other stir-fried meat and vegetable dishes; sesame flat breads (*shao bing*), which often accompany fried Chinese crullers (*you tiao*) in a Chinese breakfast and are served with Mongolian fire pot and Mongolian barbecue; steamed lotus buns, which are served with crispy-skin duck; barbecued pork buns; and scallion pancakes. The list is endless and the variety is extraordinary.

Like noodles, Chinese breads originated in the wheat-growing regions of northern China and became popular as early as the Han dynasty (206 B.C. to A.D. 220). Experts have concluded that the concept probably was foreign, evolving from foods introduced from the lands to the west. Although originally received with limited enthusiasm, in time breads and pancakes became immensely popular with both the upper and lower classes. And they came to play an important role in Chinese ritual, replacing rice on special holidays and anniversaries. On birthdays, steamed buns fashioned into peaches were served to symbolize longevity and immortality. Tinted scarlet, a color considered auspicious by the Chinese, steamed breads were presented to the gods in return for favors and were distributed on the occasion of the birth of a baby boy.

Even today, these customs are still observed. On a small island near Hong Kong, thousands of Chinese annually congregate for a Buddhist celebration called the Bun Festival. There steamed buns are presented as offerings to the gods and several sixty-foot bun mountains, each made of thousands of sweet buns, are constructed for a special race. Young men climb to the top to grab the highest bun and those who succeed are said to be blessed with good luck for the coming year.

BASIC YEAST DOUGH

FA MIAN   發麵

Chinese chefs use two types of bread dough in making steamed breads. In both doughs, they use flour, water, and lard, but the leavening agent may be plain yeast or a yeast dough starter. One might suspect that the cooked bread would be heavy from the steaming, but quite the opposite is true. Because of the lengthy rising period and the use of baking powder, the result is a light, fluffy bread.

1   Dissolve the sugar in the warm water and add the yeast. Mix lightly and let the mixture stand for 10 minutes, until foamy.
2   Place the flour in a mixing bowl and add the yeast mixture and the oil. Using a wooden spoon, mix the ingredients to a rough dough. Turn the mixture out onto a lightly floured surface and knead for 8 to 10 minutes, until the dough is smooth and elastic. If it is very sticky, knead in ¼ cup flour. (It should be soft.) Lightly grease a bowl with oil. Place the dough in the bowl and turn it so that all sides of the dough are coated. Cover the bowl with a damp cloth and let the dough rise for 4 hours in a warm area, free from drafts.
3   Uncover the dough, punch it down, and turn it out onto a lightly floured surface. Flatten the dough and make a well in the center. Place the baking powder in the well and gather up the edges around the baking powder to enclose. Pinch the edges to seal. Lightly knead the dough to incorporate the baking powder evenly. Use the prepared dough as directed. (The dough should be used immediately. If that is not possible, punch down the dough after step 2, cover with plastic wrap, and refrigerate until ready to proceed.)

LONGEVITY PEACH BUNS

¼ cup sugar
2 cups warm water
1 tablespoon active dry yeast
6 cups all-purpose flour
2 tablespoons peanut, safflower, or corn oil
2 teaspoons baking powder

SILVER-THREAD LOAVES

YING SI JUAN　銀絲捲

Although some Westerners may consider these steamed breads too sweet to serve with savory dishes, the Chinese do not. In fact, to fully satisfy their palates, sweet flavors are often paired with salty in much the same way yin is believed to complement yang. The "silver-thread" in the title refers to the delicate strands of steamed bread encased in the individual loaves.

1   Prepare the dough as directed and cut it in half. Form each half into a long snakelike roll about 1½ inches in diameter. Cut each roll into six pieces, so that you now have twelve pieces.
2   Roll out six of the twelve pieces to rectangles that are approximately 6 inches by 4 inches. Set these rectangles aside on a lightly floured tray.
3   Roll out the remaining six pieces to rectangles that are 8 inches by 4 inches. Smear the lard, butter, or sesame oil generously over the surfaces of the rectangles. Fold each one in half crosswise, so that it measures 4 inches by 4 inches, and again smear the lard over the surface. Fold each rectangle again, so that it measures 4 inches by 2 inches, and cut it crosswise into thin shreds.
4   Lightly stretch the shreds, pulling from both ends (a), and arrange in the center of each of the first six rectangles; the shreds

SILVER-THREAD LOAVES

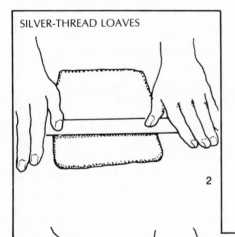

2

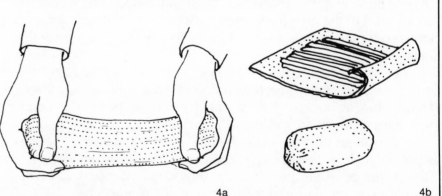

3　　　　　　　　　　　　4a　　　　　　　　　　　　4b

should run lengthwise (b). Fold in the closest end, then the sides, and finally the last end, so that the shreds are completely enclosed. Arrange the finished loaves about 1½ inches apart in several steamer trays that have been lined with wet cheesecloth or with parchment paper punched with holes. Let the loaves rise for 20 minutes.

5 Fill a wok with water level with the bottom edge of a steamer tray and heat until boiling. Place one tray over the boiling water, cover, and steam the loaves for 20 to 25 minutes over high heat, or until the loaves are puffed and springy. Steam the remaining loaves in the same manner. Cut each loaf into five or six slices and serve. To reheat, steam the loaves for 10 minutes over high heat.

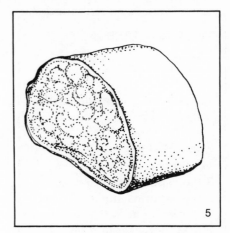

5

GOLDEN-THREAD LOAVES

JIN SI JUAN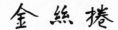

SIX FIVE-INCH LOAVES

1 recipe silver-thread loaves
   (page 50)
6 cups peanut, safflower, or
   corn oil

The simple step of deep-frying transforms silver-thread loaves into a totally new dish; the crisp, golden crust contrasts nicely with the fluffy lightness of the steamed interior. Serve these breads as a substitute for rice, as a snack, or with a hearty soup for a filling lunch or dinner.

1 Prepare the silver-thread loaves and steam as directed, but do not cut the loaves into serving slices. Leave them whole and let them cool.

2 Heat a wok, add the oil, and heat the oil to 350°. Add two or three of the loaves, depending on the size of the wok, and deep-fry, turning constantly until the loaves are golden brown. Remove with a handled strainer and drain on absorbent paper. Deep-fry the remaining loaves in the same manner. Cut each loaf into five or six slices and serve immediately.

1½ pounds barbecued pork
(page 225)

Sauce Mixture
¼ cup soy sauce
3 tablespoons oyster sauce
2 tablespoons sugar
½ tablespoon ketchup
2 teaspoons sesame oil
1½ cups water
½ teaspoon freshly ground
black pepper

Thickener
2 tablespoons cornstarch
4 tablespoons water

1 recipe basic yeast dough
(page 49)

BARBECUED PORK BUNS

CHA SHAO BAO  义 燒 包

With their fragrant oyster sauce and roasted-meat filling, barbecued pork buns have always been one of my favorite Cantonese snacks. They seem to be equally popular with the Chinese, since these buns are always one of the first snacks to sell out at bakeries and *dim sum* parlors. In some restaurants, they are made with a baking powder dough, but I prefer them with a yeast dough.

1   Cut the barbecued pork into ½-inch dice.
2   Heat a wok, add the **sauce mixture,** and heat until boiling. Add the **thickener,** stirring constantly to prevent any lumps, and cook until the sauce is very thick. Add the diced pork, toss lightly to coat with the sauce, and remove to a platter. Refrigerate until it is cool.
3   Prepare the dough as directed and cut it in half. On a lightly floured surface, form each half into a long snakelike roll about 1½ inches in diameter. Cut each roll into twelve pieces. With a cut edge down, use your fingers to flatten each piece into a 3-inch circle. The edges should be thinner than the center. Place a tablespoon of the barbecued pork mixture in the center of the dough skin. Gather the edges of the skin together (a), pressing to make a pleated finish (b). Pinch the final pleat to seal and completely enclose the filling (c). Place the finished buns about 1 inch apart on

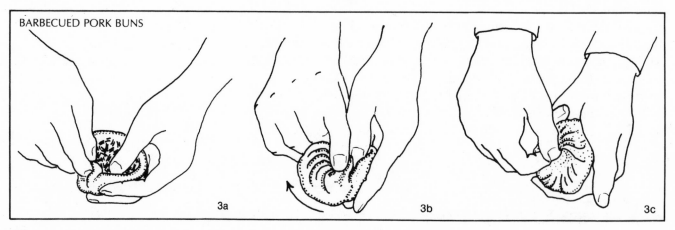
BARBECUED PORK BUNS
3a   3b   3c

several steamer trays that have been lined with wet cheesecloth or with parchment paper punched with holes. Let the buns rise for 15 minutes.

4   Fill a wok with water level with the bottom edge of a steamer tray and heat until boiling. Place one tray of buns over the boiling water, cover, and steam over high heat for 15 to 20 minutes, or until the buns are puffed and springy. Steam the remaining buns in the same manner. To reheat, steam the buns for 10 minutes over high heat.

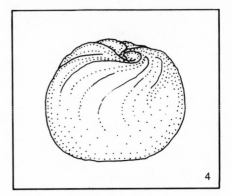

4

BUNS WITH RED BEAN FILLING

DOU SHA BAO 豆沙包

TWENTY-FOUR BUNS

1 recipe basic yeast dough
  (page 49)
1½ cups homemade red
  bean paste (page 327), or
  1½ cups canned red bean
  paste combined with 1
  tablespoon vanilla extract

Red bean paste is a popular ingredient in many Chinese puddings and pastries. Although it may be purchased ready-made in cans at any Chinese grocery store, the flavor of homemade red bean paste is far superior. Steamed buns with sweet filling are often garnished with a red stamp. A homemade stamp may be improvised by dipping the square end of a chopstick into red food coloring and pressing the tip to the top of each bun before steaming.

1   Cut the dough in half. On a lightly floured surface, form each half into a long snakelike roll about 1½ inches in diameter. Cut each roll into twelve pieces. With a cut edge down, use your fingers to flatten each piece into a 3-inch circle. The edges should be thinner and the center thicker. Place a heaping tablespoon of the red bean paste in the center of the dough skin. Gather the edges together, pinch to seal, and roll the bun into a ball. Place the buns about 1 inch apart, joined edges down, on several steamer trays lined with wet cheesecloth or with parchment paper punched with holes. Let rise for 15 minutes.

2   Fill a wok with water level with the bottom of the steamer tray and heat until boiling. Place one tray of buns over the boiling water, cover, and steam for 15 to 20 minutes over high heat, or until the buns are puffed and springy. Steam the remaining buns in the same manner. To reheat, steam the buns for 10 minutes over high heat.

THIRTY ROLLS

1 recipe basic yeast dough
(page 49)
¼ cup sesame oil

FLOWER ROLLS

HUA JUAN

In the city of Taipei, food vendors pass through the alleyways day and night hawking their offerings. One man rode a bicycle with a box strapped behind his seat filled to the brim with hot steamed bread and flower rolls. Upon hearing his call, my Chinese surrogate mother would dispatch the children to buy a supply of the buns to eat with our dinner instead of rice. Flower rolls are particularly delicious with red-cooked meats and stir-fried meat and vegetable dishes.

1   Prepare the dough as directed and cut it in half. On a lightly floured surface, roll out each half to form a rectangle approximately 18 inches long and 8 inches wide. Brush the surface of the rectangles liberally with the sesame oil. Place one rectangle directly on top of the other, with both oiled surfaces facing up (a). Starting with one of the long edges, roll up the dough jelly-roll-style (b). Pinch the two ends to seal in the sesame oil. Lightly flatten the roll with the heel of your hand and cut the roll into 2-inch pieces. Holding a chopstick perpendicular to one piece, firmly press the center in a vertical line (c). (This will cause the ends to "flower" when they are steamed.) Repeat this process for each piece. Arrange the shaped

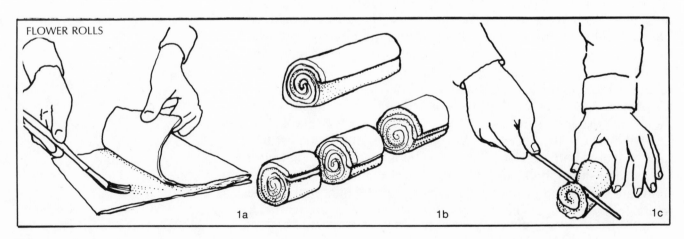

FLOWER ROLLS

1a   1b   1c

rolls about 1 inch apart on several steamer trays that have been lined with wet cheesecloth or with parchment paper punched with holes. Let the rolls rise for 15 minutes.

2   Fill a wok with water level with the bottom edge of a steamer tray and heat until boiling. Place one tray of rolls over the boiling water, cover, and steam for 15 minutes over high heat, until the rolls are light and springy. Steam the remaining rolls in the same manner. To reheat, steam for 5 minutes over high heat.

SNAIL BUNS

LUO SI JUAN   螺 絲 捲

There are no snails in this recipe. Rather, these delicately flavored steamed buns, which are served at many Sichuan and Hunan restaurants, are shaped like snails. They are often deep-fried until golden brown after having been steamed. Either way, snail buns are excellent as a substitute for rice.

1   Prepare the dough as directed and cut it in half. On a lightly floured surface, roll out each half to form a rectangle approximately 10 by 14 inches and ⅙ inch thick. Spread the surface of one rectangle with half the lard-and-sugar mixture. Starting with one of the long edges, roll up the rectangle jelly-roll-style. Pinch the two ends to seal the dough; lightly flatten the roll with the heel of your hand. Cut the roll crosswise into thin shreds. Separate the shreds into fifteen groups and let them rest. Repeat the process for the other rectangle.

2   Gather up each group of shreds and lightly stretch (a), wrapping them Maypole-style around your index finger, third finger, and thumb (b). Tuck the end underneath to secure. Repeat the procedure for all the shreds and arrange the finished buns 1 inch apart on several steamer trays that have been lined with wet cheesecloth or

THIRTY BUNS

1 recipe basic yeast dough (page 49)
½ cup melted lard (or softened butter) plus ½ cup sugar, creamed to a paste
¼ cup minced cooked ham or grated carrot

SNAIL BUNS

55

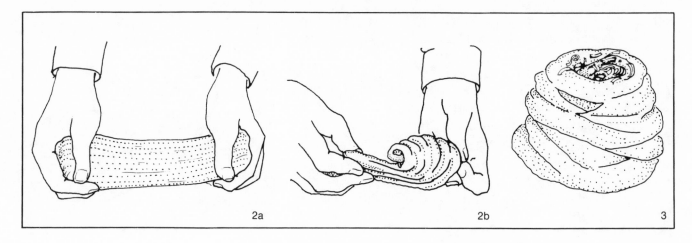

2a   2b   3

with parchment paper punched with holes. Sprinkle the tops with the minced ham or grated carrot and let the buns rise for 15 minutes.

3   Fill a wok with water level with the bottom edge of a steamer tray and heat until boiling. Place one tray of buns over the boiling water, cover, and steam for 15 minutes over high heat. Steam the remaining buns in the same manner. To reheat, steam the buns for 5 minutes over high heat.

TWENTY BUNS

½ recipe basic yeast dough
  (page 49)
¼ cup sesame oil

LOTUS BUNS

HE YE BAO 荷葉包

With a few deft movements, a yeast dough can be transformed into a number of unusual shapes, from butterflies to mock lotus leaves. Lotus buns are traditionally served with crispy-skin duck, sweet bean sauce, and scallion pieces. Once steamed, each bun contains a pocket into which stir-fried meats and vegetables can be stuffed.

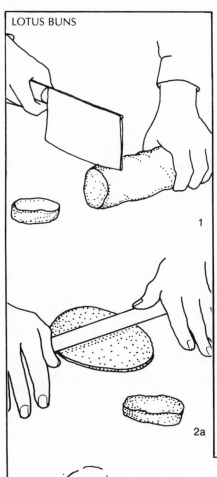

LOTUS BUNS

1

2a

1 Prepare the dough as directed and on a lightly floured surface form it into a long, snakelike roll about 1½ inches in diameter. Cut the roll into twenty pieces.

2 Place each piece, cut edge down, on the counter, and using a small rolling pin, roll out to a 3-inch circle (a). Brush the surface of the circle generously with sesame oil (b) and fold over to form a half-moon shape. With a sharp knife, lightly score the surface of the shaped bun with a diamond pattern, lengthwise and crosswise. Make two V-shaped indentations in the round edge of the bun with the end of a knife (c). Arrange the shaped buns 1 inch apart on steamer trays that have been lined with wet cheesecloth or with parchment paper punched with holes. Cover the buns with a cloth and let rise for about 15 minutes.

3 Fill a wok with water level with the bottom edge of a steamer tray and heat until boiling. Place one steamer tray over the boiling water, cover, and steam for 10 to 15 minutes over high heat, until the buns are puffed and springy. Steam the remaining buns in the same manner. To reheat the buns, steam for 5 minutes over high heat.

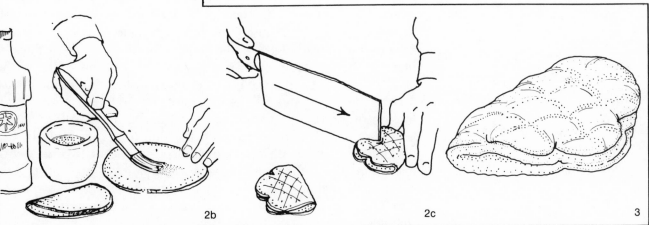

2b

2c

3

1 pound chopped pitted
dates
4 cups hot water
½ cup lard or butter, cut into
tablespoon-size pieces
½ cup sugar
1½ teaspoons lemon juice
1 teaspoon vanilla extract
1 teaspoon ground
cinnamon
1 recipe basic yeast dough
(page 49)
Red food coloring
12 pieces candied angelica

LONGEVITY PEACH BUNS

SHOU TAO

According to ancient Chinese thought, the peach symbolizes immortality and springtime. The God of Longevity is often pictured bearded and smiling, descending from a peach, or holding a peach in one hand and a staff in the other. Accordingly, steamed buns shaped like peaches are often served stacked in mountainous piles at birthday gatherings in hopes of imparting immortality and longevity to the person whose birthday is being celebrated.

1   To make the filling, place the dates with the hot water in a saucepan and heat the mixture until the water is boiling. Reduce the heat to medium and cook uncovered, stirring occasionally, for 15 to 20 minutes, or until the water has evaporated, leaving a thick paste. Cook the mixture, stirring constantly, until it is very dry. Add the lard or butter and the sugar. With a wooden spoon, stir constantly over medium heat to blend the ingredients. Cook the paste until it begins to leave the sides of the pan. Remove the pan from the heat and add the lemon juice, vanilla extract, and cinnamon. Stir to combine the ingredients evenly, and set aside to cool.
2   Prepare the dough as directed and cut it in half. On a lightly floured surface, form each half into a long snakelike roll approximately 1½ inches in diameter. Cut each roll into twelve pieces. With a cut edge down, use your fingers to flatten each piece into a 3-inch circle. The edges should be thinner and the center thicker. Place a heaping tablespoon of the date filling in the center of the dough skin (a). Gather the edges of the skin together at the center (b), pinch to seal, and roll the bun into a round ball. Lightly stretch the top of the bun to a small point (c), and using a ball of cotton, brush some red food coloring on the bun to create a blush. Cut the angelica into leaflike shapes and press one or two on top of each bun. Place the finished buns about 1 inch apart on several steamer trays that have been lined with wet cheesecloth or with parchment paper punched with holes. Let the buns rise for 15 minutes.

3 Fill a wok with water level with the bottom edge of a steamer tray and heat until boiling. Place one tray of buns over the boiling water, cover, and steam over high heat for 15 to 20 minutes, or until the buns are puffed and springy. Steam the remaining buns in the same manner. To reheat, steam the buns for 10 minutes over high heat.

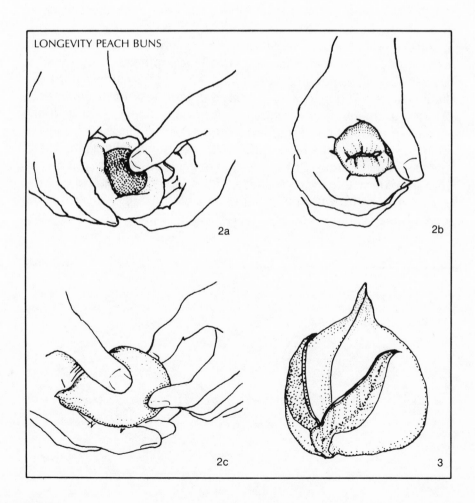

LONGEVITY PEACH BUNS

2a

2b

2c

3

TWENTY-FOUR PANCAKES

1½ cups all-purpose flour
½ cup cake flour
1 teaspoon salt
1 cup boiling water
¼ cup sesame oil
½ cup minced scallion
  greens
½ cup peanut, safflower, or
  corn oil

SCALLION CAKES

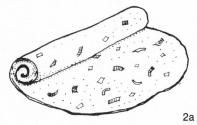

2a

SCALLION CAKES

CONG YOU BING　葱 油 餅

Scallion cakes are standard fare for a traditional Chinese breakfast with hot rice congee, but they are equally suitable for a snack or with stir-fried dishes as a rice substitute. Although most northern chefs make large, thick pancakes, I prefer smaller, thinner ones that become very crisp in frying. These cakes may be made in advance and reheated in a 350° oven for 8 to 10 minutes until crisp.

1 Place the all-purpose flour, the cake flour, and the salt in a mixing bowl and stir to blend evenly. Add the boiling water, and using a wooden spoon, mix to a rough dough. Turn the dough out onto a lightly floured surface and knead for 5 minutes, until smooth and elastic. If the dough is very sticky, knead in ¼ cup all-purpose flour. Cover the dough with a cloth and let it rest for 20 minutes.
2 On a lightly floured surface, form the dough into a long snakelike roll and cut it into twenty-four pieces. Place each piece, cut edge down, on the work surface. Using a small rolling pin, roll it out to a 4-inch circle. Brush the surface generously with sesame oil and sprinkle with minced scallion greens. Starting at the edge closest to you, roll up the circle jelly-roll-style (a). Pinch the ends to contain the scallions and sesame oil. Lightly flatten the roll (b) and

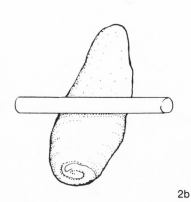

2b

2c

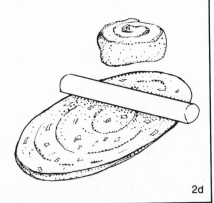

2d

60

roll it up from one end to the other, pinching the end to seal it (c). Let the pancakes rest for 20 minutes. Turn each one so that it lies flat on the work surface and press down with the palm of your hand. Roll out to a 4-inch circle (d) and place on a lightly floured tray. Stack the pancakes between lightly floured sheets of wax paper. Again let the pancakes rest for 20 minutes.

3   Heat a large frying pan, add the oil, and heat the oil to 350°. Add several of the pancakes to the oil and fry on both sides, turning once until they are golden brown and crisp, about 3 minutes. Remove and drain on absorbent paper. Fry the remaining pancakes in the same manner. Serve immediately.

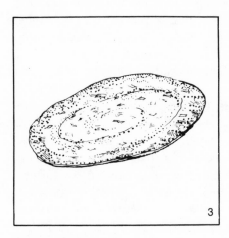

MANDARIN PANCAKES

BAO BING

TWENTY-FOUR PANCAKES

While Mandarin pancakes are usually associated with Peking duck and *mu shu* pork, they may be served with any stir-fried dish, in place of rice. They may be prepared in advance, refrigerated or frozen, and reheated about 10 minutes before serving.

2 cups all-purpose flour
1 cup boiling water
¼ cup sesame oil

1   Place the flour in a bowl. Slowly add the boiling water, mixing with a wooden spoon to form a rough dough. Let the dough cool

61

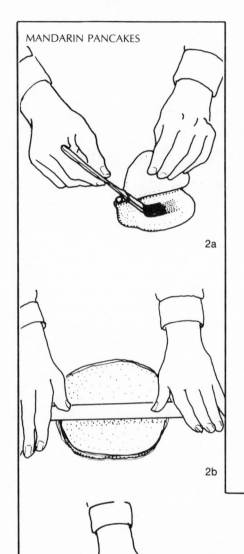

MANDARIN PANCAKES

2a

2b

slightly and turn it out onto a lightly floured surface. Knead for about 5 minutes, until smooth and elastic. Cut the dough in half. Form each half into a long snakelike roll about 1½ inches in diameter. Cut each roll into twelve pieces. Cover the dough pieces with a damp cloth to prevent them from drying out.

2 Place one piece, with a cut edge down, on the lightly floured surface. Using the palm of your hand, flatten it into a circle. Pick it up, and using your fingers, press the circle to 2 inches in diameter. Repeat the same process for another dough piece. Brush the surface of one dough circle with sesame oil, using enough oil to be generous, but not so much that it runs over the edges (a). Place another circle on top and lightly pinch the edges together to create a double circle. Repeat this process for all the dough pieces; you will have twelve double circles. Using a small rolling pin on a floured surface, roll out each double circle to 6 inches in diameter (b).

3 Heat a well-seasoned, 12-inch heavy skillet until very hot. (A bit of water sprinkled on the surface of the pan should evaporate immediately.) Place a double circle in the pan and fry for about 1 minute, twirling in a circular motion with your fingertips until it puffs in the middle (a). Turn it over and fry for another 30 seconds, twirling again. Remove and let cool for a few seconds. Carefully peel the two pancakes apart (b) and fold each one into quarters, with the cooked side on the inside (c). Repeat for the other pancakes and arrange them in a circular pattern on a plate, overlapping slightly. Cover them with a damp cloth to keep warm and moist. Just before serving, steam the pancakes for 10 minutes over high heat.

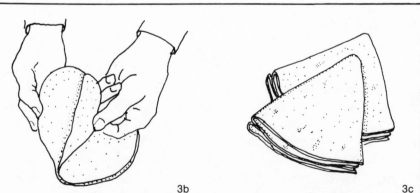

3a

3b

3c

SESAME FLAT BREADS

SHAO BING 燒 餅

Every morning for the three and a half years that I lived in Taipei, my breakfast consisted of a steaming bowl of sweet bean milk (*dou jiang*), served with a deep-fried crullerlike pastry (*you tiao*) stuffed into a flaky sesame flat bread (*shao bing*). This traditional Chinese breakfast can be as habit-forming as coffee.

In addition to being a vital element in a Chinese breakfast, *shao bing* are served with Mongolian barbecue and Mongolian fire pot. At some meals, these flaky breads take the place of rice and are served with stir-fried meat and vegetable dishes. In that case the *shao bing* are split open, stuffed with the stir-fried mixture, and eaten like a sandwich.

1   Place the flours and salt in a mixing bowl. Add the boiling water and mix with a wooden spoon to form a rough dough. Turn the dough out onto a lightly floured surface and knead for about 5 minutes, until smooth and elastic. Cover the dough with a cloth and let it rest for 30 minutes.

2   To prepare the **roux,** heat a saucepan until very hot. Add the oil and heat to 350°. Add the flour and cook over medium heat, stirring constantly until the flour is nut-brown and very fragrant. Remove from the heat and let cool.

3   On a lightly floured surface, roll out the dough to a rectangle that is approximately 14 inches long and 10 inches wide. Spread the roux evenly over the surface, stopping an inch away from each edge (a). Starting with one of the long sides, roll up the rectangle jelly-roll-style (b). Pinch the ends to seal in the roux; flatten the roll lightly with the heel of your hand. Cut the roll into twenty pieces (c) and pinch the ends of each one to prevent the roux from coming out.

4   On a lightly floured surface, roll out one dough piece to a rectangle 6 inches by 4 inches, with the pinched ends at either end of

4 cups all-purpose flour
2 cups cake flour
1½ teaspoons salt
2¾ cups boiling water

Roux
¾ cup peanut, safflower, or
   corn oil
1 cup all-purpose flour

¼ cup untoasted sesame
   seeds

SESAME FLAT BREADS

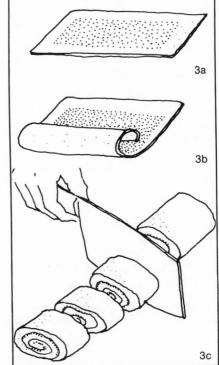

3a

3b

3c

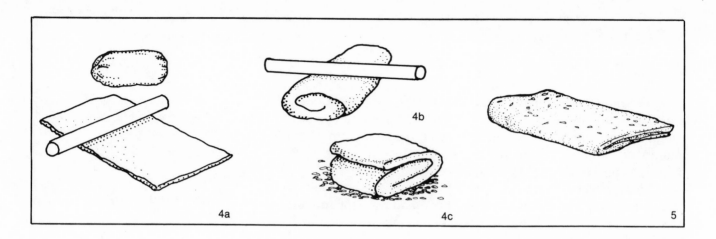

4a

4b

4c

5

the length (a). Fold the rectangle into thirds, bringing the bottom third over to the center of the length, and folding the top third down in toward the center. (This constitutes one "turn.") Turn the dough clockwise a quarter turn so that the seam is vertical (b) and roll out once again to a 6-by-4-inch rectangle. Fold into thirds to make another turn and turn the piece once again in a clockwise direction so that the seam is vertical. Dip the bottom (nonseam side) in the sesame seeds (c) and roll out to a rectangle that measures 6 inches by 4 inches. Repeat this process for the remaining dough pieces. Place the finished breads on an ungreased cookie sheet, sesame side down.

5 Preheat the oven to 400°. Bake the breads for 12 minutes, or until flaky and crisp, turning once. Serve immediately. To reheat, bake in a 350° oven for 5 to 7 minutes, until hot and crisp.

NOODLES 麵類

PLAIN THIN NOODLES

EXTRA-THIN NOODLES, AMOY-STYLE

FLAT NOODLES

Several years ago I had the privilege of watching a professional Chinese chef "throw" noodles by hand. I was mesmerized as he took a bulging piece of a soft flour-and-water dough and swung it up into the air so that it formed a thick, ropelike braid. He then proceeded to wave it wildly about, stretching and wrapping the dough around itself so that it divided into two fat strands, then four thinner ones. The process continued for about 10 minutes, with the strands multiplying and dividing with each swing. At last he held 16,000 fine, silky noodles draped over his arms. I was beside myself. And where did this wondrous scene transpire? Peking? Shandong? Hong Kong? The actual location was a Chinese restaurant kitchen in Toledo, Ohio.

What I had assumed to be a rare, ancient craft, performed by few, was once a standard skill for any well-rounded northern Chinese master chef. According to Buwei Yang Chao in *How to Cook and Eat in Chinese*, "A good northern cook, or even a cooking maid, knows how to swing noodles by hand."

Unfortunately, it appears that this once-popular craft is near extinction; one would be hard pressed to find many Chinese restaurants in the United States offering hand-swung noodles. Even in Peking, where handmade noodles were once commonplace, there remain only a few small noodle stands offering the handmade variety.

Handmade noodles aside, machine-made noodles and pasta play a prominent role in the modern Chinese diet, second only to rice. In the northern regions, where wheat is grown, noodles replace rice as the main staple for everyday meals. In the other areas, a noodle dish may be a snack, a staple food, or a meal in itself.

Like rice, wheat has long been a staple crop in China; records indicate that it was cultivated by Chinese farmers before 2800 B.C. Wheat, along with millet and barley, became the prime crop in the cool, arid regions of northern China because of its hardiness, its yield, and its high protein content. The Chinese milled the wheat and used the resulting flour to prepare a myriad of steamed breads, pancakes, and noodles.

65

THIN, STRAIGHT EGG NOODLES

THIN-EGG-NOODLE CLUSTERS

FRIED EGG NOODLES

Although noodles may seem to be a Chinese invention, anthropological clues suggest that central Asia might more properly be their source. There is unsubstantiated evidence of their presence as early as 1044 B.C., during the Etruscan era, and again later in the fifth century A.D. This refutes the commonly held belief that Marco Polo introduced the noodle to Europe after his travels to the Far East.

Once the noodle concept was introduced to ancient China, it flourished; pasta has played a prominent role in the Chinese regimen for centuries. Its popularity is easily understood: It may be eaten hot or cold; it cooks quickly; it is easily prepared; and it provides an inexpensive and nutritious filler.

Equally significant is the importance of noodles in the Chinese culture; they symbolize longevity, and to consume them is considered a means of attaining longevity. Traditionally, noodles are served on birthdays in much the same way birthday cakes are presented in the West. In view of their symbolic importance, it is not surprising to find that most noodles are very long. They are made of a number of different materials — from rice, bean curd, or pea starch to flour and water — but they are all long. They should be eaten with great relish, and with much slurping, as most Chinese eat them, for to cut the noodles is to invite ominous repercussions. (A soup spoon and chopsticks generally are used to facilitate shoveling them into the mouth.)

While the flour-and-water variety is more popular in northern China, the Cantonese prefer a flour, egg, and water noodle. Once prepared, these two doughs may be fashioned into many shapes. Hand-swung flour-and-water dough may be thrown into round, flat, or triangular noodles and macaroni. These handmade noodles have a silky texture that machine-made noodles never attain. Machine-made noodles, on the other hand, although slightly less refined in texture, are available in an amazing number of shapes, as a visit to any Chinese grocery store will prove.

Most Americans are knowledgeable about the common types of flour, egg, and water noodles but frequently are unaware of the various noodles made with rice powder, mung beans (pea starch), and bean curd.

Noodles made from rice powder, known as rice stick noodles or rice vermicelli (*mi fen*), are a variation on the traditional flour-and-water variety and are popular in the eastern and southern regions of

China. Always sold in dried form, these thin, white noodles are widely available in 8-ounce and 16-ounce bags. The uses of rice noodles are many: Once softened in warm water, they may be stir-fried with an assortment of meat, seafood, or vegetables; they may be used in a broth or soup as a delicate garnish; or they may be deep-fried in very hot oil to a light, crisp mass that serves as a bed for stir-fried dishes. Rice stick noodles will keep indefinitely, wrapped, in an airtight container in a cool, dry place. The thinnest variety is recommended for stir-fried dishes and soups. For deep-frying, thin ones are suggested, but thicker noodles may also be used.

Bean threads (*fen si*), also called cellophane noodles or pea starch noodles, are made from mung beans that are first soaked, then ground to a smooth purée, mixed with water, and strained to obtain a liquid. The liquid is dried in sheets and made into translucent noodles. When cooked, the noodles are transparent and have a smooth, gelatinous texture. After being softened in warm water, bean threads may be used in soups, stir-fried with a savory sauce, or served in cold platters or salads. They also may be deep-fried in the same manner as rice noodles to provide a crisp bed for stir-fried dishes. They absorb a considerable quantity of the liquid in which they are cooked and, since they have no flavor of their own, assume the flavor of the dish's sauce or broth. Like rice stick noodles, bean threads will keep indefinitely, wrapped, in an airtight container in a cool, dry place.

Bean curd noodles (*gan si*) are made from pressed bean curd. They are made from soybeans and so are very rich in protein and low in calories. These noodles are thin and tan. After being softened in a mixture of baking soda and water, and then rinsed, they are used primarily in cold dishes. They are usually sold packaged in plastic bags and, unfortunately, may only be available in sizable Chinese communities. An improvised version of bean curd noodles may be made by weighting down hard bean curd until most of the water has been pressed out, leaving a compact square. The square is then cut into noodlelike shreds.

In the Far East, most neighborhoods have one or two noodle makers whose shops or stands daily provide a wealth of freshly made noodles, in addition to wonton skins and dumpling wrappers. We may not be quite as lucky in the West, but most Chinese grocery

RICE STICK NOODLES

BEAN THREADS
(CELLOPHANE NOODLES)

BEAN CURD NOODLES

stores offer fresh plain noodles and egg noodles, as well as a generous selection of dried noodles that should fulfill the needs of any recipe. Fresh Chinese noodles are also available at some supermarkets. Alternatively, as outlined in the accompanying chart, fresh or dried Italian pasta may be substituted for the Chinese variety in a number of recipes. Cooking times for noodles vary greatly, depending on the thickness; they should be cooked until just tender but still slightly firm to the bite.

To many Americans a Chinese noodle dish suggests a vision of chow mein served on a bed of greasy fried noodles. This Americanized version is a far cry from the subtly seasoned and textured original. The types of noodle dishes are many and may be divided into the following categories:

SOUP NOODLES   Cooked noodles served in a rich broth with a garnish of seafood, meat, or vegetables; or, noodles simmered in a flavorful broth and topped with a mixture of seafood, meat, or vegetables.

STIR-FRIED NOODLES   Cooked noodles tossed over heat with a garnish of meat, seafood, or vegetables and cooked with a sauce. *Lo mein* dishes fall into this category.

SAUCY NOODLES   Cooked noodles served on a platter with a garnish of meat, seafood, or vegetables, and topped with a sauce or dressing. This includes both hot and cold noodle dishes.

PAN-FRIED NOODLES   Cooked noodles that are fried until crisp and golden, then topped with a garnish of stir-fried meat, seafood, or vegetables in a sauce.

CHINESE NOODLES: USES AND SUBSTITUTES

DESCRIPTION	CHINESE NAME	USE	SUBSTITUTE
Plain thin noodles (flour and water)	*gan mian* *ji mian*	soup noodle	spaghettini
Extra-thin noodles, Amoy-style (flour and water)	*mian xian*	soup noodle	vermicelli
Flat noodles (flour and water)	*gan mian bian-de* *ji mian bian-de*	soup noodle	fettucini or linguini
Thin, straight egg noodles (flour, egg, and water)	*dan mian*	stir-fried noodle pan-fried noodle saucy noodle	spaghettini
Thin-egg-noodle clusters (flour, egg, and water)	*dan mian qui*	stir-fried noodle pan-fried noodle saucy noodle	vermicelli
Fried egg noodles (flour, egg, and water)	*yi mian*	stir-fried noodle	*pancit mian* *chuka soba*
Rice stick noodles/rice vermicelli (rice powder and water)	*mi fen*	stir-fried noodle soup noodle saucy noodle	no substitute
Bean threads/ cellophane noodles (pea starch and water)	*fen si*	stir-fried noodle soup noodle saucy noodle	no substitute
Bean curd noodles (bean curd)	*gan si*	salads cold platters	no substitute

1 pound boneless center-cut
pork loin

Pork Marinade

1 tablespoon soy sauce
2 teaspoons rice wine
1 teaspoon sesame oil
2 teaspoons water
1 teaspoon cornstarch

6 dried Chinese black
mushrooms
12 dried wood ears
18 dried tiger lily buds
½ pound extra-thin noodles,
Amoy-style
½ cup peanut, safflower, or
corn oil

Minced Seasonings

1 tablespoon minced garlic
2 tablespoons minced
scallions
2 teaspoons minced
gingerroot

Pork Sauce

1 cup chicken broth
2½ tablespoons soy sauce
1 tablespoon rice wine
1 teaspoon sesame oil
1 teaspoon Chinese black
vinegar or Worcestershire
sauce
1 teaspoon sugar
½ teaspoon black pepper
1 tablespoon cornstarch

PORK AND VEGETABLE NOODLES IN BROTH

DA LU MIAN　　大滷麵

The category of "soup noodles" includes those dishes in which the cooked noodles are served in a rich broth and garnished with a saucy topping of stir-fried meat and vegetables. Like many other noodle platters, this dish may be served as a meal in itself for lunch or dinner, or as a hearty and filling snack.

1　Remove any fat or gristle from the pork loin and discard. Cut the meat, across the grain, into slices ⅛ inch thick. Cut the slices into pieces that are approximately 1½ inches square. Place the slices in a bowl, add the **pork marinade,** toss lightly, and let marinate for 20 minutes. Soften the dried mushrooms, the wood ears, and the tiger lily buds separately in hot water to cover for 20 minutes. Drain. Remove and discard the mushroom stems. Cut the mushroom caps in half. Cut away and discard the hard, bitter nib on the underside of the wood ears, and cut the wood ears into bite-size pieces, if necessary. Tie the tiger lily buds into knots.
2　Heat 2 quarts water and 1 tablespoon of the oil until boiling. Add the noodles and cook until just tender. Drain the noodles, and portion them into six soup bowls.

Soup Base
6 cups chicken broth
2 tablespoons soy sauce
2 tablespoons rice wine
2 teaspoons sesame oil
1 teaspoon salt

Thickener
3 tablespoons cornstarch
4 tablespoons water

1 pound fresh spinach,
trimmed and cleaned
3 eggs, lightly beaten

3   Heat a wok, add the remaining oil, and heat the oil to 375°. Add the pork slices and stir-fry over high heat until the meat changes color. Remove with a handled strainer and drain. Remove all but 2 tablespoons of oil from the wok and heat until very hot. Add the **minced seasonings** and stir-fry for about 10 seconds, until fragrant. Add the mushrooms, wood ears, and tiger lily buds. Stir-fry for about 15 seconds over high heat and add the **pork sauce.** Toss lightly until the sauce has thickened, add the pork slices, and stir to coat the pork. Remove the mixture from the wok and set aside.

4   Place the **soup base** in a saucepan. Heat until boiling and add the **thickener,** stirring constantly to prevent lumps. Add the spinach and remove from the heat. Add the eggs in a thin stream. Stir the soup once or twice and ladle the broth over the noodles. Spoon the pork mixture over the noodles and serve immediately.

SESAME CHICKEN WITH RICE NOODLES IN BROTH

MA YOU JI MI FEN

蔴油雞米粉

This savory Fujianese soup is traditionally served to a mother every day for one month following childbirth, for it is believed that the chicken and gingerroot rejuvenate the body.

1   Remove and discard any fat from inside the cavity and around the neck of the chicken. Cut the chicken, through the bones, into pieces about 2 inches square. Plunge the chicken pieces into boiling water for 1 minute to clean them. Rinse in cold water and drain. Soften the rice noodles in hot water to cover for 10 minutes. Drain.

2   Heat a heavy soup pot or a 3-quart Dutch oven. Add the sesame oil and heat until very hot. Add the gingerroot and stir-fry for about 5 seconds over high heat, until fragrant. Add the chicken pieces and fry in the hot oil until golden brown on both sides. Add the rice wine and heat until boiling. Add the **soup base** and heat until the liquid is boiling. Reduce the heat to low, and cook the chicken, uncovered, for 1¼ hours. Add the rice noodles and cook for 1½ minutes, or until they are very tender. Serve immediately.

SIX SERVINGS

1 small roasting chicken, 3½ to 4 pounds
½ pound rice stick noodles
¼ cup sesame oil
6 tablespoons shredded gingerroot
1 cup rice wine

Soup Base
5 cups water
2 teaspoons sugar
2 teaspoons salt

¼ cup peanut, safflower, or
　corn oil
½ pound extra-thin noodles,
　Amoy-style
6 dried Chinese black
　mushrooms
3 tablespoons dried wood
　ears
2 carrots, roll-cut into 1-inch
　pieces
1 cup straw mushrooms
¼ pound fresh snow peas,
　ends snapped

Minced Seasonings

1 tablespoon minced garlic
2 teaspoons minced
　gingerroot
1 tablespoon minced shallots

3 cups Chinese cabbage
　(Napa), in 2-inch squares

Soup Base

6 cups liquid (water plus the
　dried-mushroom liquid)
2½ tablespoons soy sauce
2 tablespoons rice wine
1 teaspoon salt
1 teaspoon sesame oil
¼ teaspoon black pepper

Thickener

¼ cup cornstarch
6 tablespoons water

1 cup 1-inch pieces of
　scallion greens
1 tablespoon sesame oil

VEGETARIAN NOODLES IN BROTH

SU CAI GEN MIAN　素菜羹麵

Western vegetarian cookery is often said to be somewhat bland, but Chinese vegetarian cuisine is just the opposite. Pungent seasonings, such as garlic, gingerroot, and sesame oil, appear frequently and contrasting textures are accentuated. This vegetarian noodle platter is a good example.

1　Heat 2 quarts water and 1 tablespoon of the oil until boiling. Add the noodles and cook until just tender. Drain the noodles, and portion them into six serving bowls.
2　Soften the dried mushrooms and wood ears separately for 20 minutes in hot water to cover. Reserve the mushroom-soaking liquid, discard the stems of the mushrooms, and cut the large caps in half. Cut away and discard the hard, bitter nib on the underside of the wood ears, and cut the wood ears into bite-size pieces, if necessary. Cook the carrot pieces for 1 minute in boiling water to cover, and refresh in cold water. Parboil the straw mushrooms and snow peas separately in boiling water to cover for 5 seconds. Remove and refresh immediately in cold water. Drain thoroughly.
3　Heat a wok, add the remaining 3 tablespoons of oil, and heat until very hot. Add the **minced seasonings** and stir-fry until fragrant, about 10 seconds. Add the harder pieces of the Chinese cabbage and stir-fry over high heat until slightly limp at the edges. Add the leafier sections and continue stir-frying for about 20 seconds over high heat. (If the cabbage is very dry, add 1 tablespoon rice wine.) Add the **soup base** (including the dried-mushroom-soaking liquid) and cook, uncovered, for 10 minutes over medium heat. Add the black mushrooms, carrot pieces, straw mushrooms, and wood ears, and continue cooking for 1 minute. Add the **thickener,** stirring constantly to prevent lumps. Add the snow peas and the scallions. Stir lightly to coat, and add the sesame oil. Toss again and spoon the mixture over the noodles. Serve immediately.

BARBECUED PORK WITH NOODLES IN BROTH

CHA SHAO TANG MIAN   义燒湯麵

This traditional Cantonese "soup noodle" dish may be found both in a sumptuous *dim sum* parlor and at a small, hole-in-the-wall noodle stand.

1   To prepare the barbecued pork, place the pork loin in a bowl with the **pork marinade.** Turn the pork to coat it with the marinade and let marinate for at least 1 hour, or overnight. Place the meat on a rack in a roasting pan. Preheat the oven to 375° and bake for 40 to 45 minutes, or until the meat is cooked. Remove, and let cool. Cut the meat into slices 1½ inches long, 1 inch wide, and about ⅛ inch thick. Cut each slice in half lengthwise. Peel away the tough outer skin from the broccoli and separate the flowerets. Roll-cut the stems into 1-inch pieces. Heat 1½ quarts salted water until boiling. Add the stem pieces and cook for ½ minute. Add the flowerets and cook for 2½ minutes, or until both stems and flowerets are just tender. Refresh immediately in cold water. Drain thoroughly.

2   Heat 2 quarts of water and 1 tablespoon oil until boiling. Add the noodles and cook until barely tender. Drain them. Portion the noodles into six soup bowls.

3   Heat a wok, add the remaining 2 tablespoons of oil, and heat until very hot. Add the **minced seasonings** and stir-fry for about 10 seconds, until fragrant. Add the **pork sauce** and stir until thickened. Add the pork slices and the broccoli. Toss lightly to coat the ingredients with the sauce, and set aside.

4   Heat the **soup mixture** until boiling and ladle it over the noodles in each bowl. Spoon some of the pork-broccoli mixture on top of each portion and serve.

SIX SERVINGS

1 pound boneless pork loin

Pork Marinade
1½ tablespoons hoisin sauce
1 tablespoon soy sauce
1 tablespoon rice wine
2 teaspoons sugar
1 teaspoon salt
1 teaspoon ketchup
½ tablespoon minced garlic

1 pound broccoli
½ pound plain thin noodles
3 tablespoons peanut, safflower, or corn oil

Minced Seasonings
1 tablespoon finely shredded gingerroot
2 tablespoons finely shredded scallions

Pork Sauce
3 tablespoons oyster sauce
2 tablespoons soy sauce
2 tablespoons rice wine
¾ teaspoon salt
1 teaspoon sesame oil
1½ teaspoons sugar
½ cup chicken broth or water
1½ teaspoons cornstarch

Soup Mixture
6 cups chicken broth
1½ teaspoons salt
1 tablespoon rice wine
½ teaspoon sesame oil
¼ teaspoon black pepper

Oyster Marinade

1 tablespoon rice wine
2 slices gingerroot, smashed
  with the flat side of a
  cleaver
2 scallions, smashed with the
  flat side of a cleaver
½ teaspoon salt

1 pint fresh, shucked oysters

Shrimp Marinade

1 tablespoon rice wine
1 teaspoon salt
½ teaspoon sesame oil

½ pound medium-sized raw
  shrimp in their shells

Scallop Marinade

1 tablespoon rice wine
2 slices gingerroot, smashed
  with the flat side of a
  cleaver
½ teaspoon salt
½ teaspoon sesame oil

½ pound fresh scallops

Fish Marinade

1 tablespoon rice wine
2 slices gingerroot, smashed
  with the flat side of a
  cleaver
½ teaspoon salt

SEAFOOD HOT POT WITH NOODLES

SAN XIAN SHA GUO MIAN 三鲜砂锅麵

Sandy pots are covered earthenware vessels. They are well suited to slow braising, since the clay conducts and distributes heat evenly, and they may be used over direct heat or in the oven. This noodle pot, with its colorful array of seafood, is a feast for the eyes and the palate. Serve it as a meal in itself or as an entrée in a banquet.

1   Prepare the individual **marinades,** pinching the gingerroot slices in them repeatedly for several minutes to impart the flavor. Discard the gingerroot slices. Mix the seafoods with their respective marinades and let marinate separately for 20 minutes.

2   Heat a wok, add the oil, and heat until almost smoking; add the cabbage pieces. Stir-fry for about 30 seconds, adding a tablespoon of the **soup base.** Add the rest of the soup base and heat until boiling. Reduce the heat to low, partially cover, and cook for 30 minutes. Meanwhile, cook the noodles in 4 quarts of boiling water until just tender. Drain and rinse the noodles. Place the noodles in a sandy pot, or in a Dutch oven. Pour the cabbage-broth mixture on top. Arrange the oysters, shrimp, scallops, and fish on top of the cabbage, keeping each one separate from the others. Sprinkle the minced leeks or scallions over the top, and cover. Cook the casserole for 5 to 7 minutes (until the seafood is just cooked) over high heat, or in a preheated 450° oven. Serve immediately from the pot.

1 pound firm-fleshed fish
  fillets, skin removed and
  diagonally cut into thin
  slices 1½ inches long and
  1 inch wide

1 tablespoon peanut,
  safflower, or corn oil
2 cups Chinese cabbage
  (Napa), cut into 2-inch
  squares

Soup Base

6 cups chicken broth
2 tablespoons rice wine
1½ teaspoons salt

½ pound flat noodles
4 tablespoons minced leeks
  or scallion greens

SAUCY SHRIMP NOODLES

XIA REN CHAO MIAN　蝦仁炒麵

This saucy Fujianese noodle platter reflects a basic characteristic of the eastern regional school — it is simple, yet with delicate seasonings accentuating the natural flavors of the ingredients. The tart and sweet tomato sauce heightens the fresh flavor of the shrimp.

1　Heat 2 quarts of water and the tablespoon of oil until boiling. Add the noodles and cook until just tender. Drain the noodles, add the tablespoon of sesame oil to them, and toss lightly. Score each shrimp along the length of the back and remove the vein; the scoring will allow the shrimp to "butterfly" when it is cooked. Rinse all the shrimp and drain thoroughly. Place the shrimp in a bowl and add the **marinade** (after having pinched the gingerroot in the rice wine repeatedly for several minutes to impart its flavor). Toss lightly and let marinate for 20 minutes. Discard the gingerroot.
2　Heat a wok, add the cup of oil, and heat the oil to 350°. Add the shrimp and stir-fry briefly until they change color and curl, about 1½ minutes. Remove them with a handled strainer, and drain. Remove all but 2 tablespoons of oil from the pan and reheat until very hot. Add the **seasonings** and stir-fry until the onions are soft and transparent. Add the **sauce** and heat until boiling. Add the cooked noodles and toss lightly. Cook for about 1 minute and add the **thickener**. Cook until the sauce has thickened and the noodles are coated. Add the cooked shrimp, toss lightly to combine the ingredients, and transfer the mixture to a platter. Serve immediately.

SIX SERVINGS

1 tablespoon peanut, safflower, or corn oil
½ pound thin, straight egg noodles
1 tablespoon sesame oil
1½ pounds raw shrimp, shelled

Shrimp Marinade

2 tablespoons rice wine
2 slices gingerroot, smashed with the flat side of a cleaver

1 cup peanut, safflower, or corn oil

Seasonings

2 medium-sized onions, shredded
1 tablespoon minced garlic
1 tablespoon minced gingerroot

Sauce

2 cups chicken broth
3 tablespoons soy sauce
2 tablespoons rice wine
1 tablespoon ketchup
1 tablespoon sugar
1 teaspoon sesame oil
½ teaspoon salt

Thickener

1 tablespoon cornstarch
2 tablespoons water

1 pound eye of the round or
  top sirloin roast

Beef Marinade

1 tablespoon soy sauce
½ tablespoon rice wine
1 teaspoon sesame oil
2 teaspoons minced garlic
2 teaspoons water
1 teaspoon cornstarch

12 dried Chinese black
  mushrooms
2 cakes bean curd
1 cup peanut, safflower, or
  corn oil
½ pound flat noodles

Minced Seasonings

2 tablespoons minced
  scallions
1 tablespoon minced
  gingerroot

2 medium-sized tomatoes,
  seeded and diced
2 green peppers, seeded and
  diced
1 tablespoon soy sauce
1 tablespoon rice wine

Soup Base

6 cups chicken broth
2 teaspoons salt
2 tablespoons soy sauce
1 tablespoon rice wine
1 teaspoon sugar
1 teaspoon sesame oil
¼ teaspoon black pepper

1 pound fresh spinach,
  trimmed and cleaned

BEEF WITH NOODLES IN A POT

NIU ROU GUO SHAO MIAN　牛肉鍋燒麵

This hearty noodle pot, with its flavorful garnish of meat and vegetables, constitutes a filling and nutritious meal.

1　Trim any fat or gristle from the beef and discard. Cut the meat, with the grain, into strips that are about 2 inches long and 2 inches thick. Cut each strip, across the grain, into slices about ⅛ inch thick. Place the meat slices in a bowl, add the **beef marinade,** toss lightly, and let marinate for 20 minutes.
2　Soften the dried mushrooms in warm water to cover for 20 minutes. Drain them, and remove and discard the stems. Cut the caps in half. Cut the bean curd into 1-inch cubes.
3　Heat 2 quarts of water and 1 tablespoon of the oil until boiling. Add the noodles and cook until barely tender. Remove, drain, and place the noodles in a heat-proof earthenware casserole or a Dutch oven.
4　Heat a wok, add the remaining oil, and heat the oil to 375°. Add half the beef slices and cook, stirring constantly over high heat, until the beef is cooked through. Remove with a handled strainer, drain, and reheat the oil. Cook the remaining beef in the same manner. Remove the oil from the wok, reserving 2 tablespoons. Clean the wok. Reheat the wok, add the 2 tablespoons of oil, and heat until very hot. Add the **minced seasonings** and stir-fry for about 10 seconds, until fragrant. Add the tomatoes, green peppers, soy sauce, and rice wine. Stir-fry for about 10 seconds. Add the mushrooms and stir-fry for another 5 seconds over high heat. Add the bean curd and the **soup base**. Heat the mixture until boiling, reduce the heat to medium, and cook, uncovered, for 8 minutes. Pour the soup mixture over the noodles. Arrange the beef slices and the spinach on top, cover, and place over high heat. Heat until the liquid is boiling and the spinach is just wilted. Remove the lid and serve.

PAN-FRIED NOODLES WITH BEEF AND BROCCOLI

NIU ROU CHAO MIAN   牛肉炒麪

Although hardly an innovative creation, this Cantonese classic is a favorite in *dim sum* houses across the globe. After tasting the crisp noodles drenched in velvety oyster sauce, contrasted with the tender beef slices and broccoli spears, one can easily understand its popularity.

1   Heat 2 quarts of water and 1 tablespoon of the oil until boiling. Add the noodles and cook until just tender. Drain the noodles, and toss them with the tablespoon of sesame oil. Place the noodles in a round cake pan or a pie plate and let cool.

2   Remove any fat or gristle from the beef and discard. Cut the meat, across the grain, into slices ⅛ inch thick. Cut the slices into pieces that are 1½ inches on each side. Place them in a bowl, add the **beef marinade,** toss lightly, and let marinate for 1 hour or longer. Drain the meat slices. Peel away the tough outer skin of the broccoli and separate the flowerets. Roll-cut the stems into 1-inch pieces. Heat 1½ quarts salted water until boiling. Add the stem pieces and cook for ½ minute. Add the flowerets and cook for 2½ minutes, or until both stems and flowerets are just tender. Refresh immediately in cold water. Drain thoroughly.

3   Heat a wok (or a cast-iron skillet), add 3 tablespoons of the oil, and heat until smoking. Invert the noodle cake into the pan and fry the noodles on both sides until golden brown, swirling the pan from time to time to move the noodles so that they cook evenly. Transfer the noodles to a deep, heat-proof platter and place in a preheated 350° oven to keep warm and crisp.

4   Reheat the wok, add the remaining oil, and heat it to 400°. Add half the beef slices and cook for about 1 minute, stirring constantly, until the beef changes color. Remove with a handled strainer, drain, and reheat the oil. Add the remaining beef slices and stir-fry in the same manner. Remove all but 2 tablespoons of oil from the wok and reheat until very hot. Add the **minced seasonings** and stir-fry until

---

SIX SERVINGS

2 cups peanut, safflower, or corn oil
½ pound thin-egg-noodle clusters
1 tablespoon sesame oil
1½ pounds eye of the round or top sirloin roast

Beef Marinade
2 tablespoons soy sauce
1 tablespoon rice wine
1 teaspoon sugar
1 teaspoon sesame oil
2 teaspoons minced garlic
2 teaspoons cornstarch
2 tablespoons water

1 pound broccoli

Minced Seasonings
2 tablespoons minced gingerroot
2 tablespoons minced scallions

Sauce
3 cups chicken broth
6 tablespoons oyster sauce
4 tablespoons soy sauce
2 tablespoons rice wine
2 teaspoons sugar
2 teaspoons sesame oil

Thickener
3 tablespoons cornstarch
4 tablespoons water

fragrant, about 10 seconds. Add the **sauce** and heat until boiling. Add the **thickener,** stirring constantly to prevent lumps. Add the beef and the broccoli. Toss lightly to coat with the sauce. Pour the mixture over the pan-fried noodles and serve immediately.

CHICKEN AND SHRIMP NOODLE PLATTER

JI SI XIA REN HUI MIAN　　　　雞絲蝦仁燴麪

The pan-fried noodle cake in this recipe may have inspired the invention of "chow mein" fried noodles sold in cans. In reality, however, one bears little resemblance to the other; the pan-fried noodles should be lightly crisp and golden brown on the outside and soft and tender inside. Although chow mein noodles generally are crisp, they lack the contrasting tenderness and delicacy of their pan-fried cousin.

1   Heat 2 quarts of water and the tablespoon of oil until boiling. Add the noodles and cook until just tender. Drain the noodles, and toss with the tablespoon of sesame oil. Place the noodles in a round cake pan or a pie plate and let cool.

2   Score each shrimp along the length of the back and remove the vein; the scoring will allow the shrimp to "butterfly" when it is cooked. Rinse all the shrimp and drain thoroughly. Place the shrimp in a bowl. Pinch the gingerroot slices in the **shrimp marinade** repeatedly for several minutes to impart the flavor to the rice wine. Discard the gingerroot. Add the marinade to the shrimp, toss lightly, and let marinate for 20 minutes. Remove the skin from the chicken breasts and discard. Cut the meat on the diagonal into thin slices about 1½ inches on each side and place them in a bowl. Add the **chicken marinade,** toss lightly, and let marinate for 20 minutes. Soften the dried mushrooms for 20 minutes in hot water to cover. Remove and discard the stems, and shred the caps.

3   Heat a wok (or a cast-iron skillet), add 3 tablespoons of the oil, and heat until smoking. Invert the noodle cake into the pan and fry

the noodles on both sides until golden brown, swirling the pan from time to time to move the noodles so that they cook evenly. Transfer the noodles to a deep heat-proof platter and place in a preheated 350° oven to keep warm and crisp.

4   Reheat the wok, add all but 3 tablespoons of the remaining oil, and heat it to 350°. Add the chicken shreds and stir-fry over high heat until they change color. Remove them with a handled strainer, and drain. Reheat the oil, add the shrimp, and stir-fry them for 1½ minutes, until cooked. Remove in the same manner and drain. Remove the oil from the wok. Reheat the pan, add the last 3 tablespoons of oil, and heat it until very hot. Add the **minced seasonings** and stir-fry for about 10 seconds, until fragrant. Add the mushroom shreds and stir-fry for about 5 seconds. Add the cabbage and carrot shreds. Toss lightly over high heat until the cabbage is just limp. Add the **sauce**. Cook until the sauce begins to boil, then add the **thickener,** stirring constantly to prevent lumps. Add the bean sprouts, chicken, scallion greens, and shrimp. Toss lightly to coat the food with sauce. Pour the mixture over the pan-fried noodles and serve immediately.

6 dried Chinese black
   mushrooms
1 cup peanut, safflower, or
   corn oil

Minced Seasonings
1 tablespoon minced
   gingerroot
1 tablespoon minced garlic

2 cups shredded Chinese
   cabbage (Napa)
4 carrots, peeled and cut
   into matchstick-size shreds

Sauce
3 cups chicken broth
4 tablespoons soy sauce
¾ teaspoon sugar
¼ teaspoon freshly ground
   black pepper
2 tablespoons rice wine
1 teaspoon sesame oil

Thickener
3 tablespoons cornstarch
5 tablespoons water

2 cups fresh bean sprouts
1 cup 1-inch pieces of
   scallion greens

1 pound boneless center-cut pork loin

Pork Marinade
1 tablespoon soy sauce
2 teaspoons rice wine
1 teaspoon sesame oil
1 tablespoon water
2 teaspoons cornstarch

2 cakes bean curd, about 3 inches square and 1 inch thick
2 medium-sized onions
1 tablespoon peanut, safflower, or corn oil
½ pound plain thin noodles
1 tablespoon sesame oil
½ cup peanut, safflower, or corn oil
1 tablespoon minced garlic

Sauce
½ cup sweet bean sauce
5 tablespoons soy sauce
1 tablespoon rice wine
2 tablespoons sugar

2 cups shredded carrot
2 cups shredded lettuce
2 cups peeled, shredded cucumber

COLD SPICY NOODLES

JIA JIANG MIAN   炸醬麵

This northern noodle platter features some of the more prominent seasonings of the cuisine of its origin — in particular, sweet bean sauce and garlic. Both flavorings contrast beautifully with the crisp, fresh vegetable shreds and tender meat and bean curd pieces.

1   Remove any fat or gristle from the pork loin and discard. Cut the meat into ½-inch dice. Place the pork in a bowl, add the **pork marinade,** toss lightly, and let marinate for 20 minutes. Place the bean curd on a plate with a paper towel on top and put a weight such as a heavy cutting board on top. (This will compress the bean curd and remove some water.) Drain and dice the bean curd, and dice the onions.
2   Heat 2 quarts of water and the tablespoon of oil until boiling. Add the noodles and cook until just tender. Lightly rinse the noodles under cold running water to remove the starch, and toss with the tablespoon of sesame oil. Arrange the noodles on a large platter or in a serving bowl.
3   Heat a wok, add the ½ cup of oil, and heat until very hot. Add the diced pork and stir-fry until the color changes. Remove with a handled strainer and drain. Reheat the oil until very hot. Add the bean curd and cook for about 1 minute, until light golden. Remove in the same manner and drain. Remove all but 2 tablespoons of oil from the wok and heat until very hot. Add the onion and garlic. Stir-fry over high heat, stirring constantly until the onion is soft and transparent. Add the **sauce.** Cook for a few minutes over high heat, stirring constantly until the sauce has thickened. Add the cooked pork and bean curd. Stir-fry to coat the ingredients with the sauce. Spoon the mixture over a third of the noodles. Arrange the shredded carrot, lettuce, and cucumbers over the remaining two thirds of the noodles in a decorative pattern next to the pork mixture. Serve at room temperature or cold. Toss lightly before portioning onto plates.

COLD TOSSED SICHUAN NOODLES

CHUAN WEI JI SI LIANG MIAN　川味雞絲凉麪

Since the climate of Sichuan and Hunan provinces is apt to be muggy and warm, cold noodle platters such as this one are extremely popular. The spicy seasonings in the sauce are intended to sensitize the palate so that the subtler flavors and the various textures may be appreciated.

1   Heat 2 quarts of water and the tablespoon of oil until boiling. Add the noodles and cook until just tender. Lightly rinse the noodles under cold running water. Drain thoroughly and toss with the tablespoon of sesame oil. Arrange the noodles on a large round platter or in a serving bowl.

2   To prepare egg sheets with the eggs, rub a nonstick frying pan or a well-seasoned wok with an oil-soaked paper towel. Heat the pan until a few drops of water sprinkled on the surface evaporate immediately. Add a quarter of the eggs and tilt the pan so that a thin pancake is formed. Cook until the pancake is lightly golden; then flip it over. Cook for a few seconds and remove. Prepare three more egg sheets in the same manner. Cut the egg sheets into matchstick-size shreds. Lightly rinse the bean sprouts in cold water and drain thoroughly.

3   Arrange the bean sprouts, the egg-sheet shreds, and the scallion greens in a decorative pattern over the noodles. Place the chicken shreds on top. Pour the **peanut dressing** over the noodles, toss lightly, and serve.

1 tablespoon peanut, safflower, or corn oil
½ pound thin, straight egg noodles
1 tablespoon sesame oil
2 "large" eggs, lightly beaten
3 cups fresh bean sprouts
1½ cups 1-inch pieces of scallion greens
2 cups shredded cooked chicken meat

Peanut Dressing
½ cup chunky peanut butter
3 tablespoons soy sauce
1½ tablespoons sugar
3 tablespoons sesame oil
1½ tablespoons Chinese black vinegar or 1 tablespoon Worcestershire sauce
1½ teaspoons chili oil
½ cup chicken broth
1 tablespoon minced garlic
1 tablespoon minced gingerroot

SIX SERVINGS

1 tablespoon peanut,
  safflower, or corn oil
½ pound thin, straight egg
  noodles
1 tablespoon sesame oil
½ pound fresh bean sprouts
1½ cups cucumber, peeled,
  seeded, and cut into
  julienne strips
1½ cups carrot, peeled and
  cut into julienne strips
½ pound medium-sized raw
  shrimp, deveined, peeled,
  and cooked
¼ cup chopped dry-roasted
  peanuts

Cold Dressing

6 tablespoons soy sauce
1 teaspoon salt
1½ tablespoons sugar
2 tablespoons sesame oil
3 tablespoons clear rice
  vinegar
2 tablespoons rice wine

COLD TOSSED NOODLE PLATTER

LIANG BAN MIAN
凉拌麵

This cold noodle platter defies regional classification; it is found in the cuisines of Peking, Sichuan, and Hunan. It is usually served in warm weather, when the crisp textures of the cold, shredded vegetables provide a tasty respite from the heat.

1 Heat 2 quarts of water and the tablespoon of oil until boiling. Add the noodles and cook until just tender. Lightly rinse the noodles under cold running water and drain thoroughly. Toss with the tablespoon of sesame oil. Arrange the noodles on a large round platter and let cool.
2 Rinse the bean sprouts and drain thoroughly. Arrange the carrots and cucumbers in two decorative rows bordering the edge of the noodles. Place the bean sprouts in the center.
3 Cut the shrimp in half lengthwise and arrange them, with the pink side up, in a circular row on top of the bean sprouts. Sprinkle the chopped peanuts on top. Before serving, pour the **cold dressing** over the noodles and toss lightly.

SIX SERVINGS

1 pound boneless center-cut
  pork loin

Pork Marinade

1 tablespoon soy sauce
2 teaspoons rice wine
1 teaspoon sesame oil
2 teaspoons water

½ pound raw shrimp, shelled

LI'S CHOP SUEY

LI GONG ZA SUI
李公什碎

The origin of chop suey is regarded by some food authorities as a controversial matter; Washington, D.C., Tokyo, and San Francisco have all been named as the site of this dish's creation. According to my Cantonese teacher, who managed to have the last word on all issues, chop suey was first prepared in the early 1900s in Tokyo for General Li Hon Chung. The general was so pleased with the dish that it was named in his honor. The following recipe offers a subtly seasoned, authentic rendition of this greatly abused classic.

1   Remove any fat or gristle from the pork loin and discard. Cut the meat, across the grain, into slices about ¼ inch thick. Cut the slices into matchstick-size shreds. Place the shreds in a bowl, add the **pork marinade,** toss lightly, and let marinate for 20 minutes.

2   Score each shrimp along the length of the back and remove the vein; the scoring will allow the shrimp to "butterfly" when it is cooked. Rinse all the shrimp lightly, and drain thoroughly. Place them in a linen dishtowel and squeeze out as much moisture as possible. Place the shrimp in a bowl. Pinch the gingerroot slices in the **shrimp marinade** repeatedly for several minutes to impart their flavor to the liquid. Add the marinade to the shrimp, toss lightly, and let marinate for 20 minutes. Discard the gingerroot.

3   Heat a wok, add the oil, and heat until smoking. Add the rice noodles and deep-fry until puffed and pale golden. This should happen almost immediately. Turn them over and deep-fry for a few seconds on the other side. Remove, and drain the noodles on absorbent paper. Transfer them to a large platter; break up the noodles with your fingertips and create a depression in the center into which the stir-fried ingredients will go. Remove the oil from the wok, reserving 9 tablespoons.

4   Reheat the wok, add 3 tablespoons of the reserved oil, and heat until very hot. Add the pork shreds and stir-fry over high heat until they have changed color and are cooked. Remove the pork and drain. Add 3 more tablespoons of the reserved oil, and heat until very hot. Add the shrimp and stir-fry over high heat until they have changed color, about 1 minute. Remove the shrimp and drain. Remove the oil from the wok.

5   Reheat the wok, add the remaining 3 tablespoons of reserved oil, and heat until very hot. Add the **minced seasonings** and stir-fry for about 5 seconds, until fragrant. Add the mushroom and green pepper shreds and stir-fry for about 10 seconds longer over high heat. Add the carrot shreds and continue stir-frying for about 1 minute. Add the bean sprouts and the **sauce**. Toss lightly over high heat, stirring constantly to prevent lumps. When the sauce has thickened, add the pork and the shrimp. Toss lightly to coat with the sauce and transfer the mixture to the platter. Serve immediately.

Shrimp Marinade

2 slices gingerroot, smashed with the flat side of a cleaver
1 tablespoon rice wine
½ teaspoon salt
½ egg white or 2 teaspoons water
1 teaspoon cornstarch

4 cups peanut, safflower, or corn oil
2 ounces rice stick noodles

Minced Seasonings

2 teaspoons minced gingerroot
2 tablespoons minced scallions

¼ cup dried Chinese black mushrooms, softened in hot water to cover, stems removed, and caps cut into matchstick-size shreds
¼ cup green pepper cut into matchstick-size shreds
½ cup carrot cut into matchstick-size shreds
4 cups fresh bean sprouts, lightly rinsed and drained

Sauce

3 tablespoons soy sauce
1½ tablespoons rice wine
1 teaspoon salt
1 teaspoon sesame oil
1 teaspoon sugar
¼ cup chicken broth
1½ teaspoons cornstarch

1½ pounds raw shrimp, shelled

Shrimp Marinade

2 slices gingerroot, smashed with the flat side of a cleaver
1 tablespoon rice wine
½ teaspoon salt
1 egg white, lightly beaten (or 1 tablespoon water)
1½ teaspoons cornstarch

1 pound rice stick noodles
7 tablespoons peanut, safflower, or corn oil

Shredded Seasonings

2 tablespoons shredded scallions
2 teaspoons shredded gingerroot

4 cups shredded Chinese cabbage (Napa)

Sauce

3 tablespoons soy sauce
1 teaspoon salt
2 tablespoons rice wine
¾ teaspoon sugar
1 teaspoon sesame oil
1½ cups chicken broth

STIR-FRIED RICE NOODLES WITH SHRIMP

XIA REN CHAO MI FEN 　蝦仁炒米粉

This Fujianese noodle platter is a savory concoction of seafood and vegetables coated with a delicately seasoned sauce. The rice stick noodles not only provide a textural contrast to the shrimp and cabbage, but act as a staple. The delicate seasonings and varied garnishes make this dish suitable as a meal in itself or as a side dish at a banquet.

1　Score each shrimp along the length of the back and remove the vein; the scoring will allow the shrimp to "butterfly" when it is cooked. Rinse all the shrimp lightly, and drain thoroughly. Place the shrimp in a linen dishtowel and squeeze out as much moisture as possible. Place the shrimp in a bowl. Pinch the gingerroot slices in the **shrimp marinade** repeatedly for several minutes to impart their flavor to the liquid. Add the marinade to the shrimp, toss lightly, and let marinate for 20 minutes. Discard the gingerroot slices. Soften the rice noodles in hot water to cover for 10 minutes. Drain them.

2　Heat a wok, add 4 tablespoons of the oil, and heat until very hot. Add half the shrimp and stir-fry over high heat for 1 minute, or until they change color and curl. Remove with a handled strainer and drain. Reheat the oil, cooking out some of the liquid that the first batch of shrimp left in the wok. Add the rest of the shrimp and cook in the same manner as the first batch. Remove the oil from the wok.

3　Reheat the wok, add the remaining 3 tablespoons of oil, and heat until very hot. Add the **shredded seasonings** and stir-fry for about 10 seconds, until fragrant. Add the shredded cabbage and stir-fry over high heat until it is slightly limp. (If the mixture is very dry, add a tablespoon of rice wine.) Add the **sauce** and heat until the mixture is boiling. Add the softened rice noodles and cook for 1½ minutes over high heat, stirring occasionally. Add the shrimp, toss lightly, and transfer the mixture to a serving bowl. Serve immediately.

DEEP-FRIED QUAIL EGG PASTRIES

NIAO CHAO WAN ZI   鳥巢丸子

There is a close similarity between this Cantonese snack and Scotch eggs, a favorite in British pubs. Both are basically an egg encased in a ground-meat mixture and covered with a coating. Rice stick noodles are used in the Chinese version; flour, eggs, and bread crumbs in the British one. The deep-fried rice noodles provide an attractive, delicately crisp exterior.

1   Devein the shrimp, rinse lightly, and drain thoroughly. Place the shrimp in a linen dishtowel and squeeze out as much moisture as possible. Remove the shrimp and mince to a paste. Plunge the water chestnuts into boiling water for a few seconds to remove the tinny flavor. Refresh them in cold water and chop coarsely. Lightly chop the meat until fluffy and place it in a mixing bowl with the shrimp paste, water chestnuts, and **pork seasonings**. Stir vigorously in one direction and throw the mixture lightly against the inside of the bowl to thoroughly combine the ingredients. Parboil the quail eggs for 5 seconds. Refresh immediately in cold water. Drain thoroughly and pat dry. Break the rice noodles into ½-inch lengths.
2   Divide the meat mixture into the same number of portions as quail eggs. Mold one portion around each quail egg. Roll each egg in the rice noodles, making sure that the meat is completely coated.
3   Heat a wok, add the oil, and heat the oil to 350°. Add half the eggs and deep-fry, turning them constantly in the hot oil for 4½ to 5 minutes, or until they are golden brown and the meat is cooked. Remove, and drain on absorbent paper. Reheat the oil, add the remaining eggs, and cook them in the same manner. Arrange the deep-fried eggs on a platter and serve immediately.

TWENTY-FIVE PASTRIES

½ pound raw shrimp, shelled
¼ cup water chestnuts
¾ pound ground pork

Pork Seasonings
1½ tablespoons soy sauce
1 tablespoon rice wine
1 teaspoon salt
1½ teaspoons sesame oil
1½ tablespoons minced scallions
2 teaspoons minced gingerroot
2 tablespoons cornstarch

1 15-ounce can quail eggs (about 25)
4 ounces rice stick noodles
8 cups peanut, safflower, or corn oil

½ pound lump crabmeat

Crabmeat Marinade
1 tablespoon rice wine
2 slices gingerroot, smashed
   with the flat side of a
   cleaver
½ teaspoon salt

6 "large" egg whites
½ cup evaporated milk
2 teaspoons cornstarch
1 tablespoon water
1 teaspoon salt
4 cups peanut, safflower, or
   corn oil
2 ounces rice stick noodles
¼ cup shredded scallions
2 ounces Chinese ham,
   sliced very thinly and cut
   into julienne strips (or
   substitute Smithfield ham
   or prosciutto)

STIR-FRIED CRABMEAT OVER RICE NOODLES

XIE CHAO XIAN NAI 蟹肉炒鮮奶

The combination of colors in this Cantonese platter — with its pink crabmeat and ivory-colored egg white mixture — suggests a hibiscus flower, with its vibrant tones of red and white. This dish, therefore, is often classified as a *fu rong* (*fu yung*), which is the Chinese name for *hibiscus*.

1   Pick over the crabmeat, discarding any shell or cartilage that may be remaining. If the crabmeat has been frozen, squeeze out any excess water. Shred the crabmeat, using your fingers. Pinch the gingerroot slices in the **crabmeat marinade** repeatedly for several minutes to impart their flavor to the mixture. Discard the gingerroot. Place the crabmeat in a bowl, add the marinade, toss lightly, and let marinate for 20 minutes. Lightly beat the egg whites until very frothy; fold in the evaporated milk. Combine the cornstarch and water to form a smooth paste and add it to the egg white mixture, along with the salt. Blend until smooth.
2   Heat a wok, add the oil, and heat until smoking. Add the rice noodles and deep-fry them until puffed and pale golden. This should happen almost immediately. Turn them over and deep-fry for a few seconds on the other side. Remove the noodles, and drain on absorbent paper. Transfer them to a large platter and lightly break up the noodles with your fingertips. Remove the oil from the wok, reserving 1 tablespoon.
3   Reheat the wok, add the tablespoon of oil, and when it is hot add the crabmeat. Stir-fry over high heat for 10 seconds, stirring constantly. Add the scallion shreds and the Chinese ham. Stir-fry for about 10 seconds over high heat; then add the egg white mixture. Cook, stirring constantly, until the egg whites have set. Pour the mixture over the fried rice noodles and serve immediately.

ANTS ON A TREE

MA YI SHANG SHU 媽蟻上樹

Most Americans balk at the title of this classic Sichuanese dish because it suggests some very adventurous eating. In fact, the bits of ground pork entwined in the soft bean threads are said to bear a resemblance to ants climbing a tree; hence the unusual title.

1   Place the ground meat in a bowl, add the **meat marinade,** toss lightly to combine, and let marinate for 20 minutes. Soften the bean threads in hot water to cover for 10 minutes.
2   Heat a wok, add the oil, and heat until hot. Add the ground meat and cook, mashing and separating it, until it changes color. Push the meat to the side of the wok, add the **minced seasonings,** and stir-fry for about 5 seconds, until fragrant. Add the chili paste and stir-fry for another 5 seconds. Add the **sauce** and the bean threads. Toss lightly to combine all the ingredients, and heat until boiling. Reduce the heat to low and cook for 8 minutes, until almost all the liquid has evaporated. Transfer the mixture to a serving bowl and sprinkle the top with the minced scallion greens. Serve immediately.

SIX SERVINGS

½ pound ground pork or beef

Meat Marinade
1 teaspoon soy sauce
1 teaspoon rice wine
½ teaspoon sesame oil

4 ounces bean threads
1 tablespoon peanut, safflower, or corn oil

Minced Seasonings
2 tablespoons minced scallions
1 tablespoon minced gingerroot
1 teaspoon minced garlic

1½ teaspoons chili paste

Sauce
2 tablespoons soy sauce
1 tablespoon rice wine
1 teaspoon salt
1 teaspoon sugar
1 teaspoon sesame oil
2 cups chicken broth

2 tablespoons minced scallion greens

MEAT DUMPLINGS

SHAO MAI

FOUR-FLAVOR DUMPLINGS

DUMPLINGS 餃子類

The Chinese New Year arrives in Taipei with much fanfare and ritual. Several weeks before the holiday, telltale signs of its advent are clearly visible; clotheslines usually festooned with laundered pantaloons and tunics become burdened with the weight of fragrant coils of freshly made sausage. The marketplace, filled to the brim with the usual bounty of shellfish, meat, and fish, offers such unusual New Year's delicacies as glutinous rice cake (*nian gao*), red and white glutinous rice balls, and mountainous stacks of dried shark's fin, bird's nests, and silver ears — prime ingredients for the New Year's banquet. The frequent boom of firecrackers exploding in the streets — set off to ward away evil spirits — becomes more pronounced as the holiday approaches, and the air fairly tingles with the electricity of expectation and excitement — for this is the most important holiday of the Chinese lunar calendar.

In Chinese homes, preparations begin at least a month in advance. Houses are cleaned from top to bottom, new clothes for the entire family are made or purchased, and the kitchen teems with activity from early morning until late at night as many dishes are made ready for the feasting. Much of the cooking for the holiday is done in advance.

In northern China a custom that has been observed for centuries still exists today; women friends and relatives gather before the holiday to prepare several hundred *jiao zi*, meat dumplings or Peking ravioli. The finished dumplings are arranged on trays and left to freeze in the chill winter air. During the holiday, a cauldron of water is boiled, the desired number of dumplings are cooked, and a hot, filling meal is ready in minutes. Often a silver coin is placed inside one of the dumplings, signifying good luck in the coming year for the recipient.

Some families prefer to pan-fry the dumplings (in this case they are called *guo tie*), creating a golden brown crust that gives the ravioli the appearance of golden coins.

The Cantonese are fond of a New Year's dumpling made of glutinous rice and a filling of powdered sesame seeds and sugar.

This pastry is believed to symbolize completeness and is served to celebrate the family unit and ensure a healthy harvest and a bountiful year. In some parts of eastern China, these dumplings are eaten two weeks after the New Year, whereas in Fujian, an eastern province north of Canton, they are consumed during the Mid-Autumn Festival and are often dusted with a mixture of sesame seeds, ground peanuts, and sugar.

Obviously, dumplings have a prominent place in Chinese cuisine; they are prepared in numerous variations for holidays and festivals and they are consumed on a daily basis in several parts of China. In the north, where wheat provides the area with its wealth of noodles and steamed breads, dumplings frequently act as a staple substitute for rice, in addition to being served as a meal in themselves. The same is true in western China. In the east and the south, dumplings are considered to be a type of *dim sum* (*dian xin*) and are commonly served as a snack with tea or wine.

The origin of dumplings is undocumented, but it is believed that these pastries, along with other wheat products, were introduced to China from the west — most likely Persia or central Asia. They quickly were adapted to Chinese ingredients and were incorporated into the daily diet. As these snacks were adopted by various cuisines, their ingredients were altered slightly, depending on the products of that area. In the north, dumplings were filled with lamb, pork, and chives. In Sichuan province, the filling included a mixture of pork, cabbage, and dried shrimp. And in the eastern and southern regions, more delicate variations of the dumpling evolved (such as *hun dun* and *shao mai*), with stuffings of shrimp, bamboo shoots, and black mushrooms. The methods of cooking dumplings have regional characteristics as well; in the north they are boiled, whereas in the east they are steamed on beds of pine needles that have been anointed with sesame oil.

By the late Sung dynasty (960 to 1279), the ancient city of Hangzhou contained a number of food shops that prepared multitudes of dumplings for the masses. Later, in the Ch'ing dynasty (1644 to 1911), dumplings of various kinds signified the arrival of the many festivals: Green dumplings with lotus root appeared during the third month of the lunar calendar. Glutinous rice dumplings with sweet bean sauce were prepared for the Kitchen God Festival, celebrated on the twenty-fourth day of the twelfth lunar month.

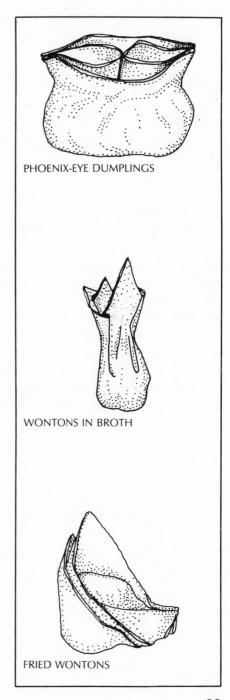

PHOENIX-EYE DUMPLINGS

WONTONS IN BROTH

FRIED WONTONS

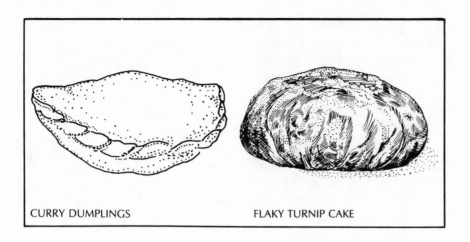

CURRY DUMPLINGS   FLAKY TURNIP CAKE

(Since these dumplings are believed to soften bones and cartilage, the initial binding of young girls' feet was performed on this day.) During the first five days of the fifth lunar month, the Dragon Boat Festival was observed, and sweet and savory dumplings wrapped in lotus leaves appeared, created as a tribute to the spirit of Chü Yuan, an ancient statesman and poet who drowned himself in the Mi-Lo River as a protest against the corruption of the government.

These snacks still exist today and are prepared as they were centuries ago — lasting remnants of traditional holiday customs.

DUMPLING SKINS

JIAO ZI PI 餃 子 皮

In Taiwan, all neighborhood markets host a noodle maker who turns out mountains of fresh noodles, wonton skins, and dumpling skins daily. The texture of these fresh pasta products is positively silky in comparison to the commercially prepared kind. Making dumpling skins at home is a time-consuming process, but the result is certainly worth the work. If necessary, however, commercial dumpling skins (goyoza) are acceptable. Dumpling skins may be frozen if tightly wrapped in plastic.

1   Place the flour in a mixing bowl and add the boiling water. With a wooden spoon, mix the ingredients to a rough dough. If the dough is too hot to handle, let it cool a bit; then turn it out onto a lightly floured surface and knead for about 5 minutes, until it is smooth and elastic. If the dough is sticky, knead in a few tablespoons of flour. Cover the dough with a towel and let it rest for 25 minutes.

2   Cut the dough in two and form each half into a long snakelike roll about 1 inch in diameter. Cut each half into twenty-five pieces. With a cut edge down, press each piece into a circle. Using a small rolling pin or a tortilla press that has been lightly floured, roll out each piece to a 3-inch circle. Cover the circles with a cloth or towel to prevent them from drying out. Use as directed in the individual recipes.

FIFTY SKINS

2½ cups all-purpose flour
1¼ cups boiling water

91

1½ cups finely minced
   Chinese cabbage (Napa)
1 teaspoon salt
¾ pound ground pork
1 cup finely minced Chinese
   garlic chives, leeks, or
   scallion greens

Dumpling Seasonings
2 tablespoons soy sauce
1 tablespoon rice wine
2 tablespoons sesame oil
1½ teaspoons minced
   gingerroot
1½ teaspoons minced garlic

50 dumpling skins (page 91)

MEAT DUMPLINGS

JIAO ZI　餃子

Meat dumplings typify the hearty, wholesome qualities of northern home-style cooking. Traditionally, they are filled with pork and cabbage, and flavored with a generous amount of Chinese garlic chives. Ten or fifteen of these delectable pastries, depending on the capacity of the diner, make a filling and nutritious meal. For a tasty variation of this recipe, lamb may be substituted for the pork.

1   Place the minced cabbage in a large mixing bowl, add the salt, toss lightly to mix evenly, and let sit for 30 minutes. (This is done to remove the water from the cabbage, so the filling will not soak through the dumpling skin.) Take a handful of minced cabbage and squeeze out as much water as possible. Place the squeezed cabbage in a mixing bowl. Squeeze out the water from the rest of the cabbage and discard the water. Add the ground pork, minced chives, and **dumpling seasonings,** and stir vigorously in one direction to combine the ingredients evenly. (If the mixture seems loose, add 2 tablespoons cornstarch to bind it together.)

2   Place a heaping tablespoon of filling in the center of each dumpling skin, and fold the skin over to make a half-moon shape. Spread a little water along the edge of the skin. Use the thumb and index finger of one hand to form small pleats along the outside edge of the skin (a); with the other hand, press the two opposite edges of the skin together to seal (b). The inside edge of the dumpling should curve in a semicircular fashion to conform to the shape of the pleated edge (c). Place the sealed dumplings (d) on a baking sheet that has been lightly dusted with cornstarch or flour.

3   In a large wok or pot, bring about 3 quarts of water to a boil. Add half the dumplings, stirring immediately to prevent them from sticking together, and heat until the water begins to boil. Add ½ cup cold water and continue cooking over high heat until the water boils. Add another ½ cup cold water and cook until the water boils again. Remove and drain. Cook the remaining dumplings in the same manner. (This is the traditional method of cooking dumplings;

MEAT DUMPLINGS

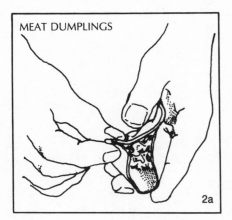

2a

92

for a simpler method, boil them for about 8 minutes, uncovered, over high heat.) Serve the boiled dumplings with one of the following dipping sauces:

DIPPING SAUCE I
½ cup soy sauce
3 tablespoons Chinese black vinegar or Worcestershire sauce

DIPPING SAUCE II
½ cup soy sauce
2 tablespoons Chinese black vinegar or Worcestershire sauce
1 tablespoon chili oil (for directions for homemade chili oil, see page 8)

Variation
Add 1 tablespoon shredded gingerroot or minced garlic to either of the above sauces.

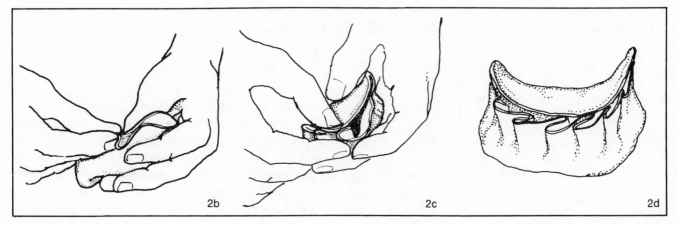

2b   2c   2d

TWENTY-FIVE DUMPLINGS

3½ tablespoons peanut, safflower, or corn oil
½ recipe meat dumplings (page 92), prepared as directed through step 2
1 cup boiling water

PAN-FRIED MEAT DUMPLINGS

GUO TIE   鍋貼

Literally translated, *guo tie* means "pot stickers," and anyone who has not used a well-seasoned pan to cook these dumplings will understand the appropriateness of this title; the dumplings often refuse to dislodge themselves from the pan. A wise and knowledgeable Chinese master chef suggested to me the helpful step of rinsing the dumplings midway, as described here.

1   Heat a large wok or a well-seasoned skillet until very hot. Add 3 tablespoons of oil and heat until very hot. Arrange the dumplings, pleated side up, to line the bottom of the pan. They should be packed closely in a circular pattern. Fry the dumplings over medium-high heat until their bottoms are a deep golden brown. Add the boiling water to the pan and cover. Reduce the heat to low and cook for about 10 minutes. Uncover, and pour out the water. Lightly rinse the dumplings for 5 seconds under hot running water to remove the excess starch. Drain. Place the pan containing the dumplings over medium-high heat. Drizzle ½ tablespoon of oil around the dumplings and fry until the bottoms are again crisp, about 2 minutes. Use a spatula to loosen any dumplings that seem to be sticking to the bottom. Invert the dumplings directly onto a platter. Serve with either of the dipping sauces on page 93.

THIRTY DUMPLINGS

1 pound raw shrimp, shelled
½ cup water chestnuts
1 ounce pork fat, finely chopped to a paste

SHRIMP BONNETS

XIA JIAO   蝦餃

Shrimp bonnets (commonly called *har gow* on Cantonese menus), are a common and popular sight in any Cantonese *dim sum* parlor. Their delicate, transparent skin is a result of the blending of two starch flours — wheat starch and tapioca starch. Wheat starch is the powder remaining from flour once the gluten has been removed, and tapioca starch is a product of the cassava root, or manioc plant, which is native to the West Indies.

1   Devein the shrimp, rinse lightly, and drain thoroughly. Place the shrimp in a linen dishtowel, and squeeze out as much excess moisture as possible. Cut the shrimp into ¼-inch dice. Plunge the water chestnuts into boiling water for a few seconds to remove the tinny flavor. Refresh in cold water and mince them. Place the shrimp, water chestnuts, pork fat, and **dumpling seasonings** in a mixing bowl. Stir the ingredients in one direction to combine evenly. Refrigerate for 20 minutes.

2   Place the wheat starch and tapioca starch in a mixing bowl, and combine well. Add the boiling water, stirring constantly to prevent lumps. Add the oil and mix to a rough dough. Turn the dough out onto a counter and knead lightly for about 2 minutes, until smooth. Cut the dough in half and form each half into a long snakelike roll about 1 inch in diameter. Cut each roll into fifteen pieces. Cover the pieces with a damp cloth.

3   Lightly grease a cleaver and place a piece of the dough, cut edge down, on the counter. Place the cleaver blade parallel to the counter, flat on the dough. Press down on the blade and turn it clockwise so that the dough is pressed out to form a thin circle about 2½ inches in diameter. Repeat the process for the remaining dough sections. Alternatively, you may use a tortilla press: Place a square of plastic wrap in the press, or lightly brush it with oil; place a section of dough, cut edge down, in the press, and press out to a thin circle.

4   Place a heaping teaspoon of the filling in the center of one circle and fold the skin over to make a half-moon shape. Use the thumb and index finger of one hand to form small pleats on the outer edge of the dumpling skin; with the other hand, press the two opposite edges of the skin together to seal. The inside edge of the dumpling skin should curve in a semicircular fashion to conform to the shape of the pleated edge. Make the remaining dumplings in the same manner. (Shrimp bonnets are formed in the same way as meat dumplings, page 92.) Place the sealed dumplings about ¼ inch apart in two steamer trays that have been lined with wet cheesecloth or with parchment paper punched with holes.

5   Fill a wok with water level with the bottom edge of a steamer tray and heat until boiling. Stack the steamer trays in the wok and cover. Steam for 12 minutes, reversing the layers after 6 minutes. Serve with soy sauce.

Dumpling Seasonings
2 teaspoons soy sauce
1 tablespoon rice wine
1 teaspoon salt
2 teaspoons sesame oil
½ teaspoon sugar
¼ teaspoon freshly ground
   white pepper
2 teaspoons minced scallions
1½ teaspoons minced
   gingerroot
1 egg white
2 tablespoons cornstarch

1¼ cups wheat starch
½ cup tapioca starch
1 cup boiling water
2 teaspoons peanut,
   safflower, or corn oil

1 pound raw shrimp, shelled
½ cup water chestnuts
1 ounce pork fat, minced to
 a paste

Dumpling Seasonings
2 teaspoons soy sauce
 (preferably light)
1 tablespoon rice wine
½ teaspoon salt
¼ teaspoon freshly ground
 white pepper
2 teaspoons sesame oil
1 teaspoon sugar
2 teaspoons minced scallions
1½ teaspoons minced
 gingerroot
½ egg white
2 tablespoons cornstarch

50 dumpling skins (page 91)
 or *shao mai* skins (page
 100)
½ cup minced cooked ham
½ cup minced hard-boiled
 egg
½ cup minced (softened)
 dried Chinese black
 mushrooms
½ cup minced scallion
 greens

FOUR-FLAVOR DUMPLINGS

SE FANG SHAO MAI

The delicate appearance of these steamed dumplings is further accentuated by their colorful garnishes. Although the shaping of the dumplings may at first seem complicated, once mastered it takes a matter of seconds. Grated carrot and minced cooked spinach may be used in addition to the listed garnishes.

1   Devein the shrimp, rinse lightly, and drain thoroughly. Place the shrimp in a linen dishtowel, and squeeze out as much moisture as possible. Mince the shrimp to a coarse paste. Plunge the water chestnuts into boiling water for a few seconds to remove the tinny flavor. Refresh them in cold water and chop coarsely. Place the shrimp, water chestnuts, pork fat, and **dumpling seasonings** in a mixing bowl. Stir vigorously in one direction to combine evenly. Refrigerate the filling for 20 minutes.

2   Place a teaspoon of filling in the center of a dumpling skin. Dip a finger in cold water and dot four points equidistant from one another at the centers and at points midway around the edge of the skin. Gather together the opposite edges of the skin (a) and press to seal them at these four points (b). The dumpling should look something like a four-leaf clover, with round openings replacing the "leaves." Further enlarge the openings with a chopstick, and fill each opening with a different minced garnish — ham, egg, mushroom, and scallion (c). Make the remaining dumplings in the same manner. Arrange the finished dumplings (d) about ¼ inch apart in two steamer trays that have been lined with wet cheesecloth or with parchment paper punched with holes.

3   Fill a wok with water level with the bottom edge of a steamer tray and heat until boiling. Stack the steamer trays in the wok, cover, and steam for 15 minutes over high heat, reversing the layers once. Serve with soy sauce. To reheat, steam for 5 minutes over high heat.

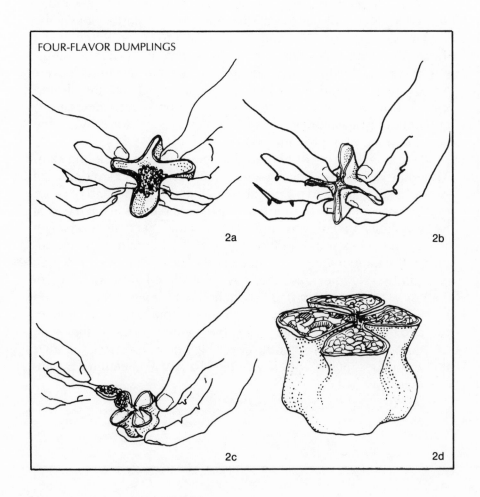

FOUR-FLAVOR DUMPLINGS

2a

2b

2c

2d

97

¼ pound raw shrimp, shelled
4 dried Chinese black
    mushrooms
½ cup water chestnuts
¾ pound ground pork
¼ cup shredded raw carrot

Dumpling Seasonings
2 teaspoons soy sauce
1 teaspoon rice wine
2 teaspoons sesame oil
¼ teaspoon freshly ground
    black pepper
2 tablespoons minced
    scallions
2 teaspoons minced
    gingerroot
2 tablespoons cornstarch

50 dumpling skins (page 91)
    or *shao mai* skins (page
    100)

PHOENIX-EYE DUMPLINGS

FENG YAN SHAO MAI 鳳眼燒賣

The phoenix, a symbol of beauty and peace, has long been revered by the Chinese. A number of dishes are said to have been inspired by this mythical bird and so bear its name. Such is the case with this dumpling, which is said to resemble the eye of a phoenix.

1   Devein the shrimp, rinse lightly, and drain thoroughly. Place the shrimp in a linen dishtowel, and squeeze out as much excess moisture as possible. Mince the shrimp to a coarse paste. Soften the dried mushrooms for 25 minutes in hot water to cover. Remove and discard the stems, and mince the caps. Plunge the water chestnuts into boiling water for a few seconds to remove the tinny flavor. Refresh them in cold water and chop coarsely. Place the shrimp paste, mushrooms, water chestnuts, ground pork, shredded carrot, and **dumpling seasonings** in a mixing bowl. Stir vigorously in one direction to combine the ingredients evenly.
2   Place a teaspoon of filling in the center of one dumpling skin. Gather the opposite edges together (a) and pinch at the midpoint of each edge to join the two sides at the center (b). (Use a dab of water as an adhesive.) Place your index fingers in the holes at each end of the dumpling and draw the opposite edges together again from each side (c), pinching at the midpoints (d). Make the remaining dumplings in the same manner. Arrange the shaped dumplings (e) ¼ inch apart on two steamer trays that have been lined with wet cheesecloth or with parchment paper punched with holes.
3   Fill a wok with water level with the bottom edge of a steamer tray and heat until boiling. Stack the steamer trays in the wok, cover, and steam for 15 minutes over high heat, reversing the trays after 8 minutes. Serve with soy sauce. To reheat, steam for 5 minutes over high heat.

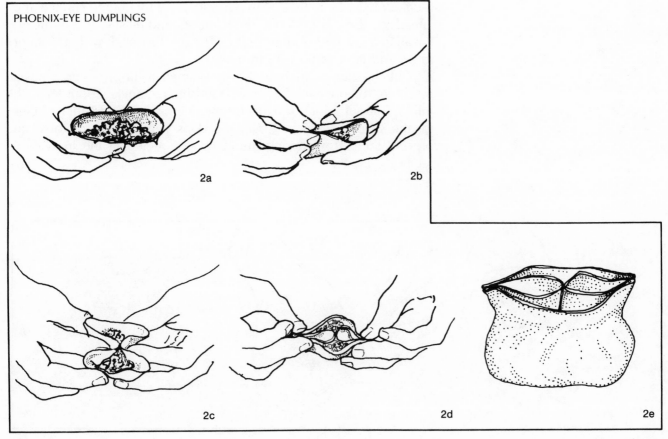

PHOENIX-EYE DUMPLINGS

2a

2b

2c

2d

2e

99

1⅓ cups all-purpose flour
1 teaspoon salt
1 "large" egg, lightly beaten
¼ cup cold water

SHAO MAI SKINS AND WONTON WRAPPERS

SHAO MAI PI, HUN DUN PI　烧賣皮窨吞皮

This versatile egg dough may be used to make egg noodles and Cantonese spring roll skins, as well as wonton wrappers and *shao mai* skins. Although commercial skins are available, the flavor and texture of the homemade variety are far superior. The wrappers or skins may be frozen if wrapped securely in plastic.

1　Place the flour and salt in a mixing bowl and combine. Add the egg and water. Using a wooden spoon, blend the mixture into a rough dough. Turn the dough out onto a lightly floured surface and knead for about 5 minutes, until smooth and elastic. If it is sticky, knead in a few tablespoons of flour. Cover the dough with a cloth or towel and let it rest for 25 minutes.

2　Cut the dough in half. Using a small rolling pin or a pasta machine, roll out each half to a paper-thin rectangle (about ¹⁄₁₆ inch thick). Cut out 3-inch squares for the wonton skins or 3-inch circles for the *shao mai* skins. Cover the skins with a cloth or towel to prevent them from drying out. Use as directed in the individual recipes.

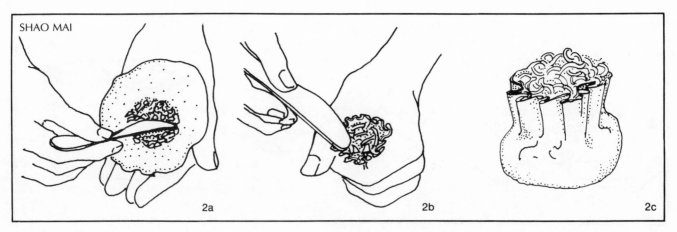

SHAO MAI

2a　　2b　　2c

SHAO MAI

SHAO MAI 燒賣

Some purists consider the addition of seafood to the traditional, all-meat *shao mai* filling an act just short of sacrilege, but I believe the shrimp adds additional depth and contrast in flavor. Shrimp, prawns, or crabmeat may be substituted for the carrot garnish to create a more exotic dumpling.

1   Devein the shrimp, rinse lightly, and drain thoroughly. Place the shrimp in a linen dishtowel, and squeeze out as much moisture as possible. Mince the shrimp to a coarse paste. Plunge the water chestnuts into boiling water for a few seconds to remove the tinny flavor. Refresh them in cold water and chop coarsely. Place the shrimp, water chestnuts, ground pork, and the **shao mai** seasonings in a mixing bowl and stir vigorously in one direction to combine the ingredients evenly.

2   Place a heaping tablespoon of filling in the center of one skin (a). Gather up the edges of the skin around the filling. Holding the *shao mai* between your thumb and index finger, lightly squeeze it to form a "waist"; at the same time, push up the filling from the bottom with the other hand, creating a flat bottom. Smooth the surface of the filling with the underside of a knife or spoon dipped in water (b). Sprinkle the surface with the shredded carrot. Make the remaining dumplings in the same manner. Arrange the shaped *shao mai* (c) about ¼ inch apart in two steamer trays that have been lined with wet cheesecloth or with parchment paper punched with holes.

3   Fill a wok with water level with the bottom edge of a steamer tray and heat until boiling. Stack the steamer trays in the wok, cover, and steam the dumplings for 15 minutes over high heat, reversing the trays after 8 minutes. To reheat, steam for 5 minutes over high heat.

THIRTY DUMPLINGS

¼ pound shrimp, shelled
½ cup water chestnuts
1 pound ground pork

Shao Mai Seasonings
2 teaspoons soy sauce
1 tablespoon rice wine
1 teaspoon salt
2 teaspoons sesame oil
½ teaspoon sugar
¼ teaspoon freshly ground
    black pepper
1 tablespoon minced
    scallions
2 teaspoons minced
    gingerroot
1 egg white
2 tablespoons cornstarch

30 *shao mai* skins (page 100)
    or dumpling skins (page
    91)
½ cup shredded carrot

¼ pound raw shrimp, shelled
4 dried Chinese black
  mushrooms
¾ pound ground pork

Shao Mai Seasonings
2 teaspoons soy sauce
1 tablespoon rice wine
1 teaspoon salt
2 teaspoons sesame oil
½ teaspoon sugar
1 tablespoon minced
  scallions
2 teaspoons minced
  gingerroot
½ egg white
2 tablespoons cornstarch

30 quail eggs, plunged
  briefly into boiling water
  and drained
30 shao mai skins (page 100)
  or dumpling skins (page
  91)

QUAIL EGG SHAO MAI

CHUN DAN SHAO MAI 鷄蛋燒賣

Here the standard Cantonese *dim sum* of *shao mai* is given an unusual touch with the addition of quail eggs in the filling. Ideally, only fresh quail eggs should be used, but canned ones, once blanched to remove the tinny flavor, are a suitable substitute.

1   Devein the shrimp, rinse lightly, and drain thoroughly. Place the shrimp in a linen dishtowel, and squeeze out as much moisture as possible. Mince the shrimp to a coarse paste. Soften the dried mushrooms in hot water to cover for 20 minutes. Remove and discard the stems, and mince the caps. Place the shrimp, mushrooms, ground pork, and the **shao mai seasonings** in a mixing bowl. Stir vigorously in one direction to combine the ingredients evenly.
2   Place a quail egg in the center of one *shao mai* skin. Shape 1 tablespoon of the filling around the quail egg. Gather up the edges of the skin around the filling. Holding the *shao mai* between your thumb and index finger, lightly squeeze it to form a "waist"; at the same time, push up the filling from the bottom with the other hand, creating a flat bottom. Smooth the surface of the filling with the underside of a spoon dipped in water. Make the remaining dumplings in the same manner. (Quail egg *shao mai* are formed in the same way as standard *shao mai,* page 000.) Arrange the shaped *shao mai,* filling side down, ¼ inch apart in several steamer trays that have been lined with wet cheesecloth or with parchment paper punched with holes.
3   Fill a wok with water level with the bottom edge of a steamer tray and heat until boiling. Stack the steamer trays in the wok and cover. Steam the dumplings for 15 minutes (reversing the order of the trays after 8 minutes) and serve with soy sauce. To reheat the *shao mai,* steam for 5 minutes over high heat.

WONTONS IN BROTH

HUN DUN TANG　雲吞湯

SIX SERVINGS

¼ pound raw shrimp, shelled
¼ cup water chestnuts
½ pound ground pork

Wonton Seasonings
2 teaspoons soy sauce
2 teaspoons rice wine
½ teaspoon salt
1½ teaspoons sesame oil
¼ teaspoon freshly ground
　black pepper
1 teaspoon minced
　gingerroot
1½ tablespoons cornstarch

30 wonton wrappers (page
100)

Literally translated, *hun dun* means "swallowing a cloud," which is very appropriate considering the appearance of the finished dish; the delicate wontons suspended in the clear chicken broth amidst the fresh green spinach do evoke (perhaps with a little imagination) clouds floating in the sky. Imagery aside, the dish is agreeable as a light lunch or dinner, or as a filling snack.

1   Devein the shrimp, rinse lightly, and drain thoroughly. Place the shrimp in a linen dishtowel, and squeeze out as much moisture as possible. Mince the shrimp to a coarse paste. Plunge the water chestnuts into boiling water for a few seconds to remove the tinny flavor. Refresh them in cold water and chop coarsely. Place the shrimp, water chestnuts, ground pork, and **wonton seasonings** in a mixing bowl. Stir vigorously in one direction to combine the ingredients evenly.
2   Using a fork (or spoon), place a scant teaspoon of the filling in the center of one wonton wrapper (a). Gather the edges of the skin together around the filling and squeeze to form a "waist" (b) — and gradually remove the fork. Squeeze the waist completely to enclose the filling. Place the finished wontons (c) on a tray that has been dusted with cornstarch or flour.

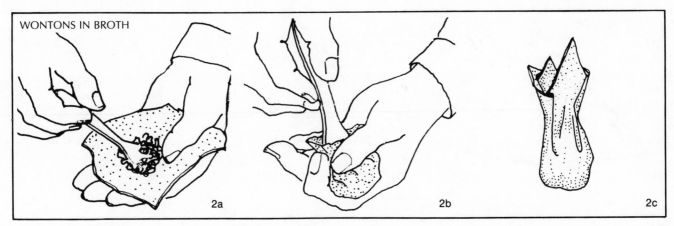

WONTONS IN BROTH

2a   2b   2c

Broth

6 cups chicken broth
1 tablespoon rice wine
1 teaspoon salt
3 tablespoons soy sauce
1 teaspoon sesame oil

1 pound fresh spinach,
    trimmed and cleaned
2 tablespoons minced
    scallion greens

3   Heat 4 quarts of water until boiling. Add the wontons and cover. Cook for 5 to 6 minutes, or until the wontons have risen to the surface. Using a handled strainer or a colander, remove the wontons. Portion them into six serving bowls.

4   Place the **broth** in a pot and heat until boiling. Add the spinach and cook briefly, just until it is barely wilted. Pour the hot soup over the wontons in the bowls. Sprinkle the top with the scallion greens and serve immediately.

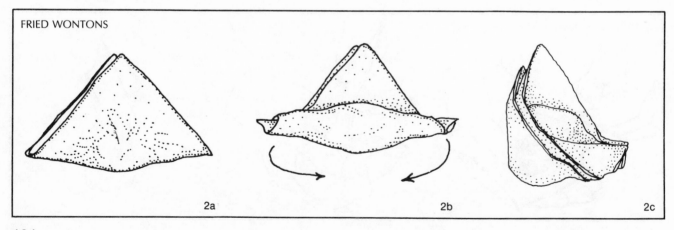

FRIED WONTONS

2a   2b   2c

FRIED WONTONS

JIA HUN DUN 炸雲吞

The versatility of wontons is apparent, since these savory pastries may be deep-fried, steamed, or boiled in a broth. Whatever the cooking method, they are appropriately served as a snack or as a light meal in themselves. I often serve fried wontons as an hors d'oeuvre with drinks. Their crisp, dry texture is excellent with wine or beer.

1   Devein the shrimp, rinse lightly, and drain thoroughly. Pat the shrimp dry with paper towels and chop coarsely. Plunge the water chestnuts into boiling water for a few seconds to remove the tinny flavor. Refresh them in cold water and chop coarsely. Place the shrimp, water chestnuts, ground pork, and **wonton seasonings** in a mixing bowl and stir vigorously in one direction to combine the ingredients evenly.

2   Place a scant teaspoon of the filling in the center of one wonton wrapper. Fold the wrapper over to form a triangle (a). Working from the longest straight edge, fold in the wrapper to a point three quarters of the length from the opposite edge (b). Dip a finger in some water and dab the ends of the triangle; press the two ends together and pinch to seal. Make the remaining wontons in the same manner. Place the finished wontons (c) on a tray that has been dusted with cornstarch or flour.

3   Heat a wok, add the oil, and heat the oil to 350°. Add about half the wontons and deep-fry for 3 to 4 minutes, until the skins are golden brown and crisp and the filling is cooked. Remove with a handled strainer, and drain on absorbent paper. Reheat the oil and deep-fry the remaining wontons in the same manner. Serve with the **sweet-and-sour dipping sauce.** (To prepare the dipping sauce, place the ingredients in a saucepan and heat until boiling and thick while stirring constantly.)

THIRTY WONTONS

¼ pound raw shrimp, shelled
½ cup water chestnuts
½ pound ground pork

Wonton Seasonings
1½ tablespoons soy sauce
2 teaspoons rice wine
½ teaspoon salt
1½ teaspoons sesame oil
¼ teaspoon freshly ground
   black pepper
1½ teaspoons minced
   gingerroot
2 teaspoons minced scallions
1½ tablespoons cornstarch

30 wonton wrappers (page
   100)
8 cups peanut, safflower, or
   corn oil

Sweet-and-Sour Dipping Sauce
3 tablespoons ketchup
3 tablespoons sugar
1 tablespoon clear rice
   vinegar
1 teaspoon salt
1 teaspoon soy sauce
½ teaspoon sesame oil
4 tablespoons water
2 teaspoons cornstarch

½ pound ground pork or
beef

Meat Marinade
1 teaspoon soy sauce
1 teaspoon rice wine
½ teaspoon sesame oil

4 tablespoons peanut,
safflower, or corn oil
¾ cup minced onion
1 tablespoon curry powder

Filling Sauce
1 teaspoon salt
2 teaspoons sugar
½ cup chicken broth

Thickener
1 tablespoon cornstarch
2 tablespoons water

2 cups all-purpose flour
1 teaspoon salt
⅔ cup shortening or lard
⅓ cup ice water

Egg Wash
1 egg, lightly beaten
1 tablespoon water
½ teaspoon salt

CURRY DUMPLINGS

JIA LI JIAO 咖喱餃

In the traditional recipe for this snack, two doughs — one that is very short, made of lard and flour, and another that is less so — are combined and folded together in a manner similar to that used in making puff pastry. Since I find this process slightly tedious, I have adapted the recipe to create a much simpler dough. Also, though traditionally the dumplings are deep-fried, I prefer to bake them. Either cooking method may be used.

1   Place the ground meat in a bowl, add the **meat marinade,** and toss lightly.
2   Heat a wok, add 2 tablespoons of oil, and heat until hot. Add the ground meat and cook over high heat, stirring constantly to break up the meat, until the meat changes color. Remove the meat, and drain.
3   Heat a wok, add the remaining 2 tablespoons of oil, and heat until very hot. Add the minced onion and stir-fry until soft and transparent. Add the curry powder and stir-fry for about 15 seconds, until very fragrant. Add the **filling sauce** and heat until boiling. Slowly add the **thickener**, stirring constantly, and cook until thick. Add the cooked meat, toss lightly to coat with the sauce, and transfer the mixture to a platter. Refrigerate until cool.
4   Combine the flour and salt in a bowl. Cut the shortening into the flour until the mixture is the consistency of cornmeal. Add the water, and mix lightly until the dough is smooth and homogeneous. (Do not overwork the dough.) Divide the dough in two, wrap each piece in plastic wrap, and refrigerate for 20 minutes.
5   Preheat the oven to 400°. Roll out half the dough to a large rectangle about ⅙ inch thick. Using a round 3-inch cookie cutter, cut out circles. Gather the scraps together into a ball and chill. Roll out the other half of the dough and cut more circles. Gather up the scraps and combine with the scraps from the first half. Roll out and cut more circles. Repeat until the dough is used up.

6 Place a teaspoon of the curry filling in the center of one dough circle and fold it over to make a half-moon shape. Pinch the two edges together to seal and enclose the filling (a). Seal the edge tightly by scalloping by hand (b) into a decorative pattern (c) or crimping with a fork. Place the finished dumplings on a baking sheet and brush with the **egg wash.** Bake for 20 minutes in the preheated oven. Cool the dumplings (d), and serve.

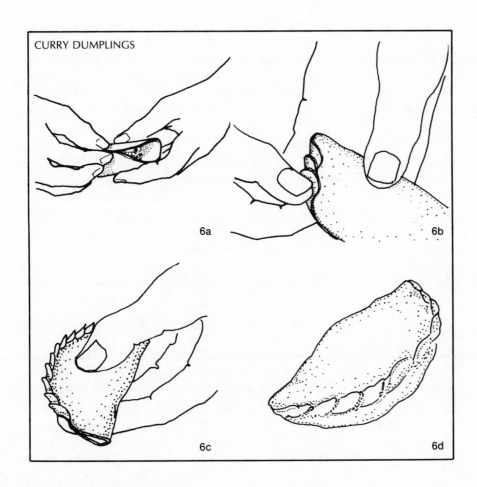

CURRY DUMPLINGS

6a

6b

6c

6d

¾ pound boneless
center-cut pork loin

Pork Marinade

2 teaspoons soy sauce
1½ teaspoons rice wine
½ teaspoon sesame oil

⅓ pound raw shrimp,
shelled

Shrimp Marinade

1 teaspoon rice wine
1 slice gingerroot, smashed
with the flat side of a
cleaver
½ teaspoon salt

4½ tablespoons peanut,
safflower, or corn oil
6 dried Chinese black
mushrooms, softened in
hot water to cover, stems
removed, and caps cut
into ¼-inch dice
½ cup minced scallions or
leeks

Filling Sauce

2 tablespoons soy sauce
1 tablespoon rice wine
½ teaspoon salt
2 teaspoons sesame oil
½ teaspoon sugar
2 tablespoons chicken broth
½ tablespoon cornstarch

SAVORY BAKED DUMPLINGS

JIU CAI SU BING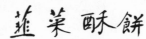

Customarily, lard is used in Chinese pastry making because it provides a flaky texture and a rich taste. Westerners, with their concern
for cholesterol, may feel more comfortable using a vegetable shortening, margarine, or half butter and half lard. I am partial to the last
combination, since the butter provides a pleasing flavor and the lard
a flaky texture.

1   Remove any fat or gristle from the pork and discard. Cut the
meat into ¼-inch dice. Place the pork in a mixing bowl, add the
pork marinade, toss lightly, and let marinate for 20 minutes. Devein
the shrimp, rinse lightly, and drain thoroughly. Pat dry with paper
towels, and cut into ¼-inch dice. Place the shrimp in a bowl, add
the **shrimp marinade,** toss lightly, and let marinate for 20 minutes.
Discard the gingerroot.
2   Heat a wok, add 2 tablespoons of oil, and heat until very hot.
Add the diced pork and stir-fry until the color changes, about 1½
minutes. Remove and drain. Add another 2 tablespoons of oil and
heat until very hot. Add the diced shrimp and stir-fry until the color
changes, about 1 minute. Remove and drain. Reheat the wok, add
the remaining ½ tablespoon of oil, and heat until very hot. Add the
mushrooms and stir-fry for about 5 seconds, until fragrant. Add the
minced scallions or leeks and stir-fry for another 10 seconds. Add
the **filling sauce** and cook, stirring constantly over high heat, until
thick. Add the pork and shrimp, toss lightly to coat with the sauce,
and remove. Transfer the mixture to a platter and refrigerate until
cool.
3   Combine the flour and salt in a bowl. Cut the shortening into the
flour until the mixture is the consistency of cornmeal. Add the ice
water and mix lightly until the dough is smooth and homogeneous. (Do not overwork the dough.) Divide the dough in two,
wrap each piece in plastic wrap, and refrigerate for 20 minutes.
4   Preheat the oven to 400°. Roll out half the dough to a large
rectangle about ⅙ inch thick. Using a round 3-inch cookie cutter,

cut out circles. Gather the scraps together into a ball and chill. Roll out the other half of the dough and cut out more circles. Gather up the scraps and combine with the scraps from the first half. Roll out and cut more circles. Repeat until the dough is used up.

5 Place a teaspoon of the filling in the center of one dough circle and fold it over to make a half-moon shape. Pinch the two edges together to seal and enclose the filling. Seal the edge tightly by scalloping by hand into a decorative pattern or crimping with a fork. (These dumplings are formed in the same manner as curry dumplings, page 106.) Place the finished dumplings on a baking sheet and brush with the **egg wash.** Bake for 20 minutes in the preheated oven. Cool the dumplings, and serve.

2 cups all-purpose flour
1 teaspoon salt
⅔ cup shortening or lard
⅓ cup ice water

Egg Wash
1 egg, lightly beaten
1 tablespoon water
1 teaspoon salt

FLAKY TURNIP CAKES

LO BO SI BING 蘿蔔絲餅

Turnip cakes are frequently served as a Chinese New Year's snack; their fried golden exteriors are said to resemble golden coins. They were so popular in my household in Taipei that we made and served them year-round. I have simplified the skin by substituting a simple dough for the more complicated one normally used, but even with this change the flavor does not differ drastically from the original recipe.

1 Place the shredded turnip in a bowl, add the salt, toss lightly, and let sit for 20 minutes. Squeeze out any water that has accumulated and set the shredded turnip aside.

2 Heat a wok, add ½ tablespoon of oil, and heat until very hot. Add the diced sausage and stir-fry over low heat, stirring constantly for about 2 minutes, until the sausage is golden and most of the fat has been rendered. Remove the sausage with a handled strainer and drain.

3 Remove all but 2 tablespoons of fat from the wok and heat until hot. Add the shredded turnip and stir-fry over high heat until tender, about 2 minutes. Add the sausage and the **filling seasoning.** Toss

TWENTY-FOUR CAKES

FLAKY TURNIP CAKE

2½ cups finely shredded Chinese turnip (daikon radish)
1 teaspoon salt
1½ cups peanut, safflower, or corn oil
½ pound Chinese pork sausage, cut into ¼-inch dice

109

Filling Seasoning

2 teaspoons rice wine
½ teaspoon salt
¼ teaspoon freshly ground
    black pepper
2 teaspoons sesame oil

2 cups all-purpose flour
1 cup cake flour
1 teaspoon salt
⅔ cup lard or butter
⅓ cup ice water

lightly over high heat for about 30 seconds. Transfer the filling to a platter and refrigerate until cool.

4   Combine the flours and salt in a mixing bowl. Add the shortening and cut it into the flour until the mixture is the consistency of cornmeal. Add the water and mix lightly until the dough is smooth and homogeneous. (Do not overwork the dough.) Wrap the dough in plastic wrap and refrigerate for 20 minutes.

5   Roll out the dough to a rectangle about ⅙ inch thick. Using a round 4-inch cookie cutter, cut out circles. Gather the scraps together into a ball and chill for 15 minutes. Roll out the dough again and cut out more circles, making twenty-four in all.

6   Place a tablespoon of the filling in the center of one dough circle. Gather up the edges of the circle and pinch to seal, enclosing the filling and forming a ball. Lightly flatten each cake into a round approximately 2½ inches wide.

7   Heat a large skillet and add the remaining oil. Heat the oil to 375°. Arrange a batch of the turnip cakes in the pan and fry over medium heat on both sides until crisp and golden brown, about 5 minutes per side. Remove with a slotted spoon and drain on absorbent paper. Reheat the oil and fry the remaining cakes in the same manner. Arrange on a platter and serve.

FRIED SHRIMP AND SWEET POTATO DUMPLINGS

XIA REN YU JIAO

蝦仁芋餃

In the original recipe for these dumplings, taro, a starchy root vegetable, is used as the base of the dough. Since this vegetable is only available on a seasonal basis in sizable Chinese communities, I often substitute sweet potato. The texture of the crust is then slightly less flaky, but the flavor is equally good.

1   Remove any fat or gristle from the pork loin and discard. Cut the meat into ¼-inch dice. Place the pork in a mixing bowl, add the **pork marinade**, toss lightly, and let the pork marinate for 20 minutes. Devein the shrimp, rinse lightly, and drain thoroughly. Pat dry with paper towels and cut into ¼-inch dice. Place the shrimp in a bowl, add the **shrimp marinade,** toss lightly, and let the shrimp marinate for 20 minutes. Discard the gingerroot.

2   Heat a wok, add 2 tablespoons of oil, and heat until very hot. Add the diced pork and stir-fry until the color changes, about 1½ minutes. Remove and drain. Add another 2 tablespoons of oil to the pan and heat until very hot. Add the diced shrimp and stir-fry until the color changes, about 1 minute. Remove and drain. Reheat the pan, add ½ tablespoon of oil, and heat until very hot. Add the black mushrooms and stir-fry until fragrant, about 5 seconds. Add the **filling sauce** and cook, stirring constantly over high heat, until thick. Add the pork and shrimp, toss lightly to coat with the sauce, and remove. Refrigerate this mixture until it is cool. Clean the wok.

3   Place the puréed sweet potato in a bowl, add the shortening, and mix until smooth. Refrigerate this mixture for 1 hour, covered, in the bowl. Add the cornstarch and salt and mix to form a smooth dough. (If the dough is too sticky, add more cornstarch.) Form the dough into a long snakelike roll about 1¼ inches in diameter and cut it into twenty-four pieces. Sprinkle them with a little cornstarch.

4   Using your fingers, flatten one dough piece into a 2½-inch circle and place a heaping teaspoon of the filling in the center. Fold the skin over to make a half-moon shape; pinch the edges together

---

TWENTY-FOUR DUMPLINGS

¾ pound boneless center-cut pork loin

Pork Marinade
2 teaspoons soy sauce
1½ teaspoons rice wine
½ teaspoon sesame oil

¼ pound raw shrimp, shelled

Shrimp Marinade
1 teaspoon rice wine
1 slice gingerroot, smashed with the flat side of a cleaver
½ teaspoon salt

8 cups peanut, safflower, or corn oil
6 dried Chinese black mushrooms, softened in hot water to cover, stems removed, and caps cut into ¼-inch dice

Filling Sauce
2 tablespoons soy sauce
1 tablespoon rice wine
½ teaspoon salt
½ teaspoon sugar
1 teaspoon sesame oil
2 tablespoons chicken broth
½ tablespoon cornstarch

1 pound sweet potato or
  taro, cooked and mashed
  to a smooth purée
4 tablespoons shortening or
  lard at room temperature
1 cup cornstarch
1½ teaspoons salt

to seal. (Handle the skins lightly and sprinkle with cornstarch if sticky.) Crimp the edge decoratively and place the dumpling on a cookie sheet that has been lightly dusted with cornstarch. Make the remaining dumplings in the same manner. (These dumplings are formed in the same manner as curry dumplings, page 106.)

5 Reheat the wok, add the remaining oil, and heat the oil to 375°. Add six or seven of the dumplings to the wok. Deep-fry over high heat until they are golden brown and crisp. Remove with a handled strainer and drain on absorbent paper. Reheat the oil, and deep-fry the remaining dumplings in the same manner. Serve hot. To reheat, bake in a 350° oven until crisp and piping hot.

SOYBEANS AND BEAN CURD 黃豆與豆腐類

Taipei is a city teeming with the smells of good food. The morning is heralded by the penetrating odor of deep-fried Chinese crullers and roasted sesame-seed rolls. At midmorning, the smell of ripe, sweet melons, pineapples, mangoes, and other subtropical fruits perfumes the air as the fruit vendor wheels his cart, bulging with the ripe offerings of the season, through the streets. Lunchtime is marked by the aroma of red-cooked beef noodles or pan-fried noodle cakes garnished with assorted meats and vegetables. And at dinnertime the smell of garlic frying in hot oil permeates the atmosphere. This was my favorite part of the day. As the sun slowly descended and a slight breeze enveloped the city in a balmy coolness, I would roam the alleyways of our neighborhood, moving from one kitchen window to the next, inhaling the assorted aromas and trying to guess the menu for that evening's dinner. I became intimate with my neighbors' palates: Those in the house to my left had a passion for hot, spicy dishes, while those to my right favored blander foods.

As evening fell after dinner, the luscious scents of crispy onion crêpes and pan-fried stuffed buns mingled with the other snacks offered at that time of day — steamed sweet corn, deep-fried sesame balls with red bean paste, and steamed peanuts. Also present throughout the day in this panorama of fragrances was a putrid smell that defied classification. What was that baffling, pungent odor, present in every part of the city? After a bit of research, I soon traced the source and discovered that it was stinky bean curd (*chou dou fu*), a favorite snack of the Chinese.

Vendors of this "unsavory" (at least to my unsophisticated palate) delicacy ran rampant all over the city with their portable deep-fryers. My Chinese surrogate sister and brothers, who were all great fans of the stuff, used to race outside, armed with empty bowls and chopsticks, at the sound of the stinky bean curd man's call. (The smell usually preceded him by two blocks, giving everyone plenty of notice.) What makes this food so fragrant is that it is actually "turned bean curd," which is made by fermenting fresh bean curd squares in a brine with assorted spices and a pickled vegetable. The

SOYBEANS AND BEAN CURD

BEAN MILK SHEETS

BEAN CURD SHEETS

resulting cakes are deep-fried in hot oil until golden and eaten with soy sauce, vinegar, mashed garlic, or chili paste.

Stinky bean curd and fresh bean curd are just two of the many products derived from the soybean — a legume that has been prominent in the Chinese diet for centuries. It is believed that soybeans were first cultivated in China and, along with wheat and millet, were a staple food for the ancient Chinese. The durability of the plant endeared it to the farmers. Bean stew was a common dish during the Han dynasty (206 B.C. to A.D. 220), and soybean milk and bean curd were also prominent in the Han diet.

Considering the many uses of this versatile legume, it is not difficult to understand why the soybean is so revered by the Chinese. It is used in making not only soy sauce but also other notable seasonings, such as sweet bean sauce or paste, hoisin sauce, and hot bean paste. Its by-products include soybean milk and its many derivatives. When ground, the soybean produces oil and flour. The fresh, green beans are cooked and served with soy sauce and sesame oil, and dried beans are fried and eaten as a snack or soaked for sprouting.

The nutritious properties of the soybean further explain why it is so popular with the health-conscious Chinese. A serving of soybeans provides more protein than the minimum body requirement. In addition, soybeans are a major source of lecithin, a vital substance that aids digestion and the absorption of fats. Bean curd has a higher protein value than the soybean in its raw state (because during its manufacture, the bean curd coagulates with most of the bean's protein, leaving much of the carbohydrates behind with the water), and it is more easily digested.

The actual process of making bean curd is relatively simple. Dried soybeans, after being soaked, are ground to a purée, mixed with water, and strained to form soybean milk. The bean milk is heated and used to make a number of by-products: Thin layers of skin from the milk are dried, forming bean milk sheets (fu pi), or rolled and deep-fried, creating bean curd sticks (fu zu). Then a coagulant is added to the heated milk and the mixture is poured into a square mold. To make bean curd sheets (bai ye), a small amount of the bean curd mixture is added and pressed to create a flat sheet. This sheet is sometimes shredded, making bean curd noodles (gan si).

Once the bean curd mixture has been pressed properly, the cakes of bean curd are removed. Although most American Oriental markets offer a choice of "soft" or "hard" bean curd, in the Orient there are usually at least three types of bean curd available. The difference in the varieties is the result of the size of the weight used and the length of pressing time. Soft bean curd is generally used for cold dishes and delicate soups; it has a loose, fragile consistency. Medium bean curd is deep-fried, used in soups, and in·some stir-fried dishes. Hard bean curd (*dou fu gan*) is more appropriate for stir-fried dishes and stewing in a *lu,* a soy-based braising mixture.

Bean curd is also fermented in rice wine and spices to make a popular seasoning (*dou fu ru*) with a slightly cheeselike flavor and pickled in a brine to make the infamous stinky bean curd.

Today, the popularity of the soybean and its many derivatives is unsurpassed. According to E. N. Anderson, Jr., and Marja L. Anderson in *Food in Chinese Culture,* edited by K. C. Chang, "A huge bowl of rice, a good mass of bean curd, and a dish of cabbages — fresh in season, otherwise pickled — is the classic fare of the everyday south Chinese world."

As most nutritionists will agree, the soybean and its many by-products are the foods of the future.

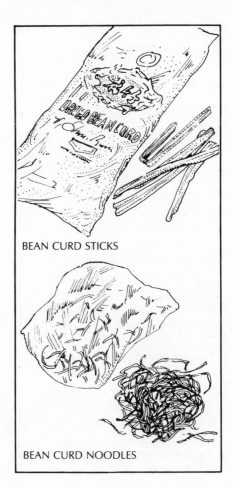

BEAN CURD STICKS

BEAN CURD NOODLES

4 cups dried soybeans
12 cups water
1 pound ground pork

Pork Seasonings
1 tablespoon soy sauce
2 teaspoons rice wine
1 tablespoon minced
   scallions
2 teaspoons minced
   gingerroot
1 egg, lightly beaten
1½ teaspoons sesame oil
1½ tablespoons cornstarch

6 cups peanut, safflower, or
   corn oil

Braising Mixture
6 cups chicken broth
6 tablespoons soy sauce
4 tablespoons rice wine
1 teaspoon salt
1 tablespoon sugar
2 scallions, smashed with the
   flat side of a cleaver
2 slices gingerroot, smashed
   with the flat side of a
   cleaver
1 whole star anise

MEATBALL AND SOYBEAN CASSEROLE

HUANG DOU ROU YUAN 黄豆肉丸

Bean stews have been a vital part of the Chinese diet since ancient times. In modern China the popularity continues, and these dishes are considered hearty, filling fare. This casserole is a fine example of such a dish.

1   Rinse the soybeans and drain. Place the soybeans in a bowl with the 12 cups of water to cover and let them soak for 8 hours or overnight. Discard any that have risen to the surface. Drain thoroughly and pat dry on a towel. Lightly chop the ground pork until fluffy. Place the meat in a mixing bowl with the **pork seasonings.** Stir the meat in one direction and throw it lightly against the inside of the bowl to thoroughly combine the ingredients evenly. Shape the meat into fifteen meatballs.

2   Heat a wok, add the oil, and heat the oil to 375°. Add the soybeans and deep-fry until golden brown, stirring constantly. Remove with a handled strainer and drain. Reheat the oil to 375° and add half the meatballs. Deep-fry the meatballs briefly in the hot oil until golden brown. Remove with a handled strainer, and drain. Reheat the oil and deep-fry the remaining meatballs in the same manner.

3   Place the soybeans and the **braising mixture** in a heavy pot or Dutch oven. Bring the liquid to a boil, reduce the heat, cover, and simmer for 20 minutes over low heat. Add the meatballs, partially cover, and simmer for 45 minutes, or until almost all the liquid has evaporated. Serve immediately.

SWEET SOYBEAN MILK

DOU JIANG   豆 漿

EIGHT CUPS

2 cups dried soybeans
8 cups water
1 cup sugar

For most Americans breakfast is not complete without a cup of coffee, whereas for many Chinese a steaming bowl of sweet soybean milk, accompanied by a sesame flat bread (*shao bing*) and a fried cruller (*you tiao*), is obligatory. A savory rendition of this dish is prepared by substituting Chinese black vinegar, chili oil, soy sauce, sesame oil, and minced scallions for the sugar. Both versions are filling, flavorful, and nutritious.

1   Rinse the soybeans in a bowl of water and discard any that rise to the surface. Place in a bowl with cold water to cover and let soak for 12 hours or overnight. Drain the soybeans.

2   In a blender, or a food processor fitted with the steel blade, purée the soybeans to a smooth paste in two or three batches, adding some of the 8 cups of water to each batch as it is blended. Line a colander with fine cheesecloth and pour the soybean mixture into the colander, adding the remainder of the water. Strain the mixture through the cheesecloth; the mixture should now resemble milk. Discard the soybean sediment. Pour the strained mixture into a saucepan, and place the pan over medium heat. Add the sugar (if the mixture is not sweet enough, add more sugar to taste) and stir constantly until the liquid is hot and the sugar is dissolved. Serve hot with sesame flat breads (page 63).

1½ pounds soybean sprouts
¾ cup red-in-snow
1 tablespoon peanut,
  safflower, or corn oil
1 teaspoon minced
  gingerroot

Sauce
1 tablespoon soy sauce
1 tablespoon rice wine
1½ teaspoons sugar
1 teaspoon sesame oil
¼ cup chicken broth or
  water

STIR-FRIED SOYBEAN SPROUTS WITH RED-IN-SNOW

HUANG DOU YA CHAO XUE LI HONG　黄豆芽炒雪裏紅

This stir-fried platter is a classic example of the blending of flavors and textures found in Chinese cuisine. The crisp freshness of the soybean sprouts mingles sensuously with the unique flavor of the preserved red-in-snow. This fragrant vegetable dish may be served hot or cold.

1　Lightly rinse the soybean sprouts and drain. Parboil the red-in-snow for 10 seconds. Immerse in cold water, and drain thoroughly.
2　Heat a wok, add the oil, and heat until very hot. Add the minced gingerroot and stir-fry for about 5 seconds, until fragrant. Add the red-in-snow and stir-fry for another 5 seconds, until fragrant. Add the soybean sprouts and the **sauce.** Bring the mixture to a boil, reduce the heat, cover, and simmer for 15 minutes. Uncover and turn the heat to high. Cook, stirring constantly, until the liquid has almost evaporated. Transfer the mixture to a platter and serve immediately.

8 dried bean curd sheets or
  bean milk sheets
¼ pound raw shrimp, shelled
½ pound ground pork

STUFFED BEAN CURD ROLLS

SAN XIAN BAI YE JUAN　三鮮百葉捲

This unusual dish originated in the eastern part of China around Shanghai. The delicate texture and flavor of the bean curd sheets are offset by the ground shrimp and meat filling. Bean curd sheets (*bai ye*) are thin sheets made from fresh bean curd and are used frequently to wrap savory fillings. Frozen sheets exported from Taiwan are available in some Chinese grocery stores. Bean milk sheets (*fu pi*) can be used if bean curd sheets are unobtainable.

1   If using the dried bean curd sheets, dissolve a teaspoon of baking soda in boiling water. Add the bean curd sheets to the water and let soak for 15 minutes, until they have lightened in color. Then place in cold water to cover for 20 minutes. Drain, and carefully squeeze out as much water as possible. Cut the sheets into rectangles that are 4 inches by 2 inches. If using the bean milk sheets, soften them in hot water for 5 minutes. Squeeze out as much water as possible and cut the sheets into rectangles that are 4 inches by 2 inches.

2   Devein the shrimp, rinse lightly, and drain thoroughly. Place the shrimp in a linen dishtowel, and squeeze out as much excess moisture as possible. Mince the shrimp to a paste. Lightly chop the ground pork until fluffy and place in a mixing bowl with the shrimp paste and the **pork seasonings.** Stir vigorously in one direction and throw the mixture lightly against the inside of the bowl to thoroughly combine the ingredients. Soften the dried mushrooms in hot water for 20 minutes, remove and discard the stems, and shred the caps.

3   Lay out one sheet on a flat surface. Form a heaping tablespoon and a half of the meat mixture into a roll about 2 inches long. Place it along a short side of the sheet and roll up. Repeat this process for the remaining meat and sheets. Place the rolls on a lightly oiled heat-proof plate and put the plate in a steamer tray.

4   Fill a wok with water level with the bottom edge of the steamer tray and heat until boiling. Place the steamer tray over the boiling water, cover, and steam for 30 minutes over high heat. Arrange the rolls on a platter. Remove the water from the wok.

5   Reheat the wok, add the oil, and heat until very hot. Add the mushroom shreds and stir-fry for 5 seconds, until fragrant. Add the **sauce** and heat until boiling. Add the bean sprouts; when the liquid comes to a boil, slowly add the **thickener,** stirring constantly to prevent lumps. Pour over the rolls and serve.

Pork Seasonings
2 tablespoons minced scallions
1 teaspoon minced gingerroot
1 tablespoon soy sauce
2 teaspoons rice wine
1 teaspoon sesame oil
1 tablespoon cornstarch

4 dried Chinese black mushrooms
1 tablespoon peanut, safflower, or corn oil

Sauce
1 cup chicken broth
1 tablespoon rice wine
¾ teaspoon salt

1 cup mung bean sprouts, lightly rinsed

Thickener
1 teaspoon cornstarch
2 teaspoons water

1½ pounds firm-fleshed fish
    fillets, such as haddock,
    sea bass, or cod

Fish Marinade

1 tablespoon rice wine
1 teaspoon salt
1 teaspoon minced
    gingerroot
1 egg white or 1 tablespoon
    water
2 tablespoons cornstarch

10 dried bean milk sheets

Paste

6 tablespoons flour
12 tablespoons (¾ cup) water

6 cups peanut, safflower, or
    corn oil

Minced Seasonings

1 tablespoon minced
    scallions
2 teaspoons minced garlic

Sweet-and-Sour Sauce

6 tablespoons ketchup
4 tablespoons clear rice
    vinegar
6 tablespoons sugar
2 teaspoons soy sauce
1 teaspoon salt
½ cup water
1 teaspoon sesame oil
2 teaspoons cornstarch

SWEET-AND-SOUR FISH SLICES

TANG CU FU PI YU JUAN　糖醋腐皮鱼捲

In this dish, the familiar classic of sweet and sour is given a new twist with the use of bean milk sheets, which not only provide a delicate, crisp coating for the fish slices, but also eliminate the mess of a batter.

1   Remove the skins from the fish fillets, if necessary, and discard. Lightly rinse the fillets and drain thoroughly. Holding the knife at a 45° angle, cut the fillets into slices that are ½ inch thick, 2 inches long, and 1 inch wide. Place the slices in a bowl, add the **fish marinade,** toss lightly, and let the fish marinate for 20 minutes. Soften the bean milk sheets in hot water for 5 minutes. Lightly squeeze out as much water as possible. Pat dry with towels. Cut the bean milk sheets into 4-inch squares. Stir the **paste** until smooth.
2   Lay out one bean curd sheet on a counter and spread the paste generously over the surface. Place a fish slice in the center and gather up the edges, bringing in the sides and folding them over and over so that the fish slice is completely enclosed in a rectangular package. Press the ends to seal. Repeat for the remaining fish slices.
3   Heat a wok, add the oil, and heat the oil to 375°. Add a few of the fish rolls and deep-fry for 3 to 4 minutes, until the fish is cooked and the rolls are lightly golden. Remove with a handled strainer, and drain. Reheat the oil, and deep-fry the remaining fish rolls in the same manner. Reheat the oil to 425°. Add all the fish rolls and deep-fry briefly, stirring constantly until they are golden brown and crisp. Drain the fish rolls on absorbent paper. Remove the oil from the wok, reserving 1 tablespoon.
4   Reheat the wok, add the tablespoon of oil, and heat until very hot. Add the **minced seasonings** and stir-fry for about 5 seconds, until fragrant. Add the **sweet-and-sour sauce** and cook until thick, stirring constantly to prevent lumps. Add the fish rolls, toss lightly to coat with the sauce, and transfer to a platter. Serve immediately.

EGGPLANT ROLLS

FU PI QIE ZI 腐皮茄子

With their minced shrimp filling, bean milk sheets, and nori sheets, the rolls below reflect both the Fujianese and Japanese influences in Taiwanese cooking. Although these rolls require more preparation than some dishes, the result is certainly worth the effort. They may be deep-fried in advance and then reheated until crisp in a 375° oven. Serve them as an hors d'oeuvre or, with rice, as an entrée.

1   Devein the shrimp, rinse lightly, and drain thoroughly. Place the shrimp in a linen dishtowel, and squeeze out as much water as possible. Mince the shrimp to a paste. Plunge the water chestnuts into boiling water for a few seconds to remove the tinny flavor. Refresh them in cold water and chop coarsely. Place the shrimp, water chestnuts, pork fat, and **shrimp seasonings** in a mixing bowl. Using your hands, stir the mixture in one direction to combine evenly. Lightly throw the mixture against the inside of the bowl. Soften the bean milk sheets in hot water for 5 minutes. Lightly squeeze out as much water as possible and trim the sheets into 6-inch squares. Trim the nori sheets to 6-inch squares. Mix the ingredients of the **paste** until smooth. Bake the eggplant strips for about 15 minutes in a preheated 375° oven until tender.

2   Lay out one bean milk sheet on a counter and spread the surface lightly with some of the paste. Place a nori sheet on top. Spread the surface of the nori sheet with one sixth of the shrimp mixture; use the underside of a spoon dipped in water to smooth the filling. Lay a strip of baked eggplant and a piece of scallion in the center and roll up the bean curd sheet, pulling as you go along to make the roll firm and compact. Make five more rolls in the same manner.

3   Heat a wok, add the oil, and heat the oil to 375°. Add the rolls and deep-fry for 5 to 6 minutes, until the filling is cooked and the rolls are lightly golden. Remove with a handled strainer, and drain. Reheat the oil to 425°. Add the fried rolls and deep-fry briefly, turning constantly, until they are crisp and golden brown. Drain on absorbent paper. Cut the rolls into 1-inch pieces and arrange on a platter. Serve immediately.

SIX SERVINGS

½ pound raw shrimp, shelled
½ cup water chestnuts
1 ounce pork fat, minced to
  a paste

Shrimp Seasonings

2 teaspoons minced
  gingerroot
1 tablespoon minced
  scallions
2 teaspoons rice wine
1 teaspoon salt
2 teaspoons sugar
1 teaspoon sesame oil
1 egg white
2½ tablespoons cornstarch

6 dried bean milk sheets
6 sheets nori (purple laver)

Paste

3 tablespoons flour
6 tablespoons water

6 strips raw eggplant,
  measuring 4 inches by
  ½ inch by ½ inch
6 pieces scallion greens,
  6 inches long
8 cups peanut, safflower, or
  corn oil

1 teaspoon baking soda
2 ounces bean curd sticks
14 fried gluten balls
10 dried wood ears
8 dried Chinese black
  mushrooms
4 cups peanut, safflower, or
  corn oil

Minced Seasonings

2 tablespoons minced
  scallions
2 tablespoons minced
  gingerroot

½ pound Chinese cabbage
  (Napa), cut into 2-inch
  squares
½ cup carrots, cut into thin
  slices

Braising Liquid

2 cups soaking liquid from
  softening the dried
  mushrooms
4½ tablespoons soy sauce
2 tablespoons rice wine
2 teaspoons sugar
2 teaspoons sesame oil
¼ teaspoon black pepper

¼ cup bamboo shoots,
  plunged briefly into
  boiling water, refreshed,
  and cut into thin slices
  about 1½ inches square

BUDDHA'S DELIGHT

LUO HAN SU CAI 羅漢素菜

This well-known vegetarian dish is one of the most popular of its kind among the Chinese. The ingredients vary from one region to the next; there sometimes may be as many as eighteen. A well-known Cantonese variation includes vegetarian loaves (mock meat rolls made with bean milk sheets) and cellophane noodles. Whatever the mix, this dish is a delectable combination of textures and flavors. Fried gluten balls are available frozen in Oriental markets. Instructions for making fried gluten balls at home appear on page 293, in the recipe for mock sweet-and-sour pork.

1   Dissolve the baking soda in 6 cups hot water and place the bean curd sticks in the water. Let soak for 1 hour. Rinse in cold water to remove the baking soda; squeeze out the water. Cut the sticks into pieces 1½ inches long. Parboil the fried gluten balls for 1 minute and rinse in cold water. Drain thoroughly and squeeze out any excess water. Soften the wood ears and the mushrooms separately in hot water for 20 minutes. Drain the wood ears and cut away the hard, bitter nib on the underside, if necessary. Cut the wood ears into pieces about 1 inch square. Drain the mushrooms, retaining 2 cups of the soaking liquid for the braising liquid. Remove and discard the stems, and cut the caps into quarters.
2   Heat a wok, add the oil, and heat the oil to 375°. Add the bean curd sticks and deep-fry, stirring constantly until the sticks are golden brown. Remove with a handled strainer, and drain. Press the sticks to squeeze out as much oil as possible. Remove the oil from the wok, reserving 3 tablespoons.
3   Reheat the wok, add the 3 tablespoons of oil, and heat until very hot. Add the **minced seasonings** and stir-fry for about 5 seconds, until fragrant. Add the mushrooms and stir-fry for another 5 seconds over high heat. Add the cabbage and the carrots. Toss lightly, adding a tablespoon of rice wine if the mixture is very dry. Cook over high heat until the cabbage is slightly limp. Add the fried gluten balls, the bean curd sticks, and the **braising liquid.** Stir the mixture,

heat until the liquid boils, reduce the heat to medium-low, and cover. Cook for 12 to 15 minutes, or until the liquid has almost completely evaporated. Add the bamboo shoots, Chinese black vinegar, and **thickener,** stirring constantly to prevent lumps. Transfer the mixture to a platter and serve immediately.

2 teaspoons Chinese black
  vinegar

Thickener
1 teaspoon cornstarch
1 tablespoon water

COLD TOSSED BEAN CURD AND CELERY SHREDS

LIANG BAN GAN SI

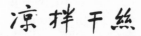

凉拌干丝

This flavorful cold salad is a familiar sight in any Sichuanese restaurant, where it is served with other small dishes to nibble on while browsing over the menu and awaiting the arrival of the meal. Although this dish is ideally suited for warm-weather eating, the contrasting textures of bean curd and celery, bathed in the fragrant sesame oil, make it popular whatever the season. Bean curd noodles (*gan si*) are usually used in this dish, but the bean curd slivers prepared here suit the purpose admirably.

1 Lightly rinse the bean curd and drain it. Place the bean curd between two pieces of muslin, cotton, or paper towel. Place a weight on top (you may use a cookie sheet weighted with books). Let sit for 2 hours. This will remove the excess liquid and compress the bean curd. Unwrap the bean curd. Holding the cleaver parallel to the cutting surface, slice the bean curd in half through the thickness. Cut the bean curd into thin slices and cut the slices into matchstick-size shreds.
2 Heat 2 quarts of water until boiling and blanch the bean curd shreds for 15 seconds. Remove and drain. Reheat the water until boiling and blanch the celery and carrot shreds for 5 seconds. Remove and refresh immediately in cold water. Drain thoroughly and pat dry.
3 Arrange the shredded bean curd, carrot, and celery in a large serving bowl. Add the **dressing,** toss lightly to coat the shreds, and serve.

SIX SERVINGS

8 cakes bean curd, about 3
  inches square and 1 inch
  thick
2 cups celery, cut into
  matchstick-size shreds
1 cup carrot, cut into
  matchstick-size shreds

Dressing
1½ teaspoons salt
2½ tablespoons sesame oil

8 cakes bean curd, 3 inches
  square and 1 inch thick
½ pound boneless center-cut
  pork loin

Pork Marinade

2 teaspoons soy sauce
½ tablespoon rice wine
½ teaspoon sesame oil
1 teaspoon cornstarch

10 dried Chinese black
  mushrooms
½ cup peanut, safflower, or
  corn oil
3 tablespoons scallions cut
  to 1-inch lengths

Braising Liquid

2 cups chicken broth
3 tablespoons soy sauce
1 tablespoon rice wine
½ teaspoon salt
¾ teaspoon sugar
1 teaspoon sesame oil
¼ teaspoon black pepper

2 carrots, parboiled for 2½
  minutes and roll-cut into
  1-inch pieces

Thickener

1½ teaspoons cornstarch
1½ tablespoons water

1 cup snow peas, ends
  snapped and veiny strings
  removed

RED-COOKED BEAN CURD

HONG SHAO DOU FU

Bean curd is ideally suited for red-cooking because it absorbs the rich braising liquid. The assorted vegetables in this dish provide color and additional flavor.

1   Rinse the bean curd lightly and drain thoroughly. Trim off any hard edges. Holding the cleaver parallel to the cutting surface, slice the bean curd cakes in half through the thickness; then cut each piece in half to form 1½-inch squares ½ inch thick. Remove and discard any fat or gristle from the pork loin. Cut the meat into slices about ¼ inch thick, 1½ inches long, and 1 inch wide, and place them in a bowl. Add the **pork marinade,** toss lightly, and let marinate for 20 minutes. Soften the dried mushrooms in hot water to cover for 20 minutes. Remove and discard the stems, and cut the caps in half.

2   Heat a wok, add the oil, and heat the oil to 375°. Add enough bean curd slices to fill the pan; fry on both sides over high heat, until golden brown. Remove, drain, reheat the oil, and fry the remaining bean curd in the same manner. Remove the oil from the wok, reserving 3 tablespoons.

3   Reheat the wok, add the 3 tablespoons of oil, and heat until very hot. Add the meat slices and stir-fry until they change color. Add the scallions and the mushrooms. Stir-fry over high heat for about 10 seconds, until fragrant. Add the **braising liquid** and heat until boiling. Add the cooked bean curd; when the liquid begins to boil, reduce the heat to medium and cook uncovered for 5 minutes. Add the carrots and cook for about 30 seconds to heat them through. With the liquid boiling, add the **thickener,** stirring constantly to prevent lumps. Add the snow peas, toss lightly to coat with the sauce, and transfer the mixture to a platter. Serve immediately.

BRAISED BEAN CURD WITH BLACK MUSHROOMS IN OYSTER SAUCE

DONG GU PA DOU FU　　冬菇扒豆腐

This Sichuanese dish was a favorite of my Chinese surrogate grandfather's. His discerning palate was highly respected in our household, and I frequently concurred with his tastes. The smoky flavor of the black mushrooms mingles harmoniously with the rich oyster sauce and provides a fine contrast to the delicate flavor of the bean curd. Ideally, the more expensive, thicker Chinese black mushrooms should be used for this dish. Some epicures praise shark's fin and bird's nest, but to my mind this simple dish rivals these delicacies.

1   Rinse the bean curd lightly and drain thoroughly. Trim off any hard edges. Holding the cleaver parallel to the cutting surface, slice each cake in half through the thickness; then cut each piece diagonally in half to form triangles. Soften the dried mushrooms for 20 minutes in hot water to cover. Remove and discard the stems, and cut the caps in half. Retain ½ cup of the soaking liquid for the braising liquid.

2   Heat a wok, add the oil, and heat the oil to 375°. Add a batch of bean curd and deep-fry in the hot oil until golden brown. Remove with a handled strainer, and drain. Reheat the oil, and deep-fry the remaining bean curd in the same manner in several batches. Remove the oil from the wok, reserving 1 tablespoon.

3   Reheat the wok, add the tablespoon of oil, and heat until very hot. Add the scallions and black mushrooms and stir-fry until fragrant, about 10 seconds. Add the **braising liquid** and bring to a boil. Add the bean curd and heat until the liquid boils again. Reduce the heat to medium and cook for 7 minutes, or until the liquid has reduced by half. Add the **thickener,** stirring constantly to prevent lumps. Add the sesame oil, toss lightly, and transfer the mixture to a platter. Serve immediately.

SIX SERVINGS

8 cakes bean curd, about 3 inches square and ½ inch thick
10 dried Chinese black mushrooms
2 cups peanut, safflower, or corn oil
3 tablespoons scallions cut into 1-inch lengths

Braising Liquid

2 cups chicken broth
½ cup mushroom-soaking liquid
3 tablespoons soy sauce
1½ tablespoons oyster sauce
1 tablespoon rice wine
1 teaspoon sugar

Thickener

1 teaspoon cornstarch
1 tablespoon water

1½ teaspoons sesame oil

8 cakes bean curd, about 3
  inches square and 1 inch
  thick
1 teaspoon dried shrimp
1 pound ground pork

Pork Seasonings
1½ tablespoons minced
  scallions
1½ teaspoons minced
  gingerroot
1 tablespoon soy sauce
2 teaspoons rice wine
1 teaspoon salt
1½ teaspoons sesame oil
¼ teaspoon freshly ground
  black pepper

3 tablespoons cornstarch
3 tablespoons peanut,
  safflower, or corn oil

Bean Curd Braising Liquid
2 cups chicken broth
1 teaspoon salt
1 tablespoon rice wine
2 tablespoons soy sauce

Thickener
1 teaspoon cornstarch
1 tablespoon water

2 tablespoons minced
  scallion greens

STUFFED BEAN CURD

XIANG DOU FU　 釀豆腐

Braised foods are usually considered hearty fare, but this Cantonese platter seems to belie that description. The ground pork, delicately seasoned with dried shrimp and other flavorings, provides a delicious contrast to the creamy bean curd.

1　Rinse the bean curd lightly and drain thoroughly. Trim off any hard edges, and cut the bean curd cakes diagonally in half to form triangles. Cut each triangle in half again, so that each cake has been cut into four triangles. Soften the dried shrimp in hot water to cover for 1 hour. Drain and mince. Lightly chop the ground pork until fluffy and place it in a mixing bowl. Add the minced shrimp and the **pork seasonings.** Stir vigorously in one direction and lightly throw the mixture against the inside of the bowl to combine evenly.

2　Using a knife and a spoon, scoop out a pocket in the longest side of one bean curd triangle. Be careful not to pierce the side. Dust the pocket with cornstarch and generously stuff with the ground pork mixture. Use the underside of a spoon dipped in water to smooth the surface. Repeat for the remaining bean curd triangles.

3　Heat a wok, add the oil, and heat the oil to 375°. Place a batch of the stuffed bean curd triangles in the pan, meat side down, and fry briefly over high heat until the meat is golden brown. Remove, reheat the oil, and fry the remaining bean curd triangles in the same manner. Add the **bean curd braising liquid** and heat until boiling. Add the stuffed bean curd, meat side down, and heat until the liquid is boiling. Reduce the heat to medium-low, cover, and cook for 10 minutes. Uncover, raise the heat to high, and remove the bean curd triangles from the wok, arranging them on a platter. Add the **thickener** to the cooking liquid, stirring constantly to prevent lumps. Pour the thickened liquid over the stuffed bean curd, sprinkle the minced scallion greens on top, and serve.

MA PO BEAN CURD

MA PO DOU FU 麻婆豆腐

This popular Sichuanese dish is said to be named after a Mrs. Chen, whose complexion was marred by prominent pockmarks. (*Ma* means pox.) Soft bean curd is traditionally used in this dish, as it provides the palate with a creamy respite from the numbing chili paste and Sichuan peppercorns.

1   Rinse the bean curd lightly and drain. Cut away any hard edges and cut the bean curd into ½-inch dice. Place the ground meat in a bowl, add the **meat marinade,** toss lightly, and let sit briefly.
2   Heat a wok, add the oil, and heat until hot. Add the meat and cook until it changes color, mashing and separating the grounds of meat with the shovel. Remove the meat with a handled strainer and heat the oil until any liquid from the meat has evaporated. Add the **minced seasonings** and stir-fry for about 10 seconds, until fragrant. Add the chili paste and stir-fry for another 5 seconds. Add the **braising liquid,** heat until boiling, and add the bean curd and meat. Return the mixture to a boil, reduce the heat to medium, and cook for about 5 minutes, uncovered, until the sauce has reduced by one fourth. With the mixture boiling, add the **thickener,** stirring constantly to prevent lumps. Transfer the mixture to a serving bowl or a platter. Sprinkle the top with the minced scallions and the Sichuan peppercorn powder.

SIX SERVINGS

8 cakes bean curd, 3 inches square and 1 inch thick
½ pound ground pork or beef

Meat Marinade

1 tablespoon soy sauce
½ tablespoon rice wine
1 teaspoon sesame oil

2 tablespoons peanut, safflower, or corn oil

Minced Seasonings

2 tablespoons minced scallions
1 tablespoon minced garlic
1 tablespoon minced gingerroot

1½ teaspoons chili paste

Braising Liquid

2 cups chicken broth
3 tablespoons soy sauce
½ teaspoon salt
1 tablespoon rice wine

Thickener

1½ teaspoons cornstarch
1½ tablespoons water

3 tablespoons minced scallion greens
1 teaspoon Sichuan peppercorns, toasted until fragrant, and pulverized

3 cakes bean curd, about 3
  inches square and 1 inch
  thick
½ pound boneless center-cut
  pork loin

Pork Marinade

2 teaspoons soy sauce
1 teaspoon rice wine
½ teaspoon sesame oil
½ teaspoon cornstarch

4 tablespoons peanut,
  safflower, or corn oil
1½ teaspoons chili paste

Sauce

3 tablespoons sweet bean
  sauce
4 tablespoons soy sauce
2 tablespoons sugar
3 tablespoons water

¾ cup carrot, parboiled for
  2½ minutes and cut into
  ½-inch dice
¾ cup English ("gourmet
  seedless") cucumber,
  seeded and cut into ½-inch
  dice, plunged into boiling
  water for 10 seconds, and
  refreshed in cold water

EIGHT-TREASURE STIR-FRIED VEGETABLES WITH MEAT

BA BAO LA JIANG

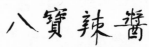

To most, the cuisine of Sichuan province brings to mind fiery seasonings and the ever-present chili pepper. Foreigners will not be disappointed when they taste the spicy sauce of this stir-fried platter. Traditionally, dried shrimp are the eighth treasure, but I have omitted them in this adapted version, leaving only seven treasures. An extra vegetable may be added in place of the missing shrimp.

1　Place the bean curd cakes between two pieces of cotton cloth or paper towels, place a cookie sheet on top of the bean curd, weight it down with some books, and let the bean curd sit for 2 hours. This will compress it and remove excess water. Cut the bean curd into ½-inch dice. Remove any fat or gristle from the pork loin. Cut the meat into ½-inch dice. Place the meat in a bowl, add the **pork marinade,** toss lightly, and let marinate for 20 minutes.
2　Heat a wok, add 2 tablespoons of the oil, and heat until very hot. Add the pork and stir-fry over high heat until the meat changes color and is cooked. Remove and drain. Remove the oil from the wok.
3　Reheat the wok, add the remaining 2 tablespoons of oil, and heat until very hot. Add the chili paste and stir-fry over high heat for 5 seconds, until fragrant. Add the **sauce** and stir-fry over high heat until the sauce starts to boil. Add the bean curd, carrots, cucum-

¾ cup water chestnuts, plunged briefly into boiling water, refreshed, and cut into ½-inch dice	¾ cup green peas (If fresh, cook for 5 minutes in boiling water and refresh in cold water. If frozen, defrost and set aside.) ¾ cup roasted, unsalted peanuts

bers, water chestnuts, and green peas. Toss lightly over high heat for a minute, until the ingredients are heated through. Add the peanuts and stir to coat with the sauce. Transfer the mixture to a platter and serve immediately.

NORTHERN-STYLE BEAN CURD

GUO TA DOU FU 鍋塌豆腐

Northern-style bean curd — or bean curd brain, as it was originally titled — is said to have been a favorite of Dowager Empress Tzu-Hsi in the nineteenth century. After you sample this dish, the reason for its popularity becomes evident: The simmered bean curd cakes, seasoned with sesame oil and chicken broth, melts in your mouth.

1   Rinse the bean curd lightly and drain thoroughly. Trim off any hard edges. Holding the cleaver parallel to the cutting surface, slice each bean curd cake in half through the thickness; then cut each piece in half to form 1½-inch squares ½ inch thick.
2   Heat a wok, add the oil, and heat the oil to 350°. Dredge each piece of bean curd in the cornstarch and then dip in the beaten egg to coat. Place a batch of bean curd in the wok and fry over medium heat until golden brown on both sides, about 3½ to 4 minutes per side. Remove with a handled strainer, and drain the bean curd. Reheat the oil, and fry the remaining bean curd in several batches. Remove the oil from the wok, reserving 1 tablespoon.
3   Reheat the wok, add the tablespoon of oil, and heat until very hot. Add the minced gingerroot and stir-fry until fragrant, about 5 seconds. Add the **bean curd cooking liquid** and heat until boiling. Add the fried bean curd and pierce the pieces of bean curd with a fork so that they will absorb the cooking liquid. Cook the bean curd, uncovered, for about 20 minutes over medium heat, or until all the liquid is absorbed. Dribble the sesame oil over the bean curd, toss lightly to coat, and transfer the bean curd to a platter. Sprinkle the minced scallions on top and serve.

EGGS 蛋類

In the Chinese culture, the birth of a child is an occasion attended by age-old customs. Tradition dictates that the mother must rest for one month, confined to the house, to adequately recuperate from the intense rigors of childbirth. During this period, friends and relatives send such varied gifts as eggs pickled in fermented wine rice (the wine is believed to "fire up" the body), chicken soup with gingerroot or sesame oil, and, in more recent times, milk powder. All of these foods are considered beneficial in restoring the body to its original state. If the baby is a boy, at the end of the month a custom called *man yue* ("a full month") is observed: Scarlet eggs are sent to relatives and friends announcing the joyous event and thanking the deities for their generosity.

Eggs, both in their natural color and dyed red, frequently are used by the Chinese on festivals and notable occasions as offerings to the supernatural powers. To the Chinese, the egg — with its yolk and white — symbolizes yin and yang, the two opposing forces of the universe.

Eggs are simmered in a fragrant tea-based solution and served during the New Year's holiday. Tea eggs are believed to "roll in," or impart, good luck for the coming year. On the occasion of the Dragon Boat Festival, celebrated on the fifth day of the fifth month of the lunar calendar, people in Hunan province eat salty duck eggs. This holiday marks the beginning of warm weather, and the preserved eggs keep beautifully in the heat.

Archeological evidence supports the belief that eggs were extremely popular among rich and poor alike even before the Han dynasty (206 B.C. to A.D. 220). During the T'ang dynasty (618 to 907), eggs with mutton and pork were cooked in hot sulfur springs and fed to invalids. Equally favored were duck, goose, quail, and peacock eggs. Turtle eggs were treasured as a delicacy for special occasions.

Since eggs are extremely perishable, preservation techniques were devised to prevent them from spoiling. Chicken eggs were smoked, red-cooked, or braised in a soy sauce–based liquid and

TEA EGGS

131

QUAIL EGGS

THOUSAND-YEAR-OLD EGGS

SALTY DUCK EGGS

simmered in a strong tea-flavored brew. Duck eggs, which were enjoyed in both sweet and savory dishes, were also packed in lime and ash and pickled in a salty brine. The resulting "pickles" were served as a garnish to rice or congee.

These preserving practices still exist today, and the methods used are almost exactly the same as those of ancient times. "Thousand-year-old" eggs are made by submerging duck eggs in a mixture of lime, pine ash, and salt, before being coated with mud and rolled in straw. The eggs are then left to ferment for fifty days. The minerals seep through the shell, changing the color, flavor, and texture of the eggs. Since the dried mud coating suggests an ancient origin and encourages the belief that the eggs may have been buried in the ground for a period, they acquired the somewhat exaggerated English name. Although many Westerners do not care for their rich, unctuous flavor and texture, thousand-year-old eggs are considered a delicacy by the Chinese and are particularly favored in cold appetizers.

Similarly, salty duck eggs are an avidly consumed variety of preserved eggs and are enjoyed in both sweet and savory dishes. To achieve the salty product, duck eggs are immersed in a saline marinade for thirty days. Like thousand-year-old eggs, these acquire a unique texture and flavor in the fermentation process; the shells take on a bluish tinge, the whites become intensely opaque, and the yolks turn deep orange. A salty duck egg with rice congee is the traditional breakfast of many southern Chinese, but salty duck eggs are enjoyed by Chinese the world over and they are sold in any well-stocked Chinese grocery store in the United States.

The reasons for the popularity of chicken eggs are obvious. In addition to their nutritional value (they contain all the essential amino acids and are an important source of protein), eggs are extremely versatile: They may be stir-fried, steamed, deep-fried, poached, or fried to form egg sheets, and are added to innumerable soups, savory concoctions, sweet pastries, and cakes. Egg yolks are used in batters and meat fillings for color and flavor; and the whites, combined with cornstarch, are added to seafood and chicken marinades to give fluffiness and firmness, or to soups to form silken threads. Furthermore, eggs are economical, filling, and easy to digest.

SALTY DUCK EGGS

XIAN DAN

Duck eggs play a prominent role in Chinese cuisine and they are more popularly used in a preserved state, rather than fresh. Once preserved in a salty brine for thirty days and cooked, they are served as a salty pickle with rice or congee or in various confections, where they provide a savory complement to the sweet pastries.

1 Rinse off the eggs and drain. Place the water, salt, rice wine, and the Sichuan peppercorns in a saucepan and heat until boiling, stirring until the salt dissolves. Remove from the heat and let cool to room temperature. Transfer the salty liquid to a large glass jar and add the eggs. Cover tightly and refrigerate for 30 days.
2 Cook the duck eggs in boiling water for 15 minutes (or the chicken eggs for 10 minutes). Serve as a pickle or use as a savory center in pastries.

TEN EGGS

10 duck eggs, or 10 "large" chicken eggs
6 cups water
1 cup salt
6 tablespoons rice wine
1 tablespoon Sichuan peppercorns

20 "large" eggs

Tea Cooking Mixture
1½ tablespoons salt
2 tablespoons soy sauce
¼ cup rice wine
3 whole star anise
2 cinnamon sticks
6 slices gingerroot, smashed
  with the flat side of a
  cleaver
½ cup black tea leaves
10 cups water

TEA EGGS

CHA YE DAN 茶葉蛋

In Taipei, tea egg vendors wheeling carts of bubbling cauldrons brimming with eggs are often seen in parks and in the parking lots of museums, beaches, and other recreational areas. The eggs make an excellent portable snack. At home, we often cooked a potload of eggs to be served as a salty pickle with rice and other simple entrées at our family meals. They reheat beautifully and the flavor is equally good whether they are hot or cold.

1   Place the eggs in a saucepan with cold water to cover. Bring the water to a boil, reduce the heat to low, and let the eggs simmer for 10 minutes, until they are hard-boiled. Refresh them in cold water. Drain the eggs and lightly tap the shells on a hard surface to crack them. Do not remove the shells.
2   Place the **tea cooking mixture** in a heavy pot and heat until boiling. Reduce the heat to low and let simmer for 20 minutes, uncovered. Add the cooked eggs and continue simmering for 45 minutes. Turn off the heat and let the eggs sit in the tea mixture until they are cool. Remove the shells and serve the eggs warm or chilled, cut into wedges.

COLD BEAN CURD APPETIZER WITH THOUSAND-YEAR-OLD EGGS

PI DAN BAN DOU FU　　　皮蛋拌豆腐

SIX SERVINGS

With its warm, muggy climate, Sichuan province is an area where cold platters are especially popular. The region's cuisine also places a strong emphasis on textures; many ingredients, such as wood ears, bamboo shoots, and water chestnuts, are admired for their textural qualities. In this cold appetizer, the spongy softness of the bean curd is contrasted with the unctuous richness of the thousand-year-old eggs.

1   Trim off any hard edges from the bean curd and remove the outer skin from all four sides, but not the top and bottom. Holding the cleaver parallel to the cutting surface, cut the bean curd through the thickness in half. Cut the bean curd into ½-inch dice and sprinkle with the salt. Remove the shells from the thousand-year-old eggs and cut each egg into six wedges.
2   Drain the bean curd thoroughly and arrange it on a platter. Arrange the wedges of thousand-year-old eggs in the center of the bean curd. Sprinkle the minced mustard greens on top, followed by the sesame oil and the soy sauce. Arrange the coriander in two piles, on either end of the platter. Toss lightly to combine the ingredients before serving.

4 cakes bean curd, about 3 inches square and 1 inch thick
1 teaspoon salt
4 thousand-year-old eggs
2 teaspoons Sichuan preserved mustard greens, rinsed and minced
¼ cup sesame oil
1½ tablespoons soy sauce
4 tablespoons coarsely chopped coriander (Chinese parsley)

1 pound cherrystone clams
½ teaspoon salt

Custard Mixture

6 whole eggs
1 teaspoon salt
2 tablespoons rice wine
1 teaspoon minced
   gingerroot
1 cup clam cooking liquid

STEAMED EGGS WITH CLAMS

HA LI ZHENG DAN   蛤蜊蒸蛋

So outstanding are the flavor and texture of this dish that, to my mind, it ranks with the likes of shark's fin soup and chicken velvet. The tender, savory custard provides the perfect foil for the seafood. Oysters, shrimp, or crabmeat may be substituted for the clams, each creating a subtle variation in flavor.

1   Rinse the clams thoroughly in cold running water to remove any sand. Place them in cold water to cover for 30 minutes; drain. Put 1 cup of water in a large pot and add the salt. Heat until boiling and add the clams. Cover and cook until the clams have just opened, shaking the pot occasionally to distribute the heat evenly.

2   Remove the clams with a handled strainer, and place them in a 1½-quart soufflé dish or a heat-proof bowl. Add 1 cup of the clam cooking liquid to the **custard mixture** while beating vigorously. Pour the custard mixture into the soufflé dish, straining it as it is added. Place the dish in a steamer tray.

3   Fill a wok with water level with the bottom edge of the steamer tray and heat until boiling. Place the steamer tray over the boiling water, cover, and steam for 12 to 15 minutes, until the custard is set. Serve immediately.

STIR-FRIED SHRIMP WITH EGG WHITE

FU RONG XIA REN

芙蓉蝦仁

One frequently finds the terms *fu jung* or *fu rong* (hibiscus) in the title of dishes containing egg whites and a garnish of crabmeat or shrimp. With a little imagination, one can envision some resemblance to the hibiscus in the fluffy, poached egg whites and the pink shrimp of the finished dish. This delicately flavored platter is excellent with rice and a steamed green vegetable.

1   Score each shrimp along the length of the back and remove the vein; the scoring will allow the shrimp to "butterfly" when it is cooked. Rinse all the shrimp and drain thoroughly. Place the shrimp in a linen dishtowel and squeeze out as much moisture as possible. Place the shrimp in a bowl with the **shrimp marinade.** Pinch the gingerroot slices repeatedly for several minutes to impart their flavor to the rice wine. Toss lightly, and let the shrimp marinate for 20 minutes. Discard the gingerroot and drain the shrimp. Beat the egg whites and cream of tartar until the egg whites are stiff. Fold the shrimp into the egg whites.
2   Heat a wok, add the oil, and heat the oil to 325°. Add the shrimp–egg white mixture and poach in the oil, stirring carefully from time to time to cook evenly. Cook for 3 to 4 minutes, until the egg whites float to the surface and the shrimp change color. Remove with a slotted spoon and drain. Remove the oil from the wok, reserving 2 tablespoons.
3   Reheat the wok, add the 2 tablespoons of oil, and heat until hot. Add the **minced seasonings** and stir-fry over high heat for about 10 seconds, until fragrant. Add the **shrimp sauce** and cook, stirring constantly to prevent lumps, until thickened. Add the poached shrimp–egg white mixture and carefully toss it in the thickened sauce. Transfer to a serving platter. Sprinkle the minced ham on top and serve.

1 pound medium-sized raw shrimp, shelled

Shrimp Marinade
2 slices gingerroot, smashed with the flat side of a cleaver
1 tablespoon rice wine
½ teaspoon salt

12 egg whites
½ teaspoon cream of tartar
4 cups peanut, safflower, or corn oil

Minced Seasonings
2 tablespoons minced scallions
2 teaspoons minced gingerroot

Shrimp Sauce
½ cup chicken broth
1 tablespoon rice wine
1 teaspoon salt
¼ teaspoon freshly ground white pepper
1 teaspoon sesame oil
1½ teaspoons cornstarch

2 tablespoons minced ham

½ pound shredded crabmeat

Crabmeat Marinade
2 slices gingerroot, smashed
  with the flat side of a
  cleaver
2 teaspoons rice wine

Crab Sauce
½ teaspoon salt
1 teaspoon sesame oil

¼ cup peanut, safflower, or
  corn oil

Minced Seasonings
1 tablespoon minced
  scallions
2 teaspoons minced
  gingerroot

Egg Mixture
6 eggs
1 teaspoon salt
¼ teaspoon freshly ground
  white pepper

1 tablespoon minced scallion
  greens

STIR-FRIED EGGS WITH CRAB

FU RONG XIE ROU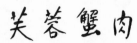

Although the term *fu rong* was originally reserved for dishes with egg whites and crabmeat or shrimp, this category was later broadened to include whole egg dishes with a garnish of pork, chicken, and beef. Any of these may be used in place of crabmeat in this dish. Most Chinese prefer that eggs be undercooked and creamy; Americans may prefer to lengthen the cooking time, producing a slightly drier version.

1   Pick over the crabmeat and remove any shell or cartilage. Shred the crabmeat and place it in a bowl. Pinch the gingerroot slices in the rice wine repeatedly for several minutes to impart their flavor. Discard the gingerroot and add the **crabmeat marinade** to the crabmeat. Toss lightly and let marinate for 20 minutes.
2   Heat a wok, add 1 tablespoon of oil, and heat until hot. Add the crabmeat and the **crab sauce**. Toss lightly over high heat until the mixture is dry, about 2 minutes, and remove. Reheat the wok. Add the remaining 3 tablespoons of oil, and heat until very hot. Add the **minced seasonings,** and stir-fry until fragrant, about 10 seconds. Lightly whisk the **egg mixture** until frothy and add to the crabmeat. Stir-fry over medium heat until the eggs are just set. Transfer to a platter, sprinkle with the minced scallion greens, and serve immediately.

FISH-FLAVORED EGG OMELET

YU XIANG HONG DAN 鱼香烘蛋

The famous Sichuanese "fish-flavored" sauce, so named because it was originally developed for fish dishes, is also a superb complement to shrimp, chicken, pork, eggplant, and eggs, as in this recipe. The fluffy omelet is an excellent foil for the spicy stir-fried topping.

1 Lightly beat the eggs until frothy and add the salt. Drain the wood ears. Cut away and discard the hard, bitter nib on the underside of the wood ears, and cut the wood ears into shreds. Cut the water chestnuts into thin slices. Remove and discard any fat or gristle from the pork loin. Cut the meat into thin slices. Shred the slices into matchstick-size shreds. Place the shreds in a bowl, add the **pork marinade,** toss lightly, and let marinate for 20 minutes.
2 Heat a wok, add 3 tablespoons of the oil, and heat the oil until very hot. Add the eggs, cover, and reduce the heat to low. Cook for about 5 minutes, until the eggs are set and the bottom is lightly golden. Uncover and turn the omelet over. Cook until golden and remove to a heat-proof platter. Keep the omelet warm while preparing the sauce.
3 Reheat the wok, add 2 tablespoons of oil, and heat until very hot. Add the shredded pork loin, and stir-fry over high heat, stirring constantly until the meat changes color. Remove and drain. Reheat the pan and add 2 tablespoons of oil. Heat the oil until very hot and add the **minced seasonings**. Stir-fry for about 10 seconds, until fragrant, and add the chili paste. Stir-fry for 5 seconds and add the water chestnuts and wood ears. Cook until the ingredients are heated through and add the **fish-flavored sauce**. Cook the sauce over high heat, stirring constantly, until thickened. Add the pork loin, toss lightly to coat with the sauce, and pour the mixture over the omelet. Sprinkle the top with the minced scallions and serve immediately.

SIX SERVINGS

8 "large" eggs
1 teaspoon salt
10 small dried wood ears, soaked for 20 minutes in hot water to cover
12 water chestnuts, plunged briefly into boiling water and refreshed
½ pound boneless center-cut pork loin

Pork Marinade

1 tablespoon soy sauce
½ tablespoon rice wine
1 teaspoon sesame oil
1 teaspoon cornstarch
1 teaspoon water

7 tablespoons peanut, safflower, or corn oil

Minced Seasonings

1 tablespoon minced scallions
1 tablespoon minced garlic
1 tablespoon minced gingerroot

1½ teaspoons chili paste

Fish-Flavored Sauce

¼ cup chicken broth
1½ tablespoons soy sauce
1 tablespoon rice wine
2 teaspoons sugar
1½ teaspoons Chinese black vinegar
1 teaspoon sesame oil
2 teaspoons cornstarch

2 tablespoons minced scallion greens

139

Egg Seasonings
1 teaspoon dried shrimp,
   soaked for 1 hour,
   drained, and minced
12 water chestnuts, plunged
   briefly into boiling water,
   refreshed, and coarsely
   chopped
1 teaspoon salt
1 tablespoon rice wine
1 tablespoon cornstarch

12 "large" egg yolks
⅔ cup chicken broth
¼ cup rendered chicken fat
2 tablespoons minced ham

NORTHERN-STYLE SCRAMBLED EGGS

LIU HUANG CAI

The Chinese title of this dish, literally translated, means "yellow flowing oil." This phrase refers to the last step of the recipe, in which the chicken fat is scrambled directly into the egg yolks. A steamed variation, in which duck fat is substituted for the rendered chicken fat, is often included as one of the entrées in a traditional Peking duck dinner. Serve this rich yet delicate platter with a steamed green vegetable and rice.

1   Place the **egg seasonings** in a mixing bowl. In a separate bowl, lightly beat the egg yolks and add the chicken broth; lightly beat to combine. Add this mixture to the egg seasonings and mix to blend.
2   Heat a wok, add 3 tablespoons of the chicken fat, and heat until hot. Add the egg mixture and slowly scramble, stirring constantly over medium heat. When the eggs have begun to set, dribble the remaining tablespoon of chicken fat around the outside of the pan. Transfer the scrambled eggs to a platter and sprinkle the top with the minced ham. Serve immediately.

Egg Mixture
5 "large" eggs
½ teaspoon salt
½ teaspoon white pepper

1 teaspoon dried shrimp,
   softened in hot water for
   1 hour
1 pound ground pork or
   beef

EGG DUMPLINGS

DAN JIAO

Dumplings of all types are a popular New Year's delicacy. In some cases, as in this dish, they are said to resemble golden coins and so serving them conveys the wish of continuing prosperity. So delectable are egg dumplings that they have become an entrée enjoyed throughout the year.

1   Beat the **egg mixture** until frothy. Drain the dried shrimp and mince finely. Chop the ground meat for a few minutes until fluffy

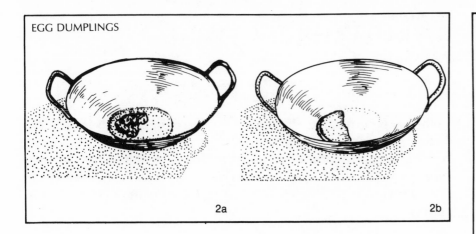

EGG DUMPLINGS

2a
2b

Meat Seasonings
1 tablespoon soy sauce
2 teaspoons rice wine
2 teaspoons sesame oil
½ teaspoon salt
2 teaspoons minced scallions
1 teaspoon minced
    gingerroot
1 tablespoon cornstarch

1½ tablespoons peanut,
    safflower, or corn oil
1 pound fresh spinach,
    trimmed and cleaned

Spinach Seasonings
½ teaspoon salt
1 tablespoon rice wine
1 tablespoon chicken broth
1 teaspoon minced garlic

Dumpling Sauce
1 cup chicken broth
2 teaspoons soy sauce
½ teaspoon sugar
½ teaspoon salt
¼ teaspoon freshly ground
    white pepper
1 teaspoon cornstarch

1 teaspoon sesame oil

and place it in a large bowl with the dried shrimp and the **meat seasonings**. Stir vigorously in one direction and throw the mixture lightly against the inside of the bowl to combine evenly.

2   Heat a wok or a nonstick frying pan and add ½ tablespoon of oil. Heat the oil, swirling it around in the pan, and add a heaping tablespoon of the egg mixture. Tilt the pan so that a thin, 3-inch pancake is formed. Place a heaping teaspoon of the ground meat mixture on one half of the pancake (a) and fold over the other half to form a half-moon shape and to seal in the meat (b). Press down along the edge of the circle with the spatula. Remove the dumpling. Make the remaining dumplings in the same manner.

3   Reheat the wok, add 1 tablespoon of oil, and heat the oil until smoking. Add the spinach and stir-fry over high heat for about 5 seconds. Add the **spinach seasonings** and continue stir-frying until the spinach is just limp. Arrange the spinach around the outer edge of a platter.

4   Reheat the wok, add the **dumpling sauce**, and add the dumplings. Cook over high heat until the sauce begins to boil. Reduce the heat to medium and continue cooking for 3 minutes. Add the teaspoon of sesame oil, toss lightly to mix, and transfer the mixture to the center of the platter. Serve immediately.

24 fresh quail eggs (or about
    1 15-ounce can)
2 15-ounce cans straw
    mushrooms
2 tablespoons soy sauce
1 pound broccoli
4 cups peanut, safflower, or
    corn oil
½ pound small fresh
    mushrooms

2 tablespoons ½-inch-long
    scallion pieces

Braising Liquid
¾ cup chicken broth
1 teaspoon salt
2 tablespoons soy sauce
    from marinating the
    quail eggs
1 tablespoon rice wine
1 teaspoon sugar
½ teaspoon sesame oil

Thickener
2 teaspoons cornstarch
1½ tablespoons water

BRAISED QUAIL EGGS WITH MUSHROOMS

YANG GU PA CHUN DAN 洋菇 扒 鷄蛋

In the Far East, fresh quail eggs are available in markets year-round. In the United States, one may find the small, spotted eggs (they look a bit like Jordan almonds) on a seasonal basis in some large Oriental grocery stores. If using fresh eggs, boil them for 5 minutes; with the canned variety, parboil for 10 seconds to remove any tinny flavor.

1   Boil the fresh quail eggs for 5 minutes (or canned ones 10 seconds). Plunge the straw mushrooms into boiling water for 15 seconds. Refresh in cold water. Drain. Place the quail eggs in a bowl, add the 2 tablespoons of soy sauce, and let marinate for 30 minutes, tossing occasionally. Peel away the tough outer skin from the broccoli and separate the flowerets. Roll-cut the stems into 1-inch pieces. Heat 1½ quarts salted water until boiling. Add the stem pieces and cook for ½ minute. Add the flowerets and cook for 2½ minutes, or until both stems and flowerets are just tender. Refresh immediately in cold water. Drain thoroughly.
2   Heat a wok, add the oil, and heat the oil to 375°. Drain the quail eggs thoroughly, reserving the soy sauce for the braising liquid. Deep-fry the quail eggs in the hot oil for 1 minute, until golden brown. Remove with a handled strainer, and drain. Reheat the oil and add the fresh mushrooms. Deep-fry for about 1½ minutes, until golden brown. Remove with a handled strainer, and drain. Remove the oil from the wok, reserving 3 tablespoons.
3   Reheat the wok (or use a heavy Dutch oven) until hot, add 2 tablespoons of the reserved oil and heat until hot. Add the scallion pieces, and stir-fry for about 10 seconds over high heat. Add the fried mushrooms and the **braising liquid**. Heat the mixture until boiling, reduce the heat to medium, and cook, uncovered, for 3 minutes. Add the straw mushrooms and the quail eggs and cook for another 2 minutes. Add the **thickener** and cook until thickened, stirring constantly. Remove and set aside to keep warm.

4 Reheat the wok, add the remaining tablespoon of oil, and heat until smoking. Add the broccoli and stir-fry over high heat for 30 seconds. Add the **broccoli sauce,** toss lightly, and arrange the broccoli around the outer edge of a large platter. Spoon the quail egg–mushroom mixture into the middle. Serve immediately.

Broccoli Sauce
1 teaspoon salt
1 tablespoon rice wine
1 tablespoon chicken broth

SWEET-AND-SOUR QUAIL EGGS

FU PI CHUN DAN 腐皮鶏蛋

SIX SERVINGS

Sweet and sour is a familiar theme in Chinese cooking, but serving the sauce with quail eggs wrapped in bean milk sheets is a flavorful twist. The crisp, bite-size eggs are excellent as an hors d'oeuvre or as a side dish in a banquet. Wonton wrappers may be substituted if bean milk sheets are unavailable.

1 Plunge the quail eggs into boiling water for 10 seconds. Immediately refresh in cold water. Drain and pat dry. Soak the bean milk sheets for 5 minutes in hot water to cover. Drain and pat dry with paper towels. Cut the bean milk sheets into twenty-four 3-inch squares. Stir the **egg paste** until smooth, adding more water if the mixture is too dry.

2 Lay out one bean milk sheet on a flat surface and spread the sheet with a little of the egg paste. Place a quail egg in the center and gather up the edges of the bean milk sheet to enclose the egg. Pinch the edges to seal the package. Repeat for the remaining squares and quail eggs.

3 Heat a wok, add the **sweet-and-sour sauce,** and cook, stirring constantly, until thickened. Transfer to a bowl and set aside. Clean the wok.

4 Reheat the wok, add the oil, and heat the oil to 375°. Add half the quail eggs and deep-fry, turning constantly in the hot oil, until crisp and golden brown. Remove with a handled strainer, drain on absorbent paper, and reheat the oil. Deep-fry the remaining quail eggs in the same manner. Transfer the quail eggs to a platter and serve with the sweet-and-sour sauce.

SIX SERVINGS

24 quail eggs (about 1 15-ounce can)
4 or 5 dried bean milk sheets

Egg Paste
1 egg, lightly beaten
2 tablespoons flour
2 tablespoons water

Sweet-and-Sour Sauce
6 tablespoons ketchup
4 tablespoons clear rice vinegar
6 tablespoons sugar
2 teaspoons soy sauce
1 teaspoon salt
½ cup water
1 teaspoon sesame oil
2 teaspoons cornstarch

6 cups peanut, safflower, or corn oil

1 pound medium-sized raw
  shrimp, shelled
1 ounce pork fat, minced to
  a paste

Shrimp Seasonings
½ tablespoon rice wine
1 teaspoon minced
  gingerroot
1 teaspoon salt
½ teaspoon freshly ground
  white pepper
½ teaspoon sesame oil

½ egg white, beaten until
  frothy
1 tablespoon cornstarch

Egg Sheets
3 "large" eggs, lightly beaten
1 teaspoon salt
½ teaspoon cornstarch
½ tablespoon water

Egg Paste
½ whole egg
2 tablespoons cornstarch

6 sheets nori (purple laver)

Shrimp Roll Sauce
⅓ cup chicken broth
2 teaspoons rice wine
½ teaspoon sesame oil
½ teaspoon cornstarch

STEAMED SHRIMP ROLLS

RU YI XIA JUAN　　如意蝦捲

Ru yi means happiness, and since the shape of these steamed shrimp rolls is reminiscent of the Chinese scepter of happiness, we find the word in the title. Once steamed, the sliced rolls may be used as a garnish in Mongolian fire pot and other soups, as well as in stir-fried vegetable dishes. Or they may be deep-fried and served with a dipping sauce.

1　Devein the shrimp, rinse lightly, and drain thoroughly. Place the shrimp in a linen dishtowel, and squeeze out as much moisture as possible. Smash the shrimp with the flat edge of a cleaver and chop to a fine paste — or use a food processor fitted with the steel blade. Place the shrimp paste and the pork fat in a large bowl; add the **shrimp seasonings**. Stir vigorously in one direction and lightly throw the mixture against the side of the bowl to combine evenly. Add the beaten egg white and mix until the paste is slightly stiff. Then add the cornstarch and continue mixing until the mixture is evenly combined. It should be stiff and slightly sticky, not loose.
2　Lightly beat the ingredients for the **egg sheets** until slightly frothy. Wipe the surface of a well-seasoned wok or a nonstick 10-inch frying pan with an oil-soaked paper towel. Heat the wok until a little water sprinkled onto the surface evaporates immediately. Remove from the heat, add one sixth of the egg mixture, and tilt the wok to form a thin, circular pancake. Place the wok back over the heat and cook until set. Flip the egg sheet and cook until lightly golden. Remove the egg sheet and set aside to cool. Trim to a square. Make five more egg sheets in the same manner.
3　Lay an egg sheet on a flat surface and spread some of the **egg paste** over the sheet. Place a nori sheet on top of the egg sheet. Spread one sixth of the shrimp mixture on the nori sheet, using the underside of a spoon dipped in water to smooth the surface. Starting at the edge nearest you, roll up the egg sheet as shown, rolling tightly as you go along. Make the remaining rolls in the same manner. Place the finished rolls, seam side down, on a lightly oiled heat-proof plate. Put the plate in a steamer tray.

4 Fill a wok with water level with the bottom edge of the steamer tray and heat until boiling. Place the steamer tray over the boiling water, cover, and steam for 12 minutes over high heat. Cut each roll into 1-inch pieces (a) and arrange the slices (b) on a platter.

5 Remove the water from the wok and reheat the wok. Add the **shrimp roll sauce** and heat until boiling and slightly thick, stirring constantly. Pour the sauce over the shrimp roll slices and serve immediately.

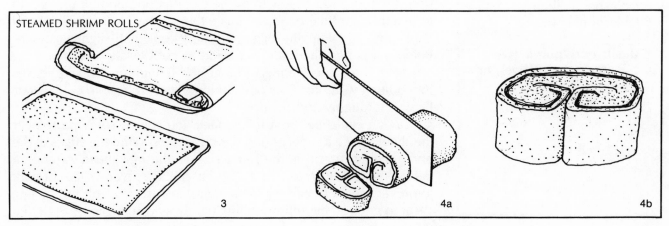

STEAMED SHRIMP ROLLS

3   4a   4b

1 pound boneless center-cut
   pork loin

Pork Marinade
1 tablespoon hoisin sauce
1 tablespoon soy sauce
¾ tablespoon sugar
2 teaspoons rice wine
½ tablespoon ketchup
1 teaspoon sesame oil
½ teaspoon salt
1 teaspoon minced garlic

Egg Sheets
5 "large" eggs, lightly beaten
1 teaspoon salt
1 teaspoon cornstarch
1 tablespoon water

6 leaves leafy lettuce or
   savoy cabbage

Paste
3 tablespoons flour
6 tablespoons water

6 sheets nori (purple laver)
6 cups peanut, safflower, or
   corn oil

NORI EGG ROLLS

ZI CAI JUAN 紫 菜 捲

Egg sheets are thin, crêpelike pancakes that are used in both Chinese and Japanese cooking. They may be used as skins or wrappings for spring rolls, or other vegetable, meat, and seafood rolls, and they may be shredded and used as a garnish in stir-fried dishes, cold salads, and soups. Nori egg rolls may be deep-fried, as in this recipe, or steamed for 8 to 10 minutes. They are traditionally served with a Sichuan peppercorn-salt. However, I prefer a light dipping sauce of soy sauce, rice vinegar, and shredded gingerroot.

1   Remove and discard any fat or gristle from the pork loin. Place the meat in a bowl, add the **pork marinade**, turn lightly to coat, and let marinate for at least 4 hours, or overnight in the refrigerator.
2   Preheat the oven to 375°. Place the meat on a rack on a roasting pan and bake for 1¼ hours, or until the meat is cooked and the outside is golden brown. Let the meat cool; then cut it, across the grain, into slices about ⅛ inch thick.
3   To make the **egg sheets**, lightly beat the ingredients until frothy. Wipe the surface of a well-seasoned wok or a 10-inch nonstick skillet with an oil-soaked paper towel. Heat the pan until a little water sprinkled onto the surface evaporates immediately. Remove from the heat, add one sixth of the egg mixture, and tilt the pan to form a thin, circular pancake. Place the pan back over the heat and cook until set. Flip the egg sheet and cook until lightly golden. Remove the egg sheet and set aside to cool. Make five more egg sheets in the same manner. Plunge the lettuce or cabbage leaves into boiling water for 5 seconds. Immediately refresh in cold water. Drain thoroughly and pat dry.
4   Lay an egg sheet on a flat surface and spread some **paste** over the sheet. Place a sheet of nori directly on top. Trim the edges of the nori sheet so that it is the same size as the egg sheet. Arrange a lettuce or cabbage leaf over the nori and place several slices of pork loin over the leaf. Starting at the edge nearest you, roll up the egg sheet to enclose the filling, rolling tightly as you go along. Spread a

little paste on the inside end of the egg sheet to seal the roll. Make five more rolls in the same manner.

5 Heat a wok, add the oil, and heat the oil to 375°. Add the rolls and deep-fry for about 5 minutes, stirring constantly until the rolls are golden brown and crisp. Drain on absorbent paper, cut into 1-inch sections, and serve.

_____

POULTRY 家禽類

When I was a child, Christmas and the New Year heralded a time of gift giving from my parents' friends, relatives, and business associates. There was always the latest Japanese electronic equipment or expensive stemware mail-ordered from glossy catalogues. If it had been a very good year, our subscription to the Fruit-of-the-Month Club would be renewed — each month a huge box bursting with a different kind of ripe, fragrant fruit would be joyfully received in our household.

Years later, I was delighted to relive the same ritual with my surrogate family in Taiwan on the occasion of the Chinese New Year. According to custom, food gifts are exchanged at this time of the year. These usually included fat links of freshly made Chinese sausage; huge bags of dried Chinese black mushrooms; dried, salted ducks; and gift boxes bursting with expensive American canned goods.

Two weeks before the holiday, one room of the house would be emptied completely in anticipation of the influx of gifts. As the New Year approached, we would watch the once-vacant space become packed with mountains of fragrant edible delicacies.

It also was not unusual to find two or three cackling chickens roaming around our back yard, compliments of one of my Chinese father's grateful customers. Obahsan, our family's stalwart old maid, would fatten them up with corn and rice for a few days before slaughtering them with her trusty cleaver. No part of the bird would be wasted; the feathers would be plucked, gathered up in a bag, and shipped off to her relatives in the country. The blood would be drained, mixed with rice, and cooked into a solid cake to be administered to my Chinese brother who suffered from anemia. (Chicken blood is believed to contain iron and vitamins and is often served shredded in soups.) The chicken itself would be cooked whole in a soy sauce braising liquid or a soup, or it would be cut up and used in several dishes.

Chicken, duck, geese, pigeon, and all types of fowl are of greatest importance to the Chinese, both symbolically and dietetically. According to ancient Chinese thought, fowl were considered more noble than four-footed animals, and the meat was considered far healthier for the body. In Chinese ritual, fowl has been used as a sacrificial offering thoughout the ages — probably because of its auspicious symbolic significance. The rooster, or cock, is the tenth symbolic animal of the Twelve Terrestrial Branches, corresponding to the zodiac sign Capricorn, and is thought to personify the warm vital component of yang, the positive element of universal life. The ancient Chinese credited the cock with supernatural powers and considered the crowing of roosters at sunrise responsible for driving away the nocturnal ghosts. White sugar cocks frequently are eaten by the bride and bridegroom at wedding ceremonies as a protection against harmful astrological powers.

The pigeon is a symbol of longevity, and in a custom dating back to the Han dynasty (206 B.C. to A.D. 220), a jade scepter, or "pigeon staff," often is presented to elderly persons as a token of long life.

Duck is the emblem of felicity and happiness, with special respect accorded to the Mandarin duck, which represents conjugal fidelity. It is said that once two ducks of this species are paired and then separated, they will pine away and die. The ancient T'ang pharmacologists recommended duck soup as a suitable means for reconciling differences between an estranged couple.

Fowl in general played a significant role in ancient Chinese pharmacology: Numerous digestive aids were prepared from the fowl gizzards. Medicines made from chicken were believed to regulate the menstrual cycle and were given to women undergoing menopause. Essences made from black-bone chicken, a species believed to have particularly healthful properties, were said to aid sufferers of consumption and feebleness. According to a Chinese friend from Peking, a popular treatment in healing broken bones was to place a freshly killed, pounded chicken on the break for three days to a week. And the eating of dove and pigeon eggs was believed to prevent smallpox.

The ancient Chinese consumed fowl in many forms — braised chicken, casseroled duck, wild duck stew, fried flesh of the crane, roasted wild goose, and wild duck stew are some of the dishes recorded from the menus of the great Han feasts. All types of fowl were available to both the common people and the upper classes,

149

and the raising of chickens was encouraged by the government as a household hobby.

Today, as in ancient times, fowl is favored fare; chicken and duck are staples of the modern Chinese diet and are admired for their delicate flavor and versatility. Both are steamed, braised, deep-fried, stir-fried, simmered in soy sauce–based liquid, stuffed, baked, and boiled in soups. And regional specialties abound: Northern chefs are masters of Peking duck and Shandong braised chicken; easterners excel in making drunken chicken and saltwater duck. In western China, the Hunanese are experts at minced squab in bamboo cups, duck breast soup, and smoked chicken, while the Sichuanese prefer crispy-skin duck, steamed duck in seasoned rice powder, and spicy stir-fried chicken with peanuts. The Cantonese offer poultry dishes ranging from roasted duck, steamed chicken with scallions, and roasted quail to fried goose with plum sauce.

Pigeons, too, serve the Chinese in gastronomic and other notable ways. An ancient Chinese practice still observed in parts of China today is the attachment of wooden pipes or whistles to the feet of domestic pigeons. As a flock of these birds circles in the sky, it creates harmonious melodies for its earthly audience below.

RED-COOKED CHICKEN

HONG SHAO JI   紅燒雞

Red-cooking, or slow cooking in a soy sauce—based liquid, is extremely popular all over China, since the preparation is simple and the flavor is complementary to rice. The cooking liquid (*lu*) may be used repeatedly to braise not only chicken, but pork, lamb, beef, liver, bean curd, and hard-boiled eggs as well. In fact, the flavor intensifies and improves with each use. One fourth of the ingredients (except the spices) should be replenished with every reuse. By the fifth use, the spices should be replaced.

1   Place the **red-cooking liquid** in a heavy pot or a Dutch oven and heat until boiling. Reduce the heat to low and let the liquid simmer, uncovered, for 30 minutes.
2   Rinse the chicken lightly, drain, and remove any fat from the cavity and neck. Place the chicken, breast side down, in the red-cooking liquid and cook for 1¼ hours, turning the chicken two or three times during the cooking. Turn off the heat and let the chicken sit in the liquid for 15 minutes; then remove it. Brush the surface of the chicken with the sesame oil. Cut the chicken, through the bones, into bite-size serving pieces as shown (discarding the backbone) and arrange them on a platter. Spoon a little of the cooking liquid over the chicken and serve.

SIX SERVINGS

Red-Cooking Liquid

1 cinnamon stick, or a piece of Chinese cinnamon bark, if available
1 whole star anise
2 pieces dried tangerine or orange peel, about 2 inches long
½ teaspoon fennel seeds
1½ cups soy sauce
⅓ cup sugar
½ cup rice wine
6 cups water

1 whole roasting chicken, 4 to 5 pounds
1 tablespoon sesame oil

RED-COOKED CHICKEN CUT UP FOR SERVING

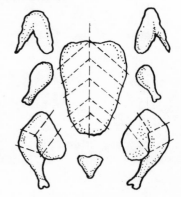

1 whole roasting chicken, 4
  to 5 pounds

Chicken Marinade
3 tablespoons rice wine
2 teaspoons salt
3 scallions, smashed with the
  flat side of a cleaver
3 slices gingerroot, smashed
  with the flat side of a
  cleaver
1 tablespoon Sichuan
  peppercorns

Smoking Mixture
4 tablespoons loose black
  tea leaves
2 tablespoons brown sugar
2 tablespoons aniseed

2 teaspoons sesame oil

HUNAN-STYLE SMOKED CHICKEN

HUNAN XUN JI　　　　湖南燻雞

In Chinese cuisine, smoking is a process used for flavoring foods
rather than cooking them; the food is first steamed or boiled until
just done; then it is suspended over the smoking mixture, which
includes black tea, brown sugar, aniseed, and sometimes flour or
rice. Heat is applied and the fragrant fumes color and flavor the
food. Chicken is a food particularly suited to this process because
the smoky flavor accentuates the delicate sweetness of the meat.

1　Rinse the chicken lightly, drain thoroughly, and remove any fat
from the cavity and neck. Rub the **chicken marinade** inside the
cavity and all over the skin. Place the chicken, with the marinade,
breast side down in a bowl and let marinate for at least 4 hours, or
overnight in the refrigerator. Transfer the chicken and the marinade
to a heat-proof bowl and place the bowl in a steamer tray. Cover the
steamer tray.
2　Fill a wok with water level with the bottom edge of the steamer
tray and heat until boiling. Place the steamer tray over the boiling
water and steam for 1 hour over high heat. Remove the chicken and
let it cool. Discard the marinade.
3　Line the inside of a wok or a deep pot with several layers of
heavy-duty aluminum foil. Place the **smoking mixture** in the wok
and stir to combine the ingredients. Place a steaming rack or a
smoking rack, or two crisscrossed chopsticks, over the smoking
mixture. Place the steamed chicken, breast side down, on the rack.
Line the inside of the wok lid, or the deep pot lid, with several layers
of heavy-duty aluminum foil, and cover the pan securely with the
lid.
4　Place the pan over high heat and smoke the chicken for 12
minutes. (Start timing when the smell of smoke becomes very pronounced.) Turn off the heat and let the chicken sit, covered, for 10
minutes; then remove it and brush the outside of the chicken with
the sesame oil. Cut the chicken, through the bones, into bite-size
pieces, as for red-cooked chicken (page 151). Discard the seasonings. Arrange the chicken on a platter and serve.

SALT-BAKED CHICKEN

YAN JIU JI　　鹽　焗　雞

Both French and Chinese chefs are fond of cooking chicken in salt because, like clay, it acts as an excellent conductor of heat, sealing in the natural juices and producing remarkably tender and moist meat. Generally the chicken is packed directly in the salt; however, I have adapted the recipe slightly by first wrapping the chicken in parchment paper or an oven-roasting bag. This prevents the juices from leaking into the salt; thus the salt may be used again and again.

1　Lightly rinse the chicken and remove any fat from the cavity and neck. Drain the chicken thoroughly and place it in a bowl. Add the **chicken marinade** and rub it inside the cavity and all over the skin. Let the chicken marinate, breast side down, for at least 2 hours, or overnight in the refrigerator. Remove from the marinade and wrap the chicken in the parchment paper, or place in the oven-roasting bag, breast side down.

2　Preheat the oven to 450°. Heat a wok or a heavy skillet and add the salt, star anise, and Sichuan peppercorns. Stir-fry over high heat, stirring constantly until the salt begins to pop and is very hot. Spoon about one third of the salt mixture into a 4-quart Dutch oven or casserole, shaping a well in the center of the salt. Place the chicken, breast side down, in the well and cover with the remaining salt. Cover the pot and place it in the preheated oven.

3　Bake the chicken for 1 hour; then remove it from the oven and let it sit in the covered pot for 10 minutes before cutting. Cut the chicken, through the bones, into bite-size pieces and arrange on a platter, as for red-cooked chicken (page 151). Discard the seasonings. Pour the **dipping sauce** into a saucepan and heat until boiling. Pour the heated sauce over the chicken and serve.

SIX SERVINGS

1 whole roasting chicken, 4 to 5 pounds

Chicken Marinade

2 tablespoons rice wine
1 tablespoon salt
3 scallions, smashed with the flat side of a cleaver
3 slices gingerroot, smashed with the flat side of a cleaver
1 whole star anise, smashed with the flat side of a cleaver
1 tablespoon Sichuan peppercorns

A 30-inch square of parchment paper or a large oven-roasting bag
4 pounds rock salt or kosher salt
3 whoie star anise, smashed with the flat side of a cleaver
1 tablespoon Sichuan peppercorns

Dipping Sauce

¼ cup chicken broth
1 teaspoon salt
1 teaspoon sesame oil
1 tablespoon shredded scallions
1 tablespoon finely shredded gingerroot

1 whole roasting chicken, 4
  to 5 pounds

Chicken Marinade
1 tablespoon salt
2 tablespoons rice wine
1 tablespoon soy sauce
3 scallions, smashed with the
  flat side of a cleaver
3 slices gingerroot, smashed
  with the flat side of a
  cleaver

⅓ cup finely shredded
  scallions
¼ cup finely shredded
  gingerroot
3 tablespoons sesame oil

Thickener
1 teaspoon cornstarch
1 tablespoon water

STEAMED CHICKEN WITH SCALLIONS

CONG YU JI　　　　葱 油 雞

Cantonese chefs are renowned for their mastery in cooking chicken, preferring to accentuate the delicate flavor rather than disguise it. Such is the case with this dish; the pungent seasonings of gingerroot and scallions highlight the flavor of the chicken meat. The technique in this recipe is also used in cooking fish.

1   Lightly rinse the chicken and drain thoroughly. Remove any fat from the cavity and neck. Place the chicken in a bowl, add the **chicken marinade,** and rub the marinade inside the cavity and all over the skin. Let the chicken marinate, breast side down, for at least 1 hour. Place the chicken, breast side up, in a heat-proof bowl or on a plate, and place in a steamer tray.
2   Fill a wok with water level with the bottom edge of the steamer tray and heat until boiling. Place the steamer tray containing the chicken over the boiling water, cover, and steam for 1 hour over high heat. Remove the chicken; drain off the liquid and set it aside; let the chicken cool slightly. Cut the chicken, through the bones, into bite-size pieces; arrange them on a platter, as for red-cooked chicken (page 151). Sprinkle the shredded scallions and gingerroot over the chicken.
3   Remove the water from the wok and reheat the wok. Add the sesame oil, and heat until smoking. Slowly pour the sesame oil over the chicken. Heat the reserved chicken cooking liquid, and skim off any fat. Slowly add the **thickener,** stirring constantly to prevent lumps. Pour over the chicken and serve immediately.

PANG PANG CHICKEN

BAN BAN JI 棒 棒 雞

This Sichuanese cold platter offers a sampling of some notable characteristics of the western regional style: The crisp, fresh cucumber slices complemented by the smooth, slippery bean threads emphasize the textural qualities in the cuisine, while the peanut butter, which forms the base for the spicy dressing, illustrates the prominent use of nuts.

1   Rinse the chicken, drain thoroughly, and remove any fat from the cavity and neck. Place the chicken, breast side down, in a soup pot, add the **chicken cooking liquid,** and heat until boiling. Reduce the heat to medium and simmer for 1 hour. Remove the chicken, let it cool, remove and discard the skin, and cut the meat into matchstick-size shreds. Retain ¼ cup of the chicken cooking liquid and add it to the **chicken dressing.** If the dressing is too thick (it should have a smooth, pouring consistency), add a little more chicken cooking liquid.

2   Slice the cucumbers lengthwise and remove the seeds. Cut each half crosswise into thirds and then cut each piece lengthwise into thin slices that are 2 inches long and 1 inch wide. Place the slices in a bowl, add the salt, toss lightly, and let sit for 20 minutes. Pour off the water that has accumulated.

3   Soften the bean threads for 10 minutes in hot water to cover. Drain, and cut them into 3-inch lengths. Blanch the bean threads in boiling water for 3 minutes. Refresh in cold water and drain. Toss the bean threads in the sesame oil and arrange them on a large round platter. Arrange the cucumber slices on top. Place the cooked chicken shreds on top of the cucumbers. Just before serving, pour the chicken dressing over all and sprinkle the top with minced scallion greens. Toss lightly and serve.

SIX SERVINGS

1 whole frying or roasting chicken, 3½ to 4 pounds

Chicken Cooking Liquid
10 cups water
⅓ cup rice wine
3 slices gingerroot, smashed with the flat side of a cleaver

Chicken Dressing
½ cup smooth peanut butter
3 tablespoons soy sauce
1 tablespoon sugar
2 tablespoons rice wine
1 tablespoon Chinese black vinegar
3 tablespoons sesame oil
2 tablespoons minced scallions
1 tablespoon minced garlic
1 tablespoon minced gingerroot
1½ teaspoons chili paste
¼ cup chicken cooking liquid

3 English ("gourmet seedless") cucumbers
2 teaspoons salt
2 ounces bean threads
2 teaspoons sesame oil

1 tablespoon minced scallion greens

1½ pounds boneless chicken
 breast meat

Chicken Marinade

2 tablespoons soy sauce
2½ tablespoons rice wine
1 teaspoon sesame oil
2 tablespoons water
1 tablespoon cornstarch

1½ cups water chestnuts
1 tablespoon sesame oil
1 pound fresh spinach,
 trimmed and cleaned

Spinach Seasonings

1 teaspoon salt
1 tablespoon rice wine
2 teaspoons minced garlic

1 cup peanut, safflower, or
 corn oil

Chicken Seasonings

3 tablespoons minced
 scallions
2 tablespoons minced
 gingerroot
2½ tablespoons minced
 garlic

2 teaspoons chili paste

STIR-FRIED CHICKEN WITH CASHEWS

YAO GUO JI　　　腰 果 雞

Sichuanese cuisine is known for its hot and spicy seasonings, and Sichuanese chefs employ a technique that further intensifies the pungent flavorings: The assorted spices are tossed in hot oil over very high heat, which enlivens the flavors and infuses the oil with the seasonings. The technique is used not only in this dish but in many other Sichuanese stir-fried platters as well.

1　Remove the skin and any fat from the chicken and cut the meat into 1-inch cubes. Place the cubes in a bowl, add the **chicken marinade,** toss lightly, and let marinate for at least 20 minutes. Plunge the water chestnuts into boiling water for a few seconds to remove the tinny flavor. Refresh them in cold water and slice thinly.

2　Heat a wok, add the tablespoon of sesame oil, and heat until smoking. Add the spinach and the **spinach seasonings.** Stir-fry, turning constantly over high heat, until the spinach is barely limp. Arrange the spinach around the outer edge of a platter.

3　Reheat the wok, add the oil, and heat the oil to 375°. Add half the chicken pieces and stir-fry over high heat, turning constantly until the meat changes color. Remove with a handled strainer, and drain. Reheat the oil. Cook the remaining chicken in the same manner. Remove the oil from the wok, reserving 2 tablespoons.

Chicken Sauce

2½ tablespoons rice wine
3½ tablespoons soy sauce
2 tablespoons sugar
1 teaspoon sesame oil
2½ teaspoons Chinese black
 vinegar
½ cup chicken broth
2 teaspoons cornstarch

1½ cups raw cashews,
 toasted in a 350° oven until
 golden

4   Reheat the wok, add the 2 tablespoons of oil, and heat until very hot. Add the **chicken seasonings** and stir-fry for about 5 seconds. Add the chili paste and stir-fry for another 5 seconds, until fragrant. Add the sliced water chestnuts and stir-fry for about 15 seconds, until heated through. Add the **chicken sauce** and heat, stirring constantly, until thick. Add the cooked chicken and the cashews. Toss lightly to coat with the sauce. Transfer the chicken to the center of the platter and serve.

CHICKEN SHISH KEBAB

JI CHUAN

The subtle and unusual seasonings of this dish set it apart from most chicken platters. I frequently serve it as an hors d'oeuvre because it goes particularly well with beer.

1   Remove the skin and any fat from the chicken and cut the meat into 1½-inch cubes. Place the cubes in a bowl. Add the **chicken marinade**, toss lightly, and let marinate for at least 1 hour. Soak the bamboo skewers in cold water to cover for 1 hour. Mix together the cornstarch and the sesame seeds.
2   Thread the chicken cubes onto the skewers. Roll the meat in the sesame seed–cornstarch mixture so that it is coated, pressing lightly so that the coating adheres to the chicken. Let the skewered chicken dry on a tray for about 15 minutes.
3   Heat a wok, add the oil, and heat the oil to 375°. Add three chicken skewers and deep-fry over high heat, turning constantly until the chicken is cooked and golden brown, about 5 minutes. Remove with a handled strainer, and drain on absorbent paper. Reheat the oil and deep-fry the remaining skewers in the same manner. Arrange all the skewers on a platter and serve immediately.

SIX SERVINGS

2 pounds boneless chicken breast meat

Chicken Marinade
2 tomatoes, peeled, seeded, and coarsely chopped
2 tablespoons minced scallions
1 teaspoon Sichuan peppercorns, roasted briefly in a pan and pulverized in a blender
1 teaspoon salt
2 tablespoons rice wine
1 teaspoon minced gingerroot
1 egg white, lightly beaten
1 teaspoon sesame oil

6 10-inch bamboo skewers
1 cup cornstarch
1 cup untoasted sesame seeds
6 cups peanut, safflower, or corn oil

2 pounds boneless chicken breast meat

Chicken Marinade

2 tablespoons soy sauce
2 tablespoons rice wine
1½ teaspoons sesame oil
1 teaspoon minced gingerroot
1 tablespoon water
1½ tablespoons cornstarch

2 cups peanut, safflower, or corn oil
2 tablespoons dried chili peppers cut into ½-inch pieces (seeds removed)
6 strips dried tangerine or orange peel about 2 inches long, softened in hot water for 20 minutes and shredded

Chicken Sauce

3 tablespoons soy sauce
2 tablespoons rice wine
1½ teaspoons sesame oil
1 tablespoon clear rice vinegar
2 teaspoons sugar
¼ teaspoon freshly ground black pepper
¼ cup chicken broth or water
1½ teaspoons cornstarch

TANGERINE PEEL CHICKEN

CHEN PI JI　陳皮雞

In the following spicy Sichuanese platter, the dried tangerine peel adds another dimension of flavor to the hot, tart sauce. Dried tangerine peel and dried orange peel are available in most Chinese grocery stores; however, fresh peel, blanched to remove any bitterness, may be substituted.

1   Remove the skin and any fat from the chicken and cut the meat into 1-inch cubes. Place the cubes in a bowl, add the **chicken marinade,** toss lightly, and let marinate for at least 20 minutes.
2   Heat a wok, add the oil, and heat the oil to 375°. Add half the chicken meat and cook, stirring constantly over high heat, until the meat changes color. Remove with a handled strainer, and drain. Reheat the oil. Cook the remaining chicken in the same manner. Remove the oil from the wok, reserving 2 tablespoons.
3   Reheat the wok, add the 2 tablespoons of oil, and heat until very hot. Add the dried pepper pieces and the tangerine peel shreds; stir-fry for about 15 seconds over high heat, stirring constantly until the peppers turn black. Add the **chicken sauce** and cook, stirring constantly, until the sauce is thick. Add the chicken meat, toss lightly to coat the pieces, and transfer the mixture to a platter. Serve immediately.

DEEP-FRIED CHICKEN PACKAGES

CAI BAO JI

菜包雞

Although this dish requires a little bit of preparation, it is certainly worth the effort. The boned chicken pieces, marinated in oyster sauce, are exquisite encased in the tender cabbage leaves and the crisp batter coating. I usually employ double-frying with this dish, cooking the packages in 350° oil early in the day. Later, just before serving, the second and final frying is done in a hotter oil. In this way, most of the preparation can be done in advance.

1   Remove the skin and any fat from the chicken and cut the meat into ¾-inch cubes. Place the cubes in a bowl, add the **chicken marinade**, toss lightly, and let marinate for at least 1 hour, or overnight in the refrigerator.

2   Holding a knife parallel to the cutting surface, trim the stem of each cabbage leaf so that it is the same thickness as the leaf itself. Blanch the leaves, a few at a time, in boiling water for 1 minute. Remove them with a slotted spoon and immediately place in cold water. Drain and pat dry with towels. Whisk the **batter** until smooth.

3   Place a tablespoon of the chicken in the middle of a cabbage leaf. Fold in the end nearest you, fold in the two sides, and fold over the far edge to enclose the chicken in a square package. Repeat for the remaining chicken and cabbage leaves.

4   Heat a wok, add the oil, and heat the oil to 375°. Dip a third of the cabbage packages in the batter, making sure that they are completely coated, and place in the hot oil. Deep-fry, turning constantly, for about 5 minutes; remove with a handled strainer, and drain on absorbent paper. Deep-fry the remaining packages in the same manner, reheating the oil between batches. Reheat the oil to 400° to 425°. Add all the packages and deep-fry until golden brown and crisp. Remove, drain on absorbent paper, cut each package crosswise in half, and arrange the packages on a platter. Serve immediately.

SIX SERVINGS

1½ pounds boneless chicken breast meat

Chicken Marinade
2 tablespoons minced scallions
1 tablespoon minced gingerroot
1 tablespoon minced garlic
3 tablespoons oyster sauce
2 tablespoons soy sauce
1 tablespoon rice wine
2 teaspoons sugar
1 teaspoon sesame oil
2 tablespoons cornstarch

18 to 24 whole cabbage leaves

Batter
1 cup all-purpose flour
1 egg, lightly beaten
1 teaspoon salt
1 cup ice water

6 cups peanut, safflower, or corn oil

1 pound boneless chicken
breast meat

Chicken Marinade

1 tablespoon soy sauce
2 teaspoons rice wine
1 teaspoon sesame oil
2 teaspoons cornstarch

½ pound fresh mushrooms,
rinsed lightly and drained
1 cup water chestnuts
4 cups peanut, safflower, or
corn oil

Minced Seasonings

1 tablespoon minced
scallions
2 teaspoons minced garlic
2 teaspoons minced
gingerroot
4 tablespoons dried
tangerine peel, softened in
hot water for 20 minutes
and shredded

½ cup carrots cut into slices
⅛ inch thick

PAPER-WRAPPED FRIED CHICKEN

ZHI BAO JI　　紙包雞

This dish illustrates an innovative technique used by Chinese chefs:
Foods are wrapped in paper and deep-fried in hot oil, thereby sealing in their juices and ensuring a tender, moist product. Wax paper,
heavy cellophane (such as oven-roasting bags cut into squares),
parchment paper, or rice paper (an edible sheet found in some
Chinese stores) may be used. Chicken, pork, and shrimp all may be
prepared in this manner and are excellent as an hors d'oeuvre or as
an entrée with accompanying dishes.

1   Remove the skin and any fat from the chicken and cut the meat
into ¾-inch cubes. Place the cubes in a bowl, add the **chicken
marinade,** toss lightly, and let marinate for 20 minutes. Thinly slice
the fresh mushrooms. Plunge the water chestnuts into boiling water
for a few seconds to remove the tinny flavor. Refresh them in cold
water and slice them thinly.
2   Heat a pan, add 4 tablespoons of the oil, and heat until very hot.
Add the **minced seasonings** and stir-fry over high heat for 10 seconds, until fragrant. Add the chicken cubes, mushrooms, water
chestnuts, carrot slices, and **chicken sauce.** Toss lightly over high
heat, stirring constantly until the sauce has thickened. Remove the
mixture from the wok.

Chicken Sauce

1½ tablespoons soy sauce
1 tablespoon rice wine
1 teaspoon sugar
½ teaspoon salt
1 teaspoon sesame oil
1 teaspoon Chinese black
vinegar or Worcestershire
sauce
1 teaspoon cornstarch

36 5-inch squares heavy-duty
cooking cellophane or
parchment paper
36 4-inch pieces of kitchen
twine

3 Place a tablespoon of the chicken mixture in the center of each square of cellophane. Gather up the edges of the cellophane, twist to seal, and tie securely with the kitchen twine.

4 Reheat the wok, add the remaining oil, and heat the oil to 350°. Add a third of the cellophane packages and deep-fry in the hot oil for 3 minutes, stirring constantly. Remove with a handled strainer and drain on absorbent paper. Deep-fry the rest in the same manner. Arrange the packages on a platter and serve immediately.

BARBECUED CHICKEN LIVERS AND PORK SLICES

FENG GAN ROU CHUAN   鳳肝肉串

The contrasting textures and flavors of the pork loin, scallions, and chicken livers marinated in the flavorful mixture of plum sauce, hoisin sauce, and soy sauce make this unusual platter truly delicious. For the sake of authenticity as well as aesthetics, I use bamboo skewers for this dish, soaking them in cold water for 1 hour to prevent them from burning in the intense heat.

1 Remove any fat or gristle from the pork loin and discard. Cut the meat into twenty-four thin slices. Cut the chicken livers in half at the natural division, and remove and discard any fat. Cook the chicken livers for about 1 minute in boiling water, and drain thoroughly. Place the pork loin and the liver in separate bowls and add half of the **marinade** to each bowl. Toss lightly and let marinate for at least 20 minutes. Soak the skewers for 1 hour in cold water to cover.

2 Lay a slice of pork loin on a flat surface and place a piece of scallion and half a liver in the center. Roll up the pork loin to enclose the scallion and liver and thread onto a bamboo skewer. Repeat for the remaining pork slices, livers, and scallion pieces, using four of each on each skewer.

3 Preheat the broiler and place the pork skewers on a jelly-roll pan. Pour the marinade over the skewers and broil for 10 minutes, turning once and brushing occasionally with the marinade, until the pork slices and chicken livers are cooked. Serve immediately.

SIX SERVINGS

1½ pounds boneless center-cut pork loin
12 whole chicken livers

Marinade
½ cup hoisin sauce
¼ cup plum sauce
¼ cup soy sauce
¼ cup rice wine
3 tablespoons sugar
1 teaspoon sesame oil
3 cloves garlic, smashed with the flat side of a cleaver

6 10-inch bamboo skewers
24 1-inch pieces of scallion, white part only

2 pounds chicken livers

Liver Marinade

4 scallions, smashed with the flat side of a cleaver
3 slices gingerroot, smashed with the flat side of a cleaver
1½ tablespoons soy sauce
2 tablespoons rice wine
1½ teaspoons minced garlic

6 cups peanut, safflower, or corn oil

Liver Sauce

¼ cup ketchup
2 teaspoons soy sauce
½ teaspoon salt
2 teaspoons Chinese black vinegar
1½ tablespoons sugar
1 teaspoon sesame oil
¼ cup water

SWEET-AND-SOUR GLAZED CHICKEN LIVERS

SAO ZHU FENG GAN　燒焗鳳肝

In Chinese cuisine, liver, whether from the pig, cow, duck, or chicken, is treated with a versatility rarely found in other cuisines. It is deep-fried, stir-fried, pan-fried, simmered in a soy-based marinade, and used as a garnish in soups. In this Cantonese platter, the crisp, deep-fried livers are coated in a light sweet-and-sour glaze. It is suitable as an hors d'oeuvre, an appetizer, or an entrée served with rice.

1   Rinse the chicken livers lightly and drain thoroughly. Separate the livers at the natural division, and remove and discard any fat. Place the livers in a bowl, add the **liver marinade**, toss lightly, and let marinate for 20 minutes. Discard the scallions and gingerroot. Drain the livers.
2   Heat a wok, add the oil, and heat the oil to 375°. Add the livers, covering the oil with the wok lid to prevent the oil from splashing. Uncover, and deep-fry the livers for about 4 minutes, stirring occasionally, until golden brown. Remove with a handled strainer. Drain the livers and remove the oil from the wok.
3   Reheat the wok, add the **liver sauce,** and heat until boiling, stirring constantly over high heat. Add the livers and cook, stirring constantly over high heat, until the liquid has reduced to a thick glaze. Serve immediately.

ROASTED DUCK SALAD

LI ZI BAN HUO YA 荔枝拌火鴨

Normally I am not fond of sweet fruits in savory salads and shun such all-American favorites as Waldorf salad and chicken salad with grapes; but, surprisingly, I enjoy the flavor of the lychees in this dish. Their freshness and crisp texture provide a superb contrast to the vegetables, the rich duck meat, and the creamy sesame dressing. Sesame paste is the traditional base for the dressing, but smooth peanut butter is an excellent substitute.

1   Place the bean sprouts in a colander and pour boiling water over them. Immerse immediately in cold water and drain. Soften the bean threads for 10 minutes in hot water to cover. Drain thoroughly, and cut into 3-inch lengths. Cook the bean threads in boiling water for 3 minutes. Rinse in cold water, drain thoroughly, and place in a bowl. Add the **bean thread dressing** and toss lightly. Arrange the bean threads on a large platter.

2   Place the bean sprouts over the bean threads; then arrange the carrots in a border around the bean sprouts. Toward the center, arrange the shredded green peppers and egg sheets in two separate circles. Arrange the shredded duck meat on top. Finally, arrange the lychee halves, cut edge down, in a crown over the shredded meat. Just before serving, pour the **salad dressing** over the salad. Toss lightly and portion onto plates.

To make the **egg sheets:** Lightly beat the eggs, salt, and water until frothy. Wipe the surface of a well-seasoned wok or a 10-inch non-stick skillet with an oil-soaked paper towel. Heat the pan until a little water sprinkled onto the surface evaporates immediately. Remove the pan from the heat and add one quarter of the egg mixture; tilt the pan to form a thin, circular pancake. Place the pan back over the heat and cook until set. Flip the egg sheet over and cook until lightly golden. Make three more egg sheets in the same manner. Cool the egg sheets before shredding.

SIX SERVINGS

1½ cups fresh bean sprouts, rinsed and drained
2 ounces bean threads

Bean Thread Dressing

½ teaspoon salt
1 teaspoon sesame oil
1 tablespoon chicken broth

1½ cups carrot cut into matchstick-size shreds
2 green peppers, cored, seeded, and cut into matchstick-size shreds
1 cup shredded egg sheets (see below)
1 pound boned, roasted duck meat, cut into matchstick-size shreds
1 cup canned lychees, drained and cut in half lengthwise

Salad Dressing

¼ cup sesame paste or smooth peanut butter
3 tablespoons clear rice vinegar
3 tablespoons soy sauce
1 tablespoon sugar
2 teaspoons salt
3 tablespoons sesame oil
½ cup chicken broth

Egg Sheets

4 eggs
½ teaspoon salt
1 tablespoon water

163

18 chicken wings

Marinade

2 tablespoons soy sauce
1½ tablespoons rice wine
½ teaspoon salt
¼ teaspoon freshly ground
   black pepper
3 slices gingerroot, smashed
   with the flat side of a
   cleaver
4 scallions, smashed with the
   flat side of a cleaver
2 cloves garlic, smashed with
   the flat side of a cleaver

2 egg yolks
1½ cups cornstarch
6 cups peanut, safflower, or
   corn oil

Lemon Sauce

2 tablespoons freshly
   squeezed lemon juice
1 tablespoon sugar
1 teaspoon salt
1 teaspoon sesame oil
1 teaspoon cornstarch
6 tablespoons chicken broth

LEMON CHICKEN WINGS

NING MENG FENG YI 檸檬鳳翼

Lemon chicken is a popular Cantonese entrée of boned, fried chicken lightly glazed with a tart, lemony sauce. Chicken wings, marinated and deep-fried to a golden crispness, are equally delicious when coated with a lemon sauce. Serve the wings as an hors d'oeuvre with drinks or as an entrée with rice. Lemon chicken wings reheat beautifully in a 375° oven.

1   Rinse the chicken wings and drain thoroughly. Cut each wing in two at the "elbow" and place in a bowl. Add the **marinade,** toss lightly, and let marinate for at least 1 hour, or overnight in the refrigerator. Discard the gingerroot, scallions, and garlic, and add the egg yolks to the wings. Toss lightly to coat with the yolks. Dredge each wing in the cornstarch, pressing lightly to make sure the cornstarch adheres.
2   Heat a wok, add the oil, and heat the oil to 375°. Add half the wings and deep-fry over high heat for about 5 minutes, stirring constantly. Remove the chicken wings with a handled strainer, and drain. Reheat the oil and deep-fry the remaining wings in the same manner. Reheat the oil to 425°. Add all the wings and deep-fry a second time, until crisp and golden brown. Drain the wings and remove the oil from the wok.
3   Reheat the wok, add the **lemon sauce,** and heat, stirring constantly, until thick. Add the fried wings, toss them in the sauce, and transfer to a platter. Serve immediately.

CHICKEN WINGS IN OYSTER SAUCE

HAO YU BAO FENG YI 蠔油爆鳳翼

The thrifty Chinese savor every part of the chicken's anatomy, and wings are no exception; they are braised, deep-fried, boiled, and used in soups. In this dish, they are simmered to a succulent tenderness in rich oyster sauce.

1   Cut each chicken wing in two at the "elbow." Place the wings in a bowl, add the **marinade**, toss lightly, and let marinate for 20 minutes. Peel away the tough outer skin from the broccoli and separate the flowerets. Roll-cut the stems into 1-inch pieces. Heat 1½ quarts salted water until boiling. Add the stem pieces and cook for ½ minute. Add the flowerets and cook for 2½ minutes, or until both stems and flowerets are just tender. Refresh immediately in cold water. Drain thoroughly.

2   Heat a wok and add the oil. Heat the oil to 375°. Drain the wings and add the marinade to the **braising sauce**. Add half the wings to the oil and deep-fry over high heat until golden brown. Remove with a handled strainer, and drain. Reheat the oil, and deep-fry the remaining wings in the same manner. Remove all but 1 tablespoon of oil from the wok and heat until very hot. Add the **seasonings** and stir-fry over high heat for about 10 seconds, until fragrant. Add the braising sauce and the chicken wings. Heat until the liquid is boiling, reduce the heat to medium, partially cover, and cook for 45 minutes, until the wings are tender. With the liquid boiling, add the **thickener**, stirring constantly to prevent lumps. Set aside and keep warm. Clean the wok.

3   Reheat the wok, add 1 tablespoon of the oil used for deep-frying, and heat until very hot. Add the minced garlic and stir-fry until fragrant, about 5 seconds. Add the broccoli and stir-fry until heated through, about 10 seconds. Add the **broccoli sauce,** and stir-fry for about 10 more seconds over high heat. Arrange the broccoli around the outer edge of a platter. Place the chicken wings in the center, cover with their sauce, and serve.

SIX SERVINGS

18 chicken wings

Marinade
1½ tablespoons soy sauce
1 tablespoon rice wine
1 teaspoon sesame oil

1 pound broccoli
2 cups peanut, safflower, or corn oil

Braising Sauce
3 tablespoons oyster sauce
1½ tablespoons soy sauce
3 tablespoons rice wine
1½ teaspoons sugar
1 cup chicken broth

Seasonings
12 1-inch pieces of scallion, white part only
12 paper-thin slices of gingerroot

Thickener
1 teaspoon cornstarch
1 tablespoon water

2 teaspoons minced garlic

Broccoli Sauce
1 tablespoon rice wine
¾ teaspoon salt
2 tablespoons chicken broth

1 whole duck, 5½ to 6
  pounds
2 tablespoons soy sauce

Duck Sauce

1½ tablespoons ketchup
1 tablespoon rice wine
1 teaspoon salt
1 tablespoon sugar
¼ teaspoon freshly ground
  black pepper
½ cup chicken broth or
  water

6 cups peanut, safflower, or
  corn oil
1 cup shredded onions
2 teaspoons minced garlic
2 navel oranges, peeled and
  sectioned

Thickener

2 teaspoons cornstarch
1½ tablespoons water

STEAMED DUCK WITH ORANGES

ZHU ZHI MEN YA   桔汁燜鴨

Like the French, the Chinese are partial to the combination of oranges and duck. In this platter the duck is first deep-fried in hot oil to give it a golden brown color and render some of the fat. Then the whole bird is steamed with oranges and other seasonings, resulting in a superb mingling of flavors. This dish is an excellent companion to rice.

1 Rinse the duck, drain, and remove any fat from the cavity and neck. Using a heavy cleaver, cut the duck, through the bones, into bite-size serving pieces. Place the pieces in a bowl, add the soy sauce, and toss lightly to coat. Let sit for 15 minutes. Drain the pieces, and add the soy sauce to the **duck sauce.**
2 Heat a wok, add the oil, and heat the oil to 400°. Add half the duck pieces, covering the oil with the wok lid to prevent the oil from splashing. Uncover, and deep-fry the duck pieces for about 2 minutes, until golden brown. Remove with a handled strainer, and drain. Reheat the oil, and deep-fry the remaining duck in the same manner. Remove the oil from the wok, reserving 2 tablespoons.
3 Reheat the wok, add the 2 tablespoons of oil, and heat until hot. Add the shredded onions and stir-fry over high heat, stirring constantly until the onion is soft and transparent. Add the minced garlic and stir-fry for about 5 seconds, until fragrant. Add the orange sections and stir-fry for another 5 seconds. Add the duck sauce, and heat until boiling. Add the **thickener,** stirring constantly to prevent lumps. Arrange the duck pieces in a heat-proof 2-quart soufflé dish or bowl. Pour the thickened sauce on top. Place in a steamer tray. Clean the wok.
4 Fill the wok with water level with the bottom edge of the steamer tray and heat until boiling. Place the steamer tray over the boiling water, cover, and steam for 1 hour over high heat. Remove and arrange the duck pieces on a platter. Skim the fat off the sauce and pour the sauce over the duck pieces. Serve immediately.

STIR-FRIED DUCK WITH PINEAPPLE

FENG LI CHAO YA PIAN 鳳梨炒鴨片

Judging from the frequency with which one encounters the combination of poultry and fruit in Cantonese dishes, one can rightfully deduce that the chefs from this region are fond of the contrasting flavors of these ingredients. Duck is often prepared with oranges, plums, lychees, or pineapple. In this dish, the mellow richness of the duck meat is a superb partner for the tart sweetness of the pineapple. Ideally, fresh pineapple should be used; if it is unavailable, canned pineapple may be substituted.

1 Remove the skin and any fat from the duck; cut the meat into 1-inch cubes. Place the cubes in a bowl. Pinch the gingerroot slices in the **duck marinade** repeatedly for several minutes to impart the flavor. Add the marinade to the duck meat, toss lightly, and let marinate for 20 minutes. Discard the gingerroot.

2 Heat a wok, add the oil, and heat the oil to 375°. Drain the duck meat and add half of it to the hot oil. Cook the meat, stirring constantly, until it changes color. Remove with a handled strainer, and drain. Reheat the oil, and cook the remaining duck meat in the same manner. Remove the oil from the wok, reserving 2 tablespoons.

3 Reheat the wok, add the 2 tablespoons of oil, and heat until very hot. Add the **minced seasonings** and stir-fry until fragrant, about 5 seconds. Add the green pepper and stir-fry for another 5 seconds. Add the pineapple and the **duck sauce.** Stir-fry over high heat until the sauce has thickened, add the duck meat, toss lightly, and transfer to a platter. Serve immediately.

SIX SERVINGS

2 pounds boned duck meat

Duck Marinade

1½ teaspoons salt
2 tablespoons rice wine
3 slices gingerroot, smashed with the flat side of a cleaver
2 teaspoons cornstarch

1½ cups peanut, safflower, or corn oil

Minced Seasonings

1 tablespoon minced scallions
2 teaspoons minced gingerroot

1 cup green pepper, cored, seeded, and cut into 1-inch cubes
1½ cups pineapple cut into 1-inch cubes

Duck Sauce

5 tablespoons pineapple juice
1½ teaspoons salt
½ teaspoon freshly ground black pepper
1 teaspoon sesame oil
1 teaspoon cornstarch

1 whole duck, 5½ to 6 pounds

Duck Marinade

5 scallions, smashed with the flat side of a cleaver
6 slices gingerroot, smashed with the flat side of a cleaver
1 tablespoon rice wine
2 tablespoons salt
2 teaspoons Sichuan peppercorns
1 whole star anise, smashed with the flat side of a cleaver

2 tablespoons soy sauce
1 cup cornstarch
10 cups peanut, safflower, or corn oil

CRISPY-SKIN DUCK

XIANG SU YA 香酥鴨

The extraordinary contrast of textures in crispy-skin duck may be one reason for the popularity of this Sichuanese dish. The combination of cooking methods accounts for the result: The steaming gently cooks the meat, leaving it juicy and succulently tender, while the deep-frying further seals in the meat juices and makes the skin beautifully crisp.

1   Rinse the duck, drain, and remove any fat from the cavity and neck. Rub the **duck marinade** inside the cavity and all over the skin. Place the duck, breast side down, in a bowl with the marinade, and let marinate for at least 1 hour. Transfer the duck and the marinade to a heat-proof plate or bowl; arrange the duck breast side up. Place the plate or bowl in a steamer tray.
2   Fill a wok with water level with the bottom edge of the steamer tray and heat until boiling. Place the steamer tray over the boiling water, cover, and steam the duck for 2 hours over high heat. (Replenish the boiling water when necessary.) Remove the duck, discard the marinade, and let the duck cool. Rub the soy sauce all over the outside of the duck and then dredge the duck in the cornstarch; press lightly to make the cornstarch adhere to the skin. Let the duck dry for 15 minutes. Remove the water from the wok.
3   Reheat the wok, add the oil, and heat the oil to 425°. Slowly lower the duck into the hot oil and deep-fry it on both sides, ladling the oil over the top, until the skin is crisp and golden brown. Drain the duck and cut it, through the bones, into bite-size pieces. Arrange the duck pieces on a platter, as for red-cooked chicken (page 151). Serve the duck plain or with steamed lotus buns (page 56) and sweet bean sauce or hoisin sauce.

CANTONESE-STYLE ROASTED DUCK

YUE SHI KAO YA 粵式烤鴨

Though roasted duck is considered by most to be an exclusive specialty of northern China, Cantonese chefs prepare a variation that rivals even Peking duck in flavor—the famous Cantonese-style roasted duck. The two do have their similarities: The skin of both is basted with a syrup, so that it will be crisp and golden, and both ducks are served with Mandarin pancakes (page 61) and either sweet bean sauce or hoisin sauce.

1   Rinse the duck, drain, and remove the fat from the cavity and neck. Pinch the scallions and the gingerroot in the **duck marinade** repeatedly for several minutes to impart their flavor. Rub the marinade inside the cavity and all over the skin. Let the duck marinate for at least 2 hours, or overnight in the refrigerator. Discard the scallions and gingerroot.

2   Bring about 4 quarts of water to a boil. Wrap a length of twine around each wing. Grab the ends of the twine and use them to suspend the duck over the water. Ladle the boiling water over the duck for 1 minute (this will clean it and open the pores of the skin). Drain thoroughly.

3   Place the **coating mixture** in a large pan and heat until boiling. Hold the duck over the boiling mixture in the same manner as above, and baste the duck for several minutes. Hang the duck in a cool, dry place or near a fan. Place a pan underneath the duck to catch the drippings. Do not touch the duck, or the cooked skin will have spots. Let the duck dry for 4 hours, or overnight if possible.

4   Preheat the oven to 375°. Place the duck breast side up on a rack in a roasting pan and roast for 2 hours, turning several times. Let the duck cool briefly, and cut it, through the bones, into bite-size pieces, as for red-cooked chicken (page 151). Serve with Mandarin pancakes and sweet bean sauce or hoisin sauce.

SIX SERVINGS

1 whole duck, 5½ to 6 pounds

Duck Marinade
1½ teaspoons salt
1½ teaspoons five-spice powder
½ teaspoon freshly ground black pepper
4 scallions, smashed with the flat side of a cleaver
4 slices gingerroot, smashed with the flat side of a cleaver

Coating Mixture
4 tablespoons honey
2 cups boiling water
1 tablespoon clear rice vinegar
3 tablespoons rice wine

1 head leafy or Boston
lettuce
4 cups peanut, safflower, or
corn oil
1 ounce rice stick noodles
2 1-pound squabs
1 pound boneless center-cut
pork loin

Meat Seasonings

1½ tablespoons soy sauce
1 tablespoon rice wine
1½ teaspoons sesame oil
3 tablespoons water

Minced Seasonings

2 tablespoons minced
scallions
1 tablespoon minced
gingerroot
¼ cup dried Chinese black
mushrooms, softened for
20 minutes in hot water,
stems removed, and caps
coarsely chopped
1½ cups water chestnuts,
plunged briefly into
boiling water, refreshed,
and coarsely chopped

Meat Sauce

1 teaspoon salt
2½ tablespoons soy sauce
1 tablespoon rice wine
1 teaspoon sugar
1½ teaspoons sesame oil
¼ cup water
1 teaspoon cornstarch

STIR-FRIED MINCED SQUAB

CHAO GE SONG 炒鴿鬆

This dish is a fine example of the best in Chinese cuisine; the pungency of the fresh gingerroot, the crispness of the lettuce, and the crunchiness of the fried noodles provide a combination of superb flavors and textures. If squab is unavailable, Rock Cornish hen or dark chicken meat may be substituted.

1   Rinse the lettuce and separate the leaves. Drain thoroughly and lightly pound each leaf with the flat side of a cleaver. Arrange the flattened leaves on a platter and set aside.
2   Heat a wok, add the oil, and heat the oil to 425°, or until smoking. Add the rice noodles and deep-fry for about 5 seconds, until puffed and pale golden. Turn over immediately and cook briefly on the other side. Drain on absorbent paper. Arrange the noodles on a platter and lightly break them up with your fingers. Remove the oil from the wok, reserving 7 tablespoons.
3   Bone the squabs, remove the skin, and mince the meat. Remove any fat and gristle from the pork loin and discard; mince the meat. Place the minced meats in a bowl, add the **meat seasonings,** toss lightly, and let marinate for 20 minutes.
4   Reheat the wok, add ¼ cup of the reserved oil, and heat until hot. Add the minced meats and stir-fry over high heat, mashing and separating the pieces, until the color changes. Remove and drain. Reheat the wok, add the remaining 3 tablespoons of oil, and heat until very hot. Add the **minced seasonings** and stir-fry over high heat, turning constantly until fragrant, about 10 seconds. Add the mushrooms and stir-fry for another 5 seconds, turning constantly. Add the water chestnuts and stir-fry for about 15 seconds, until heated through. Add the **meat sauce** and stir-fry, stirring constantly until thick. Add the cooked meat, toss lightly in the sauce, and spoon the mixture over the fried rice noodles. To serve, place some of the stir-fried meat and fried rice noodles in a lettuce leaf, roll up, and eat.

RED-COOKED SQUAB

HONG SHAO GE ZI　紅燒鴿子

Game birds, such as squab, are especially popular with the Cantonese, and the chefs from Canton use a great deal of imagination in preparing them. Perhaps one of the simplest and tastiest cooking methods is simmering in a soy sauce–based marinade, as in this recipe. The spicy cooking liquid is equally suitable for cooking other poultry and meats, and the flavor of the liquid increases with each use.

1   Rinse the squabs and drain them thoroughly.
2   Place the **seasonings** in a square of cheesecloth, gather up the edges, and tie securely to make a spice bag. Place the seasonings and the **red-cooking liquid** in a large pot and heat until boiling. Reduce the heat to low and simmer, uncovered, for 45 minutes. Add the squabs and heat until boiling. Reduce the heat to low and simmer the squabs for about 35 minutes, turning them several times. Remove the squabs and cut each one into four pieces. Spoon a little of the cooking liquid over the squabs and serve.

SIX SERVINGS

6 squabs, about 1 pound each

Seasonings
1 tablespoon Sichuan peppercorns
1 whole star anise
2 strips dried tangerine or orange peel, about 2 inches long
1 cinnamon stick
3 whole cloves

Red-Cooking Liquid
6 cups water
½ cup rice wine
1½ cups soy sauce
4 tablespoons rock sugar, chopped coarsely

SEAFOOD 海鮮類

The magnificent scenic beauty of Hong Kong is legendary. The breathtaking panoramic skyline has inspired numerous writers to produce stunning prose, and the mystique of this Far Eastern city is such that Hong Kong is a frequent backdrop for sizzling spy thrillers and torrid romances. So it was with a great deal of excitement that I prepared for my first visit to this famed colony, poring over guidebooks by the score at the public library.

"Rugged peaks studded with skyscrapers and surrounded by azure waters" was what one travel author had written about the stunning aerial view of Hong Kong. Sadly, on the day my plane landed, the entire area was shrouded in a muggy fog so thick the runway was barely perceptible, even as the wheels of the plane touched down. The view from the taxi window as we sped into the city was hardly more enlightening. That night I felt quite let down as I crawled into my bunk at the hostel, but I vowed that I would rise at dawn to view the magnificent vistas of the city.

Bright sunlight awakened me the next morning and joyfully I ran to the window. The view that greeted me from our fifteen-story high-rise located in the inner recesses of Hong Kong was not at all what I expected. Instead of "rugged peaks" and "azure waters," I glimpsed endless tenement rooftops brimming with all types of seafood drying in the blistering sun. Later, on a jaunt through the neighborhood, I passed row after row of shopfronts displaying dried fish maw, shark's fin, and bird's nest, with signs proclaiming WHOLESALE PURVEYORS OF DRIED SEA PRODUCTS. The air fairly reeked of the sea and its products.

The sea dominates the atmosphere of Hong Kong: It surrounds the island in varying shades of azure and aquamarine, it provides a portion of the population with their livelihood, and it furnishes an inexhaustible supply of food products. Seafood is plentiful and readily available at a very reasonable price here and one immediately senses its importance to the Chinese. It figures prominently in the diets of all Chinese and is consumed in all forms; though fresh seafood is readily available, dried seafood is eaten frequently and preferred by some as a flavorful and nutritious garnish to rice.

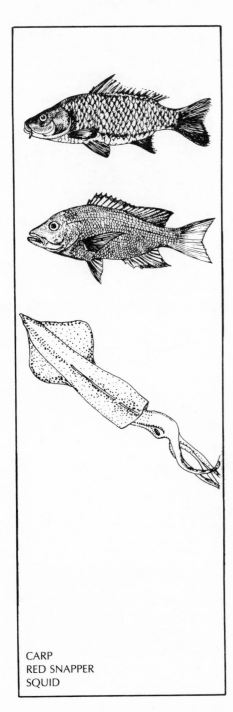

CARP
RED SNAPPER
SQUID

Because China abounds in rivers, lakes, streams, canals, and ponds (not to mention the fact that a large portion of the country borders the sea), numerous freshwater and saltwater fish, shellfish, crustaceans, and mollusks are available and have enjoyed prominence throughout Chinese history.

The ancient Chinese were the first to employ nets, weirs, rods, and lines in fishing. The legendary Emperor Fu Hsi, who ruled China from 2953 B.C. to 2838 B.C., is credited with teaching his people how to weave nets, in addition to showing them how to utilize the many food products of the sea. Later, fishing became an enjoyable and lucrative pastime, and during the T'ang dynasty (618 to 907), fish farming became extremely popular.

Fish and "sea savories," as shellfish were called, became mainstays of the ancient Chinese diet. Clams, mussels, shrimp, and oysters were particularly relished by the officials of the Imperial Court; the finest specimens were sent off to the Imperial kitchens before the rest of the daily catch reached the marketplace. Red-bellied trout and striped mullet were both highly prized, and flatfish such as sole and halibut were also very popular.

Fish relishes, too, were very much in demand. These fermented pastes contained fish, notably carp and mullet, with the addition of rice, salt, and occasionally milk products. Some of the relishes were extremely sophisticated, with special emphasis placed on aesthetics; one was composed of paper-thin slices of pink fish flesh arranged like the petals of a blooming hibiscus.

Fish is highly regarded by the Chinese not only as a source of food. Owing to its plentiful numbers and the speed with which it reproduces, the fish is a symbol of regeneration, and since it is a creature seemingly content with its environment, it signifies harmony. Fish frequently swim in pairs and are therefore emblematic of the joys of union. Accordingly, a pair of fish is customarily given as a betrothal gift to a future bride. Also, by tradition, fish are served at the end of a banquet; a whole fish is displayed on the banquet table at the New Year to represent bounty, wealth, and abundance. Fish were often presented as offerings in ancient ceremonial worship, and certain species were prized for their beauty.

Certain seafoods signified events in the ancient culinary calendar: The appearance of crab claws in the marketplace heralded the Mid-Autumn Festival (the fifteenth day of the eighth lunar month), whole

173

crabs and clams bespoke the arrival of winter, and in Suzhou, a city renowned for its culinary refinement, sea scallops were eaten to mark the arrival of summer.

The popularity of these foods has not diminished. All types of fish and shellfish are notably evident in the modern Chinese diet. In their fresh state, they are seasoned with light, delicate flavorings — such as gingerroot, scallions, and rice wine — to highlight their natural, sweet flavors. (The Chinese believe that the flavor of freshwater fish is sweeter and more refined than that of saltwater species.) The cooking methods used are generally characterized by extremely high temperatures and brief cooking times, as in stir-frying, steaming, and deep-frying. These same foods in dried form play a prominent role in Chinese cuisine as flavorings in soups, stir-fried dishes, braised stews, and fillings or stuffings.

The accompanying Seafood Glossary offers some background information, starting with the most commonly served foods of this category.

SEAFOOD GLOSSARY

FISH   Freshness is a trait particularly stressed by the Chinese where fish is concerned. Fish are often purchased live and then stored in large tanks until they are ready to be cooked. When purchasing a whole fish, the following guidelines should be used in determining the freshness: (1) The flesh should be firm, springing back when pressed. (2) The eyes should be clear, well-rounded, and not sunken. (3) The gills should be bright red. (4) The fish should have a mild, fresh odor, especially in the gills.

Although Chinese do prepare and serve fillets and steaks, the majority of their dishes call for a whole fish with head and tail intact. It is believed that in this form the natural juices are retained with less chance of the flesh drying out. The tongue and cheeks of certain fish are greatly relished. Some of the most notable varieties of freshwater fish used by the Chinese are carp, buffalo, bream, trout, and grouper. Of the saltwater fish, sea bass, sole, turbot, porgy, butterfish, whitefish, flounder, and shark are widely used. Shad, millet, and perch, all extremely popular, defy classification, since they migrate seasonally from the ocean into the rivers. Eel and turtle are favored as well.

SHRIMP   Unlike the fairly limited selection of shrimp found in most American markets, numerous sizes are available in the Far East. They are most often stir-fried, deep-fried, boiled, or minced to a paste. In Hunan, miniature shrimp the size of rice grains are collected from mountain streams and cooked with squash in a soup. Miniature shrimp are also used in a fermented paste prepared in southern China. This paste is used as a pungent flavoring and is an extremely rich form of calcium and protein. These same shrimp are dried and used as a seasoning in fillings, soups, and vegetable dishes.

PRAWNS   Although something of an expensive delicacy, prawns are used extensively in Chinese cooking. Like shrimp, they may be stir-fried, deep-fried, or boiled. Prawns are also extremely tasty when braised (dry-cooked) and served cold with assorted dipping sauces.

CRAB   As with fish and other seafoods, freshwater crabs are preferred by the Chinese to the saltwater variety because the flavor is considered more delicate. Several kinds of crab are found in the many fresh waters of China, as well as in the China Sea. Crab are customarily steamed, stir-fried, or deep-fried.

LOBSTER   Lobster — or sea dragon, as it is commonly called in the Far East — is rarely consumed in areas other than southernmost China. Even here it is only enjoyed by a select few because of its exorbitant price. The spiny lobster, native to the Far East, does not have large claws; the bulk of its meat is in the tail, and the texture is thought to be coarser than that of the American East Coast lobster. Lobster should always be purchased live and cooked as soon as possible. The Chinese serve this seafood steamed, stir-fried, or sliced cold in salads.

SCALLOPS   Scallops are greatly admired for their sweet, delicate flavor and unique texture. Fresh scallops are available exclusively in the coastal regions, where they are stir-fried and poached. Dried scallops, a delicacy popular throughout China, are used as a flavoring in soups, braised stews, and vegetable dishes.

CLAMS   Clams are generally enjoyed by the Chinese living in coastal areas. Some of the more exotic varieties favored by the Chinese are not available in American markets, but cherrystones, littlenecks, and razor clams are consumed regularly. Simplicity is stressed when cooking clams; steamed or boiled clams with a dipping sauce are commonly served with wine. Clams are also stir-fried, stuffed, and simmered.

OYSTERS   Contrary to the popular Western belief that oysters are an aphrodisiac, the Chinese feel that the opposite is true, so this shellfish is rarely eaten in the nocturnal hours. Oysters are often served as a snack with wine, and are stir-fried, deep-fried, and used in soups and omelets. Dried oysters are used in stuffings, soups, and stir-fried dishes. In southern China, oysters and seasonings are reduced to a thick, pungent sauce (oyster sauce) and used as a flavoring in vegetable, meat, and seafood dishes.

SQUID   Squid has been a popular food in China since ancient times. It is enjoyed both fresh and dried. Dried squid is softened in hot water, and, like the fresh variety, scored into decorative shapes and used in stir-fried dishes or parboiled and served with a dipping sauce. In the Far East, strips of dried squid are sold by street vendors with grills as a snack that is eaten like beef jerky. Squid meat has an unusually high protein content and it is available not only fresh and dried, but frozen, canned, and salted as well. Cuttlefish, a cousin to squid with short tentacles and a thick body, is also very popular, particularly with the southern Chinese.

ABALONE   Abalone is a large univalve mollusk found in the warm waters of the Pacific. Most abalone is dried or canned, but frozen abalone is shipped to some parts of the United States. Abalone is prepared in a number of ways: It is used in cold platters, stir-fried with vegetables, and cooked in soups and stews. The liquid from canned abalone is often used in soups and stews for additional flavor.

DRIED JELLYFISH   This delicacy is found in most large Chinese grocery stores and is admired for its crunchy, resilient texture. The jellyfish is generally dried and salted, then formed into round sheets or strips. A lengthy soaking period is required to remove the surface salt. It is used in cold platters, salads, and congee.

SHARK'S FIN   Shark's fin is, as the name implies, the fin of the shark. In some Chinese grocery stores, the entire fin, with the cartilage and gelatinous needles, is available. But the dried gelatinous needles, often slightly preconditioned, are most widely sold. A lengthy soaking period and precooking time is necessary to rid this food of its fishy flavor, for it is relished merely for its texture. Shark's fin may be added to soups, braised with meats, or used in savory pastries. It is also extremely nutritious.

BIRD'S NEST   Bird's nest has been used by the Chinese since the beginning of the Ming dynasty (1368 to 1644). This delicacy is made from a combination of seaweed and the saliva of a swallow that inhabits the Malay Archipelago. The gathering of the nests is a perilous procedure, which accounts for the formidable expense of this food. There are two types of bird's nest: The more precious are white nests, made entirely from the saliva; black nests are those dotted with feathers and bits of seaweed. White nests are gathered once a year, while black nests are gathered twice. Both varieties are extremely nutritious and are reputed to possess powers of restoring youth. Once this dried delicacy has been soaked in water, it is used as a garnish in sweet and savory soups. Like shark's fin, it is admired for its texture.

SEA CUCUMBERS   Although sea cucumbers are foreign to the Western palate, they are enjoyed by the Chinese. This spineless creature, which inhabits the bottom of the ocean, is collected and dried. Once it has been soaked, the texture becomes gelatinous and slightly resilient. It is then stuffed, braised, or stir-fried. As with other specialty seafoods, it is considered a delicacy and is generally reserved for special occasions.

SIX SERVINGS

1½ pounds firm-fleshed, 1-inch-thick fish steaks (such as halibut or swordfish), or bluefish fillets

Fish Marinade
½ teaspoon salt
3 tablespoons soy sauce
1 tablespoon rice wine
1 tablespoon sugar
3 scallions, smashed with the flat side of a cleaver
3 slices gingerroot, smashed with the flat side of a cleaver

Smoking Mixture
¼ cup brown sugar
½ cup black tea leaves
3 tablespoons aniseed

2 teaspoons sesame oil

SIX SERVINGS

1½ pounds firm-fleshed fish fillets (such as haddock, cod, sea bass, pickerel, or lake trout)

SMOKED FISH STEAKS

XUN YU 燻 魚

Smoking is not usually used as a *cooking* method in Chinese cuisine; most foods are steamed or boiled before they are smoked, and the tea-laden fumes add color and flavor. Delicate foods such as fish, however, are cooked and smoked simultaneously, which produces tender, moist, and fragrant results.

1 Rinse the fish steaks, drain thoroughly, and pat dry. Pinch the scallions and the gingerroot slices in the **fish marinade** repeatedly for several minutes to impart their flavors. Place the steaks in a heat-proof dish and rub the marinade all over them. (If using fillets, place them skin side down.) Let marinate for at least 1 hour in the refrigerator.
2 Preheat the oven to 475°. Cover a shallow pan (such as a cake pan or pie plate) inside and out with several layers of heavy-duty aluminum foil. Place the **smoking mixture** in the pan, making sure the ingredients are well combined. Place the pan on the lowest shelf of the preheated oven.
3 When the mixture begins to smoke, place the heat-proof dish containing the steaks on the middle shelf of the oven. Bake for 10 minutes; then turn off the oven and let the fish sit for 5 minutes. Remove the fish and brush with the sesame oil. Serve hot or cold.

STIR-FRIED FISH ROLLS WITH BROCCOLI

SHENG CHAO YU QIU   生炒魚球

I was first served this memorable dish in a restaurant in Canton at a banquet in celebration of my husband's birthday. The delectable fish rolls, with their smoky black-mushroom and Chinese-ham filling, form an elegant platter befitting any special occasion.

1 Rinse the fillets lightly and drain thoroughly. Pat them dry and remove the skin. Holding the blade of a cleaver or a chef's knife at a

178

45° angle to the cutting surface, cut the fillets into slices about 1½ inches long, 1 inch wide, and ⅛ inch thick. Place the slices in a bowl. Pinch the gingerroot slices in the **fish marinade** repeatedly for several minutes to impart the flavor to the rice wine. Add the fish marinade and the egg white to the fish slices. Toss lightly and let marinate for 20 minutes. Drain the mushrooms. Remove and discard the stems. Cut the caps into matchstick-size shreds about 1 inch long. Cut the Chinese ham into shreds the same size. Peel away the tough outer skin from the broccoli and separate the flowerets. Roll-cut the stems into 1-inch pieces.

2   Heat 1½ quarts salted water until boiling. Add the stem pieces and cook for ½ minute. Add the flowerets and cook for 2½ minutes, or until both stems and flowerets are just tender. Refresh immediately in cold water. Drain thoroughly.

3   Arrange the fish slices on a flat surface. Generously sprinkle the top of a fish slice with cornstarch. Place a strip of ham and a strip of mushroom crosswise at one end of the fish slice and roll it up so that they are completely enclosed. Lightly squeeze each roll to secure it, so that it won't open while cooking. (You may piece together a fish slice using any little bits, with cornstarch as an adhesive.) Make the remaining rolls in the same manner.

4   Heat a wok, add the oil, and heat the oil to 375°. Add a third of the fish rolls and cook for about 2 minutes over high heat, carefully stirring all the while, until the rolls are cooked. Remove with a handled strainer, and drain. Reheat the oil and deep-fry the remaining rolls in the same manner, reheating the oil between batches. Remove the oil from the wok, reserving 2 tablespoons.

5   Reheat the wok, add the 2 tablespoons of oil, and heat until very hot. Add the **minced seasonings** and stir-fry over high heat for about 10 seconds, until fragrant. Add the broccoli and toss lightly over high heat for 15 seconds. Add the **fish sauce.** Stir slowly until the sauce has thickened. Add the fish rolls and toss lightly, and carefully, to coat with the sauce. Transfer the mixture to a platter and serve immediately.

Fish Marinade

1 tablespoon rice wine
1 teaspoon salt
2 slices gingerroot, smashed with the flat side of a cleaver

1 egg white, lightly beaten
5 dried Chinese black mushrooms, softened in hot water to cover for 20 minutes
4 paper-thin slices (about 2 ounces) Chinese ham, Smithfield ham, or prosciutto
1 pound broccoli
3 tablespoons cornstarch
4 cups peanut, safflower, or corn oil

Minced Seasonings

1 tablespoon minced scallions
2 teaspoons minced gingerroot

Fish Sauce

¼ cup chicken broth
1 tablespoon rice wine
1 teaspoon salt
½ teaspoon sugar
1 teaspoon sesame oil
1 teaspoon cornstarch

2 pounds firm-fleshed,
  skinned fish fillets (such as
  haddock, cod, or pickerel)

Fish Marinade
1 tablespoon rice wine
2 slices gingerroot, smashed
  with the flat side of a
  cleaver
1 teaspoon salt

½ cup cornstarch
2 cups peanut, safflower, or
  corn oil

Fish Sauce
½ cup chicken broth
2 tablespoons rice wine
1 teaspoon salt
¼ teaspoon freshly ground
  white pepper

Thickener
1 teaspoon cornstarch
1 tablespoon water

2 tablespoons scallion oil
  (see below)

Scallion Oil
2 tablespoons peanut,
  safflower, or corn oil
2 tablespoons sesame oil
½ cup shredded scallions

SCALLION-OIL FILLETS

CONG YOU YU PIAN 葱油魚片

Scallion oil is a pungent seasoning held in high regard by a number of eastern Chinese chefs. My chef-teacher substituted this fragrant oil for sesame oil in a number of recipes. Notice how it accentuates the fresh, sweet flavor of the fried fillets.

1   Rinse the fillets lightly, drain thoroughly, and place in a mixing bowl. Pinch the gingerroot in the **fish marinade** repeatedly for several minutes to impart the flavor to the rice wine. Add the marinade to the fillets, toss lightly, and let marinate for 20 minutes. Discard the gingerroot slices.
2   Dredge the fillets in the cornstarch, pressing lightly to be sure the cornstarch adheres.
3   Heat a wok, add the oil, and heat the oil to 400°. Add half the fillets and fry on both sides, over high heat, for about 5 minutes, until the fish is golden brown and flaky. Remove and drain. Reheat the oil. Fry the remaining fillets in the same manner. Arrange the fish on a platter. Remove the oil from the wok.
4   Reheat the wok, add the **fish sauce,** and heat until boiling. Add the **thickener,** stirring constantly to prevent lumps. Slowly pour the thickened sauce over the fish fillets. Sprinkle the scallion oil on top and serve immediately.

To make the **scallion oil:** Heat the peanut, safflower, or corn oil and the sesame oil in a wok until smoking. Add the scallions and turn off the heat. Cover, and let the mixture sit for 20 minutes. Strain the oil, discarding the scallions.

SHANGHAI-STYLE FISH BALLS IN BROTH

SHANGHAI YU WAN　　　　上 海 魚 丸

Fish balls are a popular delicacy among the Chinese. In this eastern version, the scallions and gingerroot lend a delicate flavor to the fish meat, and the egg white adds a fluffy lightness. The quantity of chicken broth in the recipe may be increased so that the dish may be served as a soup.

1　Remove the skin from the fillets and rinse them lightly. Drain and pat dry. Mince the fish to a smooth paste using a blender or a food processor fitted with the steel blade, or by hand with two cleavers. Place the fish paste in a mixing bowl, add the salt, and refrigerate for 10 minutes. Pinch the gingerroot and scallions in the **fish marinade** repeatedly for several minutes to impart their flavors. Discard the scallions and gingerroot and slowly add the marinade to the fish paste, stirring vigorously in one direction. Add the egg white and stir vigorously for about 5 minutes. Lightly throw the mixture against the inside of the bowl to combine evenly.

2　Heat a wok, add 2 quarts of cold water, and turn off the heat. Dip your hands in water to prevent the fish paste from sticking. Shape the paste into balls about ½ inch in diameter, dropping each one into the water as it is finished. Once all the balls have been added to the water, turn the heat to high and bring the water to a boil. Reduce the heat to medium and cook the fish balls for 5 minutes, or until they rise to the surface. Remove them with a slotted spoon and place in a serving bowl. Remove the water from the wok.

3　Reheat the wok, add the **sauce base,** and heat until boiling, stirring constantly. Add the spinach, sesame oil, and white pepper. Cook for about 30 seconds, until the spinach is barely limp, and pour the mixture over the fish balls. Serve immediately.

⅔ pound firm-fleshed fish fillets (such as cod, haddock, whitefish, or pickerel)
1 teaspoon salt

Fish Marinade
4 scallions, smashed with the flat side of a cleaver
4 slices gingerroot, smashed with the flat side of a cleaver
1 tablespoon rice wine
½ cup cold water

1 egg white

Sauce Base
2 cups chicken broth
2 tablespoons rice wine
1½ teaspoons cornstarch
1 teaspoon salt

½ pound fresh spinach, trimmed and cleaned
1 teaspoon sesame oil
¼ teaspoon freshly ground white pepper

1 whole firm-fleshed fish
  (such as sea bass, pickerel,
  or lake trout), about 3½
  pounds

Fish Marinade

1 tablespoon rice wine
1 teaspoon salt
2 slices gingerroot, smashed
  with the flat side of a
  cleaver
2 scallions, smashed with the
  flat side of a cleaver

Fish Poaching Liquid

1 tablespoon peanut,
  safflower, or corn oil
3 tablespoons rice wine
5 quarts boiling water

Fish Sauce

2½ tablespoons soy sauce
1 teaspoon salt
2½ tablespoons sugar
1½ tablespoons Chinese
  black vinegar
1½ cups fish poaching liquid

POACHED WEST LAKE FISH

XI HU CU YU 西湖醋魚

Hangzhou, an ancient city in eastern China, is famous for its refined cuisine and exquisite scenery. A specialty of this region is West Lake fish. One restaurant in Hangzhou has a large sign that reads: IF YOU WANT GOOD FISH, EAT WEST LAKE FISH. One can well understand this message after tasting this dish.

1   Direct the fishmonger to clean the fish through the gills, if possible, leaving the belly intact. Scale the fish, rinse thoroughly, and drain. Holding the knife at a 45° angle to the fish, make deep scores crosswise along the length of the fish, an inch apart, from the dorsal fin to the tail. Turn the fish over and repeat for the other side. Pinch the gingerroot slices and the scallions in the **fish marinade** repeatedly for several minutes to impart their flavors to the rice wine. Rub the marinade all over the outside of the fish and into the scores. Let the fish marinate for 30 minutes. Discard the gingerroot and scallions.

2   Heat a large wok, add the oil, and heat until hot. Add the remaining ingredients of the **fish poaching liquid** and heat until boiling. Slowly lower the fish into the poaching liquid and heat until boiling. Turn off the heat, cover, and let the fish sit for 20 minutes, or until the fish flakes when prodded with a chopstick or a fork. If the fish is not done, turn the heat to low and cook for 5 minutes.

Fish Seasonings	**Thickener**
¼ cup finely shredded gingerroot	1 tablespoon cornstarch
¼ cup finely shredded scallions	3 tablespoons water
1 fresh red chili pepper, seeds removed and shredded finely	
½ teaspoon freshly ground white pepper	

Using slotted utensils, carefully lift the fish and transfer it to a platter. Add 1½ cups of the fish poaching liquid to the **fish sauce.** Sprinkle the **fish seasonings** over the fish. Remove the liquid from the wok.

3   Reheat the wok, add the fish sauce, and heat it until boiling. Slowly add the **thickener,** stirring constantly to prevent lumps. Pour the thickened sauce over the fish and serve immediately.

STEAMED FISH FILLETS IN BLACK BEAN SAUCE

DOU SHI ZHENG YU   豆 豉 蒸 魚

Few seasonings complement the delicate flavor of fresh fish as ideally as fermented black beans. Though the beans may be salty and strong-tasting on their own, combined in a sauce with the rice wine, sugar, and chicken broth, they accentuate the sweet flavor of the fish fillets rather than mask it.

1   Rinse the fillets lightly and pat them dry. Place the fillets in a mixing bowl. Pinch the gingerroot slices in the **fish marinade** repeatedly for several minutes to impart the flavor to the rice wine. Add the marinade to the fish fillets, toss lightly, and let marinate for 20 minutes. Discard the gingerroot and arrange the fillets in a heatproof pie plate or quiche pan.

2   Heat a wok, add the oil, and heat until very hot. Add the **minced seasonings,** stir-fry for about 10 seconds (until fragrant), and add the **fish sauce.** Heat the mixture until boiling and cook for about 2 minutes, stirring constantly. Pour the sauce over the fish fillets. Place the pie plate or quiche pan in a steamer tray.

3   Fill a wok with water level with the bottom edge of the steamer tray and heat until boiling. Place the steamer tray over the boiling water, cover, and steam the fish for 10 minutes over high heat, or until it flakes when prodded with a chopstick or a fork. Serve immediately.

SIX SERVINGS

1½ pounds firm-fleshed, skinned fish fillets (flounder, sole, pickerel, lake trout)

Fish Marinade

2 slices gingerroot, smashed with the flat side of a cleaver
1 tablespoon rice wine
1 teaspoon salt

2 tablespoons peanut, safflower, or corn oil

Minced Seasonings

1 tablespoon fermented black beans, rinsed, drained, and minced
2 teaspoons minced garlic
1 tablespoon minced scallions

Fish Sauce

¼ cup chicken broth
1 tablespoon soy sauce
1 tablespoon rice wine
½ teaspoon sugar
¼ teaspoon black pepper

183

1 whole firm-fleshed fish
(such as flounder, red
snapper, pickerel, or lake
trout), about 3½ pounds

Fish Marinade
2 teaspoons salt
1 tablespoon rice wine
2 slices gingerroot, smashed
with the flat side of a
cleaver

8 dried Chinese black
mushrooms
5 paper-thin slices (about 2
ounces) Chinese ham,
Smithfield ham, or
prosciutto
1 tablespoon soy sauce

Fish Seasonings
2 tablespoons shredded
scallions
2 tablespoons shredded
gingerroot

2 tablespoons sesame oil

STEAMED FISH WITH HAM AND MUSHROOM SLICES

HUO TUI DONG GU ZHENG YU 火腿冬菇蒸魚

The savory richness of Chinese ham and black mushrooms provides a superb contrast to fresh fish. Topped with fragrant shreds of fresh scallion and gingerroot, this dish is pleasing to both the eye and the palate.

1   Direct the fishmonger to clean the fish through the gills, if possible, leaving the belly intact. Scale the fish, rinse thoroughly, and drain. Holding the knife at a 45° angle to the fish, make deep scores crosswise along the length of the fish, an inch apart, from the dorsal fin to the tail. Pinch the gingerroot slices and the scallions in the rice wine repeatedly for several minutes to impart their flavors. Rub the **fish marinade** all over the outside of the fish and into the scores. Let the fish marinate for 30 minutes. Discard the gingerroot and scallions. Soften the dried mushrooms for 20 minutes in hot water to cover. Remove and discard the stems, and cut the caps in half. Cut the ham into pieces 2 inches long.
2   Arrange the fish on a heat-proof platter, scored side up, and stuff a ham slice and a mushroom half into each of the scores. Sprinkle the soy sauce over the fish and place the platter in a steamer tray.
3   Fill a wok with water level with the bottom edge of the steamer tray and heat until boiling. Place the steamer tray containing the fish over the boiling water, cover, and steam for 15 to 17 minutes over high heat, or until the fish flakes when prodded with a chopstick or a fork. Remove the platter and sprinkle the **fish seasonings** over the fish. Remove the water from the wok.
4   Reheat the wok, add the sesame oil, and heat until smoking. Pour the sesame oil over the fish. Serve immediately.

SWEET-AND-SOUR FISH WITH PINE NUTS

SUNG ZI CHUAN YU　　　松子全魚

Sweet-and-sour fish is a dish found in all regional cuisines, but it is the addition of buttery pine nuts that distinguishes this eastern version from all others.

1 Direct the fishmonger to clean the fish through the gills, if possible, leaving the belly intact. Scale the fish, rinse thoroughly, and drain. Holding the knife at a 45° angle to the fish, make deep scores crosswise along the length of the fish, an inch apart, from the dorsal fin to the tail. Turn the fish over and repeat on the other side. Pinch the scallions and gingerroot slices in the **fish marinade** repeatedly for several minutes to impart their flavors to the rice wine. Rub the marinade all over the outside of the fish and into the scores. Let the fish marinate for 20 minutes. Discard the gingerroot and scallions.
2 Rub the egg yolk over the fish and coat the fish with the cornstarch, making certain that the scores are also coated.
3 Heat a wok, add the oil, and heat the oil to 425°. Holding the fish curled in a semicircular shape so that the scores are open, slowly lower the fish into the hot oil. Deep-fry the fish over high heat for about 10 minutes, or until the meat is flaky and the outside is crisp and golden brown. (Ladle hot oil over the fish as it is frying.) Remove the fish, drain, and arrange on a platter. Remove the oil from the wok, reserving 2 tablespoons.
4 Reheat the wok, add the 2 tablespoons of oil, and heat until very hot. Add the **fish seasonings** and stir-fry for about 1 minute over high heat, until the onion shreds are soft and transparent. Add the **fish sauce** and cook, stirring occasionally, until the sauce has thickened. Pour the sauce over the fish and sprinkle the pine nuts on top. Serve immediately.

SIX SERVINGS

1 whole firm-fleshed fish (sea bass, pickerel, or lake trout), about 3½ pounds

Fish Marinade
1 tablespoon rice wine
2 scallions, smashed with the flat side of a cleaver
2 slices gingerroot, smashed with the flat side of a cleaver
¾ teaspoon salt

1 egg yolk
1 cup cornstarch
8 cups peanut, safflower, or corn oil

Fish Seasonings
½ cup shredded onions
½ cup shredded green peppers
1 tablespoon minced garlic

Fish Sauce
5 tablespoons ketchup
5 tablespoons sugar
5 tablespoons clear rice vinegar
2 teaspoons soy sauce
½ teaspoon salt
½ teaspoon sesame oil
½ cup water
1½ teaspoons cornstarch

1 ounce pine nuts, roasted in a 325° oven until golden

1 whole firm-fleshed fish
(such as sea bass,
haddock, pickerel, or lake
trout), about 3½ pounds

Fish Marinade

2 slices gingerroot, smashed
with the flat side of a
cleaver
1 tablespoon rice wine
2 tablespoons soy sauce

Fish Braising Liquid

4 cups chicken broth or
water
¼ cup soy sauce
2 tablespoons rice wine
2 teaspoons sugar
1 teaspoon sesame oil

½ pound boneless center-cut
pork loin

Pork Marinade

1 tablespoon soy sauce
½ tablespoon rice wine
1 teaspoon sesame oil
1 teaspoon cornstarch
½ tablespoon water

2 cups peanut, safflower, or
corn oil

RED-COOKED YELLOW FISH

HONG SHAO HUANG YU

Although red-cooking is frequently used for preparing tough cuts of meat, admirable results occur when the method is used to braise a whole fish. The pungent seasonings of scallions, gingerroot, and garlic with the rich, soy-based sauce transform any fish into a delectable platter that is excellent served with rice.

1   Direct the fishmonger to clean the fish through the gills, if possible, leaving the belly intact. Scale the fish, rinse thoroughly, and drain. Holding the knife at a 45° angle to the fish, make deep scores crosswise along the length of the fish, an inch apart, from the dorsal fin to the tail. Pinch the gingerroot slices in the **fish marinade** repeatedly for several minutes to impart the flavor. Rub the marinade all over the outside of the fish and into the scores. Let the fish marinate for 30 minutes. Discard the gingerroot and drain the fish, adding the fish marinade to the **fish braising liquid.**
2   Remove any fat or gristle from the pork loin and discard. Cut the pork, across the grain, into slices ⅛ inch thick. Cut the slices into matchstick-size shreds. Place the pork shreds in a bowl, add the **pork marinade,** toss lightly, and let marinate for 20 minutes.
3   Heat a wok, add the oil, and heat the oil to 400°. Slowly lower

Fish Seasonings	Thickener
6 dried Chinese black mushrooms, softened in hot water for 20 minutes, stems removed, and caps shredded	1 tablespoon cornstarch
	2 tablespoons water
1 tablespoon minced garlic	½ cup bamboo shoots, blanched briefly and cut into matchstick-size shreds
2 tablespoons minced scallions	2 tablespoons finely shredded gingerroot

the fish into the pan and fry, constantly ladling the oil over the fish, for 5 minutes over high heat. Remove and drain. Remove the oil from the pan, reserving 4 tablespoons.

4 Reheat the wok, add 3 tablespoons of the reserved oil, and heat until very hot. Add the pork, stir-fry over high heat until the shreds turn color, remove, and drain. Add the rest of the reserved oil, heat until very hot, add the **fish seasonings,** and stir-fry for about 10 seconds, until fragrant. Add the pork shreds and the fish braising liquid, and heat until boiling. Add the fish, scored side up, and heat until the liquid boils. Reduce the heat to medium, cover, and cook for 12 to 15 minutes, or until the fish flakes when prodded with a chopstick or a fork. Using slotted utensils, carefully lift the fish and transfer it to a platter. Heat the sauce until boiling, and add the **thickener,** stirring constantly to prevent lumps. When the sauce has thickened, add the bamboo shoots. Toss lightly and pour the sauce over the fish. Sprinkle the shredded gingerroot over the fish and serve immediately.

2 pounds medium-sized raw
   shrimp in their shells

Shrimp Marinade
2 tablespoons rice wine
2 slices gingerroot, smashed
   with the flat side of a
   cleaver

2½ tablespoons cornstarch
8 cups peanut, safflower, or
   corn oil

Shrimp Seasonings
2½ teaspoons salt
3 tablespoons minced garlic

CRISPY-FRIED SHRIMP WITH GARLIC

YAN SU XIA   鹽 酥 蝦

This apparently simple eastern dish is actually an unusual mélange of texture and flavor. The shrimp are superb, deep-fried to a crisp, golden color and lightly seasoned with salt and minced garlic.

1   Cut away the legs and antennae of the shrimp, if remaining. Devein the shrimp using a needle or a toothpick, and rinse the shrimp thoroughly. Pat them dry and place them in a mixing bowl. Pinch the gingerroot slices in the rice wine repeatedly for several minutes to impart the flavor; add the **shrimp marinade** to the bowl. Toss the shrimp lightly and let them marinate for 20 minutes. Discard the gingerroot. Add the cornstarch to the shrimp and toss lightly.

2   Heat a wok, add the oil, and heat the oil to 425°. Add the shrimp and deep-fry over high heat for about 2½ minutes, turning constantly until golden brown and crisp. Remove with a handled strainer, and drain. Remove the oil from the wok.

3   Reheat the wok until very hot. Add the fried shrimp and the **shrimp seasonings.** Toss lightly over high heat for about 20 seconds, until fragrant. Transfer the mixture to a platter and serve immediately.

1 whole firm-fleshed fish
   (such as sea bass, haddock, carp, pickerel, or
   lake trout), about 3½
   pounds

SICHUANESE BRAISED FISH IN SPICY SAUCE

DOU BAN JIAN YU   豆 瓣 煎 魚

In Chinese cuisine, gingerroot, scallions, rice wine, and vinegar are invariably used in the preparation of fish. It is believed that these ingredients remove any undesirable fishy flavors. In this dish all four of these seasonings are employed, along with chili paste, resulting in a superb mingling of flavors.

1 Direct the fishmonger to clean the fish through the gills, if possible, leaving the belly intact. Scale the fish, rinse thoroughly, and drain. Holding the knife at a 45° angle to the fish, make deep scores crosswise along the length of the fish, an inch apart, from the dorsal fin to the tail. Pinch the gingerroot slices in the **fish marinade** repeatedly for several minutes to impart the flavor to the rice wine. Rub the marinade all over the outside of the fish and into the scores. Let the fish marinate for 30 minutes. Discard the gingerroot and drain the fish.

2 Heat a wok, add the oil, and heat the oil to 400°. Slowly lower the fish into the hot oil and deep-fry, constantly ladling the oil over the fish, over high heat for 5 minutes, until golden. Remove and drain. Remove the oil from the wok, reserving 2 tablespoons.

3 Reheat the wok, add the 2 tablespoons of oil, and heat until very hot. Add the **minced seasonings,** and stir-fry for 10 seconds, until fragrant. Add the chili paste and stir-fry for another 5 seconds. Add the wood ears, toss lightly, and add the **fish braising sauce;** heat until boiling. Slowly lower the fish into the sauce, scored side up, and heat until the liquid is boiling. Cover, reduce the heat to medium, and cook for about 12 minutes, or until the meat flakes when prodded with a chopstick or a fork. Using slotted utensils, transfer the fish to a platter. Heat the sauce until boiling and slowly add the **thickener,** stirring constantly to prevent lumps. When the sauce has thickened, add the sesame oil, toss lightly, and pour the sauce over the fish. Sprinkle the minced scallion greens over the fish and serve immediately.

Fish Marinade

2 slices gingerroot, smashed with the flat side of a cleaver
1 tablespoon rice wine
½ teaspoon salt

2 cups peanut, safflower, or corn oil

Minced Seasonings

2 tablespoons minced scallions
1½ tablespoons minced gingerroot
1½ tablespoons minced garlic

1½ teaspoons chili paste
10 dried wood ears, softened in hot water for 20 minutes, drained, and shredded

Fish Braising Sauce

2 cups chicken broth
1½ tablespoons soy sauce
½ teaspoon salt
1 tablespoon rice wine
½ tablespoon sugar
1 tablespoon Chinese black vinegar

Thickener

1 tablespoon cornstarch
2 tablespoons water

1 teaspoon sesame oil
2 tablespoons minced scallion greens

189

24 medium-sized dried
    Chinese black mushrooms

Mushroom Seasonings

1 tablespoon soy sauce
1 tablespoon rice wine
1 teaspoon sesame oil
½ teaspoon sugar
2 tablespoons mushroom-
    soaking liquid
2 scallions, smashed with the
    flat side of a cleaver
2 slices gingerroot, smashed
    with the flat side of a
    cleaver

Shrimp Sauce

½ cup chicken broth
Mushroom-steaming liquid
½ teaspoon salt
2 teaspoons rice wine
1½ teaspoons cornstarch

¾ pound raw shrimp, shelled
½ ounce pork fat, minced to
    a paste

BLACK MUSHROOMS STUFFED WITH SHRIMP

XIA REN XIANG DONG GU 蝦仁釀冬菇

The rich, smoky flavor of dried Chinese black mushrooms is superbly contrasted with the delicate sweet flavor of the minced shrimp filling. If possible, large, thick black mushroom caps should be used, as they are superior in flavor to the small, thin ones and more attractive.

1   Rinse the dried mushrooms and soften them for 20 minutes in hot water to cover. Add 2 tablespoons of the soaking liquid to the **mushroom seasonings.** Remove and discard the mushroom stems; place the caps in a heat-proof bowl, add the mushroom seasonings, toss lightly, and place the bowl in a steamer tray. Fill a wok with water level with the bottom edge of the steamer tray. Place the steamer tray over the water, cover, and steam the mushroom caps for 15 minutes over high heat. Let the mushrooms cool, drain off the liquid in the bowl, and add it to the **shrimp sauce,** discarding the scallions and gingerroot. Set the shrimp sauce aside.

2   Devein the shrimp, rinse lightly, and drain thoroughly. Place the shrimp in a linen dishtowel and squeeze out as much moisture as possible. Mince the shrimp to a paste using a blender or a food processor fitted with the steel blade, or with two cleavers. Place the shrimp paste in a mixing bowl, and add the minced pork fat and **shrimp seasonings.** Stir vigorously in one direction and lightly throw the mixture against the inside of the bowl to combine evenly.

3   Sprinkle the inside of a mushroom cap with a little bit of cornstarch and spoon shrimp paste generously into the cap. Smooth the surface with the underside of a spoon dipped in water. Stuff the remaining caps in the same manner and place them on a lightly greased heat-proof plate. Put the plate in a steamer tray. Following the procedure described in step 1, steam for 7 minutes over high heat.

4   Heat a wok, add 1 tablespoon of oil, and heat until smoking. Add the minced garlic and stir-fry over high heat for 5 seconds. Add

the spinach, toss lightly, and add the **spinach seasonings.** Toss briefly over high heat until the spinach is slightly wilted. Arrange the spinach around the outer edge of a platter. Place the steamed mushroom caps in the center of the platter.

5 Reheat the wok, add the shrimp sauce, and stir until the sauce thickens. Pour the sauce over the mushrooms and serve immediately.

Shrimp Seasonings
¾ teaspoon salt
1½ teaspoons rice wine
1 teaspoon sesame oil
½ teaspoon minced
    gingerroot
½ egg white
1½ tablespoons cornstarch

2 tablespoons cornstarch
1 tablespoon peanut,
    safflower, or corn oil
1 teaspoon minced garlic
1 pound fresh spinach,
    trimmed and cleaned

Spinach Seasonings
2 teaspoons rice wine
1 tablespoon chicken broth
½ teaspoon salt
½ teaspoon sesame oil

1½ pounds medium-sized raw shrimp, shelled

Shrimp Marinade

1 teaspoon salt
1 tablespoon rice wine
2 slices gingerroot, smashed with the flat side of a cleaver
1 teaspoon sesame oil

3 English ("gourmet seedless") cucumbers or 6 pickling cucumbers
4 cups peanut, corn, or safflower oil
2 ounces rice stick noodles

Minced Seasonings

2 teaspoons minced gingerroot
1 tablespoon minced scallions

Shrimp Sauce

2 teaspoons soy sauce
1½ tablespoons rice wine
¾ teaspoon sugar
¾ teaspoon salt
1 teaspoon sesame oil
2½ tablespoons chicken broth

2 cups pine nuts, roasted in a 325° oven until golden brown

STIR-FRIED SHRIMP WITH CUCUMBERS AND PINE NUTS

SUNG ZI XIA REN 松子蝦仁

This dish reflects three basic characteristics of eastern regional cooking: It is exquisite in appearance, rich in flavor, and sweet in taste. Tiny river shrimp are traditionally used in the recipe because of their sweet and delicate flavor, but even frozen saltwater shrimp are delicious when prepared in this manner.

1   Score each shrimp along the length of the back and remove the vein; the scoring will allow the shrimp to "butterfly" when cooked. Rinse all the shrimp and drain thoroughly. Place the shrimp in a linen dishtowel and squeeze out as much moisture as possible. Place the shrimp in a bowl. Pinch the gingerroot slices in the **shrimp marinade** repeatedly for several minutes to impart the flavor. Add the marinade to the shrimp, toss lightly, and let marinate for 20 minutes. Discard the gingerroot slices. Trim the ends off the cucumbers and discard. Cut the cucumbers in half lengthwise, remove the seeds, and cut each half lengthwise into thirds. Roll-cut the lengths into 1-inch pieces.

2   Heat a wok, add the oil, and heat the oil to 425°, or until smoking. Drop the rice noodles into the hot oil and deep-fry very briefly until they are puffed and lightly golden. (This should take no longer than 5 seconds.) Turn the noodles over and fry for a few seconds more. Remove them and drain on absorbent paper. Transfer the noodles to a platter and break them up lightly with your fingertips; make a slight depression in the center. Remove the oil from the wok, reserving ½ cup.

3   Reheat the wok, add 6 tablespoons of the oil, and heat until very hot. Drain the shrimp and add half of them to the hot oil. Stir-fry over high heat for about 1 minute, or until the shrimp change color. Remove with a handled strainer, and drain. Reheat the oil until very hot and stir-fry the remaining shrimp in the same manner. Remove the oil from the wok.

4   Reheat the wok, add the remaining 2 tablespoons of oil, and

heat until very hot. Add the **minced seasonings** and stir-fry for about 10 seconds, until fragrant. Add the cucumber pieces and stir-fry over high heat for about 30 seconds, until the cucumbers are heated through. Add the **shrimp sauce** and the shrimp. Toss lightly over high heat for about 20 seconds; then add the pine nuts. Toss lightly to combine the mixture, and spoon it over the fried noodles. Serve immediately.

HUNDRED-CORNER SHRIMP BALLS

BAI JIAO XIA QIU 　　百角蝦球

These puffs are so named because of their light coating of bread cubes. Serve them as finger food with drinks or as an entrée accompanied by Sichuan-peppercorn salt for dipping.

1   Devein the shrimp, rinse lightly, and drain thoroughly. Place the shrimp in a linen dishtowel and squeeze out as much moisture as possible. Mince the shrimp to a smooth paste using a blender or a food processor fitted with the steel blade, or by hand with two cleavers. Place the shrimp paste in a mixing bowl, and add the pork fat, water chestnuts, and **shrimp seasonings.** Stir to combine, and add the cornstarch. Stir vigorously in one direction and lightly throw the mixture against the inside of the bowl to combine evenly.

2   Cut the bread into ¼-inch cubes. Spread the cubes out on a cookie sheet and let them dry for 2 hours, turning occasionally.

3   Dip your hands in water to prevent the shrimp paste from sticking. Shape the paste into balls ¾ inch in diameter. Roll the shrimp balls in the bread cubes, pressing lightly to make sure that the cubes adhere firmly.

4   Heat a wok, add the oil, and heat the oil to 350°. Add a third of the shrimp balls and deep-fry, turning constantly over high heat, for about 4 minutes, or until the shrimp paste is cooked and the balls are golden. Remove with a handled strainer, and drain on absorbent paper. Reheat the oil and deep-fry the remaining shrimp balls in the same manner, reheating the oil between batches. Arrange the shrimp balls on a platter and serve immediately.

SIX SERVINGS

1 pound raw shrimp, shelled
1 ounce pork fat, minced to a paste
½ cup water chestnuts, plunged briefly into boiling water, refreshed, and coarsely chopped

Shrimp Seasonings
1 tablespoon rice wine
1 teaspoon salt
1 teaspoon minced scallions
1 teaspoon minced gingerroot
1 egg white
1 teaspoon sesame oil

3 tablespoons cornstarch
12 slices sandwich bread, crusts removed
8 cups peanut, safflower, or corn oil

2 pounds large prawns or
shrimp, in their shells

Prawn Marinade

1½ tablespoons rice wine
2 slices gingerroot, smashed
with the flat side of a
cleaver
½ teaspoon salt

4 cups peanut, safflower, or
corn oil

Minced Seasonings

2 tablespoons minced
scallions
1½ tablespoons minced
garlic
1 tablespoon minced
gingerroot

1½ teaspoons chili paste

Prawn Sauce

5 tablespoons ketchup
2 tablespoons rice wine
1½ tablespoons sugar
1 teaspoon salt
6 tablespoons water
1½ teaspoons cornstarch

SPICY PRAWNS IN TOMATO SAUCE

GAN SHAO MING XIA　　　乾燒明蝦

Although some Americans consider shrimp or prawns served in the shells to be a nuisance to eat, the Chinese feel that the shell preserves the natural juices and prevents the meat from overcooking. Serve this spicy Sichuanese dish with rice and a stir-fried green vegetable for a simple yet superb meal.

1　Devein the prawns using a needle or a toothpick. Rinse lightly, drain thoroughly, and pat dry. Pinch the gingerroot slices in the **prawn marinade** repeatedly for several minutes to impart the flavor to the rice wine. Place the prawns in a mixing bowl, add the prawn marinade, toss lightly, and let marinate for 20 minutes. Drain the prawns and discard the gingerroot and scallions.
2　Heat a wok, add the oil, and heat the oil to 375°. Add half the prawns, and deep-fry for about 4 minutes over high heat, stirring constantly. Remove with a handled strainer, and drain. Reheat the oil and deep-fry the remaining prawns in the same manner. Remove the oil from the wok, reserving 1 tablespoon.
3　Reheat the wok, add the tablespoon of oil, and heat until very hot. Add the **minced seasonings** and stir-fry for about 10 seconds, until fragrant. Add the chili paste and stir-fry for about 5 seconds over high heat. Add the **prawn sauce** and stir until it begins to thicken. Add the cooked prawns, toss lightly to coat with sauce, and transfer the mixture to a platter. Serve immediately.

CRAB IN SWEET-AND-SOUR SAUCE

CU LIU XIE ROU 醋溜蟹肉

The sweet, delicate flavor of fresh crabmeat provides a perfect foil for piquant sweet-and-sour sauce. Soft-shell or blue crab are ideally suited to this tasty Cantonese dish, as are Dungeness and Alaskan king crab legs.

1   Plunge the crabs into boiling water for about a minute; rinse them in cold water. Twist off and discard the apron. Remove the upper shell of the crab and reserve the roe. Remove and discard the spongy gill tissue from inside the crab. Rinse the bodies and drain well. Cut away the last two hairy joints of the legs. Cut each crab into four to six pieces, cutting so that a portion of the body is attached to one or two legs. Place the crab pieces and the roe in a mixing bowl. Pinch the gingerroot slices in the rice wine repeatedly for several minutes to impart the flavor, and add the **crab marinade** to the bowl. Toss lightly, and let the crab marinate for 20 minutes. Discard the gingerroot. Add the cornstarch and toss lightly to coat the pieces of crab.

2   Heat a wok, add the oil, and heat the oil to 400°. Add half the crab pieces and deep-fry for about 4 minutes over high heat, until golden brown and crisp. (The roe should be cooked only briefly, about 1 minute.) Remove and drain the pieces. Reheat the oil and deep-fry the remaining crab in the same manner. Remove the oil from the wok, reserving 2 tablespoons.

3   Reheat the wok, add the 2 tablespoons of oil, and heat until very hot. Add the **minced seasonings** and stir-fry for about 10 seconds over high heat, until fragrant. Add the **crab sauce** and stir-fry until it begins to thicken. Add the fried crab pieces and the roe, and toss lightly to coat with the sauce. Transfer the mixture to a platter and serve immediately.

SIX SERVINGS

6 medium-sized live blue crabs, about 5 ounces each

Crab Marinade
2 tablespoons rice wine
3 slices gingerroot, smashed with the flat side of a cleaver

1 cup cornstarch
6 cups peanut, safflower, or corn oil

Minced Seasonings
2 tablespoons minced scallions
1 tablespoon minced garlic

Crab Sauce
5 tablespoons ketchup
4 tablespoons clear rice vinegar
5 tablespoons sugar
¾ teaspoon salt
1 teaspoon soy sauce
½ teaspoon sesame oil
6 tablespoons water
2 teaspoons cornstarch

6 medium-sized live blue
   crabs, about 5 ounces
   each

Crab Marinade

2 tablespoons rice wine
3 slices gingerroot, smashed
   with the flat side of a
   cleaver

1 cup cornstarch
6 cups peanut, safflower, or
   corn oil

Minced Seasonings

1 tablespoon minced
   scallions
1 tablespoon minced garlic

2 green peppers, cored,
   seeded, and roll-cut into
   1-inch pieces

Crab Sauce

1½ tablespoons sweet bean
   sauce
1½ tablespoons soy sauce
1 tablespoon rice wine
1 tablespoon sugar
¼ cup water

CRAB IN SWEET BEAN SAUCE

JING JIANG XIE ROU　京醬蟹肉

The richness of the sweet bean sauce in this dish clearly accentuates the delicate sweetness of the crabmeat. The additional seasonings — green pepper, scallions, and garlic — combine to create a flavor that is unusually tasty, and excellent with white rice.

1   Plunge the crabs into boiling water for about 1 minute; rinse them in cold water. Twist off and discard the apron. Remove the upper shell of the crab and reserve the roe. Remove and discard the spongy gill tissue from inside the crab. Rinse the bodies and drain well. Cut away the last two hairy joints of the legs. Cut each crab into four to six pieces, cutting so that a portion of the body is attached to one or two legs. Place the crab pieces and the roe in a mixing bowl. Pinch the gingerroot slices in the rice wine repeatedly for several minutes to impart the flavor, and add the **crab marinade** to the crab pieces. Toss lightly, and let the crab marinate for 20 minutes. Discard the gingerroot. Add the cornstarch and toss lightly to coat the pieces of crab.

2   Heat a wok, add the oil, and heat to 400°. Add half the crab pieces and deep-fry for about 4 minutes over high heat, until golden brown and crisp. (The roe should be cooked only briefly, about 1 minute.) Remove and drain the pieces. Reheat the oil, add and deep-fry the remaining crab in the same manner. Remove the oil from the wok, reserving 2 tablespoons.

3   Reheat the wok, add the 2 tablespoons of oil, and heat until very hot. Add the **minced seasonings** and stir-fry for about 10 seconds over high heat. Add the green peppers and stir-fry for another 10 seconds. Add the **crab sauce** and cook until the sauce begins to thicken after boiling. Add the crab pieces and the roe, and toss lightly to coat with the sauce. Transfer the mixture to a platter and serve immediately.

LOBSTER CANTONESE

YUE SHI CHAO LONG XIA　　粵式炒龍蝦

A New England purist at heart, I had always maintained that the only way to serve lobster was boiled with drawn butter; any other method was desecration of the highest order. My point of view changed radically, however, one evening many years ago when I was served this famous Cantonese dish. It is also excellent when prepared with shrimp.

1 Using a sharp cleaver or a large chef's knife, cut through the undershell of the lobster lengthwise, cutting through the head and back toward the tail, splitting the lobster in two. Remove the sand sac from the head and remove the intestinal tract. Cut off and discard the tip of the head with the eyes and the antennae. Cut off and discard the legs. Cut the body, through the shell, into pieces about 2 inches square.

2 Chop the ground meat until fluffy, place it in a mixing bowl, add the **pork marinade**, and toss lightly.

3 Heat a wok, add the oil, and heat until very hot. Add the **minced seasonings** and stir-fry for about 10 seconds, until fragrant. Add the ground pork and stir-fry, mashing and stirring the meat to separate the grounds, for about a minute (until the color changes). Add the lobster pieces and stir-fry for about 1 minute over high heat. Add the **lobster sauce** and heat until boiling. Cover and cook for about 3 minutes over high heat. Uncover, and slowly add the **thickener**, stirring constantly to prevent lumps. When the sauce has thickened, turn off the heat and slowly add the beaten eggs in a thin stream around the side of the wok. Stir once or twice and transfer the mixture to a platter. Sprinkle the minced scallion greens on top and serve immediately.

Thickener
1½ teaspoons cornstarch
1 tablespoon water

2 eggs, lightly beaten
1 tablespoon minced scallion greens

2 live lobsters, 1½ to 2 pounds each
½ pound ground pork

Pork Marinade
2 teaspoons soy sauce
1 teaspoon rice wine
½ teaspoon sesame oil
1 teaspoon water

2 tablespoons peanut, safflower, or corn oil

Minced Seasonings
1 tablespoon minced garlic
2 teaspoons minced gingerroot
1 tablespoon minced scallions
2 tablespoons fermented black beans, rinsed, drained, and minced

Lobster Sauce
1 cup chicken broth
2½ tablespoons soy sauce
2 tablespoons rice wine
1 teaspoon sugar
¼ teaspoon freshly ground black pepper
1 teaspoon sesame oil

2 pounds steamers or
   littleneck clams
1 cup water
½ teaspoon salt

Clam Marinade
½ cup clam cooking liquid
1 cup Shaohsing or another
   good-quality rice wine
½ cup chicken broth
1 teaspoon salt
4 cloves garlic, smashed with
   the flat side of a cleaver
4 scallions, smashed with the
   flat side of a cleaver
6 slices gingerroot, smashed
   with the flat side of a
   cleaver

DRUNKEN CLAMS

XIAN XIAN   鹹 蜆

Although some Chinese insist that the clams found in the Far East are more tender and sweet than those found in the United States, I must admit partiality to those found in New England. Littleneck and soft-shelled clams are both excellent in this dish.

1   Rinse the clams thoroughly in cold running water to remove any sand; place them in cold water to cover for 30 minutes. Drain them; place the 1 cup water and ½ teaspoon salt in a large pot. Heat until boiling and add the clams. Cover, and reduce the heat to low. Cook, shaking the pot occasionally, until the clams are just open. Remove the pot from the heat and transfer the clams to a bowl. Add ½ cup of the clam cooking liquid to the **clam marinade** and add the marinade to the bowl. Toss lightly to coat the clams with the marinade; refrigerate for at least 3 hours, turning the clams from time to time. Serve cold.

5 fresh or frozen lobster
   tails, about 5 to 6 ounces
   each, or 1½ pounds
   cooked lobster meat

Lobster Seasonings
1 teaspoon salt
2 tablespoons lemon juice

6 dried vermicelli sheets or
   2 ounces bean threads

THREE-FLAVOR LOBSTER SLICES

SAN WEI LONG XIA   三 味 龍 蝦

Although Sichuanese cuisine is renowned for its fiery seasonings and spicy flavors, several dishes from this area are more subtle and delicate. Such is the case with this platter, a specialty frequently served at the opening of a Chinese banquet. Dried vermicelli sheets, which are available at most Chinese markets, are made from the starch of mung beans. They have no flavor and are used as a base for a number of Chinese cold platters.

1   If the lobster tails are still in the shell, cut the shell down the back with a pair of kitchen shears. Fill a pan with 3 quarts of water and add the **lobster seasonings**. Heat until boiling, add the lobster

tails, and cook for 5 minutes (begin timing after the water boils again). Remove the tails, let them cool, and remove the meat from the shells. (If the lobster meat is already cooked, omit this step.) Holding the knife at a 45° angle to the meat, cut it crosswise into paper-thin slices.

2   Soften the vermicelli sheets or bean threads in hot water to cover for 10 minutes. Drain; cut the vermicelli sheets into strips 1 inch wide or the bean threads into 3-inch lengths. Cook the vermicelli sheets or the bean threads for 1 minute in boiling water. Refresh immediately in cold water. Drain thoroughly and mix with the **vermicelli seasonings**. Place the vermicelli sheets or bean threads on a platter and arrange the lobster slices overlapping in a circular pattern on top.

3   Place the **sesame sauce, peppercorn sauce,** and **ginger sauce** in separate small bowls. Serve the lobster slices with the three dipping sauces.

Vermicelli Seasonings
1 teaspoon sesame oil
½ teaspoon salt

Sesame Sauce
½ cup sesame paste or
   smooth peanut butter
3 tablespoons soy sauce
1 tablespoon sugar
2 tablespoons sesame oil
2 teaspoons Chinese black
   vinegar
1 tablespoon minced
   gingerroot
1 tablespoon minced
   scallions
1 tablespoon minced garlic
1 teaspoon chili oil or chili
   paste
¼ cup chicken broth or
   water

Peppercorn Sauce
1 tablespoon Sichuan
   peppercorns, roasted for 5
   minutes and pulverized
2 tablespoons minced
   scallions
2 tablespoons minced
   gingerroot
1½ tablespoons Chinese
   black vinegar
1 tablespoon sugar
1½ tablespoons sesame oil
¼ cup soy sauce
½ teaspoon salt

Ginger Sauce
¼ cup clear rice vinegar
2 tablespoons finely
   shredded gingerroot
¾ teaspoon salt
½ teaspoon sugar

2 pounds fresh scallops

Scallop Marinade

2 tablespoons rice wine
2 slices gingerroot, smashed
  with the flat side of a
  cleaver
2 scallions, smashed with the
  flat side of a cleaver
½ teaspoon salt

1 pound broccoli
2 tablespoons peanut,
  safflower, or corn oil

Scallop Seasonings

1½ tablespoons shredded
  scallions
1 tablespoon finely shredded
  gingerroot
2 teaspoons finely sliced
  garlic

Scallop Sauce

8 tablespoons chicken broth
2 tablespoons rice wine
1 teaspoon salt
½ teaspoon sugar
1½ teaspoons sesame oil
¼ teaspoon freshly ground
  white pepper
1½ teaspoons cornstarch

STIR-FRIED SCALLOPS WITH BROCCOLI

BI LU XIAN BEI 碧綠鮮貝

This stir-fried platter illustrates the delicate seasonings and crisp textures that give Cantonese cuisine its great reputation. High heat and a short cooking time are essential to the success of this dish.

1   Rinse the scallops lightly and drain. Holding the knife blade parallel to the cutting surface, slice each scallop in half through the thickness, as shown on page 201. Place the scallops in a mixing bowl. Pinch the gingerroot and the scallions in the **scallop marinade** repeatedly for several minutes to impart their flavors to the rice wine. Add the marinade to the scallops, toss lightly, and let marinate for 20 minutes. Discard the scallions and gingerroot.
2   Peel the tough outer skin from the broccoli and separate the flowerets. Roll-cut the stems into 1-inch pieces. Heat 1½ quarts of salted water until boiling. Add the stem pieces and cook for ½ minute. Add the flowerets and cook for 2½ minutes, or until both stems and flowerets are just tender. Refresh immediately in cold water. Drain thoroughly.
3   Heat 2 quarts of water until boiling. Add the scallops and cook them for 30 seconds, until they change color. Drain thoroughly.
4   Heat a wok, add the oil, and heat until very hot. Add the **scallop seasonings** and stir-fry for about 10 seconds over high heat. Add the **scallop sauce** and cook, stirring constantly, until it thickens. Add the broccoli and scallops. Toss lightly to coat with the sauce and transfer the mixture to a platter. Serve immediately.

SCALLOPS IN OYSTER SAUCE

HAO YOU XIAN BEI　　蠔油鮮貝

The fragrant seasonings of scallion and gingerroot accentuate the sweet flavor of fresh scallops. Add a light coating of oyster sauce and the result is a unique blending of flavors.

1　Rinse the scallops lightly and drain thoroughly. Holding the knife blade parallel to the cutting surface, slice each scallop in half through the thickness, as shown. Place the scallops in a bowl. Pinch the gingerroot in the **scallop marinade** repeatedly for several minutes to impart the flavor to the rice wine. Add the marinade to the scallops, toss lightly, and let marinate for 20 minutes. Discard the gingerroot slices. Prepare the **shredded seasonings** and place them in ice water to cover for 20 minutes. Drain the shredded seasonings and place them on a platter.

2　Heat a wok, add the 6 cups of water and the rice wine, and heat until boiling. Add the scallops and poach for about 30 seconds, until barely cooked. Remove the scallops with a slotted spoon and arrange them over the shredded seasonings. Remove the liquid from the wok.

3　Reheat the wok, add the **oyster sauce**, and heat until boiling. Cook for about 1 minute, until slightly thickened. Pour the sauce over the scallops, toss lightly, and serve.

SIX SERVINGS

2 pounds fresh scallops

Scallop Marinade
2 tablespoons rice wine
2 slices gingerroot, smashed with the flat side of a cleaver
½ teaspoon salt

Shredded Seasonings
3 tablespoons finely shredded gingerroot
3 tablespoons finely shredded scallions

6 cups water
2 tablespoons rice wine

Oyster Sauce
3 tablespoons oyster sauce
2 tablespoons soy sauce
2 tablespoons rice wine
2 teaspoons sugar
1½ teaspoons sesame oil
¼ cup water

PARALLEL-CUTTING
A SCALLOP

3 pints freshly shucked
   oysters

Oyster Marinade
1 tablespoon rice wine
2 slices gingerroot, smashed
   with the flat side of a
   cleaver

2 English ("gourmet
   seedless") cucumbers
2 tablespoons peanut,
   safflower, or corn oil

Minced Seasonings
1 tablespoon minced
   gingerroot
2 tablespoons minced
   scallions

2 13-ounce cans golden
   needle mushrooms,
   drained and blanched for
   10 seconds

Oyster Sauce
¼ cup chicken broth
1½ tablespoons rice wine
1 teaspoon salt
½ teaspoon sugar
¼ teaspoon white pepper
1 teaspoon sesame oil
1½ teaspoons cornstarch

STIR-FRIED OYSTERS WITH GOLDEN NEEDLE MUSHROOMS

JIN GU SHENG HAO   金菇生蠔

A contrast of flavors, textures, and colors is essential to any respectable Chinese dish. When judged on these counts, this dish certainly wouldn't be found lacking. The plump oysters, poached to perfection, are superbly complemented by the crisp cucumber slices and golden needle mushrooms. Golden needle, or *enoki*, mushrooms are available in cans at all Chinese markets. They are also sold fresh in season at some produce stands and supermarkets.

1   Rinse the oysters carefully in a colander to remove any bits of shell. Drain thoroughly and place the oysters in a bowl. Pinch the gingerroot slices in the rice wine repeatedly for several minutes to impart their flavor. Add the **oyster marinade** to the oysters, toss lightly, and let marinate for 20 minutes. Discard the gingerroot.
2   Cut the cucumbers in half lengthwise and remove the seeds. Cut each half crosswise into 2-inch lengths. Cut each piece lengthwise into paper-thin slices.
3   Heat 2 quarts of water until boiling and add the oysters. Blanch the oysters for 10 seconds, until the edges just begin to curl. Drain thoroughly.
4   Heat a wok, add the oil, and heat the oil until very hot. Add the **minced seasonings** and stir-fry over high heat for about 10 seconds, until fragrant. Add the cucumber slices and the golden needle mushrooms and stir-fry for about 15 seconds, until heated through. Add the **oyster sauce** and heat until the sauce starts to thicken. Add the cooked oysters, toss lightly, and transfer the mixture to a platter. Serve immediately.

FRIED OYSTER ROLLS

ZHA SHENG HAO 炸 生 蠔

Fresh oysters are greatly relished in the province of Fujian. There the plumpest and freshest are dipped in batter and deep-fried until golden brown. Equally popular is a coating of bread crumbs, which, to my mind, tends to be lighter and more delicate than the flour-egg batter. Serve these delectable rolls as an hors d'oeuvre.

1   Carefully rinse the oysters in a colander to remove any bits of shell. Drain thoroughly and place the oysters in a bowl. Pinch the gingerroot and the scallions in the rice wine repeatedly for several minutes to impart their flavors. Add the **oyster marinade** to the oysters, toss lightly, and let marinate for 20 minutes. Discard the gingerroot and scallions. Soak the skewers in water to cover for 1 hour. Heat the **dipping sauce** until thick, and transfer to a serving bowl.

2   Heat 2 quarts of water until boiling and add the oysters. Blanch the oysters for 10 seconds, until the edges just begin to curl. Drain thoroughly. Carefully thread the oysters onto the skewers, distributing them evenly among the skewers.

3   Dredge the oysters in the **oyster coating**, making certain that they are completely covered. Dip the oysters in the eggs and then dredge in the bread crumbs, once again making certain that all sides are covered. Lightly press the oysters to make sure the bread crumbs adhere.

4   Heat a wok, add the oil, and heat the oil to 375°. Add half the oyster rolls and deep-fry for about 5 minutes, until the rolls are golden brown and crisp. Remove and drain on absorbent paper. Reheat the oil and deep-fry the remaining oyster rolls in the same manner. Arrange the rolls on a platter and serve immediately with the dipping sauce.

SIX SERVINGS

2 pints freshly shucked oysters

Oyster Marinade
1 tablespoon rice wine
2 scallions, smashed with the flat side of a cleaver
2 slices gingerroot, smashed with the flat side of a cleaver

12 10-inch bamboo skewers

Dipping Sauce
1 tablespoon ketchup
1 tablespoon soy sauce
2 teaspoons Chinese black vinegar
1 tablespoon sugar
1 teaspoon sesame oil
1 tablespoon minced garlic
2 teaspoons minced gingerroot
¼ cup water
1½ teaspoons cornstarch

Oyster Coating
1 cup cornstarch
1 teaspoon salt
¼ teaspoon freshly ground black pepper

2 eggs, lightly beaten
4 cups bread crumbs
10 cups peanut, safflower, or corn oil

1 pound cleaned fresh squid meat (buy about 1⅓ pounds of squid to obtain this amount)
½ pound raw shrimp, shelled

Seafood Marinade

1 tablespoon rice wine
1 teaspoon salt
½ teaspoon sesame oil
1 teaspoon cornstarch

½ pound boneless center-cut pork loin

Pork Marinade

2 teaspoons soy sauce
1 teaspoon rice wine
½ teaspoon sesame oil
1 teaspoon cornstarch
2 teaspoons water

8 dried Chinese black mushrooms
3 cups peanut, safflower, or corn oil

Minced Seasonings

2 tablespoons minced scallions
1 tablespoon minced gingerroot

1 cup thinly sliced water chestnuts, plunged briefly into boiling water and refreshed

THREE TREASURES OVER SIZZLING RICE

SAN XIAN GUO BA　　三鲜锅巴

The most familiar version of "sizzling rice," a popular Sichuanese specialty, is made with shrimp and snow peas in a light sweet-and-sour sauce. There are, however, countless variations of this dish made with an assortment of seafood, meat, and vegetable garnishes; this is one of them. Sea scallops cut in half through the thickness may be substituted for the squid.

1　Clean the squid. Make a lengthwise cut in a body sac to open it up and form a flat piece. Rinse lightly and drain. Holding the cleaver at a 45° angle to the squid, on the inside surface (not the skin side) make deep scores at ⅙-inch intervals lengthwise across the body sac. (The scores should be deep, but be careful not to cut through to the other side.) Turn the squid and make scores at ⅙-inch intervals perpendicular to the first scores, to create a diamond pattern. Repeat for all the body sacs. Score the back flaps in the same manner. Cut the squid into 1-inch squares and place the pieces in a bowl. Separate the tentacles and add them to the bowl. Score each shrimp along the back and remove the vein; the scoring will allow the shrimp to "butterfly" when it is cooked. Rinse all the shrimp and drain thoroughly. Place the shrimp in the bowl with the squid, add the **seafood marinade**, toss lightly, and let marinate for 20 minutes. Discard the gingerroot.
2　Remove any fat or gristle from the pork loin and discard. Cut the meat, across the grain, into slices ⅛ inch thick. Cut the slices into pieces 1½ inches long and 1 inch wide. Place the pieces in a bowl, add the **pork marinade**, toss lightly, and let marinate for 20 minutes. Soften the dried mushrooms for 20 minutes in hot water to cover. Remove and discard the stems, and cut the caps in half.
3　Heat a wok, add 1 cup of oil, and heat until very hot, about 400°. Add the squid and shrimp, toss lightly until both change color (about 1 minute), remove with a handled strainer, and drain. Reheat the oil, add the pork slices, stir-fry until the meat changes color, remove, and drain. Remove the oil from the wok, reserving 2 tablespoons.

4 Reheat the wok, or heat a casserole, add the 2 tablespoons of oil, and heat until very hot. Add the **minced seasonings** and stir-fry for about 10 seconds, until fragrant. Add the mushroom caps and water chestnuts. Toss over high heat for about 1 minute. Add the **three-treasure sauce** and heat until it starts to thicken. Add the snow peas, pork loin, shrimp, and squid. Stir, and turn the heat to low.

5 Heat a wok, add the remaining 2 cups of oil, and heat it to 400°. Add the rice cakes, a few at a time, and deep-fry, stirring constantly, until they puff up and become golden. Transfer the cakes to a deep platter. Pour the seafood mixture over the rice cakes; the combination of the hot oil from the rice cakes and the seafood sauce will produce a sizzling sound. Serve immediately.

Three-Treasure Sauce
2½ cups chicken broth
2½ tablespoons soy sauce
½ teaspoon salt
1 tablespoon rice wine
½ teaspoon sugar
¼ teaspoon black pepper
1 tablespoon cornstarch

1 cup snow peas, ends trimmed and veiny strings removed
12 sizzling rice cakes, about 3 inches square (page 36)

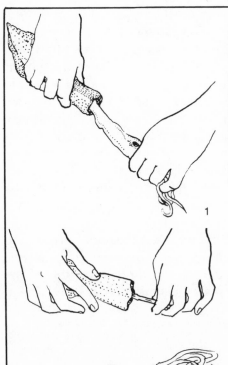

HOW TO CLEAN SQUID

1 Pull the head and body apart. Cut off the tentacles just below the eyes, reserving the tentacles and body sac.
2 Remove and discard the transparent quill from the inside of the body sac.
3 Gently pull the back flaps from the body sac and reserve them. Peel off and discard the purple membrane covering the body sac and the back flaps.
4 Slice the squid body lengthwise and use as directed.

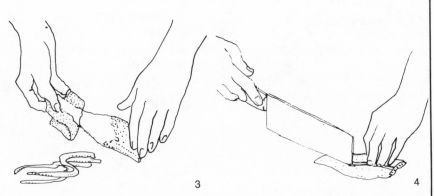

1½ pounds cleaned fresh
squid meat (buy about 2
pounds of squid to obtain
this amount)

Squid Marinade
2 tablespoons rice wine
2 slices gingerroot, smashed
with the flat side of a
cleaver
1 teaspoon salt

3 English ("gourmet
seedless") cucumbers
1½ teaspoons salt
1½ teaspoons sesame oil

Squid Dressing
¼ cup soy sauce
1 tablespoon sugar
1 tablespoon clear rice
vinegar
1½ tablespoons sesame oil
2 teaspoons minced
gingerroot
1 tablespoon minced
scallions
2 teaspoons chili oil or chili
paste

SPICY SQUID FLOWERS

HONG YOU YU HUA 紅油魷花

Squid is a seafood frequently overlooked by many Americans, but it is a popular delicacy with the Chinese. Chefs use their cleavers to score the meat into myriad shapes. Once blanched, the pieces are transformed into delicate designs.

1   Make a lengthwise cut in a body sac of the squid to open it up and form a flat piece. Rinse lightly and drain. Holding the cleaver at a 45° angle to the squid, on the inside surface (not the skin side) make deep scores at ⅙-inch intervals lengthwise across the body sac. (The scores should be deep, but be careful not to cut through to the other side.) Turn the squid and make scores at ⅙-inch intervals perpendicular to the first scores, to create a diamond pattern. Repeat for all the body sacs. Score the back flaps in the same manner. Cut the squid into 1-inch squares and place the pieces in a bowl. Separate the tentacles and add them to the bowl. Pinch the gingerroot slices in the **squid marinade** repeatedly for several minutes to impart the ginger flavor to the rice wine. Add the marinade to the squid, toss lightly, and let marinate for 20 minutes. Discard the gingerroot. Cut the cucumbers in half lengthwise. Remove the seeds and cut each half crosswise into 2-inch pieces. Cut each piece lengthwise into paper-thin slices and place them in a mixing bowl. Add the salt, toss lightly, and let sit for 20 minutes. Drain the cucumbers, pat dry, toss with the sesame oil, and arrange in a mound on a platter.
2   Heat 3 quarts of water until boiling. Add the squid pieces and cook for about 1 minute, until the pieces "blossom" into flowers and change color. Drain thoroughly, and arrange on top of the cucumbers. Just before serving, pour the **squid dressing** on top and toss lightly.

STIR-FRIED SQUID WITH HOT RED PEPPERS

GONG BAO YOU YU JUAN　宮保鮏魚捲

In the Orient, whole squid are treated and dried until they look something like leather. This preserves them beautifully, but the flavor becomes extremely fishy. Though the Chinese use dried squid in this recipe, I prefer the fresh variety; the spicy sauce highlights the sweet flavor of the fresh meat.

1　Make a lengthwise cut in a body sac of the squid to open it up and form a flat piece. Rinse lightly and drain. Holding the cleaver at a 45° angle to the squid, on the inside surface (not the skin side) make deep scores at 1/6-inch intervals lengthwise across the body sac. (The scores should be deep, but be careful not to cut through to the other side.) Turn the squid and make scores at 1/6-inch intervals perpendicular to the first scores, to create a diamond pattern. Repeat for all the body sacs. Score the back flaps in the same manner. Cut the squid into 1-inch squares and place the pieces in a bowl. Separate the tentacles and add them to the bowl. Pinch the gingerroot slices in the **squid marinade** repeatedly for several minutes to impart the flavor to the rice wine. Add the marinade, toss lightly, and let marinate for 20 minutes. Discard the gingerroot. Cut the dried chili peppers into 1-inch pieces and shake out the seeds.
2　Heat 3 quarts of water until boiling. Add the squid pieces and cook for about 1 minute, until they change color and "blossom" into flowers. Drain thoroughly.
3　Heat a wok, add the oil, and heat until very hot. Add the chili peppers and stir-fry over high heat for about 30 seconds, until they turn black. Add the minced garlic and stir-fry for about 10 seconds. Add the **squid sauce** and stir-fry until it begins to thicken. Add the cooked squid pieces, toss lightly to coat with the sauce, and transfer the mixture to a platter. Serve immediately.

SIX SERVINGS

1½ pounds cleaned fresh squid meat (buy about 2 pounds of squid to obtain this amount)

Squid Marinade
2 tablespoons rice wine
3 slices gingerroot, smashed with the flat side of a cleaver
1 teaspoon salt
1 teaspoon cornstarch

10 dried chili peppers
3 tablespoons peanut, safflower, or corn oil
2 teaspoons minced garlic

Squid Sauce
¼ cup soy sauce
2 tablespoons rice wine
2 tablespoons sugar
1 tablespoon Chinese black vinegar
1½ teaspoons sesame oil
1 teaspoon cornstarch
¼ cup chicken broth or water

2 pounds cleaned fresh
   squid meat, body sacs only
   (buy about 2½ pounds of
   squid)
1 tablespoon minced pork
   fat

Squid Seasonings
2 teaspoons rice wine
1 teaspoon salt
2 egg whites, lightly beaten
1 teaspoon finely minced
   gingerroot
2 tablespoons cornstarch

10 Sichuan peppercorns
1 tablespoon salt
6 cups peanut, safflower, or
   corn oil

DEEP-FRIED SQUID BALLS

ZHA MO YU WAN　　炸墨魚丸

The innovativeness of Chinese cooking is clearly demonstrated in
this dish. The squid meat is pounded into a paste, shaped into balls,
and deep-fried. The resulting product is slightly crisp and bursting
with the sweet freshness of the squid meat. This Taiwanese specialty
is ideally served as an hors d'oeuvre.

1 Rinse the body sacs lightly. Pat dry, removing as much excess
moisture as possible. Using a blender or a food processor fitted with
the steel blade, chop the squid meat to a smooth paste. (Or chop it
by hand with a meat mallet.) Place the paste and pork fat in a mixing
bowl. Slowly add the **squid seasonings** to the squid paste, mixing
vigorously and continuously in one direction for 5 minutes. Refrigerate for 1 hour.
2 To make the Sichuan-peppercorn salt, toast the Sichuan peppercorns in a dry skillet over low heat for 5 minutes, until they are
fragrant and golden. Pulverize the peppercorns in a blender. Stir the
powder into the salt and transfer the mixture to a small serving dish.
3 Heat a wok, add the oil, and heat the oil to 375°. Turn the heat
to low. Dip your hands in water to prevent the squid paste from
sticking. Shape the paste into balls ½ inch in diameter. Add a third
of the balls to the oil and turn the heat to high. Deep-fry the balls,
turning constantly, for 3½ minutes, or until golden and cooked
through. Remove with a handled strainer, and drain on absorbent
paper. Reheat the oil and deep-fry the remaining balls in the same
manner, reheating the oil between batches. Arrange the fried squid
balls on a platter and serve immediately with the Sichuan-
peppercorn salt.

STIR-FRIED ABALONE WITH BLACK MUSHROOMS IN OYSTER SAUCE

HAO YOU BAO YU　　蠔油鮑魚

Abalone is a delicacy much admired by Chinese chefs for its distinctly chewy texture. In this dish that texture is contrasted with the spongy richness of Chinese black mushrooms and oyster sauce.

1   Drain the abalone and remove any hard outer edges. Cut the abalone into paper-thin slices and blanch the slices for 10 seconds in boiling water. Drain thoroughly. Soften the dried mushrooms for 20 minutes in hot water to cover. Remove and discard the stems; cut any large caps in half. Trim away any reedy tips. Cut out V-shaped wedges around the edge of each cap to form a decorative pattern. Trim the bamboo shoot to a V-shaped wedge and cut it into thin slices.

2   Rinse the lettuce, drain, and trim away any hard stems. Heat a wok, add 1 tablespoon of oil, and heat until smoking. Add the lettuce leaves and the **vegetable seasonings**. Stir-fry lightly over high heat until the lettuce is just wilted. Arrange the lettuce around the outer edge of a platter.

3   Reheat the wok, add the remaining 2 tablespoons of oil, and heat until very hot. Add the **minced seasonings** and stir-fry for about 10 seconds, until fragrant. Add the mushrooms and stir-fry for about 5 seconds; then add the **abalone sauce**. Stir-fry, turning constantly, until the sauce thickens; then add the bamboo shoot and abalone slices. Toss lightly to coat with the sauce and transfer the mixture to the center of the platter. Serve immediately.

SIX SERVINGS

A 1-pound can of abalone
10 dried Chinese black
　　mushrooms
1 whole canned bamboo
　　shoot, plunged briefly into
　　boiling water, refreshed,
　　and drained
1 pound leafy lettuce
3 tablespoons peanut,
　　safflower, or corn oil

Vegetable Seasonings
½ tablespoon chicken broth
½ teaspoon salt
½ teaspoon sesame oil

Minced Seasonings
1 tablespoon minced
　　gingerroot
2 tablespoons minced
　　scallions

Abalone Sauce
½ cup chicken broth
1½ tablespoons oyster sauce
1 tablespoon soy sauce
1 tablespoon rice wine
1½ teaspoons sugar
1 teaspoon sesame oil
1½ teaspoons cornstarch

1 whole roasting chicken,
about 4½ pounds

Chicken Marinade

2 tablespoons soy sauce
2 scallions, smashed with the
flat side of a cleaver
2 slices gingerroot, smashed
with the flat side of a
cleaver
1 tablespoon rice wine

Chicken Braising Mixture

4 cups chicken broth
3 tablespoons soy sauce
1½ tablespoons rice wine
1 teaspoon sugar

4 cups peanut, safflower, or
corn oil
2 ounces shark's fin needles
(see next page)

Chicken Seasonings

4 Chinese dried black
mushrooms, softened in
hot water to cover, stems
removed, and caps
shredded
4 tablespoons finely
shredded Chinese ham,
Smithfield ham, or
prosciutto
2 tablespoons finely
shredded scallions
1 tablespoon finely shredded
gingerroot

BRAISED CHICKEN WITH SHARK'S FIN

YU CHI SHAO JI　　　魚翅燒雞

Dried shark's fin is available in Chinese grocery stores in two forms — the whole fin or just the gelatinous needles. This eastern dish, which uses the needles, is a delightful departure from the usual Cantonese rendition of shark's fin.

1　Remove and discard any fat from the cavity and neck of the chicken. Rinse the chicken lightly and place it in a bowl. Rub the **chicken marinade** all over the chicken and inside the cavity. Let marinate for 1 hour. Drain the chicken, discard the scallions and gingerroot, and add the liquid to the **chicken braising mixture**.

2　Heat a wok, add the oil, and heat the oil to 400°. Slowly lower the chicken into the hot oil and deep-fry on both sides, over high heat, until golden brown. (Ladle hot oil over the chicken as it is frying.) Remove and drain. Remove the oil from the wok.

3　Place the chicken and the braising mixture in a heavy casserole or a Dutch oven. Heat the mixture until boiling. Reduce the heat to low, cover, and cook for 45 minutes. Add the shark's fin needles and the **chicken seasonings**. Continue cooking, covered, for 30 minutes. Remove the chicken, let it cool slightly, and cut it, through the bones, into bite-size serving pieces, as for red-cooked chicken (page 151). Arrange the pieces on a platter.

4　Heat the braising mixture until boiling and slowly add the **thickener**, stirring constantly to prevent lumps. Add the Chinese black vinegar and the shredded bamboo shoots. Toss lightly, and pour the mixture over the chicken pieces. Serve immediately.

Thickener
1½ tablespoons cornstarch
3 tablespoons water

1½ teaspoons Chinese black
vinegar

½ cup bamboo shoots,
plunged briefly into
boiling water, refreshed,
and cut into matchstick-
size shreds

TO PREPARE SHARK'S FIN NEEDLES:

1   Place the shark's fin needles in a pan with cold water to cover. Add 2 tablespoons rice wine, 2 scallions smashed with the flat side of a cleaver, and 2 gingerroot slices smashed with the flat side of a cleaver. Heat the mixture until just below the boiling point, turn the heat to low, and let simmer for ½ hour.

2   Remove the pan from the heat and let cool to room temperature. Rinse the shark's fin needles, discarding the gingerroot and scallion. Repeat step 1 in its entirety. Let cool to room temperature.

3   Discard the liquid, scallions, and gingerroot and rinse the shark's fin needles lightly.

---

6 dried sea cucumbers
(*bêche-de-mer*)

Preconditioning Seasonings
2 tablespoons rice wine
4 scallions, smashed with the
flat side of a cleaver
4 slices gingerroot, smashed
with the flat side of a
cleaver

2 tablespoons peanut,
safflower, or corn oil

Sea Cucumber Seasonings
2 tablespoons shredded
scallions
2 tablespoons shredded
gingerroot
8 dried Chinese black
mushrooms, softened,
stems removed, and caps
quartered

Sea Cucumber Sauce
1½ cups chicken broth
6 tablespoons soy sauce
1 tablespoon rice wine
2 teaspoons sugar

Thickener
1 tablespoon cornstarch
2 tablespoons water

1 teaspoon sesame oil

BRAISED SEA CUCUMBERS WITH CHINESE BLACK MUSHROOMS

DONG GU HAI SHEN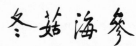

Although many Americans may balk at the idea of eating sea cucumbers, for the Chinese they are a treat reserved for only the most special occasions.

1   Place the sea cucumbers in a heavy soup pot with cold water to cover and add the **preconditioning seasonings**. Let them soak for 12 hours in the refrigerator. Place the pot over high heat and bring the liquid to a boil. Reduce the heat to low and let simmer for 1½ hours. Remove the pot from the heat and let the water cool to room temperature. Drain the sea cucumbers and make a cut lengthwise in each one along the flat side. Remove the entrails and scrape out the insides. Place the sea cucumbers in cold water to cover and let them soak for another 12 hours in the refrigerator. Cut each sea cucumber crosswise into thirds.
2   Heat a wok, add the oil, and heat until very hot. Add the **sea cucumber seasonings** and stir-fry over high heat for about 10 seconds, until fragrant. Add the **sea cucumber sauce** and heat until boiling. Add the sea cucumber pieces and heat until the mixture begins to boil. Reduce the heat to low, partially cover, and cook for about 20 minutes. Uncover, and turn the heat to high. Slowly add the **thickener**, stirring constantly to prevent lumps. Add the sesame oil, toss lightly, and transfer the mixture to a platter. Serve immediately.

PORK 猪肉類

The Chinese pork butcher in our small neighborhood market in Taipei was a jovial fellow given to regaling his favorite customers with witty anecdotes, but when it came time to do business, his mood immediately turned sober; he took his meat very seriously. Every morning at six, he would arrive at his humble stand with two massive sides of freshly slaughtered pig slung over his Vespa scooter. His first order of business was to hang the carcasses from the meat racks positioned on the side of his concession.

After scrubbing down the counter and rinsing off his cleaver and knife, he would begin to cut up the meat. Working methodically and with the confidence of a man who knows his business, he would divide the pig into loin, shoulder, leg, belly, and feet. The innards — liver, intestines, and kidney — would be cleaned and hung up for sale. The next twenty minutes would be devoted to arranging the cuts of meat to display their finest features; the importance of this procedure was evident as he painstakingly positioned each piece of meat until he was satisfied with its appearance. Although he was one of many butchers selling pork in the marketplace, his meat always stood out for its high quality and attractive arrangement. No meat would be sold until the daily routine had been completed.

The pig — or "long-nosed general," as it is sometimes affectionately called — was among the first animals domesticated in China. Raising pigs appears to have been a widespread practice; excavations of an ancient Chinese village dating back to 2000 B.C. have uncovered evidence of pig remains in most dwellings.

Whereas beef is the most popular meat in the Western diet, pork has assumed this role for the Chinese. So prominent is pork, in fact, that the Chinese word for meat can also be used to mean pork. During the T'ang dynasty (618 to 907) pork was prepared in a number of ways: A tart, rich porridge of pig, chicken, goat, deer, and seasonings was very popular. Wild boar and dried and pickled pork were savory companions to rice. Overconsumption of pork and meat was frowned upon, however, by the T'ang pharmacologists.

213

Marco Polo attested to the fondness for pork among the southern Chinese during the Sung dynasty (960 to 1279). After observing the volume of this meat sold daily in the market of Hangzhou, he recorded, "Each day each shop hangs sides of pork — not less than ten sides. In two holidays of wintertime, each shop sells tens of sides daily." The popularity of pork was not restricted to the gentry; the lower classes also ate much pork, and particularly savored the lung, kidneys, liver, and heart.

The pig has served a crucial role of religious significance as a sacrificial offering. Meat and fish historically have been the main ingredients of feast and ritual dishes, but the presentation of a whole pig was an honor reserved for the most revered deities. A roast pig was offered annually in the celebration of *Ching-ming,* the Festival of the Dead.

The symbolic significance of the pig is equally notable. It is the last animal of the Twelve Terrestrial Branches, corresponding to the astrological sign of Pisces. The wild boar symbolizes the wealth of the forest.

The popularity of the pig continues to the present day. The reasons are obvious: The meat is highly versatile and reasonably priced, and the subtle flavor complements many ingredients. The pig is easily raised on little feed — often scraps — and in turn produces a meat rich in vitamins and minerals.

The Chinese allow no waste. Every part of the pig's anatomy is utilized. The meat may be stir-fried; deep-fried; steamed; braised; red-cooked; white-cooked; ground and used in fillings and sau-

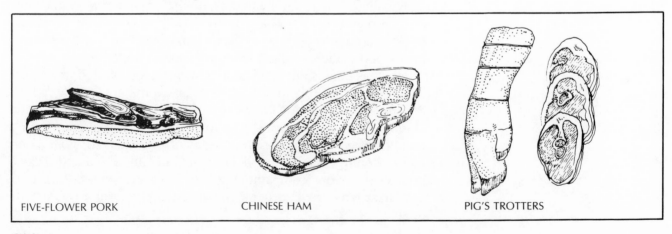

FIVE-FLOWER PORK   CHINESE HAM   PIG'S TROTTERS

sages; or dried and salted, producing a popular garnish for rice. The feet are red-cooked, stewed, braised, chilled in aspic, pickled in vinegar, or cooked in soups. The kidney and liver are stir-fried, simmered, deep-fried, or cooked in soups. Pig's ear, a celebrated Chinese delicacy, is cooked, shredded, and served cold with a spicy dressing. Even the brain is cooked — deep-fried in a batter, fritter-style.

Perhaps one of the simplest yet most classic pork recipes is Tung-po pork, a braised meat dish invented by the celebrated Chinese poet Su Tung-po. He immortalized the dish in a poem titled "Eating Pork":

Huang Chou produces good pork
Which is cheap as dirt
The rich spurn and won't eat it.
The poor know not how to cook it.
Keep the fire low,
Use very little water,
Give it plenty of water to get tender
I take a bowl of pork first thing in the morning
I like it this way — mind your own business!

STANDARD AMERICAN CUTS OF PORK AND THEIR APPROPRIATE CHINESE COOKING METHODS

SECTION	CUT OF MEAT	SUITABLE COOKING METHOD
Shoulder	blade, Boston roast, pork butt, Boston butt	red-cook, simmer, braise, grind for filling and sausage
	picnic shoulder	red-cook, simmer, braise, white-cook, grind for filling and sausage, preserve by salting and drying
Loin	chops, roasts, tenderloin	stir-fry, deep-fry, braise, steam, barbecue, grind for filling and sausage
	ribs	deep-fry, steam, braise, simmer, cook in soups, barbecue
	fatback	add to filling for flavor and body, render to a cooking oil
Belly	fresh bacon ("five-flower pork")	red-cook, braise, simmer, steam, deep-fry, roast, preserve by salting and drying
Pork Leg	fresh ham	stir-fry, steam, braise, red-cook, simmer, deep-fry, grind for filling
	center roast, sirloin	simmer, red-cook, steam, white-cook, grind for filling, cure to make Chinese ham
	shank	red-cook, steam, white-cook, preserve by salting and drying
Feet	hocks and trotters	red-cook, braise, simmer, white-cook, cook in soups

PORK SLICES WITH GARLIC SAUCE

SUAN NI BAI ROU 蒜泥白肉

There are many parallels in French and Chinese cooking methods. One example is white-cooking, used in this recipe. This process is almost identical to the French practice of *cuire à blanc*. The cooked meat maintains its original color and provides an attractive contrast to the dark, pungent sauce. The meat is traditionally sliced for serving with a generous border of fat, lending a richness that most Chinese savor.

1   Rinse the ham and drain. Place the **white-cooking liquid** in a pot. Add the meat and heat the mixture until boiling. Reduce the heat to low and simmer, uncovered, for 1 hour, turning the meat from time to time. Remove the meat and let it cool to room temperature. Add the 2 tablespoons of white-cooking liquid to the **garlic sauce.**
2   Cut the meat, across the grain, into paper-thin slices. If possible, there should be a border of fat on each slice. Blanch each slice quickly in boiling water and arrange the meat slices in an overlapping circular pattern on the plate. Before serving, pour the garlic sauce on top. Garnish with sprigs of coriander, if desired, and serve.

SIX SERVINGS

1½ pounds fresh ham or center-cut pork loin, with a thin border of fat

White-Cooking Liquid
3 slices gingerroot, smashed with the flat side of a cleaver
3 scallions, smashed with the flat side of a cleaver
3 tablespoons rice wine
2 quarts water

Garlic Sauce
3 tablespoons soy sauce
1 tablespoon minced garlic chopped into a smooth paste
1½ teaspoons sugar
2 teaspoons sesame oil
2 teaspoons chili oil or chili paste
2 tablespoons white-cooking liquid

1½ pounds boneless
   center-cut pork loin

Pork Marinade
1½ tablespoons soy sauce
1½ tablespoons rice wine
1 teaspoon sesame oil
1 tablespoon cornstarch
2 tablespoons water

10 dried wood ears, softened
   in hot water to cover for
   20 minutes
2 cups peanut, safflower, or
   corn oil

Minced Seasonings
3 tablespoons minced
   scallions
2 tablespoons minced
   gingerroot
2 tablespoons minced garlic

2 teaspoons chili paste
2 cups sliced water
   chestnuts, plunged into
   boiling water for a few
   seconds and immediately
   refreshed

STIR-FRIED PORK WITH FISH-FLAVORED SAUCE

YU XIANG ROU SI 魚香肉絲

The so-called fish-flavored sauce in this dish is found in a number of Sichuanese platters, and it is equally delicious with eggplant, beef, or eggs. This classic version illustrates well the sensual qualities of Sichuan cuisine: The fiery seasonings sensitize the palate to the textures of the wood ears and water chestnuts.

1   Remove any fat or gristle from the pork loin and discard. Cut the meat, across the grain, into slices ⅛ inch thick. Cut the slices into matchstick-size shreds. Place the shreds in a bowl, add the **pork marinade,** toss lightly, and let marinate for 30 minutes. Cut away and discard the hard, bitter nib from the wood ears, and shred the wood ears.

2   Heat a wok, add the oil, and heat the oil to 400°. Add half the pork shreds and stir-fry over high heat, stirring constantly until the shreds change color. Remove with a handled strainer, and drain. Reheat the oil and stir-fry the remaining shreds in the same manner. Remove the oil from the wok, reserving 2 tablespoons.

3   Reheat the wok, add the 2 tablespoons of oil, and heat until very hot. Add the **minced seasonings** and stir-fry for about 10 seconds, until fragrant. Add the chili paste, stir-fry for about 5 seconds, and add the water chestnuts and the wood ears. Toss lightly over high heat for 20 seconds and add the **fish-flavored sauce.** Stir-fry until the sauce thickens, add the pork shreds, toss lightly to coat with the sauce, and transfer the mixture to a platter. Serve immediately.

Fish-Flavored Sauce
4 tablespoons soy sauce
2 tablespoons rice wine
1 tablespoon sugar
2 teaspoons Chinese black
   vinegar
1 teaspoon sesame oil
¼ teaspoon freshly ground
   black pepper
¼ cup water
2 teaspoons cornstarch

CHINESE-STYLE PORK STEAK

ZHONG SHI ZHU PAI 中式猪排

Although this dish might not be considered a classic Chinese platter, its delectable flavor has made it a contemporary favorite of many Chinese. The tart sauce provides an excellent contrast to the snowy grains of steamed rice.

1   Remove any fat or gristle from the pork loin and discard. Cut the meat, across the grain, into slices ¼ inch thick. Using the blunt edge of the cleaver, lightly pound the pork slices in a diamond pattern, to tenderize the meat. Cut the slices lengthwise in half and place them in a bowl. Add the **pork marinade,** toss lightly, and let marinate for at least 3 hours, or overnight in the refrigerator. Peel the onions and shred them lengthwise.

2   Heat a wok, add the oil, and heat until very hot, about 400°. Add half the pork slices, and fry on both sides until golden. Remove and drain. Reheat the oil. Add the remaining pork slices and fry in the same manner. Remove the oil from the wok, reserving 2 tablespoons.

3   Reheat the wok, add the 2 tablespoons of oil, and heat until very hot. Add the shredded onions and stir-fry over high heat, stirring constantly until soft and transparent. Add the **pork sauce** and toss lightly until the sauce has thickened a bit. Add the cooked pork slices, toss lightly to coat with the sauce, and transfer the mixture to a platter. Serve immediately over rice.

SIX SERVINGS

2 pounds boneless
  center-cut pork loin

Pork Marinade
1 tablespoon soy sauce
1 tablespoon rice wine
1 teaspoon sesame oil
2 teaspoons cornstarch
1 tablespoon water
2 teaspoons minced garlic

2 medium-sized onions
6 tablespoons peanut,
  safflower, or corn oil

Pork Sauce
6 tablespoons chicken broth
  or water
3 tablespoons soy sauce
3 tablespoons ketchup
1½ tablespoons Chinese
  black vinegar
1½ tablespoons sugar
½ teaspoon freshly ground
  black pepper
1 teaspoon cornstarch

219

1 pound boneless center-cut
pork loin

Pork Marinade

1 tablespoon soy sauce
1 tablespoon rice wine
1 teaspoon sesame oil
2 teaspoons cornstarch
1 tablespoon water

1 ounce bean threads
3 eggs, lightly beaten
½ cup peanut, safflower, or
corn oil
½ cup shredded (softened)
Chinese black mushroom
caps
1 cup shredded Chinese
cabbage (Napa)
1 cup shredded leeks or
scallion greens
3 cups bean sprouts, lightly
rinsed

Pork Sauce

3 tablespoons soy sauce
½ teaspoon salt
2 tablespoons rice wine
½ teaspoon sugar
¼ teaspoon freshly ground
black pepper
¼ cup chicken broth or
water
1½ teaspoons cornstarch

STIR-FRIED VEGETABLES AND PORK WITH EGG CAP

HE CAI DAI MAO

This dish typifies the mild flavors and delicate seasoning often used in the north. Since wheat is a major staple crop in northern China, meat and vegetable dishes there are commonly served with steamed bread or pancakes, instead of rice. This one is served with Mandarin pancakes (page 61) and sweet bean sauce or hoisin sauce.

1   Remove any fat or gristle from the pork loin and discard. Cut the meat, across the grain, into slices ⅛ inch thick. Cut the slices into matchstick-size shreds. Place them in a bowl, add the **pork marinade,** toss lightly, and let marinate for 20 minutes. Soften the bean threads in hot water for 10 minutes; then cut into 6-inch lengths.
2   Rub the surface of a well-seasoned wok or an omelet pan with an oil-soaked cloth or paper towel and heat until a few drops of water sprinkled on the surface evaporate immediately. Add the beaten eggs and tilt the pan so that the eggs form a thin pancake about 8 inches in diameter. Cook the pancake (egg cap) over medium heat until golden and set. Flip it over and cook briefly on the other side. Remove and set aside.
3   Heat a wok, add the oil, and heat until very hot. Add the pork shreds and stir-fry until they change color, about 1 minute. Remove and drain. Remove the oil from the wok, reserving 3 tablespoons.
4   Reheat the wok, add the 3 tablespoons of oil, and heat until very hot. Add the black mushrooms and stir-fry for about 10 seconds, until fragrant. Add the cabbage and the leeks or scallions. Toss lightly over high heat for 1 minute. Add the softened bean threads, the cooked pork, and the bean sprouts, and cook for 1 minute. Add the **pork sauce** and stir-fry over high heat until the sauce is thick. Transfer the mixture to a platter. Place the egg cap on top, completely covering the stir-fried mixture. Serve with scallion brushes, sweet bean sauce, and Mandarin pancakes. Each person spreads some sweet bean sauce on a Mandarin pancake with a scallion brush, puts some of the stir-fried mixture on top, rolls up the pancake, and eats.

SHREDDED PORK WITH SWEET BEAN SAUCE

JING JIANG ROU SI

京醬肉絲

This flavorful stir-fried platter illustrates well the subtle seasoning that makes northern Chinese cuisine so popular. The saucy richness of the sweet bean sauce contrasts beautifully with the shredded scallions and steamed Mandarin pancakes (page 61).

1   Remove any fat or gristle from the pork loin and discard. Cut the meat, across the grain, into slices 1/8 inch thick. Cut the slices into matchstick-size shreds. Place the shreds in a bowl, add the **pork marinade,** toss lightly, and let marinate for 20 minutes.
2   Heat a wok, add the oil, and heat the oil to 400°. Add half the pork shreds and stir-fry over high heat, turning constantly until the shreds change color. Remove with a handled strainer, and drain. Reheat the oil, and stir-fry the remaining pork in the same manner.
3   Drain the scallion shreds and arrange them in a mound on a platter. Heat the wok, and add the **pork sauce.** Stir-fry the sauce over high heat until it thickens. Add the cooked pork shreds, toss lightly, and place over the scallions on the platter. Toss lightly before serving with Mandarin pancakes.

SIX SERVINGS

2 pounds boneless
   center-cut pork loin

Pork Marinade
2 tablespoons soy sauce
1 tablespoon rice wine
3 tablespoons water
1 teaspoon sesame oil
1 teaspoon cornstarch

2 cups peanut, safflower, or
   corn oil
2 cups finely shredded
   scallions or leeks, placed
   in cold water to cover

Pork Sauce
1½ tablespoons sweet bean
   sauce
2 tablespoons soy sauce
1½ tablespoons rice wine
1½ tablespoons sugar
5 tablespoons water

1½ pounds boneless
   center-cut pork loin

Pork Marinade
2 tablespoons soy sauce
2 tablespoons rice wine
1 teaspoon salt
1½ teaspoons sugar
½ teaspoon five-spice
   powder
2 tablespoons minced
   scallions
2 teaspoons minced
   gingerroot

1½ cups cornstarch
3 whole eggs, lightly beaten
4 cups raw cashews, coarsely
   chopped
6 cups peanut, safflower, or
   corn oil

CASHEW-COATED PORK SLICES

YAO GUO ROU PIAN 腰果肉片

A traditional Chinese banquet begins with a period of drinking and toasting, and at this time several dishes are usually served. These dishes are often deep-fried ones, because the dry, crisp texture is complementary to wine. Cashew-coated pork slices are a good example of dishes in this category.

1 Remove any fat or gristle from the pork loin and discard. Cut the meat, across the grain, into slices ⅛ inch thick. Cut the slices into pieces that are approximately 2 inches square. Place the slices in a mixing bowl and add the **pork marinade.** Toss lightly and let marinate for at least 3 hours, or overnight in the refrigerator.

2 Dredge each pork slice in the cornstarch, dip in the beaten egg, and coat with the chopped cashews. (Drain each piece before dipping it into the cashews.) Lightly press the meat slices so that the cashews adhere to them. Arrange the meat slices on a tray and let them dry for 20 minutes.

3 Heat a wok, add the oil, and heat the oil to 375°. Add a third of the pork slices and deep-fry over high heat for about 2½ minutes, turning constantly until the meat is cooked and golden brown. Remove with a handled strainer, and drain on absorbent paper. Reheat the oil. Deep-fry the remaining slices in the same manner, reheating the oil between batches. Arrange the slices on a platter and serve immediately.

SWEET-AND-SOUR PORK

GU LU ROU　　咕 嚕 肉

Although sweet-and-sour pork often seems a cliché in Chinese cuisine, any collection of classical pork recipes would be incomplete without it. This version is a delicious contrast to the ersatz renditions one often finds in American Cantonese restaurants.

1　Remove any fat or gristle from the pork loin and discard. Cut the meat into 1-inch cubes. Place the cubes in a bowl, add the **pork marinade,** toss lightly, and let marinate for at least 1 hour. Roll-cut the green peppers into 1-inch pieces. Add the egg yolks to the pork cubes and stir to coat. Dredge the pork cubes in cornstarch, lightly squeezing each piece to make sure the cornstarch adheres. Place the cubes on a tray to air-dry for 1 hour.

2　Heat a wok, add the oil, and heat the oil to 400°. Add a third of the pork cubes and deep-fry over high heat for about 3 minutes, stirring constantly until the meat is cooked and golden. Remove with a handled strainer, and drain. Reheat the oil. Deep-fry the remaining pork in the same manner, reheating the oil between batches. Strain the oil to remove bits of cooked cornstarch. Reheat the oil to 425°. Add all the pork cubes and deep-fry for about 1 minute, turning constantly, until the cubes are crisp and golden brown. Remove, and drain thoroughly. Remove the oil from the wok, reserving 2 tablespoons.

3　Reheat the wok, add the 2 tablespoons of oil, and heat until very hot. Add the garlic and green peppers. Stir-fry for about 1 minute over high heat. Add the pickled carrots and the pineapple. Stir-fry for another minute and add the **sweet-and-sour sauce.** Heat the mixture, stirring constantly, until it begins to thicken. Add the fried pork cubes and toss lightly to coat with the sauce. Transfer the mixture to a platter and serve immediately.

To make the **pickled carrots:** Place the carrot pieces in a bowl and add the remaining ingredients. Toss lightly and marinate for 12 hours (or overnight) in the refrigerator. Toss the carrots occasionally, if possible.

SIX SERVINGS

2 pounds boneless pork loin

Pork Marinade

2 tablespoons rice wine
1½ tablespoons soy sauce
1 teaspoon sesame oil

2 green peppers, cored and
　seeded
2 egg yolks
2 cups cornstarch
8 cups peanut, safflower, or
　corn oil
1½ tablespoons minced
　garlic
2 cups pickled carrots (see
　below), drained
1 cup pineapple chunks

Sweet-and-Sour Sauce

⅔ cup water
4 tablespoons ketchup
3 tablespoons vinegar
3 tablespoons sugar
2 teaspoons soy sauce
1 teaspoon salt
½ teaspoon sesame oil
2 teaspoons cornstarch

Pickled Carrots

2 cups carrots roll-cut into
　1-inch pieces
3 tablespoons clear rice
　vinegar
3 tablespoons sugar
3 slices gingerroot, smashed
　with the flat side of a
　cleaver

1½ pounds boneless
center-cut pork loin

Pork Marinade

1 tablespoon soy sauce
2 teaspoons rice wine
1 teaspoon sesame oil
1 egg yolk
1½ tablespoons cornstarch

5 dried Chinese black
mushrooms

Mushroom Marinade

1 tablespoon soy sauce
1 teaspoon sesame oil

6 scallions, white part only
1 pound broccoli
½ cup cornstarch
6 cups peanut, safflower, or
corn oil

Minced Seasonings

2 tablespoons minced
scallions
1 tablespoon minced
gingerroot

STUFFED PORK ROLLS

BI LU YE JI JUAN　碧綠野雞捲

These golden-hued stuffed rolls are said to resemble chicken meat, which explains the term *ji juan* (chicken rolls) in the Chinese title. In my Chinese household, we often served this dish during Chinese New Year, since the rolls faintly resemble gold bars or ingots (foods that resemble gold or money are eaten at this time with the wish of achieving prosperity in the coming year).

1   Remove any fat or gristle from the pork loin and discard. Cut the meat, across the grain, into slices about ¼ inch thick. Using the blunt edge of the cleaver, lightly pound the pork slices in a diamond pattern to tenderize the meat. Cut the slices lengthwise into pieces 3 inches long and 2 inches wide. Place the pieces in a bowl, add the **pork marinade,** toss lightly, and let marinate for 30 minutes. Soften the dried mushrooms for 20 minutes in hot water to cover. Remove and discard the stems, and cut the caps into matchstick-size shreds. Add the mushroom shreds to the **mushroom marinade,** and toss lightly. Cut the scallions into 3-inch pieces. Peel away the tough outer skin from the broccoli and separate the flowerets. Roll-cut the stems into 1-inch pieces.

2   Heat 1½ quarts salted water until boiling. Add the stem pieces and cook for ½ minute. Add the flowerets and cook for 2½ minutes, or until both stems and flowerets are just tender. Refresh immediately in cold water. Drain thoroughly.

3   Place the pork slices on a flat surface. Put a mushroom shred and a piece of scallion in the middle of one slice across the length; roll up the slice to enclose the mushroom and scallion. Make the remaining pork rolls in the same manner. Dredge the pork rolls in the cornstarch, lightly pressing the meat to make sure the cornstarch adheres.

4   Heat a wok, add the oil, and heat the oil to 400°. Add a third of the pork rolls and deep-fry for about 4 minutes, turning constantly over high heat. Remove with a handled strainer, and drain. Reheat the oil. Deep-fry the remaining rolls in the same manner, reheating the oil between batches. Remove the oil from the wok, reserving 2 tablespoons.

5 Reheat the wok, add the 2 tablespoons of oil, and heat until very hot. Add the **minced seasonings** and stir-fry over high heat for about 10 seconds, until fragrant. Add the broccoli and stir-fry for about 30 seconds over high heat. Add the **pork sauce,** and toss lightly until it thickens. Add the pork rolls, toss lightly to coat with the sauce, and transfer the mixture to a platter. Serve immediately.

Pork Sauce

1 tablespoon soy sauce
1½ tablespoons rice wine
1 teaspoon salt
¼ teaspoon freshly ground
   black pepper
½ teaspoon sugar
¼ cup chicken broth
1 teaspoon cornstarch

BARBECUED PORK LOIN

CHA SHAO ROU

Barbecued pork loin is extremely versatile: It may be sliced and served by itself as an appetizer, stir-fried in meat and vegetable platters, or used in a stuffing for steamed lotus buns (page 56).

1 Remove most of the fat and all the gristle from the pork loin and discard. Cut the meat, with the grain, into strips about 3 inches thick. Place the meat in a mixing bowl. Add the **pork marinade**, toss lightly, and let marinate for 4 hours, or overnight in the refrigerator, turning occasionally.

2 Preheat the oven to 375°. Arrange the meat strips on a rack in a roasting pan and bake for 45 minutes, or until the inside is cooked and the outside is brown. Let cool slightly, slice, and serve.

SIX SERVINGS

2 pounds boneless
   center-cut pork loin

Pork Marinade
2 tablespoons hoisin sauce
2 tablespoons soy sauce
1½ tablespoons rice wine
2½ tablespoons sugar
1 teaspoon salt
1 tablespoon ketchup
1½ tablespoons minced
   garlic

225

2 pounds boneless
   center-cut pork loin or
   tenderloin

Pork Marinade

3 tablespoons soy sauce
1½ tablespoons sweet bean
   sauce or hoisin sauce
2 tablespoons rice wine
1 teaspoon sesame oil
1 tablespoon sugar
½ teaspoon five-spice
   powder
3 slices gingerroot, smashed
   with the flat side of a
   cleaver
2 cloves garlic, smashed with
   the flat side of a cleaver
3 scallions, smashed with the
   flat side of a cleaver

12 10-inch bamboo skewers
1 pound salt pork

BAKED GOLDEN COINS

JIN CHIAN ROU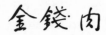

Glazed with a light coating of sweet bean sauce and baked until golden brown, these succulent pork slices are said to resemble golden coins — hence their poetic title. The salt pork slices merely provide flavor and moistness to the lean meat pieces. Serve these tender slices stuffed into steamed lotus buns (page 56) or between slices of bread.

1   Remove any fat or gristle from the pork loin and discard. Cut the meat, across the grain, into slices ⅙ inch thick. Cut each slice lengthwise into thirds. Place the slices in a bowl, add the **pork marinade,** toss lightly, and let marinate for at least 3 hours, or as long as overnight. Soak the bamboo skewers in water to cover for 1 hour. Blanch the salt pork in boiling water for 1 minute; rinse it in cold water. Remove the rind and cut the salt pork into slices about ¼ inch thick. Cut the slices into pieces the same size as the pork.
2   Thread the skewers with alternating slices of pork loin and salt pork. Place the skewers in a roasting pan and baste with the marinade. Bake the pork slices for about 20 minutes, turning and basting occasionally. Remove the pork slices from the skewers and arrange on a platter. Discard the salt pork slices. Serve.

SHREDDED EGG BALLS

DONG PO XIU QIU 東坡綉球

SIX SERVINGS

According to an ancient Chinese custom, a maiden of marrying age would throw an embroidered ball of silk or a bouquet *(xiu qiu)* to a group of her suitors. The young man fortunate enough to catch the missile would then become her husband. These steamed meatballs bear some resemblance to this bouquet.

1   Lightly chop the meat until fluffy and place it in a mixing bowl. Add the **meat seasonings** and stir vigorously in one direction to combine evenly. Lightly throw the meat against the inside of the bowl for 1 minute. Form the mixture into 1-inch meatballs.

2   Wipe the surface of a well-seasoned wok or a nonstick skillet with an oil-soaked paper towel. Heat the pan until hot. Add a third of the beaten eggs and tilt the pan so that the eggs form a thin pancake. Cook over medium heat until the egg sheet is firm. Flip it over and cook for 5 seconds. Remove, cool, and cut into thin shreds. Make two more egg sheets in the same manner, and shred them. Roll the meatballs in the egg shreds, making sure they are completely coated.

3   Lightly coat a heat-proof plate with oil. Arrange the meatballs on the plate about ½ inch apart. Sprinkle any remaining egg shreds over the meatballs. Place the plate in a steamer tray.

4   Add water to wok to reach the bottom edge of the steamer tray and heat until boiling. Place the steamer tray over the boiling water, cover, and steam for 20 minutes over high heat. Remove the water from the wok.

5   Reheat the wok, add the tablespoon of oil, and heat until smoking. Add the spinach and the **spinach seasonings.** Toss lightly over high heat until the spinach begins to wilt slightly. Arrange the spinach around the outer edge of a platter and place the steamed egg balls in the center.

6   Reheat the wok, add the **egg ball sauce,** and heat, stirring constantly, until slightly thick. Pour the sauce over the egg balls and serve immediately.

¾ pound ground pork or beef

Meat Seasonings

2 teaspoons dried shrimp, softened for 1 hour in hot water, drained, and minced
½ cup chopped (softened) Chinese black mushroom caps
2 teaspoons minced gingerroot
1½ tablespoons soy sauce
½ teaspoon salt
1½ teaspoons sesame oil
1 tablespoon cornstarch

4 eggs, lightly beaten
1 tablespoon peanut, safflower, or corn oil
1 pound fresh spinach, trimmed and cleaned

Spinach Seasonings

½ teaspoon salt
1 teaspoon minced garlic
1 teaspoon sesame oil

Egg Ball Sauce

½ cup chicken broth
1 tablespoon rice wine
1 teaspoon salt
¼ teaspoon freshly ground white pepper
1 teaspoon cornstarch

2 pounds Chinese cabbage
  (Napa)
4 tablespoons peanut,
  safflower, or corn oil
1 tablespoon rice wine
4 cups chicken broth or
  water
1½ pounds ground pork butt
  or picnic shoulder

Pork Seasonings

1½ teaspoons salt
2 teaspoons sesame oil
1 tablespoon rice wine
1 tablespoon minced
  scallions
1 teaspoon minced
  gingerroot
1½ tablespoons cornstarch

Pork Coating

1 tablespoon cornstarch
1½ tablespoons soy sauce
1 tablespoon water

Broth Seasonings

¾ teaspoon salt
1 tablespoon soy sauce

LION'S HEAD

SHI ZI TOU 獅 子 頭

This famous eastern dish was once reserved for banquets because of the quantity of meat called for in the recipe. In recent times, however, it has joined the ranks of the family-style platters and it is now regularly served at home. The large meatballs are said to look like a lion's head, and the cabbage, slightly browned and wilted at the edges, suggests a lion's mane.

1 Rinse the cabbage and drain thoroughly. Remove and set aside four of the big outer leaves. Cut the remaining leaves into 2-inch squares and discard the core.

2 Heat a wok, add 1 tablespoon of oil, and heat until smoking. Add the harder sections of cabbage and stir-fry for about 1 minute over high heat, stirring constantly. Add the leafier sections and sprinkle the tablespoon of rice wine over the cabbage. Stir-fry for another minute and add the chicken broth. Cook the mixture for about 10 minutes over high heat; then transfer it to a heavy 3-quart casserole or a Dutch oven.

3 Lightly chop the ground pork until fluffy and place it in a mixing bowl. Add the **pork seasonings** and stir vigorously in one direction for about 5 minutes. Lightly throw the meat against the inside of the bowl to combine evenly. Divide the meat into four portions and form them into oval meatballs.

4 Reheat the wok, add the remaining 3 tablespoons of oil, and heat until very hot. Dip the meatballs in the **pork coating** and slide them into the pan. Pan-fry the meatballs over high heat until brown. Remove them with a slotted spoon, and drain. Arrange the meatballs on the cabbage in the casserole and cover with the four reserved cabbage leaves. Cover the pot.

5 Preheat the oven to 400°. Bake the casserole for 1 hour. Add the **broth seasonings,** stir, and bake for 10 more minutes. Serve immediately.

BIRD'S NEST MEATBALLS

NIAO CHIAO ROU WAN 烏巢肉丸

Few cuisines treat the meatball as imaginatively as the Chinese: In addition to the usual forcemeat base, ingredients such as carrots, water chestnuts, black mushrooms, and dried shrimp are often included. Also, the outside may be coated with sesame seeds, rice, ground nuts, or, as in this case, rice noodles. These meatballs, rolled in rice stick noodles and deep-fried until golden brown, look something like the outside of a bird's nest.

1   Lightly chop the ground pork until fluffy and place it in a mixing bowl. Add the water chestnuts. Soften the black mushrooms for 20 minutes in hot water to cover. Remove and discard the stems and finely chop the caps. Add the mushrooms to the bowl, along with the shredded carrots and the **meatball seasonings.** Stir vigorously in one direction and lightly throw the mixture against the inside of the bowl to combine evenly.
2   Lightly break the rice noodles into pieces ½ inch long.
3   Form the meat into balls about ½ inch in diameter and roll each one in the rice noodles, pressing lightly to make sure the outside is completely coated and the rice noodles adhere well.
4   Heat a wok, add the oil, and heat the oil to 350°. Add a third of the meatballs and deep-fry over high heat, turning constantly until the meat is cooked and the noodles are golden. Remove with a handled strainer, and drain on absorbent paper. Reheat the oil. Deep-fry the remaining meatballs in the same manner, reheating the oil between batches. Arrange the meatballs on a platter and serve immediately.

SIX SERVINGS

1 pound ground pork
1 cup water chestnuts, plunged briefly into boiling water, refreshed, and coarsely chopped
6 dried Chinese black mushrooms
1½ carrots, shredded finely

Meatball Seasonings
1½ tablespoons minced scallions
2 teaspoons minced gingerroot
2 tablespoons soy sauce
1 tablespoon rice wine
1½ teaspoons sesame oil
1½ tablespoons cornstarch

2 ounces rice stick noodles
6 cups peanut, safflower, or corn oil

2 pounds boneless pork butt
  or fresh ham
3 cakes bean curd, about 3
  inches square and 1 inch
  thick
3 green peppers, seeded and
  cored
2 leeks, cleaned
3 cups peanut, safflower, or
  corn oil
1 tablespoon minced garlic
1½ teaspoons chili paste

Pork Sauce

2 tablespoons sweet bean
  sauce
¼ cup soy sauce
2 tablespoons sugar
3 tablespoons rice wine
¼ cup water

DOUBLE-COOKED PORK SLICES

HUI GUO ROU　　　回鍋肉

To my mind, this dish ranks as one of the best that Sichuanese cuisine has to offer. The marriage of flavorings among the pork loin, green peppers, and bean curd slices, all glazed with the sweet and spicy sauce, is superb. Fresh green garlic is traditionally used in the Far East, but I find that a combination of leeks and garlic makes an excellent substitute.

1   Rinse the meat and place it in a pot with water to cover. Heat until the water is boiling, reduce the heat to low, and cook for 1½ hours, turning the meat occasionally. Remove the meat from the pot and let it cool to room temperature. Cut the meat, across the grain, into slices ⅛ inch thick. Cut the slices into 2-inch squares. Cut the bean curd into slices that are 1½ inches long and 1 inch wide. Roll-cut the green peppers into 1-inch pieces. Slice the leeks lengthwise in half and cut them into 1-inch pieces.

2   Heat a wok, add the oil, and heat the oil to 400°. Drain the bean curd slices and deep-fry them in batches over high heat until golden brown, about 2 minutes. Remove with a handled strainer, and drain. Reheat the oil between batches.

3   Reheat the oil to 425°. Add the pork slices and deep-fry, stirring constantly over high heat, for 2 minutes. Add the green peppers and leeks. Deep-fry over high heat for 1 minute. Remove all the food and drain. Remove the oil from the wok, reserving 1 tablespoon.

4   Reheat the wok, add the tablespoon of oil, and heat until very hot. Add the minced garlic and stir-fry over high heat for 10 seconds, until fragrant. Add the chili paste and stir-fry for 5 seconds. Add the **pork sauce.** Toss lightly until the sauce begins to boil and thicken. Add the pork, green peppers, leeks, and bean curd. Toss to coat with the sauce, transfer to a platter, and serve immediately.

TUNG-PO PORK

DONG PO ROU 東坡肉

Su Tung-po, the famed poet, statesman, and gourmet of the Sung dynasty, was admired for his many talents. He is credited with inventing this savory dish; the combination of slow-simmering and steaming reduces the sauce to a lustrous glaze and transforms the meat to a buttery tenderness.

1   Heat 2 quarts of water until boiling. Place the meat in the water and cook it for 2 minutes. Rinse the meat in cold water and drain thoroughly.

2   Place the meat, skin side down, in a heavy casserole or a Dutch oven. Sprinkle the rock sugar on top. Pour the **braising sauce** over the meat and rub the sugar and sauce into the meat. Put the lid securely on the pot and mix the **luting paste** until smooth. Spread the luting paste around the rim of the lid, making sure that there are no openings between the lid and the casserole. Place the pot over medium heat and cook for 10 minutes. Reduce the heat to low, and simmer for 2 hours. Remove the pan from the heat and let it sit for 10 minutes. Cut away the hardened luting paste and discard. Skim most of the fat from the braising sauce and discard.

3   Transfer the pork, skin side up, to a heat-proof bowl and pour the braising sauce on top. Place the bowl in a steamer tray.

4   Fill a wok with water level with the bottom edge of the steamer tray and heat until boiling. Place the steamer tray over the boiling water, cover, and steam for 1½ hours over high heat. Remove the pork and cut, across the grain, into slices ½ inch thick. Skim off any fat remaining on the braising sauce, discard the scallions and gingerroot, and pour the sauce over the pork. Serve immediately.

SIX SERVINGS

3½ to 4 pounds fresh belly pork or 4½ pounds pork picnic shoulder
4 tablespoons rock sugar, lightly pounded to a coarse powder

Braising Sauce

½ cup soy sauce
⅓ cup rice wine
5 slices gingerroot, smashed with the flat side of a cleaver
4 scallions, smashed with the flat side of a cleaver

Luting Paste

6 tablespoons all-purpose flour
3 tablespoons water

2 pounds spareribs

Sparerib Marinade
1 tablespoon minced garlic
2 tablespoons curry powder
2 tablespoons soy sauce
2 tablespoons rice wine
1 teaspoon salt
¼ teaspoon freshly ground
  black pepper

1 egg, lightly beaten
1½ cups cornstarch
6 cups peanut, safflower, or
  corn oil

INDONESIAN SPARERIBS

YIN DU JIAN PAI GU 印度煎排骨

Fragrant and deep-fried until crisp and golden, these spicy spareribs are excellent as an hors d'oeuvre or snack. Accompanied by a stir-fried vegetable and a light soup, they also make a tasty and filling meal.

1   Direct the butcher to cut the slab of spareribs in half crosswise, so that they measure about 3 inches in length. Separate the ribs, cutting between the bones. Place the pieces in a bowl, add the **sparerib marinade,** toss lightly, and let marinate for at least 3 hours, or overnight in the refrigerator. Add the egg and stir to coat the ribs. Dredge the spareribs in cornstarch, lightly squeezing each piece to make sure the cornstarch adheres. Place the coated ribs on a tray and let them air-dry for 1 hour.
2   Heat a wok, add the oil, and heat the oil to 400°. Add a third of the spareribs and deep-fry over high heat for about 5 minutes, turning constantly until the ribs are cooked and golden brown. Remove with a handled strainer, and drain on absorbent paper. Reheat the oil. Deep-fry the remaining ribs in the same manner, reheating the oil between batches. Arrange the ribs on a platter and serve.

HOME-STYLE SPARERIBS

JIA CHANG PAI GU 家常排骨

I was first served this dish at an excellent eastern restaurant in Taipei, and the wrapping and baking of the spareribs in aluminum foil intrigued me. The head chef, when questioned, admitted that he had adapted the dish from the classic version, which called for a paper wrapping. He assured me, however, that the flavor of the adapted version remained true to that of the traditional recipe.

1   Direct the butcher to cut the slab of spareribs crosswise into thirds so that they measure 1½ to 2 inches in length. Separate the ribs, cutting between the bones. Place the pieces in a bowl, add the **sparerib marinade,** toss lightly, and let marinate for at least 3 hours, or overnight in the refrigerator. Discard the scallions and gingerroot, drain the ribs, and add the marinade to the **braising mixture.** Cut the aluminum foil into 6-inch squares, one for each sparerib piece.
2   Heat a wok, add the oil, and heat the oil to 425°. Add a third of the spareribs and deep-fry over high heat for about 3 minutes, stirring constantly until the ribs are golden. Remove with a handled strainer, and drain. Reheat the oil. Deep-fry the remaining spareribs in the same manner, reheating the oil between batches. Remove the oil from the wok, reserving 1 tablespoon.
3   Reheat the wok, add the tablespoon of oil, and heat until very hot. Add the **minced seasonings** and stir-fry for about 10 seconds, until fragrant. Add the braising mixture and heat until boiling. Add the spareribs. Heat the mixture until boiling, reduce the heat to medium, partially cover, and cook for 30 minutes, tossing occasionally. Uncover, turn up the heat, and cook the sauce to a syrupy glaze, stirring constantly. Discard the star anise and cinnamon sticks.
4   Preheat the oven to 450°. Wrap each sparerib piece in a square of aluminum foil and place the wrapped pieces on a baking sheet. Bake for 10 minutes. Transfer the ribs to a platter and serve immediately.

SIX SERVINGS

3 pounds "country-style" spareribs

Sparerib Marinade
1½ tablespoons soy sauce
2 tablespoons rice wine
1 teaspoon salt
6 scallions, smashed with the flat side of a cleaver
6 slices gingerroot, smashed with the flat side of a cleaver

Braising Mixture
3 cups chicken broth or water
3 tablespoons soy sauce
2 tablespoons rice wine
1½ tablespoons sugar
1 whole star anise
2 cinnamon sticks

Aluminum foil
6 cups peanut, safflower, or corn oil

Minced Seasonings
2 tablespoons minced scallions
1 tablespoon minced gingerroot

233

3 pounds spareribs

Sparerib Marinade
3 tablespoons soy sauce
2 tablespoons rice wine
1 teaspoon sesame oil
1 tablespoon minced garlic

Sparerib Sauce
6 tablespoons soy sauce
2 tablespoons rice wine
1½ tablespoons sugar
6 tablespoons chicken broth
  or water
1 teaspoon cornstarch

3 cups peanut, safflower, or
  corn oil

Minced Seasonings
2 tablespoons fermented
  black beans, rinsed,
  drained, and coarsely
  chopped
1 tablespoon minced
  gingerroot
2 tablespoons minced
  scallions

1 tablespoon minced dried
  chili peppers
1 tablespoon minced scallion
  greens

STEAMED SPARERIBS IN BLACK BEAN SAUCE

SHI ZHI PAI GU　　　豉汁排骨

In the traditional version of this dish, the spareribs are first deep-fried, then braised in the black bean sauce. I prefer to steam the spareribs, giving the dish a subtler, more refined flavor. Either method will provide an exquisitely savory concoction that is the perfect foil for white rice.

1　Direct the butcher to cut the slab of spareribs crosswise into thirds so that they measure 1½ to 2 inches in length. Separate the ribs, cutting between the bones. Place the pieces in a bowl, add the **sparerib marinade,** toss lightly, and let marinate for at least 3 hours, or overnight in the refrigerator. Drain the spareribs and add the marinade to the **sparerib sauce.**
2　Heat a wok, add the oil, and heat the oil to 425°. Add a third of the spareribs and deep-fry over high heat for about 3 minutes, stirring constantly until the ribs are golden. Remove and drain. Reheat the oil. Deep-fry the remaining spareribs in the same manner, reheating the oil between batches. Remove the oil from the wok, reserving 2 tablespoons.
3　Reheat the wok, add the 2 tablespoons of oil, and heat until very hot. Add the **minced seasonings** and stir-fry for about 10 seconds, until fragrant. Add the sparerib sauce and heat until boiling. Cook for about 1 minute, until the sauce has thickened, and add the spareribs. Toss lightly to coat with the sauce and transfer to a heat-proof bowl or a pie plate. Sprinkle the minced chili peppers over the spareribs. Place the bowl in a steamer tray and cover. Clean and dry the wok.
4　Fill the wok with water level with the bottom edge of the steamer tray and heat until boiling. Place the steamer tray over the boiling water, cover, and steam for 45 minutes over high heat. Sprinkle the minced scallion greens over the spareribs and serve immediately.

CHINESE PORK SAUSAGE

LA CHANG 腊腸

Sausage is a specialty made once a year by many Chinese families before the New Year's Festival. At this time, a pig is slaughtered in preparation for the holiday. The air is cool enough to permit hanging the sausages outside to dry. The following recipe is Cantonese, accounting for the addition of honey and the resulting sweet flavor. Traditionally, a very strong rice wine is used to provide extra flavor and to help preserve the meat.

1   Chop the pork fat and place it in a mixing bowl along with the ground pork and the **sausage seasoning.** Stir vigorously in one direction and lightly throw the mixture against the inside of the bowl. Let the meat marinate overnight in the refrigerator.

2   Rinse the sausage casing and carefully attach it to the end of a funnel. Tie the other end of the casing. Push the ground meat mixture into the funnel and squeeze the casing to distribute the meat evenly throughout. The sausage should be loosely packed. Once all the meat has been stuffed into the casing, tie off the funnel end. Tie the casing at 4-inch intervals, and prick the sausage all over with a pin. Refrigerate it at least overnight, but preferably two or three days, before cooking.

3   Pan-fry the sausage in a little bit of oil, or steam it for 10 minutes over high heat. Slice and serve, or use as directed in individual recipes.

SIX SERVINGS

1½ pounds pork fat
2 pounds ground pork picnic shoulder, pork loin, or fresh ham

Sausage Seasoning
¾ cup Kaoliang liquor or Scotch
1½ tablespoons salt
¼ cup honey
1 teaspoon five-spice powder

10 feet sausage casing

BEEF AND LAMB 牛羊肉類

One chilly March evening several years ago, three friends and I had the pleasure of dining at the Barbecue Chi Restaurant in Peking. After a frantic half-hour taxi ride — weaving in and out of a sea of cyclists silhouetted in the dusk, and accompanied by the majestic strains of "The Hearts of the Yunnan People Are Turned to Chairman Mao" blaring from the radio — we arrived at our destination. The restaurant is situated in the northern sector of the city on South Lake, which provides a cool sanctuary for diners during the summer months when the unrelenting heat forces a number of the city's restaurants to close.

The Barbecue Chi (barbecue meats) Restaurant has maintained an outstanding reputation for more than a century. The specialty of the house is Mongolian barbecue, a dish made with paper-thin slices of only the most tender beef and lamb dipped in a sauce of rice wine, ginger-flavored water, shrimp oil, soy sauce, and other seasonings of the diner's choice, then grilled over a charcoal brazier. The fuel used is limited to cypress and willow, as these woods are believed to provide the most fragrant smoke. Once cooked to a turn with Mongolian chopsticks some two feet long, the meat slices are stuffed into a hot, flaky sesame roll (*shao ping*), sprinkled with shredded scallions, and eaten immediately.

According to Kenneth Lo, an eminent authority on Chinese cuisine, barbecued meats were first introduced in Peking toward the end of the Ming dynasty (1368 to 1644). The emperor at that time liked to cater to the culinary tastes of the many dignitaries and princes visiting the Imperial Palace, and his Mongolian guests were keen on beef and lamb.

For most ancient Chinese, however, the cow was a beast of burden rather than a source of food. "Do not eat the cow, for it is a hardworking and sympathetic beast," states an early proverb. Oxen were work animals, and rulers generally prohibited their slaughter except as a sacrifice to honor particularly revered officials or ancestors.

The ox or bull is the second symbolic animal of the Twelve Terrestrial Branches, corresponding to the astrological sign Taurus, and is emblematic of spring and agriculture. Each year on the fifth of February, a ceremony called Meeting of the Spring is conducted, with the cow playing the leading role. A huge clay image of a cow, along with numerous smaller ones, is carried to a designated field. While the field is plowed, the huge cow is beaten with sticks, representing the arrival of spring. The observers then disperse, carrying the smaller images and bits of soil to their own fields. The soil is then sprinkled over their own land in hopes of cultivating a good crop.

The cow's ritual importance notwithstanding, beef was consumed on occasion in ancient China. During the Han dynasty (206 B.C. to A.D. 220), stews were made with beef and turnip, a combination still popular today, or beef and sonchus, a wild grass. Beef flank was apparently a feast dish; meatballs made of beef, pork, mutton, and rice were generally reserved for the elderly, as was beef marinated in good wine. Salt-cured beef was served with rice or millet, stir-fried, or cooked in soups. Beef was also pounded, mixed with salt, millet, and yeast, and fermented to a relish. Though during the T'ang dynasty (618 to 907) and Sung dynasty (960 to 1279) beef was not a favorite food, beef tea was a popular beverage that supposedly possessed strengthening powers. Similarly, beef bone marrow was recommended for blood disorders and fatigue.

The number of beef dishes in modern Chinese cuisine has been on the increase in recent years — perhaps because of Western influences — but chicken, pork, and fish are still far more prominent. All parts of the animal are used and many cooking methods are employed. Although there are beef dishes in most of the regional cuisines, the largest number is found in the northern and western schools. The reasons are obvious: The greatest concentrations of Moslems are in these areas (beef and lamb figure prominently in the Moslem diet because pork is prohibited) and oxen are used in the western provinces to haul salt from the mines. In Hunan province, braised beef and beef tendons are favorite dishes. The tendons, which have a slightly gelatinous, resilient texture, are extremely nutritious and are said to prolong life. Smoked beef is frequently served with wine, and tangerine-peel beef is a well-loved garnish for rice. (Dairy products have never played a substantial role in the Chinese diet, but in some areas of northern China and in Yunnan province, milk products such as cheese, fried milk, and yogurt are commonly consumed.)

Like beef, lamb and mutton are favored by the present-day Moslems, and these meats were sometimes eaten by the ancient Chinese. During the Han dynasty, boiled or roasted mutton was an important offering and was served during the Chinese New Year, the Summer Festival, and other important holidays. Lamb flank, shoulder, and stomach were used in Han feast dishes, whereas lamb with assorted seasonings over noodles was a popular snack. Believed to have beneficial properties, lamb was suggested fare for the infirm.

During the Sung dynasty, cooking with lamb and kid became widespread among all classes. Milk-steamed lamb and lamb's head are examples of the unusual delicacies of this period. In the ancient city of Kaifeng, large shops specializing in roast lamb flourished.

With the takeover of China by the Mongolian rulers in the Yüan dynasty (1271 to 1368), mutton became a regular item on the Imperial menu. According to existing records, an average of four or five sheep were slaughtered daily and huge vats for boiling whole sheep were installed in the Imperial kitchens. Whole lamb was also prepared in a manner similar to roast suckling pig; the unskinned animal was put in a pit lined with red-hot stones, covered with willow branches, and sealed with mud. Lamb and mutton were present in a variety of forms in Mongolian dishes: Wontons were made with a dough of bean paste and a filling of minced lamb and dried tangerine peel, boiled, and served in lamb broth; and Mongolian meat cakes consisted of almost every edible portion of sheep, stewed, minced, and mixed with yams, cheese, and eggs. Mongolian fire pot, barbecued or scorched lamb, lamb shish kebab, and thrice-cooked lamb became popular in Peking restaurants. Lamb is believed to have a warming effect on the body, so these dishes were especially popular in cold weather. Even mutton wine, with an alcohol level of more than 9 percent, was brewed by the Mongols. Today the major consumption of lamb still occurs in northern China, but the meat is eaten on occasion in the southern and western regions, particularly during the winter months when hearty lamb stews are common fare.

The Chinese rarely draw a distinction between lamb, mutton, or goat, as the same Chinese word is used for all three. The lamb represents filial piety because the young animals habitually assume a kneeling position, suggesting respect, while nursing. The sheep is the eighth symbolic animal of the Twelve Terrestrial Branches, corresponding to Scorpio on the zodiac.

Whatever the method of preparation, including those outlined in the following recipes, it seems safe to conclude that one's culinary odds will be much higher than those given by the poet Yüan Mei when he wrote, "There are seventy-two ways of cooking lamb. Of these, only eighteen or nineteen are palatable."

STANDARD AMERICAN CUTS OF LAMB AND THEIR APPROPRIATE CHINESE COOKING METHODS

SECTION	CUT OF MEAT	SUITABLE COOKING METHOD
Neck	neck meat	braise, simmer, roast, grind for filling
Shoulder, Foreshank, Hindshank	blade chop, arm chop, shoulder roasts, foreshank, hindshank	braise, simmer, roast, grind for filling, barbecue
Breast	riblets, roasts, spareribs	steam, braise, simmer, grind for filling, cook in soups
Rib	rib chops, rib roast, crown roast	stir-fry, steam, deep-fry, roast, barbecue
Loin and Sirloin, Flank	loin chops, loin roasts, sirloin chops and roasts	stir-fry, deep-fry, roast
Leg	whole leg, sirloin half, center leg, shank half	stir-fry, steam, roast, barbecue

STANDARD AMERICAN CUTS OF BEEF AND THEIR APPROPRIATE CHINESE COOKING METHODS

SECTION	CUT OF MEAT	SUITABLE COOKING METHOD
Chuck (blade portion, arm half, and shoulder)	chuck roasts, chuck steaks	braise, simmer, stir-fry, deep-fry, steam, grind for filling
Foreshank, Brisket	foreshank, brisket	braise, simmer, grind for filling
Rib	rib roasts	stir-fry, steam, smoke
Plate ("white abdomen")	Yankee pot roast, short ribs, spareribs	braise, simmer, barbecue, cook in soups
Loin, Hip	loin roasts, loin steaks, sirloin steaks, sirloin roasts, tenderloin	stir-fry, deep-fry, steam, smoke
Flank	flank steak, London broil	stir-fry, deep-fry, steam, smoke
Round	rump roast, bottom round, shank, sirloin tip, eye of the round, top round	simmer, braise, stir-fry, deep-fry, smoke
Oxtail	oxtail	braise, simmer, cook in soups
Variety Meats	tongue, derma, liver, tripe	stir-fry, braise, simmer, deep-fry, cook in soups

SLICED BEEF IN HOT SAUCE

MA LA NIU ROU　麻辣牛肉

The *ma la* in the title refers to the numbingly spicy flavor of the Sichuan peppercorns, which sensitize the palate and accentuate the unique contrast of textures: the crisp cucumber slices and smooth vermicelli sheets bathed in the peppery sauce combine with the beef to create an unforgettable dish. Bean threads (cellophane noodles) may be used in place of the vermicelli sheets.

1　Rinse the beef and place it in a pot with 4 cups of cold water. Heat until boiling, reduce the heat to low, and simmer the beef, uncovered, for about 1 hour, until tender. Remove the beef from the pot and let it cool. Cut the beef, across the grain, into slices ⅛ inch thick. Cut the slices into pieces 1½ inches long and 1 inch wide.
2　Soften the vermicelli sheets for 10 minutes in hot water to cover. Drain the sheets and cut them into strips 1 inch wide. Cook the strips in boiling water for 1 minute. Refresh them in cold water, drain thoroughly, and place in a bowl. Add the **vermicelli seasonings,** toss lightly, and arrange the vermicelli strips on a platter.
3　Cut the cucumbers in half lengthwise and remove the seeds. Cut each half crosswise into 1½-inch pieces and cut each piece lengthwise into paper-thin slices. Place the cucumber slices in a bowl, add the 2 teaspoons of salt, toss lightly, and let sit for 20 minutes. Drain the cucumbers, rinse off the salt with cold water, and pat the slices dry. Arrange the slices on top of the vermicelli strips. Arrange the beef slices in the center of the cucumber strips.
4　Heat a wok, add the Sichuan peppercorns, and stir-fry for 5 minutes over medium heat, stirring constantly until the peppercorns are fragrant and golden brown. Pulverize the peppercorns in a blender or a food processor fitted with the steel blade. Add the Sichuan peppercorn powder to the **beef seasonings.** Just before serving, pour the sauce over the beef and arrange the coriander around the edge of the platter. Toss lightly and serve.

SIX SERVINGS

1 pound top sirloin roast or eye of the round roast
5 dried vermicelli sheets

Vermicelli Seasonings
½ teaspoon salt
¾ teaspoon sesame oil

2 English ("gourmet seedless") cucumbers
2 teaspoons salt
1 tablespoon Sichuan peppercorns

Beef Seasonings
2 tablespoons minced scallions
2 tablespoons minced gingerroot
¼ cup soy sauce
1 tablespoon Chinese black vinegar or Worcestershire sauce
2 tablespoons sesame oil
2 teaspoons sugar
½ teaspoon salt

1 bunch coriander (Chinese parsley), rinsed and drained

1½ pounds beef tenderloin
  or sirloin

Beef Marinade
1 tablespoon rice wine
2 slices gingerroot, smashed
  with the flat side of a
  cleaver
1½ tablespoons soy sauce
1 teaspoon sugar
1 teaspoon sesame oil
1 tablespoon cornstarch

8 "large" eggs
¾ teaspoon salt
1 cup peanut, safflower, or
  corn oil
3 tablespoons minced
  scallions
1 tablespoon minced scallion
  greens

STIR-FRIED BEEF WITH EGGS

HUA DAN NIU ROU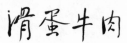

The standard Western version of steak and eggs can hardly be considered a "gourmet" item, but the Chinese rendition is a memorable and savory delicacy. The fluffy scrambled eggs contrast in taste and texture with the tender beef slices.

1   Remove any fat or gristle from the beef and discard. Cut the meat, across the grain, into slices ⅛ inch thick. Cut each slice into pieces 1½ inches long and 1 inch wide. Place the pieces in a bowl, add the **beef marinade**, toss lightly, and let marinate for at least 2 hours. Discard the gingerroot slices and drain the meat. Beat the eggs lightly until frothy, adding the salt.
2   Heat a wok, add the oil, and heat the oil to 400°. Add the beef slices and cook over high heat for about 1 minute, stirring constantly until the pieces change color. Remove with a handled strainer, and drain. Remove the oil from the wok, reserving 3 tablespoons.
3   Reheat the wok, add the 3 tablespoons of oil, and heat until very hot. Add the minced scallions and stir-fry for 10 seconds, until fragrant. Add the eggs and stir-fry over medium-high heat until they begin to set. Add the beef slices and toss lightly. Cook for a bit longer and transfer the mixture to a platter. Sprinkle the minced scallion greens on top and serve immediately.

STIR-FRIED BEEF WITH SCALLIONS

CONG BAO NIU ROU 葱爆牛肉

The subtle seasoning of northern cooking is apparent in this stir-fried platter, with its light glaze of soy sauce and sugar and the scallion garnish. This home-style dish is delicious whether it is served with Mandarin pancakes (page 61) or with rice.

1   Remove any fat or gristle from the beef and discard. Cut the meat, across the grain, into slices about ⅛ inch thick. Cut each slice into pieces about 1½ inches long and 1 inch wide. Place the pieces in a bowl, add the **beef marinade**, toss lightly, and let marinate for at least 1 hour. Drain the meat.

2   Heat a wok, add the oil, and heat the oil to 400°. Add half the beef and deep-fry over high heat, stirring constantly until the pieces change color, about 1½ minutes. Remove with a handled strainer, and drain. Reheat the oil and deep-fry the remaining beef in the same manner. Remove the oil from the wok, reserving 2 table-spoons.

3   Reheat the wok, add the 2 tablespoons of oil, and heat until very hot. Add the shredded scallions and stir-fry for about 1 minute over high heat. Add the cooked beef pieces and the **beef sauce**. Toss lightly to coat the meat and scallions with the sauce. Add the sesame oil, toss lightly, and transfer the mixture to a platter. Serve immediately.

SIX SERVINGS

2 pounds beef sirloin or
   tenderloin

Beef Marinade
2 tablespoons minced garlic
4 tablespoons soy sauce
2 tablespoons rice wine
1 tablespoon sugar
2 tablespoons cornstarch

2 cups peanut, safflower, or
   corn oil
4 cups shredded scallion
   greens or leeks

Beef Sauce
6 tablespoons soy sauce
1½ tablespoons sugar

1½ teaspoons sesame oil

1 pound beef sirloin or
tenderloin

Beef Marinade

2 tablespoons soy sauce
1 tablespoon rice wine
1 teaspoon sesame oil
1 teaspoon sugar
¼ teaspoon freshly ground
black pepper
¼ teaspoon five-spice
powder
1 teaspoon minced
gingerroot
2 teaspoons minced scallions

2 carrots, parboiled for 2
minutes
36 snow peas, ends snapped
and veiny strings removed
36 6-inch squares of
parchment paper or wax
paper
8 cups peanut, safflower, or
corn oil

PAPER-WRAPPED FRIED BEEF

ZHI BAO NIU ROU   纸包牛肉

Paper-wrapped foods are found in both French and Chinese
cuisines. While the French generally bake the food in a hot oven,
the Chinese prefer to deep-fry in hot oil. The results, however, are
similar: The wrapped food steams in its own juices, becoming both
fragrant and tender.

1   Remove any fat or gristle from the beef and discard. Cut the
meat, across the grain, into slices ⅛ inch thick. Cut the slices into
36 pieces about 1½ inches long and 1 inch wide. Place the slices in
a bowl, add the **beef marinade**, toss lightly, and let marinate for at
least 3 hours, or overnight in the refrigerator. Cut four evenly spaced
V-shaped grooves lengthwise in each carrot (use either a knife or the
tip of a vegetable peeler), and then cut the carrots into thin slices.
Rinse the snow peas and drain.
2   Lightly brush the center of one square of parchment paper with
sesame oil and place a piece of meat over the oil. Put a snow pea on
top of the meat and place two or three carrot slices along the length
of the snow pea. Fold the paper in half to form a triangular package
(a), and fold the edges together to form pleats and to seal in the meat
(b). Twist the ends to seal (c). Repeat for each package. Alternatively, follow the method shown in steps d through g.
3   Heat a wok, add the oil, and heat the oil to 350°. Add a third of
the packages and deep-fry, stirring constantly, for about 2½ minutes, until the packages puff slightly and the meat is cooked. Remove with a handled strainer, and drain on absorbent paper. Reheat
the oil to 350° and deep-fry the remaining packages in the same
manner, reheating the oil between batches. Arrange the packages
on a platter and serve immediately.

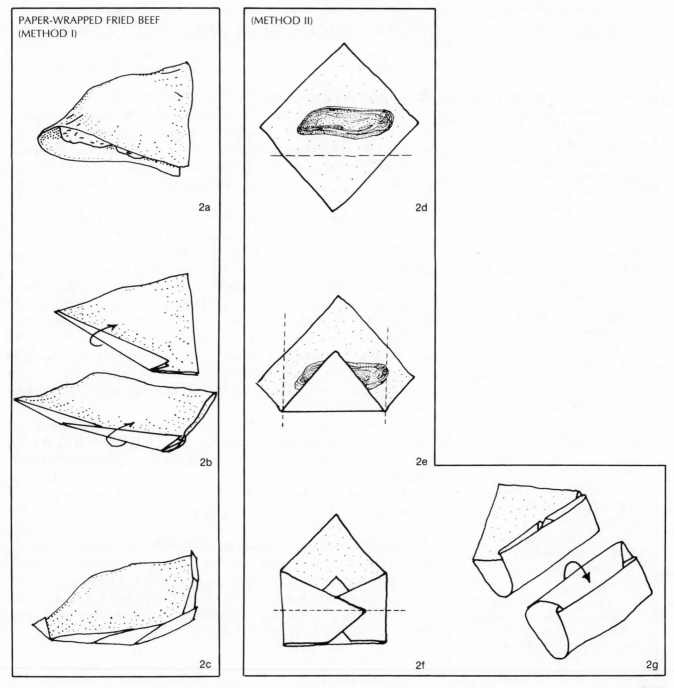

PAPER-WRAPPED FRIED BEEF
(METHOD I)

2a

2b

2c

(METHOD II)

2d

2e

2f

2g

245

DRY-COOKED BEEF WITH VEGETABLES

GAN PIAN NIU ROU SI 乾煸牛肉丝

In Sichuan province, cattle are used as work animals, hauling salt and other provisions. Once old age inhibits their usefulness, they are slaughtered for consumption. The meat is extremely tough; accordingly, most Sichuanese chefs cook beef in very hot oil far longer than any Western chef would dare. The cooked meat in this dish is dry, crisp, and tender, combining well with the spicy seasonings.

1½ pounds eye of the round roast or top sirloin roast

Beef Marinade

2 tablespoons soy sauce
1 tablespoon rice wine
1 teaspoon sesame oil
1 tablespoon water

4 cups peanut, safflower, or corn oil
2 ounces rice stick noodles

Minced Seasonings

1 tablespoon minced scallions
2 teaspoons minced gingerroot
3 tablespoons minced garlic

2 teaspoons chili paste
1½ cups shredded celery
2 cups shredded carrots

Beef Sauce

3 tablespoons chicken broth
2 tablespoons soy sauce
1 tablespoon rice wine
1½ teaspoons sugar
1½ teaspoons sesame oil
1½ teaspoons Chinese black vinegar
½ teaspoon Sichuan peppercorns, toasted (in a heavy skillet over low heat for 2 minutes) and pulverized

1   Remove any fat or gristle from the beef and discard. Cut the meat, across the grain, into slices ¼ inch thick. Cut the slices into matchstick-size shreds and place them in a bowl. Add the **beef marinade**, toss lightly, and let marinate for 20 minutes.
2   Heat a wok, add the oil, and heat the oil until smoking, about 425°. Add the rice noodles and deep-fry them until puffed and pale golden. This should happen almost immediately. Turn them over and deep-fry for a few seconds on the other side. Remove, and drain the noodles on absorbent paper. Transfer them to a platter and lightly break up the noodles with your fingertips. Leave a slight depression in the middle of the platter. Remove all but 1 cup of oil from the wok.
3   Reheat the oil to 425°. Drain the beef and add half of the shreds to the hot oil. Deep-fry, stirring constantly over high heat for 3½ minutes, or until the beef is golden brown and slightly crisp. Remove with a handled strainer, and drain. Reheat the oil and deep-fry the remaining beef shreds in the same manner. Remove the oil from the wok, reserving 3 tablespoons.
4   Reheat the wok, add the 3 tablespoons of oil, and heat until very hot. Add the **minced seasonings** and stir-fry for about 5 seconds, until fragrant. Add the chili paste and stir-fry for another 5 seconds. Add the celery and carrot shreds, and continue stir-frying over high heat for about 3 minutes, until they are tender. Add the **beef sauce** and the cooked meat shreds. Toss lightly to coat with the sauce. Pour the mixture over the rice noodles and serve immediately.

STIR-FRIED BEEF WITH GREEN PEPPERS

CHING JIAO NIU ROU SI 青椒牛肉絲

The leanness of flank steak makes it a particularly good cut of beef for stir-frying, but eye of the round or top sirloin also does nicely. When the meat has been shredded and marinated, it assumes a tenderness comparable to sirloin or tenderloin. This is an excellent version of a well-known Cantonese dish.

1   Remove any fat or gristle from the beef and discard. Cut the meat, across the grain, into slices about ⅛ inch thick. (You may partially freeze the meat to facilitate cutting.) Cut each slice into matchstick-size shreds and place them in a bowl. Add the **beef marinade**, toss lightly, and let marinate for 30 minutes. Cut the green peppers into matchstick-size shreds. Drain the beef.

2   Heat a wok, add the oil, and heat the oil to 400°. Add a third of the meat shreds and deep-fry, stirring constantly over high heat for about a minute, until the pieces change color. Remove with a handled strainer, and drain. Reheat the oil and deep-fry the remaining beef in the same manner, reheating the oil between batches. Remove the oil from the wok, reserving 2 tablespoons.

3   Reheat the wok, add the 2 tablespoons of oil, and heat until very hot. Add the **minced seasonings** and stir-fry over high heat for about 10 seconds, until fragrant. Add the green pepper shreds and stir-fry for about 1 minute over high heat. Add the **beef sauce** and toss lightly until the sauce begins to thicken. Add the cooked beef pieces, and toss lightly to coat with the sauce. Transfer the mixture to a platter and serve immediately.

SIX SERVINGS

2 pounds flank steak, eye of the round roast, or sirloin roast

Beef Marinade
2 tablespoons soy sauce
1 tablespoon rice wine
1 teaspoon sesame oil
2 teaspoons cornstarch
2 tablespoons water

6 medium-sized green peppers, cored and seeded
2 cups peanut, safflower, or corn oil

Minced Seasonings
2 tablespoons minced scallions
2 tablespoons minced garlic
2 tablespoons fermented black beans, rinsed, drained, and coarsely chopped
1 tablespoon minced gingerroot

Beef Sauce
1 tablespoon soy sauce
2 tablespoons rice wine
2 teaspoons sugar
⅓ cup chicken broth
2 teaspoons sesame oil
1 tablespoon cornstarch

2½ pounds eye of the round
roast or flank steak

Beef Marinade

3 tablespoons rice wine
2 slices gingerroot, smashed
with the flat side of the
cleaver
¾ teaspoon salt

4 strips dried tangerine or
orange peel, about 2
inches long
¼ cup 1-inch pieces dried
chili peppers
4 cups peanut, safflower, or
corn oil
4 tablespoons sesame oil

Beef Seasonings

1 tablespoon Sichuan
peppercorns
1 whole star anise
1 cinnamon stick

Braising Liquid

1½ tablespoons soy sauce
3 tablespoons rice wine
3 tablespoons sugar
1½ cups water

1 teaspoon clear rice vinegar

CINNAMON-FLAVORED BEEF

GUI PI NIU ROU 桂皮牛肉

Since ancient times the Chinese have felt the pungent seasoning cinnamon to be particularly appealing with beef. During the Han dynasty, beef was seasoned with gingerroot and cinnamon, then grilled or barbecued. These spicy beef slices are equally delectable served hot with rice or at room temperature on a bed of shredded lettuce as an appetizer.

1   Remove any fat or gristle from the beef and discard. Cut the meat, across the grain, into slices about ¼ inch thick. Cut the slices into pieces about 1½ inches long and 1 inch wide. Place the meat in a bowl, add the **beef marinade**, toss lightly, and let marinate for at least 3 hours, or overnight in the refrigerator. Soften the dried tangerine peel for 30 minutes in hot water to cover. Then cut it into julienne strips. Shake out the seeds from the chili peppers.
2   Heat a wok, add the 4 cups of oil, and heat the oil to 400°. Drain the beef slices and discard the gingerroot. Add a third of the beef slices to the hot oil and deep-fry for 3 or 4 minutes, stirring constantly until the beef is golden brown and slightly crisp. Remove with a handled strainer, and drain. Reheat the oil and deep-fry the remaining beef in the same manner, reheating the oil between batches. Remove the oil from the wok.
3   Reheat the wok, add 2 tablespoons of the sesame oil, and heat the oil until smoking. Add the chili pepper pieces and stir-fry over high heat, stirring constantly until the peppers turn black. Remove the peppers with a slotted spoon and set aside. Add the **beef seasonings** and the tangerine peel. Stir-fry over high heat for about 20 seconds; then add the **braising liquid**. Add the beef pieces and heat the mixture until boiling. Reduce the heat to low, partially cover, and cook for 40 minutes, stirring occasionally. The sauce should be reduced to a third of its original amount. Uncover, turn the heat to high, and continue cooking the beef, stirring constantly until the sauce has reduced to a thick glaze. Add the cooked chili peppers, the remaining 2 tablespoons of sesame oil, and the rice vinegar. Toss lightly, transfer the mixture to a platter, and serve immediately.

BRAISED SOY SAUCE BEEF

HONG SHAO NIU ROU 紅燒牛肉

In this simple braised dish the slow-cooking process heightens the licorice flavor of the star anise and the mellow richness of the soy sauce. Serve it hot with rice or cold over shredded lettuce.

1   Remove any fat or gristle from the beef and discard. Cut the meat into 1-inch cubes.

2   Heat a 3-quart casserole or a Dutch oven, add the oil, and heat until very hot. Add half the meat cubes and fry over high heat until golden brown on all sides. Remove the meat. Reheat the oil, and fry the remaining beef cubes in the same manner.

3   Remove the oil from the casserole and add the beef and the **braising mixture**. Heat the liquid until boiling. Reduce the heat to low and simmer, covered, for 1½ hours, or until the meat is tender; stir occasionally. The sauce should be reduced to about ½ cup. If not, turn the heat to high and reduce the sauce, stirring constantly. Remove the star anise, scallions, and gingerroot. Transfer the beef and sauce to a bowl and serve hot or cold.

SIX SERVINGS

2 pounds boneless stewing
   beef, such as chuck or
   shin
¼ cup peanut, safflower, or
   corn oil

Braising Mixture
3 scallions, smashed with the
   flat side of a cleaver
3 slices gingerroot, smashed
   with the flat side of a
   cleaver
1 whole star anise
1 cup water
¼ cup rice wine
¼ cup soy sauce
1 tablespoon sugar

2 pounds top sirloin roast or eye of the round roast

Beef Marinade
¼ cup hoisin sauce
½ cup soy sauce
¼ cup rice wine
3 tablespoons sugar
1 tablespoon minced garlic
1 tablespoon minced gingerroot
¼ cup water

3 tablespoons sesame oil
6 cups fresh bean sprouts, lightly rinsed
4 cups shredded scallion greens or leeks
1½ cups ginger water (Pinch 6 slices gingerroot, smashed with the flat side of a cleaver, in 1½ cups water repeatedly for 1 minute.)

MONGOLIAN BARBECUE

MENG GU KAO ROU 蒙古烤肉

This northern specialty can be successfully duplicated at home with a heavy steel Genghis Khan grill (available in Oriental markets) or an ordinary hibachi or barbecue covered with several layers of heavy-duty aluminum foil pierced with holes. Leg of lamb also may be used in this dish, which is ideally served stuffed in sesame flat breads (page 63) or steamed lotus buns (page 56).

1   Remove any fat or gristle from the beef and discard. Cut the meat, across the grain, into slices about ⅛ inch thick. (You may freeze the beef to facilitate cutting.) Cut the slices into 2-inch squares and place the squares in a bowl. Add the **beef marinade**, toss lightly, and let marinate for at least 4 hours, or overnight in the refrigerator.
2   Prepare a charcoal fire and wait until the coals are red; then place the Genghis Khan grill over the charcoal grill. Or you may place the Genghis Khan grill over an electric hot plate. Heat the grill until water sprinkled on the surface evaporates immediately. Brush the surface with sesame oil. Arrange slices of beef on the grill, wait 15 seconds, and sprinkle 1 cup bean sprouts and ⅔ cup scallions on top of the beef. Using chopsticks, toss the mixture and pour ¼ cup of ginger water over all. When the meat and vegetables are cooked, remove and serve in sesame flat breads or steamed lotus buns. Repeat for the remaining meat and vegetables.

RED-COOKED OXTAIL

HONG SHAO NIU WEI 紅燒牛尾

Although Taipei is just north of the tropical zone, the winters there can be extremely cold and raw; and there is little central heating. This hearty stew was a favorite cold-weather dish in our Chinese household. Accompanied by rice and a green vegetable, it makes a filling, nutritious, and inexpensive meal.

1   Rinse the oxtail sections and drain. Blanch for 1 minute in boiling water, remove, and rinse in cold water. Drain thoroughly.
2   Heat a heavy 3-quart casserole or a Dutch oven, add the oil, and heat the oil until very hot. Add the onion and stir-fry until soft and transparent. Add the oxtail sections and brown lightly on all sides. Add the **braising mixture** and heat until boiling. Reduce the heat to low, partially cover, and simmer for 3 hours, or until the oxtail is very tender and the braising mixture has reduced and become somewhat thick. Place the oxtails in a serving bowl and strain out the seasonings from the braising liquid. Heat the strained liquid until boiling. Add the **thickener** and heat until the sauce has thickened, stirring constantly to prevent lumps. Pour the sauce over the oxtails and serve immediately.

SIX SERVINGS

3 pounds oxtail, separated into sections at the joints
2 tablespoons peanut, safflower, or corn oil
1 medium-sized onion, diced

Braising Mixture

6 cups water
6 tablespoons soy sauce
3 tablespoons rice wine
1 tablespoon sugar
1 whole star anise
1 cinnamon stick
2 strips dried tangerine or orange peel, about 2 inches long
3 scallions, smashed with the flat side of a cleaver
3 slices gingerroot, smashed with the flat side of a cleaver

Thickener

2 teaspoons cornstarch
1 tablespoon water

2½ pounds boned shoulder of lamb or boned leg of lamb, shank half

Seasoning Mixture

1½ tablespoons sweet bean sauce
2 tablespoons soy sauce
1 tablespoon rice wine
1 tablespoon sugar
1 whole star anise, smashed with the flat side of a cleaver
2 scallions, smashed with the flat side of a cleaver
2 slices gingerroot, smashed with the flat side of a cleaver
2 cloves garlic, smashed with the flat side of a cleaver

Thickener

3 tablespoons chicken broth
1 teaspoon cornstarch

STEAMED LAMB IN SWEET BEAN SAUCE

JIANG YANG ROU

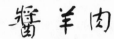

Steamed lamb has been a popular Mongolian specialty since the Sung dynasty, when it was first introduced to Peking by the northern tribesmen. Over the years it was refined by the Han chefs until it became the dish below — a subtle delicacy with seasonings of sweet bean sauce and star anise. Serve these fragrant lamb slices on steamed lotus buns (page 56) or with rice.

1   Trim all but a thin layer of fat from the lamb. Place the lamb in a bowl. Rub the **seasoning mixture** all over the lamb. Let the lamb marinate for at least 1 hour or, if possible, overnight in the re-frigerator. Place the lamb in a heat-proof bowl or deep plate and pour the seasoning mixture on top. Place the bowl in a steamer tray.
2   Fill a wok with water level with the bottom edge of the steamer tray and heat until boiling. Place the steamer tray over the boiling water, cover, and steam for 1 hour and 15 minutes over high heat, or until the lamb is just pink in the center. Remove the lamb from the bowl and let it stand for 10 minutes. Cut the lamb, across the grain, into thin slices and arrange the slices on a platter.
3   Skim any fat from the liquid in the bowl and strain out the seasonings. Discard the seasonings. Heat the sauce until boiling and slowly add the **thickener**, stirring constantly. When the sauce has thickened, pour it over the lamb slices. Serve with steamed lotus buns or rice.

BRAISED LAMB IN ASPIC

DONG YANG ROU 凍羊肉

According to Buwei Yang Chao in *How to Cook and Eat in Chinese*, this northern dish should be served with "wine and good company," which explains why it is such a popular Chinese New Year's offering. While the Chinese turnip in the recipe is merely used to impart flavor and is generally discarded, my Chinese surrogate mother liked to serve the braised turnip pieces on the side.

1   Remove all but a very thin layer of fat from the lamb. Blanch the meat in boiling water for 1 minute. Rinse the meat in cold water, and drain. Place the meat in a heavy 3-quart pot or a Dutch oven, add the **braising mixture**, and heat until boiling. Reduce the heat to low and cook, uncovered, for 1 hour. Peel the turnip and roll-cut it into 1-inch cubes. Add the turnip cubes to the lamb and continue cooking over low heat for 30 minutes, or until the lamb is very tender. Remove the lamb from the pot and let it sit for 10 minutes. Cut the lamb into 1-inch cubes. Discard the turnip pieces and the seasonings in the braising liquid and skim any fat from the braising liquid.

2   Continue cooking the braising liquid over medium heat until it has reduced to 1½ cups. Soften the gelatin in the ¼ cup cold water and slowly heat, stirring constantly, until the gelatin has dissolved. Add the gelatin to the reduced braising liquid and stir to combine.

3   Arrange the cooked lamb cubes in the bottom of a 1-quart rectangular mold or terrine and pour the reduced braising liquid on top. Chill the mold for 6 hours, or until it is set. Run a sharp knife around the edge of the mold and unmold the lamb onto a platter. Cut the mold into slices ½ inch thick and arrange on the platter. Sprinkle the top with the shredded gingerroot. Garnish with fresh coriander, if desired.

2 pounds boned shoulder or breast of lamb

Braising Mixture
4 tablespoons soy sauce
3 tablespoons rice wine
1 teaspoon salt
2 teaspoons sugar
7 cups water
4 scallions, smashed with the flat side of a cleaver
4 slices gingerroot, smashed with the flat side of a cleaver
2 cloves garlic, smashed with the flat side of a cleaver
1 whole star anise
1 cinnamon stick

½ pound Chinese turnip (daikon radish)
1 tablespoon unflavored gelatin
¼ cup cold water
3 tablespoons finely shredded gingerroot

2½ pounds blade or rib lamb
chops

Braising Liquid
6 cups water
1 whole star anise
1 teaspoon Sichuan
　peppercorns
2 2-inch strips dried
　tangerine or orange peel
1 cinnamon stick
4 scallions, smashed with the
　flat side of a cleaver
4 slices gingerroot, smashed
　with the flat side of a
　cleaver
2 tablespoons rice wine
1 tablespoon soy sauce
1 teaspoon salt

Dipping Sauce
4 tablespoons soy sauce
1½ tablespoons rice wine
1½ tablespoons Chinese
　black vinegar
1½ tablespoons sugar
1½ teaspoons chili oil or
　chili paste
2 teaspoons sesame oil
2 tablespoons minced
　scallions
1 tablespoon minced
　coriander (optional)
2 teaspoons minced garlic
2 teaspoons minced
　gingerroot

FINGER LAMB IN DIPPING SAUCE

ZHA YANG PAI　　炸羊排

The Mongolian custom of eating with one's hands offended many ancient Chinese, who considered it primitive. Later this attitude seems to have softened considerably as "grab-your-own-lamb" dishes gained popularity in Peking restaurants. Perhaps the extraordinary flavor of these tender lamb chops dipped in pungent sauce was partially responsible for the Chinese gourmands' change of attitude.

1　Direct the butcher to cut the chops crosswise, through the bones, into pieces 2 inches long. Remove any excess fat and discard. Blanch the lamb chop pieces in boiling water for 1 minute. Drain thoroughly.
2　Place the **braising liquid** in a heavy pot or casserole. Heat the mixture until boiling, reduce the heat to low, and cook for 20 minutes. Add the lamb chop pieces and heat until boiling. Reduce the heat to medium and cook, uncovered, for 35 minutes, or until the lamb is tender. Remove the lamb and arrange it on a platter. (Reserve the braising liquid and use it again.) Serve the lamb pieces with the **dipping sauce**.

LAMB SHISH KEBAB

KAO YANG ROU CHUAN 烤羊肉串

I first tasted this delicious dish several years ago at the famous Peking restaurant known as the Sick Duck. The skewered meat offers a pleasant departure from the usual repertory of stir-fried platters.

1   Remove all but a thin layer of fat from the lamb. Cut the meat into 1-inch cubes. Place the lamb cubes in a bowl, add the **lamb marinade**, toss lightly, and let marinate for at least 3 hours, or overnight in the refrigerator. One hour before cooking, soak the bamboo skewers in cold water to cover for 1 hour. (This will prevent them from burning during cooking.)
2   Loosely thread an equal number of lamb cubes onto each skewer. Reserve the marinade for basting.
3   Broil the meat about 4 inches from the source of heat for 3½ to 4 minutes on each side, turning once and basting occasionally. Cook the lamb until medium-rare. Serve the lamb with steamed lotus buns (page 56) and sweet bean sauce.

SIX SERVINGS

2 pounds boned shoulder or leg of lamb

Lamb Marinade
4 tablespoons soy sauce
2 tablespoons rice wine
2 teaspoons sesame oil
1 teaspoon Sichuan peppercorns, toasted (in a heavy skillet over low heat for 2 minutes) and pulverized
¼ teaspoon freshly ground black pepper
1 teaspoon five-spice powder
1 tablespoon minced gingerroot
1 tablespoon minced garlic

6 10-inch bamboo skewers

255

2½ pounds blade or rib lamb
  chops

Lamb Marinade

3 tablespoons soy sauce
2 tablespoons rice wine
2 teaspoons sesame oil
1 teaspoon salt
3 scallions, smashed with the
  flat side of a cleaver
3 slices gingerroot, smashed
  with the flat side of a
  cleaver
1 teaspoon five-spice powder
1 teaspoon sugar
½ teaspoon Sichuan
  peppercorns, toasted (in a
  heavy skillet over low heat
  for 2 minutes) and
  pulverized

1 head leafy lettuce, rinsed
  and drained thoroughly
1 cup cornstarch
6 cups peanut, safflower, or
  corn oil

DEEP-FRIED LAMB CHOPS

JING SHAO YANG ROU　京燒羊肉

Although the double-cooking employed in this recipe may seem bothersome to some people, each step in the preparation of this dish contributes to the exquisite flavor. The deep-frying renders the fat and produces a crisp, golden skin.

1　Direct the butcher to cut the chops crosswise, through the bones, into pieces 2 inches long. Remove and discard any excess fat. Place the lamb pieces in a bowl and add the **lamb marinade**. Toss lightly and let marinate for at least 4 hours, or overnight in the refrigerator. Cut the lettuce into strips ½ inch wide and arrange them in a mound on a platter. Drain the lamb pieces and dredge them in the cornstarch, lightly pressing each piece to make sure the cornstarch adheres.
2　Heat a wok, add the oil, and heat the oil to 400°. Add a third of the lamb pieces and deep-fry, turning constantly over high heat, for about 3½ minutes, until the chops are cooked and the outside is crisp and golden. Remove with a handled strainer, and drain on absorbent paper. Reheat the oil and deep-fry the remaining chops in the same manner, reheating the oil between batches. Arrange over the shredded lettuce, and serve immediately.

STIR-FRIED LAMB WITH SCALLIONS

CONG BAO YANG ROU 葱 爆 羊 肉

While many Chinese generally do not care for lamb because of its strong flavor, this northern dish has become popular throughout China. One can hardly discern any flavor of lamb, since the meat slices are redolent of garlic and scallions.

1　Remove any fat or gristle from the lamb and discard. Cut the meat, across the grain, into slices about ⅛ inch thick. Cut the slices into pieces that are 1½ inches long and 1 inch wide. Place the pieces in a bowl, add the **lamb marinade**, toss lightly, and let marinate for 30 minutes.

2　Heat a wok, add the oil, and heat the oil to 400°. Add half the lamb and stir-fry over high heat, stirring constantly until the lamb changes color. Remove the meat and drain. Reheat the oil and stir-fry the remaining lamb pieces in the same manner. Remove the oil from the wok, reserving 3 tablespoons.

3　Reheat the wok, add the 3 tablespoons of oil, and heat until very hot. Add the garlic and the shredded scallions. Stir-fry over high heat for about 30 seconds. Add the cooked lamb and the **lamb sauce**. Toss lightly and transfer the mixture to a platter. Serve immediately.

2 pounds boned leg of lamb, shank half

Lamb Marinade
2½ tablespoons soy sauce
1½ tablespoons rice wine
1½ teaspoons sugar
2 tablespoons water
1 tablespoon cornstarch

1 cup peanut, safflower, or corn oil
6 cloves garlic, sliced very thinly
5 cups shredded scallion greens or leeks

Lamb Sauce
2 tablespoons soy sauce
2 tablespoons rice wine
2 teaspoons clear rice vinegar
1 tablespoon sesame oil

257

1½ pounds boned leg of
  lamb, shank half

Lamb Marinade

1 tablespoon soy sauce
½ tablespoon rice wine
1 teaspoon sugar
1 tablespoon minced
  gingerroot
1 tablespoon water
2 teaspoons cornstarch

10 dried wood ears
1½ cups water chestnuts
1½ cups peanut, safflower,
  or corn oil

Minced Seasonings

2 tablespoons minced
  scallions
1 tablespoon minced garlic

1½ teaspoons chili paste

Lamb Sauce

3 tablespoons soy sauce
1 tablespoon rice wine
1½ tablespoons sugar
1½ teaspoons Chinese black
  vinegar
¼ cup chicken broth or
  water
1 teaspoon cornstarch

SICHUAN LAMB

CHUAN SHI YANG ROU 川 式 羊 肉

This tasty stir-fried platter is distinctly Sichuanese in character, as evidenced by the pungent seasonings and the textural delicacies, wood ears and water chestnuts. Serve this spicy platter with a steamed green vegetable and rice for a filling and nutritious meal.

1   Remove any fat or gristle from the lamb and discard. Cut the meat, across the grain, into slices ⅛ inch thick. Cut the slices into pieces 1½ inches long and 1 inch wide. Place the pieces in a bowl, add the **lamb marinade**, toss lightly, and let marinate for 1 hour. Soften the wood ears for 20 minutes in hot water to cover; drain thoroughly. Cut away and discard the hard, bitter nib on the underside of the wood ears and cut the wood ears into thin shreds. Plunge the water chestnuts into boiling water for a few seconds to remove the tinny flavor. Refresh them in cold water and slice thinly.

2   Heat a wok, add the oil, and heat the oil to 400°. Drain the lamb pieces and add half to the hot oil. Stir-fry over high heat, turning constantly until the lamb changes color. Remove and drain. Reheat the oil and stir-fry the remaining lamb in the same manner. Remove the oil from the wok, reserving 3 tablespoons.

3   Reheat the wok, add the 3 tablespoons of oil, and heat until very hot. Add the **minced seasonings** and stir-fry for about 10 seconds, until fragrant. Add the chili paste and stir-fry for another 5 seconds. Add the wood ears and water chestnuts and stir-fry over high heat for about 20 seconds, until they are heated through. Add the **lamb sauce** and stir-fry until the sauce begins to thicken. Add the cooked lamb pieces, toss lightly to coat with the sauce, and transfer the mixture to a platter. Serve immediately.

VEGETABLES 蔬菜類

Winter comes hard to Taipei. The normally balmy air takes on a raw, chilling edge. The sky, which reflects the seasonal changes by its color, turns gray and threatening. Since central heating is virtually nonexistent, layers of clothing are donned and voluminous down quilts, unpacked from storage, are thrown over beds. In the mornings, seats are hard to come by at the *dou jiang* stands, as most of the city's residents combat the winter chill by downing a bowl of hot, filling soybean milk. At night, the unique call of the sweet potato vendor is heard as he roams the alleyways, peddling his hot snack. He wheels a portable charcoal stove filled with sizzling potatoes and carries a scale for measuring the weight and calculating the cost of each purchase.

Every evening, my Chinese surrogate sister and brothers would pile out of the house at the sound of the sweet potato call and buy a hot potato for their bedtime snack. I, on the other hand, had fallen into the habit of purchasing a whole catty of potatoes. At first my surrogate siblings were quite surprised, since I normally shunned large quantities of any food, being constantly on a diet. In time they came to appreciate my ingenuity: I wrapped each potato in foil, bundled the lot in a towel, and carefully tucked the hot package between my sheets. The Japanese have their hot bricks and the British their hot water bottles, but I had my sweet potatoes. In the morning, the same potatoes — now slightly crushed by my nocturnal tossings — would be donated to the family's breakfast. They were sliced, fried to a crisp golden brown, and served with the morning congee or rice.

In the winter marketplace, in addition to sweet potatoes, the stalls are heaped with other winter vegetables. Numerous green cabbages and winter bamboo shoots, the tastiest and most prized of the bamboo family, line the shelves.

Taiwan is an agricultural paradise. Because the northern half of the island suffers through chilling temperatures several months of the year and the southern half is drenched in sunshine and humid heat, both tropical vegetables and those that grow best in cooler temperatures thrive. China, too, with its varied climate and fertile

BAMBOO SHOOTS
CHINESE EGGPLANT
BITTER GOURD
DAIKON RADISH
LUFFA SQUASH

259

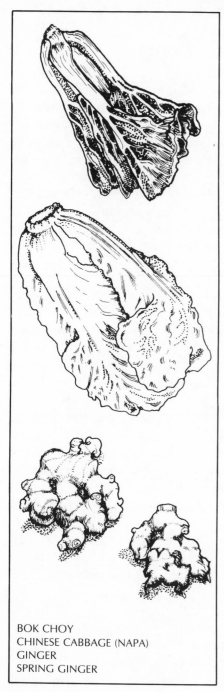

BOK CHOY
CHINESE CABBAGE (NAPA)
GINGER
SPRING GINGER

acreage, is a land of agricultural promise. The economy is largely agrarian, and has been since the beginning of civilization. The ancient Chinese were accomplished farmers, raising crops of beans, mallow, melons, turnips, gourds, Chinese leeks, cabbage, amaranth, garlic, water chestnuts, and bamboo shoots.

Later, as China opened her doors to the outside world, a host of new vegetables was introduced: Spinach and celery came from Nepal, and kohlrabi and garden peas were brought by the Europeans. Because of horticultural experimentation, the native vegetables also increased in numbers and varieties. As farming methods and transportation improved, so too did the availability of these products. Vegetables came to be obtainable year-round, and they were enjoyed by the wealthy and poor alike. Hence they came to assume a prominent role in the Chinese diet and in Chinese cuisine.

Vegetables served other purposes as well. Lotus root, rhubarb, kohlrabi, and the licorice plant were believed to possess medicinal properties and were prescribed as tonics. Garlic, leeks, and shallots were said to warm the body. During the Han dynasty (206 B.C. to A.D. 220), these and other strong-smelling vegetables were hung from doors and gates in the summertime to ward off disease, poisonous insects, and other evils. And most vegetables were used as offerings for the deities.

The Chinese classify vegetables into three categories: root, leafy, and fruit. Root vegetables include carrots, turnips, potatoes, taro, bamboo shoots, water chestnuts, lotus root, and gingerroot. Members of the leafy category are Chinese cabbage, watercress, spinach, amaranth, ''vegetable hearts,'' mustard greens, and edible chrysanthemums. The fruit family includes tomatoes, cucumbers, eggplant, winter melon, peas, and the many gourd varieties.

Stir-frying and steaming are the preferred cooking methods employed in hot vegetable dishes because these two processes preserve the vitamins, fresh flavors, crunchy textures, and bright colors of each vegetable.

Many vegetables also appear in cold salads. For hygienic reasons, vegetables are rarely eaten raw. They are plunged into boiling water and refreshed immediately in cold water before being used in salads and other cold dishes. A great deal of attention is paid to combining foods with contrasting flavors, colors, and textures: Shredded ham, chicken, or pork as well as dried jellyfish and shrimp are paired with bean sprouts, celery, carrots, peppers, green beans, cucumbers, eggplant, or Chinese turnip. Noodles, bean threads, agar-agar, and vermicelli sheets are used as textural bases. The dressings are numerous and may vary from a delicate vinegar—sesame oil creation to a hot and spicy peanut butter or sesame paste sauce. Since most parts of China experience a summer season of sorts, salads have become an ideal hot-weather dish. Their cool, crisp textures are pleasing to the palate and their preparation is quite simple.

Pickled vegetables also enjoy a prominent position in the Chinese diet, as they have for many centuries. In ancient China, fresh vegetables were scarce, owing to seasonal agricultural factors and lack of adequate refrigeration. To preserve these and other foods, methods such as smoking, drying, steeping, pickling, and salting were employed.

It is believed that the first Chinese pickles were salted and dried during the T'ang dynasty (618 to 907). Shortly thereafter, a vinegar-based brine was used to preserve vegetables. Even in these early times, a selection of vinegars was available: Rice, peaches, wheat, and grape juice were fermented to make vinegar, and kumquat leaves and peach blossoms were added to enhance the flavor. Water chestnuts, bamboo shoots, and mustard greens were all pickled in this manner.

Salt and wine were used in fermenting some vegetables. Pickled cabbage, or sauerkraut, is the most notable example of this process. It is said that the oldest form of sauerkraut was invented by Chinese workers building the Great Wall during the Han dynasty. They subsisted on a diet of cabbage and rice and used rice wine to preserve the cabbage from summer to winter. When the Tatars overran China, they sampled the pickled cabbage and adapted it to their own tastes, substituting salt for rice wine. It was in this form that sauerkraut was introduced to Europe.

Pickles are served as a piquant garnish to rice and congee, or as a pungent seasoning in cooked dishes. In modern China, most people eat large quantities of vegetables and pickles, for obvious reasons — they are flavorful, inexpensive, and nutritious.

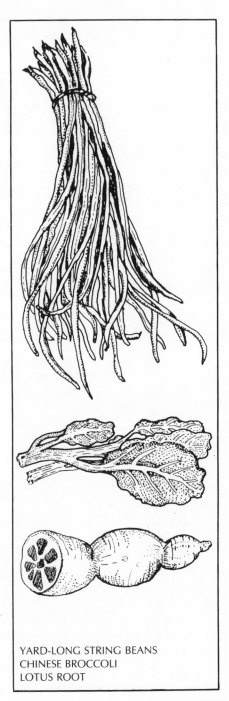

YARD-LONG STRING BEANS
CHINESE BROCCOLI
LOTUS ROOT

261

2 pounds celery hearts
1½ tablespoons powdered
  mustard
1 tablespoon boiling water
1 tablespoon rice wine
1 teaspoon salt
2 teaspoons sugar
1 tablespoon sesame oil

CELERY HEARTS IN MUSTARD SAUCE

JIE MO CHIN CAI 芥末青菜

In Chinese restaurants in the Far East, an empty stomach is never neglected for long. Small dishes of peanuts and pickled salads are served as soon as the diners sit down, so that they may nibble while planning their order. This spicy dish is often served in Peking restaurants.

1 Rinse the celery hearts and peel away the tough skin, if necessary. Cut off the root ends and leafy tops. Cut the celery in half lengthwise and cut each half into 2-inch pieces. Blanch the celery pieces in boiling water for 1 minute. Refresh immediately in cold water, drain thoroughly, and pat dry. Place the celery pieces in a bowl.

2 Mix the mustard powder and the boiling water to a smooth paste. Add the rice wine and combine well. Cover the mixture with a plate and let it sit for 10 minutes. Add the salt, sugar, and sesame oil to the mustard mixture and stir until smooth. Add the dressing to the celery pieces, toss lightly to coat them, and refrigerate for 1 hour before serving.

1 Chinese turnip (daikon
  radish), about ½ pound
4 carrots, peeled
6 pickling cucumbers or 2
  English ("gourmet
  seedless") cucumbers
1 tablespoon salt

CANTONESE PICKLED VEGETABLES

YUE SHI PAO CAI 粤式泡菜

Pao cai, or pickled vegetable salads, are found all over China, but they differ from place to place depending on the local products and flavorings. This sweet-and-sour version can stand alone, but it is often used as a colorful garnish for sweet-and-sour shrimp or pork.

1 Peel the turnip and cut off the root and stem ends. Cut the turnip lengthwise in half. Then cut each half lengthwise into thirds and

roll-cut each section into 1-inch pieces. Roll-cut the carrots into 1-inch pieces. Cut the cucumbers in half lengthwise. Remove any seeds and cut each half lengthwise into thirds. Roll-cut the cucumbers into 1-inch pieces. Place the vegetables in a mixing bowl, add the salt, toss lightly, and let sit for 2 hours. Drain off any water that has collected and pat the vegetables dry.

2   Combine the sugar and rice vinegar, stirring until the sugar has dissolved. Add this mixture and the gingerroot slices to the vegetables, and toss lightly to coat. Refrigerate for at least 3 hours, or overnight, before serving.

> 8 tablespoons sugar
> 8 tablespoons clear rice
>   vinegar
> 12 thin slices gingerroot,
>   smashed with the flat side
>   of a cleaver

STIR-FRIED LETTUCE WITH STRAW MUSHROOMS

CAO GU PA CAI   草菇扒菜

Lettuce holds a special place in the hearts of the Chinese. This leafy vegetable symbolizes prosperity because the Chinese name is similar in sound to the word for *thriving*. Consequently, it is often served at Chinese New Year celebrations.

1   Discard any wilted leaves from the lettuce and cut away any stem ends. Rinse the lettuce, drain thoroughly, and pat dry. Cut the leaves lengthwise into 1-inch strips. Blanch the straw mushrooms for 10 seconds in boiling water; drain, and refresh in cold water. Drain again.

2   Heat a wok, add 1 tablespoon of oil, and heat until smoking. Add the lettuce and the **lettuce seasonings.** Stir-fry over high heat for about 1 minute, until the lettuce is slightly wilted. Arrange the lettuce around the outer edge of a platter.

3   Reheat the wok, add the remaining tablespoon of oil, and heat until very hot. Add the **minced seasonings** and stir-fry over high heat until fragrant, about 10 seconds. Add the straw mushrooms and toss lightly for about 15 seconds. Add the **oyster sauce** and cook for about 1½ minutes, or until the sauce has thickened. Spoon the mushrooms and the sauce into the center of the platter and serve immediately.

> SIX SERVINGS
>
> 1½ pounds leafy or Boston
>   lettuce
> 2 15-ounce cans straw
>   mushrooms, drained
> 2 tablespoons peanut,
>   safflower, or corn oil
>
> **Lettuce Seasonings**
> ¾ teaspoon salt
> 1 tablespoon rice wine
> ½ teaspoon sesame oil
>
> **Minced Seasonings**
> 1 tablespoon minced
>   scallions
> 2 teaspoons minced
>   gingerroot
>
> **Oyster Sauce**
> 2 tablespoons soy sauce
> 1 tablespoon oyster sauce
> 1 teaspoon sugar
> ½ teaspoon sesame oil
> ½ cup chicken broth
> 1½ teaspoons cornstarch

1½ pounds boneless
center-cut pork loin

Pork Marinade

2 tablespoons soy sauce
1 tablespoon rice wine
½ teaspoon sugar
1 teaspoon minced
gingerroot
1 teaspoon minced scallions
1 tablespoon cornstarch

1 pound green beans
2 ounces bean threads

Bean Thread Seasonings

1 teaspoon salt
1 teaspoon sesame oil

1 cup peanut, safflower, or
corn oil

Dressing

¼ cup soy sauce
1½ teaspoons salt
1 tablespoon sugar
2 tablespoons sesame oil
2 tablespoons clear rice
vinegar
2 tablespoons rice wine

2 dried red chili peppers,
seeded and shredded

THREE-FLAVOR TOSSED SALAD

LIANG BAN SAN SI　凉拌三丝

Although Peking is in the north of China, its summers are long and sultry. Cold vegetable dishes and salads, similar to this platter, are extremely popular in the hot weather. Serve this dish as the first course of a banquet or as a filling, one-dish lunch or dinner.

1　Remove any fat or gristle from the pork loin and discard. Cut the meat, across the grain, into slices ⅛ inch thick. Cut the slices into matchstick-size shreds. Place the shreds in a bowl, add the **pork marinade,** toss lightly, and let marinate for 20 minutes.
2　Snap off the ends of the green beans and cut the beans into 2-inch lengths. Cook the beans in salted boiling water for about 2 minutes, or until tender. Refresh immediately in cold water and drain thoroughly.
3　Soften the bean threads for 10 minutes in hot water to cover. Drain them; then cook for 5 minutes in boiling water. Rinse the bean threads in cold water, drain thoroughly, and add the **bean thread seasonings**. Arrange the bean threads on a platter.
4　Heat a wok, add the oil, and heat until very hot. Add the pork shreds, toss lightly over high heat until they change color, and remove. Drain thoroughly. Arrange the green beans on top of the bean threads and place the meat shreds in a mound on top of the green beans. Clean the wok.
5　Reheat the wok, and add the **dressing** and the chili peppers. Heat the mixture until boiling and cook for 1 minute. Pour over the salad and serve.

SICHUAN PICKLED CUCUMBER SLICES

SI CHUAN MA LA HUANG GUA 四川麻辣黄瓜

SIX SERVINGS

From all outward appearances, this dish may seem quite simple, but the complexity of flavors in the sauce is unusual. All of the ingredients lend their individual flavors to create a taste that is simultaneously sweet, sour, hot, and numbing. Contrasted with the cool crispness of the cucumbers, the overall effect is exquisite.

1   Rinse the cucumbers, drain, and pat dry. Cut the cucumbers lengthwise in half, remove any seeds, and cut into slices about 4 inches long and 1 inch thick. Place the slices in a bowl, add the salt, toss lightly, and let sit for 30 minutes. Pour off any water that has accumulated. Rinse the cucumbers lightly, drain thoroughly, and pat dry. Place the cucumbers in a bowl and add the shredded gingerroot and fresh chili pepper.

2   Heat a wok, add the sesame oil, and heat until smoking. Add the Sichuan peppercorns and stir-fry over high heat for about 30 seconds, until fragrant. Add the dried chili peppers and stir-fry for about 30 seconds, until they turn black. Pour this mixture into the bowl containing the cucumbers, toss lightly, and let cool. Add the rice vinegar and sugar, toss to coat, and let the mixture sit for at least 6 hours in the refrigerator. Serve.

1 pound pickling or English ("gourmet seedless") cucumbers

1 tablespoon salt

½ cup finely shredded gingerroot, soaked in cold water for 20 minutes

1 fresh red chili pepper, seeded and cut into thin shreds

½ cup sesame oil

1 teaspoon Sichuan peppercorns

¼ cup dried chili peppers seeded and cut into ¼-inch lengths

3 tablespoons clear rice vinegar

1½ tablespoons sugar

1 pound Chinese cabbage
  (Napa)
1 Chinese turnip (daikon
  radish), about ½ pound
4 carrots, peeled

Pickling Mixture
10 cups warm water
5 tablespoons salt
¼ cup rice wine

1½ tablespoons Sichuan
  peppercorns
3 fresh red chili peppers,
  seeded and cut into
  ¼-inch lengths
12 slices gingerroot,
  smashed with the flat side
  of a cleaver

SICHUAN PICKLED SALAD

SI CHUAN PAO CAI　四川泡菜

According to my Sichuanese teacher, the flavor of this pickling marinade doesn't begin to "ripen" until the second use. In the Far East, starters are available from small Sichuanese restaurants. For those less fortunate, perseverance is the key; just realize that your second batch will be better than the first. The traditional pickle is made with cabbage, carrots, and Chinese turnip, but green beans and cucumbers may also be used.

1   Rinse the cabbage lightly, drain, and pat dry. Remove and discard the core, and cut the leaves into 2-inch squares. Lightly bruise the cabbage pieces by smashing them with the flat side of a cleaver. Spread the cabbage pieces out on a tray and let them air-dry for 1 hour, turning once. Peel the turnip, and cut off the root and stem ends. Cut the turnip lengthwise in half. Then cut each half lengthwise into thirds and roll-cut each piece into 1-inch pieces. Roll-cut the carrots into 1-inch pieces.
2   Pour the **pickling mixture** into a glass jar or a pickling crock. Stir to dissolve the salt. Add the Sichuan peppercorns and let the liquid cool to room temperature. Add the chili peppers and the gingerroot. Add the vegetables and stir again. The liquid should cover the vegetables. If not, add more water. Cover tightly and let sit for 3 days at room temperature. Remove the vegetables and serve. Refrigerate the marinade and use it again, adding 2 tablespoons each of salt and rice wine every time, plus enough water to cover the vegetables.

STIR-FRIED HOT AND SOUR CABBAGE

SUAN LA BAI CAI 酸辣白菜

Chinese cabbage is one of the most versatile vegetables. It can be stir-fried, steamed, pickled, or cooked in soups, and its taste lends a pronounced flavor to any dish. Fortunately, several varieties are now available in most supermarkets. For this spicy northern dish, I prefer to use the one called Napa, which is available in both supermarkets and Chinese grocery stores.

1   Discard any wilted leaves from the cabbage and cut away any stem sections from the leaves. Cut the leaves into 2-inch squares and separate the hard pieces from the leafy pieces.

2   Heat a wok, add the oil, and heat until smoking. Add the hard cabbage pieces and stir-fry over high heat, stirring constantly for 30 seconds. Add the rice wine and continue stir-frying for another 30 seconds. Add the leafier cabbage pieces and stir-fry for about 1 minute, stirring constantly. Remove the cabbage and set aside.

3   Reheat the wok, add the sesame oil, and heat until very hot. Add the **cabbage seasonings** and stir-fry for about 1 minute, until the dried chili peppers have turned black. Add the gingerroot shreds and stir-fry for 10 seconds, until fragrant. Add the cooked cabbage and stir-fry for about 30 seconds. Add the **cabbage sauce** and toss lightly over high heat. Cook until the sauce begins to thicken. Transfer the mixture to a platter and serve immediately.

SIX SERVINGS

2 pounds Chinese cabbage (Napa)
1 tablespoon peanut, safflower, or corn oil
1 tablespoon rice wine
1 tablespoon sesame oil

Cabbage Seasonings
1 tablespoon Sichuan peppercorns
6 dried chili peppers, seeded and cut into ¼-inch lengths

2 tablespoons finely shredded gingerroot

Cabbage Sauce
1 tablespoon soy sauce
1 tablespoon rice wine
¾ teaspoon salt
2 teaspoons sugar
2 teaspoons Chinese black vinegar
1 teaspoon cornstarch

2 pounds eggplant
1 teaspoon salt

Eggplant Sauce
¼ cup soy sauce
1 tablespoon rice wine
1 tablespoon clear rice
  vinegar
2 teaspoons sugar
1 tablespoon minced
  scallions
1½ tablespoons minced
  garlic
2 tablespoons sesame oil
2 teaspoons chili oil or chili
  paste

SPICY STEAMED EGGPLANT

ZHENG QIE ZI 蒸茄子

The Chinese eggplant, unlike its American cousin, is long, thin, and about the size of a zucchini. It is also an extremely versatile vegetable; its tender flesh absorbs flavors and is the perfect carrier for both spicy and delicate sauces. If Chinese eggplant are unavailable, use small, tender eggplant. This dish may be served hot or cold.

1   Peel the eggplant and cut off the ends. Cut the eggplant in half lengthwise and cut each half into strips about 1 inch thick. Cut the strips into pieces 2 inches long. Place the eggplant in a bowl, add the salt, toss lightly, and let sit for 1 hour. Pour off any water that has accumulated.
2   Fill a wok with water level with the bottom edge of a steamer tray and heat until boiling. Place the eggplant on a heat-proof plate, place the plate in a steamer tray, and cover. Place the steamer tray over the boiling water and steam the eggplant for 20 minutes, or until tender. Pour the **eggplant sauce** over the steamed eggplant, and serve.

2 cups shredded English
  ("gourmet seedless")
  cucumbers
2 cups shredded carrots
⅔ pound fresh bean sprouts
¼ pound medium-sized
  shrimp, peeled, deveined,
  and cooked
3 tablespoons dry-roasted
  peanuts, coarsely chopped

COLD CHINESE SALAD

LIANG BAN DOU YA CAI 凉拌豆芽菜

The light sesame oil–based vinaigrette in this northern salad provides a piquant contrast to the fresh vegetable shreds, sliced shrimp, and minced peanut topping. Shredded chicken or pork may be substituted for the shrimp. In a cold salad such as this, it is traditional and more refined to trim the ends of the bean sprouts, but this procedure is optional.

1   Combine the shredded cucumbers with two thirds of the shredded carrots. Place the mixture in the center of a large platter. Arrange the remaining carrot shreds around the outer edge of the platter. Place the bean sprouts around the cucumber-carrot mixture.

2 Holding a cleaver or a large chef's knife parallel to the cutting surface, slice the shrimp in half lengthwise. Arrange the shrimp, pink (uncut) side up, on top of the bean sprouts. Sprinkle the crushed peanuts over all. Before serving, pour the **Chinese vinaigrette** on the salad. Toss lightly and serve.

STIR-FRIED BROCCOLI IN OYSTER SAUCE

HAO YU JIE LAN CAI

Chinese broccoli differs from its Western relative in that the stems are longer, the flowerets are tiny, and the flavor is slightly bitter. It is available year-round at most Chinese markets, but if you cannot obtain it, substitute Western broccoli.

1 Peel away the tough outer skin of the broccoli and separate the flowerets. Roll-cut the stems into 1-inch pieces. Soften the dried mushrooms for 20 minutes in hot water to cover. Remove and discard the stems; cut the caps in half.

2 Heat 3 quarts salted water until boiling. Add the broccoli stem pieces and cook for ½ minute. Add the flowerets and cook for 1½ minutes, or until both stems and flowerets are just tender. Refresh immediately in cold water. Drain thoroughly.

3 Heat a wok, add the oil, and heat until very hot. Add the **minced seasonings** and stir-fry for 10 seconds, until fragrant. Add the mushroom halves and stir-fry for about 5 seconds. Add the broccoli and toss lightly over high heat until the broccoli is heated through. Add the **oyster sauce** and heat until thickened, tossing lightly to coat the broccoli. Transfer the mixture to a serving platter. Serve immediately.

SIX SERVINGS

2 pounds Chinese broccoli
8 dried Chinese black
   mushrooms
2 tablespoons peanut,
   safflower, or corn oil

Minced Seasonings
1 tablespoon minced
   scallions
1 tablespoon minced
   gingerroot
1 tablespoon minced garlic

Oyster Sauce
3 tablespoons oyster sauce
2 tablespoons soy sauce
1 tablespoon rice wine
1 teaspoon sugar
1 teaspoon sesame oil
6 tablespoons chicken broth
   or water
2 teaspoons cornstarch

2 pounds yard-long string
 beans
½ pound ground pork or
 beef

Meat Seasonings
1 teaspoon soy sauce
1 teaspoon rice wine
½ teaspoon sesame oil

6 cups peanut, safflower, or
 corn oil
1 tablespoon dried shrimp,
 softened for 1 hour in hot
 water to cover and minced
5 tablespoons minced
 Sichuan preserved mustard
 greens, rinsed lightly and
 drained

Green Bean Sauce
1½ tablespoons soy sauce
1 tablespoon rice wine
1½ teaspoons sugar
1 tablespoon water

2 tablespoons minced
 scallion greens
1 teaspoon sesame oil

DRY-COOKED STRING BEANS

GAN BIAN SI JI DOU　　乾煸四季豆

Yard-long string beans have become more readily recognizable to Americans as the demand for Chinese ingredients has increased. Now these long beans are available seasonally in most Chinese markets and the seeds are sold in major seed catalogues. Western string beans may be used in this recipe.

1　Snap off both ends of the beans. Cut the beans on the diagonal into 2-inch pieces. Rinse the beans and drain thoroughly. Lightly chop the ground meat until fluffy. Place the meat in a bowl, add the **meat seasonings,** and stir vigorously in one direction to combine evenly.

2　Heat a wok, add the oil, and heat the oil to 400°. Add a third of the beans, covering the wok with the dome lid as they are placed in the oil to prevent the oil from splashing. Deep-fry the beans for about 3½ minutes, stirring constantly until they are tender and golden brown at the edges. Remove with a handled strainer, and drain. Reheat the oil and deep-fry the remaining beans in the same manner, reheating the oil between batches. Remove the oil from the wok, reserving 2 tablespoons.

3　Reheat the wok, add the 2 tablespoons of oil, and heat until very hot. Add the ground meat and stir-fry until the color changes, mashing and chopping to separate the grounds. Push the meat to the side and add the minced shrimp and the preserved mustard greens. Stir-fry over high heat for about 15 seconds, until fragrant. Add the fried beans and the **green bean sauce,** and return the meat to the center of the pan. Toss lightly to coat the beans with the sauce. Add the minced scallion greens and the sesame oil. Toss lightly and transfer the mixture to a platter. Serve immediately.

BRAISED CELERY HEARTS WITH DRIED SHRIMP

XIA MI CHING CAI　　　　蝦米芹菜

The subtle flavorings and refined seasonings that mark eastern cooking are clearly illustrated in this vegetable dish. The full, rich taste of the celery hearts is offset by the savory chicken broth and pungent dried shrimp.

1　Rinse the celery hearts and peel away the tough skin, if necessary. Cut off the root ends and leafy tops. Cut the celery in half lengthwise and cut each half into 2-inch pieces.

2　Heat a wok, add the sesame oil, and heat until very hot. Add the **minced seasonings** and stir-fry over high heat for 10 seconds, until fragrant. Add the celery and the **braising mixture**. Heat until boiling, partially cover, and reduce the heat to medium. Cook for 15 minutes, stirring occasionally, until the celery is tender. Slowly add the **thickener**, stirring constantly to prevent lumps. Transfer the mixture to a bowl, sprinkle with the minced scallion greens, and serve.

SIX SERVINGS

2 pounds celery hearts
1 tablespoon sesame oil

Minced Seasonings

1 teaspoon dried shrimp, softened for 1 hour in hot water to cover and minced
1 tablespoon minced scallions
1 tablespoon minced gingerroot

Braising Mixture

2 tablespoons rice wine
1 teaspoon salt
1½ cups chicken broth
1½ teaspoons sugar
¼ teaspoon freshly ground white pepper

Thickener

1½ teaspoons cornstarch
1½ tablespoons water

1 tablespoon minced scallion greens

1¼ pounds ground pork or
beef

Meat Seasonings
1½ tablespoons soy sauce
1 tablespoon rice wine
2 teaspoons sesame oil
1 tablespoon minced
gingerroot
1 tablespoon minced
scallions
1½ tablespoons cornstarch

1 tablespoon dried shrimp,
softened for 1 hour in hot
water to cover and minced
6 medium-sized green
peppers, cored and
seeded
2 tablespoons cornstarch
3 tablespoons peanut,
safflower, or corn oil

Minced Seasonings
1 tablespoon fermented
black beans, rinsed,
drained, and minced
1 tablespoon minced garlic
1 tablespoon minced
scallions

STUFFED PEPPERS IN BLACK BEAN SAUCE

XIANG QING ZHAO 釀青椒

The black bean sauce in this dish is quite subtle, yet substantial enough to complement the green peppers and meat filling. Raw shelled shrimp may be substituted for the pork for a flavorful variation; in that case, omit the dried shrimp.

1   Lightly chop the ground meat until fluffy. Place the meat in a mixing bowl, and add the **meat seasonings** and the minced shrimp. Stir vigorously in one direction to combine evenly. Lightly throw the mixture against the inside of the bowl.
2   Lightly dust the cavity of each green pepper with the cornstarch. Stuff a portion of the ground meat mixture into each pepper. Using the underside of a spoon dipped in water, smooth the surface of the filling.
3   Heat a wok, add the oil, and heat until very hot. Place half the peppers, filling side down, in the hot oil. Fry for a minute over high heat until the filling is golden brown. Remove the peppers and reheat the oil. Fry the remaining peppers in the same manner. Reheat the oil, add the **minced seasonings,** stir-fry for about 10 seconds (until fragrant), and add the **sauce.** Add the green peppers, filling side down, and heat the mixture until boiling. Cover, reduce the heat to medium, and cook for about 10 minutes, until the meat is cooked and the peppers are tender. Uncover, turn the heat to high, and reduce the sauce to a coating consistency. Transfer the stuffed peppers to a platter, meat side up, and pour the sauce over the top. Serve immediately.

Sauce

1 cup chicken broth	¾ teaspoon sugar
1½ tablespoons soy sauce	½ teaspoon salt
1½ tablespoons rice wine	1 teaspoon cornstarch

STUFFED CUCUMBERS

XIANG DA HUANG GUA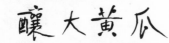

The tender flesh of the cucumber is superbly complemented by the savory forcemeat filling in this eastern dish, which is excellent accompanied by rice. Zucchini may be substituted for the cucumber for an equally delectable variation.

1   Cut each cucumber lengthwise in half and scoop out the seeds and the centers. Cut each half crosswise into thirds. Sprinkle the cucumber cavities with cornstarch. Plunge the water chestnuts into boiling water for a few seconds to remove the tinny flavor. Refresh them in cold water and chop coarsely. Lightly chop the meat until fluffy. Place it in a mixing bowl with the water chestnuts and the **meat seasonings**. Stir vigorously in one direction and lightly throw the mixture against the inside of the bowl to combine evenly. Stuff the cucumbers with the ground meat mixture and smooth the surface with the underside of a spoon dipped in water.

2   Heat a wok, add the oil, and heat until very hot. Place a third of the cucumbers (or as many as the wok will hold) meat side down in the bottom of the wok. Fry over medium-high heat for about 1 minute, until golden brown. Remove with a slotted spoon. Fry the remaining cucumbers in the same manner. Add the **braising mixture** to the wok, heat until boiling, and add the cucumbers, meat side up. Cover the pan and heat until the liquid boils again. Turn the heat to medium-low and simmer for 15 minutes, or until the meat is cooked and the cucumbers are tender. With a slotted spoon, remove the cucumbers and arrange them on a platter. Heat the braising mixture until boiling, add the **thickener,** stirring constantly to prevent lumps, and heat until thickened. Pour the sauce over the cucumbers, sprinkle the tops with the minced scallion greens, and serve immediately.

SIX SERVINGS

3 medium-sized English ("gourmet seedless") cucumbers
2 tablespoons cornstarch
½ cup water chestnuts
1 pound ground pork or beef

Meat Seasonings
1½ tablespoons soy sauce
1 tablespoon rice wine
½ teaspoon salt
1½ teaspoons sesame oil
1 tablespoon minced scallions
2 teaspoons minced gingerroot
1½ tablespoons cornstarch

3 tablespoons peanut, safflower, or corn oil

Braising Mixture
2 cups chicken broth
1 tablespoon soy sauce
1 tablespoon rice wine
½ teaspoon salt
½ teaspoon sugar

Thickener
1½ teaspoons cornstarch
1 tablespoon water

2 tablespoons minced scallion greens

1 pound fresh scallops

Scallop Marinade
1 tablespoon rice wine
2 slices gingerroot, smashed
   with the flat side of a
   cleaver
½ teaspoon salt

1½ pounds carrots
   (preferably big ones),
   cooked in boiling water for
   2 minutes and refreshed
1½ pounds English
   ("gourmet seedless")
   cucumbers

Vegetable Sauce
2 cups chicken broth
1½ tablespoons rice wine
1 teaspoon salt
½ teaspoon sugar

Thickener
2 teaspoons cornstarch
1 tablespoon water

VEGETABLE BALLS WITH SCALLOPS

GAN BEI LIANG SE QIU　干貝两色球

This delicate vegetable platter is often served at Chinese New Year because the spheres of carrots and cucumbers are said to resemble money. (Foods resembling money are eaten then in hopes of achieving prosperity during the coming year.) Dried scallops, a savory delicacy used as a pungent seasoning, are traditional in this recipe, but I have adapted the original to create a more delicately seasoned platter.

1 Rinse the scallops lightly and drain thoroughly. Holding a cleaver or a chef's knife parallel to the cutting surface, slice each scallop in half through the thickness (see page 201). Cut each half into matchstick-size shreds. Place the shredded scallops in a bowl. Pinch the gingerroot slices in the **scallop marinade** repeatedly for several minutes to impart the flavor to the rice wine. Add the marinade to the scallops, toss lightly, and let marinate for 20 minutes. Discard the gingerroot.

2 Peel the carrots and cucumbers and cut off the ends. Using a melon baller, cut the vegetables into balls. Heat 3 quarts of salted water until boiling and add the carrot balls. Cook for about 2 minutes over medium heat, add the cucumber balls, and continue cooking for 2 more minutes. The carrot and cucumber balls should be tender. Remove and drain.

3 Heat a wok, add the **vegetable sauce,** and heat until boiling. Add the carrot and cucumber balls and cook for 30 seconds. Add the **thickener,** stirring constantly to prevent lumps. When the sauce has thickened, add the scallop shreds. Stir to blend, taste the sauce for seasoning, and adjust if necessary. Transfer the mixture to a bowl and serve immediately.

FIVE-TREASURE VEGETABLE PLATTER

WU SI SU CAI

五色蔬菜

Although Sichuanese cuisine is best known for its fiery, spicy seasonings, there are a number of more mild-flavored banquet dishes. This platter is such a dish. The vegetables used may be varied according to seasonal availability.

1   Peel the baby carrots and trim the ends. Peel the asparagus to within a few inches of the tip and break off the tough end. Heat a quart of salted water until boiling. Add the fresh asparagus and cook for 7 minutes, covered. Drain, and refresh in cold water. Add the carrots to the boiling water. Cook the carrots for 4 minutes, uncovered. Drain, and refresh in cold water.

2   Cut out the stem of each tomato and make a shallow cross in the skin at the opposite end, cutting through the skin only. Plunge the tomatoes into boiling water for 20 seconds, until the skin puckers, and refresh immediately in cold water. Drain, and peel the skin. Cut each tomato into quarters and remove the seeds.

3   Pour two thirds of the **vegetable cooking mixture** into a wok or saucepan and heat until boiling. Add the asparagus and carrots, and cook for 2 minutes. Remove the vegetables with a slotted spoon and heat the mixture until boiling. Add the straw mushrooms and baby corn ears and cook for 1 minute. Remove with a slotted spoon and again heat the mixture until boiling. Add the tomatoes and cook for about 1 minute. Remove the tomatoes with a slotted spoon. Discard the liquid.

4   Place the straw mushrooms in the center of a large round platter and arrange the remaining vegetables, except the tomatoes, decoratively in individual piles around them. Arrange the tomatoes in a circle between the mushrooms and the other vegetables.

5   Pour the remainder of the vegetable cooking mixture into a saucepan or wok and heat until boiling. Slowly add the **thickener,** stirring constantly to prevent lumps. Add the sesame oil, stir to combine, and pour the sauce over the vegetables. Serve immediately.

SIX SERVINGS

1 pound baby carrots
1 pound fresh asparagus (or 2 cans white asparagus, drained and blanched briefly in boiling water)
3 medium-sized tomatoes

Vegetable Cooking Mixture

6 cups chicken broth
3 tablespoons rice wine
2 teaspoons salt

1 15-ounce can straw mushrooms, drained and blanched briefly in boiling water
1 can baby corn ears, drained and blanched briefly in boiling water

Thickener

2 teaspoons cornstarch
1 tablespoon water

1 teaspoon sesame oil

275

½ pound boneless center-cut pork loin

Pork Marinade
1 tablespoon soy sauce
1 tablespoon rice wine
1 teaspoon sesame oil
1 tablespoon water
2 teaspoons cornstarch

18 Shanghai spring roll (or *lumpia*) wrappers
1 tablespoon sugar
½ cup coarsely chopped peanuts
1 cup peanut, safflower, or corn oil
¼ cup shredded (softened) Chinese black mushrooms
1 cup shredded leeks or 1-inch scallion green pieces
3 cups fresh bean sprouts

Pork Sauce
1½ tablespoons soy sauce
1 tablespoon rice wine
1 teaspoon sesame oil
½ teaspoon sugar
¼ cup chicken broth
2 teaspoons cornstarch

STUFFED PANCAKES

SHI JING LIANG CAI 十錦涼菜

The Festival of the Dead is a Chinese holiday celebrated 106 days after the winter solstice. On this day, ancestors' graves are visited and offerings are presented to their departed souls. Traditionally, no fires are lit for three days before the holiday, so it has become known as the "cold foods" festival. Cold dishes, like this one, are prepared in advance and eaten cold or at room temperature.

1   Remove any fat or gristle from the pork loin and discard. Cut the meat, across the grain, into slices ⅛ inch thick. Cut the slices into matchstick-size shreds. Place the shreds in a bowl, add the **pork marinade**, toss lightly, and let marinate for 20 minutes. Separate the wrappers and steam them briefly. Mix the sugar and peanuts.
2   Heat a wok, add the oil, and heat the oil to 400°. Add the pork shreds and stir-fry over high heat until they change color, about 1 minute. Remove with a handled strainer, and drain. Remove the oil from the wok, reserving 5 tablespoons.
3   Reheat the wok, add 2 tablespoons of the oil, and heat until very hot. Add the shredded mushrooms and stir-fry for about 10 seconds, until fragrant. Add the shredded leeks and stir-fry for another 30 seconds. Add the pork, the bean sprouts, and the **pork sauce.** Toss lightly over high heat until the sauce thickens. Transfer the mixture to a platter. Clean the wok.

Minced Vegetable Seasonings	**Vegetable Sauce**
1 tablespoon minced garlic	1 teaspoon salt
2 tablespoons minced salted Chinese turnip, rinsed and drained	1 tablespoon rice wine
	1 teaspoon sugar
	⅓ cup chicken broth
2 cups shredded Chinese cabbage (Napa)	2 teaspoons cornstarch
2 cups finely shredded carrots	½ cup hoisin sauce

4   Reheat the wok, add the remaining 3 tablespoons of oil, and heat until very hot. Add the **minced vegetable seasonings** and stir-fry for about 10 seconds, until fragrant. Add the cabbage and carrot shreds. Toss lightly over high heat for 2 minutes, until the shreds are tender. Add the **vegetable sauce.** Stir-fry over high heat, stirring constantly until the sauce thickens. Transfer this mixture to another platter. To eat, spread a little hoisin sauce over a spring roll wrapper, sprinkle on some chopped peanuts, portion some of each stir-fried mixture on top, and roll up.

DEEP-FRIED MUSHROOMS WITH PINE NUTS

SONG ZI YANG GU   松子洋菇

For centuries, nuts have been relished by the Chinese. Pine nuts have been cultivated since the T'ang dynasty, and they are added to numerous dishes for flavor and texture. In this dish they provide a buttery though crisp accompaniment to the tender mushrooms. Serve the fried mushrooms as an hors d'oeuvre or first course with the tart dipping sauce.

1   Lightly rinse the mushrooms and drain thoroughly. Pat dry. Mix the eggs with the soy sauce and black pepper. Put the flour, egg mixture, and pine nuts in separate deep dishes. First dredge the mushrooms in the flour, shaking out the excess, then dip them in the eggs, again draining away the excess, and finally coat with the pine nuts. Arrange the coated mushrooms on a tray and let them dry for 1 hour.
2   Heat a wok, add the oil, and heat the oil to 400°. Add a few of the coated mushrooms and deep-fry, turning constantly, for 2½ minutes, until the mushrooms are tender and the pine nuts are golden brown. Remove with a handled strainer, and drain on absorbent paper. Reheat the oil and deep-fry the remaining mushrooms in the same manner, reheating the oil after each batch. Serve with the **dipping sauce.**

SIX SERVINGS

1½ pounds fresh button mushrooms
3 eggs, lightly beaten
2 tablespoons soy sauce
¼ teaspoon freshly ground black pepper
2 cups all-purpose flour
3 cups coarsely chopped pine nuts
6 cups peanut, safflower, or corn oil

Dipping Sauce
½ cup soy sauce
3 tablespoons Chinese black vinegar
1 tablespoon finely shredded gingerroot

STIR-FRIED EGGPLANT WITH FISH FLAVOR

YU XIANG QIE ZI   魚香茄子

1½ pounds eggplant
½ pound ground pork or
    beef

Meat Marinade
2 teaspoons soy sauce
1 teaspoon rice wine
½ teaspoon sesame oil

6 cups peanut, safflower, or
    corn oil

Minced Seasonings
2 tablespoons minced
    scallions
2 teaspoons minced
    gingerroot
1½ tablespoons minced
    garlic

2 teaspoons chili paste

Fish-Flavored Sauce
2 tablespoons soy sauce
1 tablespoon rice wine
1 tablespoon sugar
1½ tablespoons Chinese
    black vinegar
1 teaspoon sesame oil

The "fish-flavored" sauce in this dish is simultaneously sweet, tart, and spicy. Its origin is traced to Sichuan, where the innovative chefs initially developed this sauce for the preparation of fish. They soon found that it complemented pork, chicken, and eggplant as well.

1   Rinse the eggplant, cut off the stems, and cut the eggplant lengthwise in half. Cut each half into slices ½ inch thick and cut the slices into pieces 3 inches long and 1 inch wide. Lightly chop the meat until fluffy and place it in a bowl. Add the **meat marinade,** toss lightly, and let the meat sit for 10 minutes.
2   Heat a wok, add the oil, and heat the oil to 400°. Add a third of the eggplant slices, covering the wok with the dome lid as they are placed in the oil to prevent the oil from splashing. Deep-fry the slices for about 3 minutes, or until tender. Remove with a handled strainer, and drain. Reheat the oil and deep-fry the remaining eggplant in the same manner, reheating the oil between batches. Remove the oil from the wok, reserving 2 tablespoons.
3   Reheat the wok, add the 2 tablespoons of oil, and heat until very hot. Add the ground meat and stir-fry until the color changes, mashing and chopping to separate the grounds. Push the meat to the side and add the **minced seasonings.** Stir-fry for about 10 seconds, until fragrant. Add the chili paste and stir-fry for about 5 seconds. Add the **fish-flavored sauce,** return the meat to the center of the pan, and toss over high heat until the sauce thickens. Add the fried eggplant, toss lightly to coat with the sauce, and transfer the mixture to a platter. Serve immediately.

VEGETARIAN DISHES 素菜類

The Kuantu Temple, a Buddhist-Taoist sanctuary founded in 1661, lies at the intersection of two rivers about an hour's drive from Taipei. Visitors can view several lavishly decorated temples containing gilded statues of Buddha and Matsu, the Holy Mother, or they can wander in the 320-foot-long Buddha Cave, which contains a small statue of the thousand-handed Goddess of Mercy flanked by her four fierce-looking protectors. Chinese from all parts of Taiwan flock here to sightsee, to pursue religious meditation, and to partake of the superb vegetarian food prepared in the temple's kitchens and served in its famous restaurant.

On a recent visit to Taiwan, I and fourteen fellow American food professionals had the honor of dining in the Kuantu Temple restaurant, where reservations are hard to come by. We feasted our way through a magnificent twelve-course meal that included cold asparagus spears with mock ham; braised Chinese black mushrooms coated in sesame seeds; deep-fried oyster mushrooms in batter; vegetarian dumplings with shredded spring ginger; a mixed vegetarian platter with fresh broccoli spears, water chestnuts, *enoki* mushrooms, cucumbers, and silver tree ears; and two soup pots — one with hairy seaweed and assorted vegetables and the other with steamed wheat gluten, pickled mustard cabbage, bamboo shoots, and straw mushrooms. The meal ended with a huge platter of fresh sliced fruit and a cold, sweet soup garnished with fresh pineapple, watermelon, and silver tree ears.

The quality and magnificence of the dishes was in no way diminished by the lack of meat. If anything, it was enhanced. Furthermore, we were all impressed by the level of sophistication that Chinese vegetarian cuisine has achieved.

To trace its creation and development, one must go back to the introduction of Buddhism and Taoism to China, for it was in the kitchens of these monasteries that vegetarian cuisine was conceived and refined. Although undocumented, it appears that Buddhism was first introduced to China from India before the first century A.D. The movement did not gain strength, however, until the Han dynasty (206 B.C. to 220 A.D.) when it was paired with Taoism, which preached simplicity and harmony with nature and was founded by Lao-tze, an eminent Chinese philosopher. The two religions had strong similarities in ideology and dietary practices: The Buddhists refrained from eating meat because they believed in reincarnation and abhorred killing any living animal; the Taoists abstained from eating meat and grains in order to achieve immortality and unity with the natural order of the universe. Both factions encouraged a diet of vegetables, herbs, plants, nuts, and seeds. The only major difference in the regimens of these two groups was that the Buddhists shunned garlic, onions, leeks, scallions, and the like (hun cai), believing that these spicy seasonings disrupted the internal tranquility of the body, whereas the Taoists credited many of these plants with medicinal value.

As Buddhism and Taoism became more widespread, the number of temples increased. Pilgrimages were made to the monasteries in observance of holidays and for religious meditation. In ancient China, these refuges also provided lodging and refreshment for travelers. Visitors sampled the food and slowly developed a taste for the cuisine. Gradually, restaurants and food stands offering vegetarian fare opened. While many of the pastries and snacks had once been eaten in observance of Buddhist festivals, they now became available on a seasonal basis in the marketplaces.

As the cuisine became more popular, the ancient chefs, particularly in eastern China, used their expertise and imagination to create an impressive repertory of delicate and sophisticated dishes. Imitations of chicken, goose, duck, ham, and fish were refined and perfected to the point where one was hard pressed to distinguish them from their models. Various ingredients were used to make these creations resemble the original foods as much as possible: Mock duck and goose were made from fried bean curd sheets; mock shrimp balls were created with potatoes and carrots; turtles were fashioned out of mushrooms and cucumbers; mock eels were formed with seaweed, turnips, mushrooms, and bamboo shoots; and imitation crab was created with bean curd.

Protein-rich foods such as soybeans and their by-products — bean curd, soybean milk, bean milk sheets, and bean curd sheets — figure prominently in vegetarian cookery. Wheat gluten (mian jin), the spongy material remaining after the starch in a flour dough has been removed, is another product available in several forms. Rolled into balls and deep-fried (*mian jin pao*), it is then stuffed with a variety of fillings; separated into chunks and steamed, with the resulting material (*kao fu*) braised and simmered, it is rolled into cylinders. This ingredient (*su chang*) is then used in stir-fried platters or braised and served cold in slices.

Naturally, vegetables themselves — fresh, dried, salted, or pickled — play a substantial role in vegetarian cooking. Preserved vegetables also are used as seasonings, and condiments such as pickled bean curd (*dou fu ru*) and hot sauces and pastes with a vegetable base provide additional seasoning for bland dishes. Nuts of all types figure prominently in a meatless diet; other foods used in vegetarian cookery include seaweed (in its many forms), noodles, and grains.

Today in the Far East, many Chinese still observe a reformed regimen of the Buddhist and Taoist dietary practices: Some abstain from eating meat each day before noon, while others will eat no meat on the second and sixteenth days of each month. In China, Buddhist teachings and temples gradually are being restored after the repression of the Cultural Revolution, and in Taiwan there are still a considerable number of Buddhist temples like the Kuantu and eateries that serve magnificent vegetarian fare in the memorable and refined style of the ancient Chinese master chefs.

FRIED WHEAT GLUTEN
STEAMED WHEAT GLUTEN

2 cups water
4 tablespoons honey
1 teaspoon salt
½ pound raw cashews
6 cups peanut, safflower, or
  corn oil

CRUNCHY CASHEWS

JIA YAO GUO　炸 腰 果

The Rong Shing Restaurant in Taipei is known for its superb Sichuanese cuisine. Once they are seated, diners are treated to a number of small snacks to munch on. These crunchy cashews were a favorite of mine. I would alternate mouthfuls of the cashews with sips of cold beer, becoming quite content even before the food was served.

1   Place the water, honey, and salt in a saucepan. Stir to dissolve the honey. Add the cashews and heat the mixture until boiling. Reduce the heat to medium and cook, uncovered, for 15 minutes. Remove the cashews from the water, drain thoroughly, and place them on a tray to air-dry for 1 hour, turning occasionally.
2   Heat a wok, add the oil, and heat the oil to 350°. Add the cashews and deep-fry over high heat, turning constantly for about 3½ minutes, until the cashews are golden brown. Remove the nuts with a handled strainer and spread them out on brown paper to drain. (Do not use paper towels, as the nuts will stick.) Let cool completely, and serve.

MOCK SHRIMP BALLS

SU CHA WAN ZI 素炸丸子

These golden-fried balls, with their pinkish hue, truly do resemble shrimp balls, in appearance if not in flavor. Served piping hot, they make a superb hors d'oeuvre or an unusual vegetable entrée.

1   Assemble the ingedients of the **mock shrimp mixture** and combine them in descending order, stirring vigorously after each addition. Add the egg white and stir vigorously in one direction until the mixture is smooth. Add the cornstarch and stir again until smooth. If the mixture is very soft, add another tablespoon of cornstarch and mix well. Refrigerate the mixture for about 1 hour.
2   Heat a wok, add the oil, and heat the oil to 350°. Shape the mock shrimp mixture into balls about ½ inch in diameter and carefully slide about a third of them into the hot oil. Turn up the heat to high and deep-fry the balls, stirring constantly, for about 3½ minutes, until they are golden brown and cooked through. Remove with a handled strainer, and drain on absorbent paper. Reheat the oil. Deep-fry the remaining balls in the same manner, reheating the oil between batches. Arrange the fried balls on a platter and serve immediately.

SIX SERVINGS

Mock Shrimp Mixture
3 cups firmly packed mashed boiling potatoes, still hot
½ cup minced raw carrot
¼ cup blanched, chopped water chestnuts
1 tablespoon minced scallions
2 teaspoons minced gingerroot
1½ teaspoons salt
1 tablespoon rice wine
1½ teaspoons sesame oil

1 egg white, lightly beaten
¼ cup cornstarch
6 cups peanut, safflower, or corn oil

12 small dried Chinese black
  mushrooms
1 19-ounce can winter
  bamboo shoots, plunged
  briefly into boiling water,
  refreshed, and drained
4 cups peanut, safflower, or
  corn oil
1 teaspoon minced garlic
1 pound fresh spinach,
  trimmed and cleaned

Spinach Seasonings
1 tablespoon rice wine
¾ teaspoon salt

Minced Seasonings
2 teaspoons minced scallions
1 teaspoon minced
  gingerroot

Black Mushroom Sauce
3 tablespoons soy sauce
2 tablespoons rice wine
2 teaspoons sugar
½ cup mushroom-soaking
  liquid

Thickener
1½ teaspoons cornstarch
1 tablespoon water

1½ teaspoons sesame oil

TWO WINTERS

CHAO SUAN DONG

The title of this colorful vegetable platter refers to the winter varieties of black mushrooms and bamboo shoots commonly used in the
dish. The flavor and quality of these two vegetables are believed to
be at their best during the colder months. Whatever the season, this
dish will please both the eye and the palate.

1   Soften the dried mushrooms for 20 minutes in hot water to
cover. Remove and discard the stems. Retain ½ cup of the mushroom-soaking liquid. Trim each bamboo shoot to a rectangle and
cut three V-shaped wedges lengthwise in each side. Then cut the
bamboo shoot crosswise into slices about ⅛ inch thick.
2   Heat a wok, add 1 tablespoon of oil, and heat until smoking.
Add the minced garlic and stir-fry for about 3 seconds; then add the
spinach and the **spinach seasonings**. Toss lightly over high heat until
the spinach is slightly wilted. Arrange the spinach around the outer
edge of a platter.
3   Reheat the wok, add the remaining oil, and heat the oil to 400°.
Add the black mushrooms and the bamboo slices and deep-fry,
stirring constantly, for about 1½ minutes over high heat. Remove
with a handled strainer, and drain. Remove the oil from the wok,
reserving 1 tablespoon.
4   Reheat the wok, add the tablespoon of oil, and heat until very
hot. Add the **minced seasonings** and stir-fry for about 10 seconds,
until fragrant. Add the **black mushroom sauce** (including the ½ cup
of mushroom-soaking liquid) and heat until boiling. Add the fried
mushrooms and bamboo shoots. Cover, and cook for 1½ minutes
over high heat. Uncover, and slowly add the **thickener**, stirring
constantly to prevent lumps. When the sauce has thickened, add
the sesame oil, toss lightly, and transfer the mixture to the center of
the platter. Serve immediately.

BROCCOLI IN MOCK CRABMEAT SAUCE

SU XIE JIE LAN

素蟹芥蘭

The minced soft bean curd and shredded carrot arranged on crisp stir-fried broccoli spears are meant to resemble flecks of crabmeat and pinkish roe.

1   Peel away the tough outer skin of the broccoli and separate the flowerets. Roll-cut the stems into 1-inch pieces. Heat 2 quarts salted water until boiling. Add the stem pieces and cook for ½ minute. Add the flowerets and cook for 2½ minutes, or until both stems and flowerets are just tender. Refresh immediately in cold water. Drain thoroughly.
2   Mash the bean curd with a fork and add the ½ teaspoon sesame oil.
3   Heat a wok, add 1 tablespoon of oil, and heat until very hot. Add the **minced seasonings** and stir-fry for about 10 seconds, until fragrant. Add the broccoli and the **broccoli sauce**. Toss lightly over high heat and cook for about 1 minute. Transfer the mixture to a platter. Clean the wok.
4   Reheat the wok, add the remaining oil, and heat until very hot. Add the mashed bean curd and toss lightly over high heat for 30 seconds. Add the **mock crabmeat sauce** and stir. Cook for about 20 seconds, stirring constantly until the mixture begins to bubble. Slowly add the **thickener**, stirring constantly, and cook until thickened. Pour the mixture over the broccoli and sprinkle the minced carrot over the top. Serve immediately.

1½ pounds broccoli
1 cake bean curd, about 3 inches square and 1 inch thick
½ teaspoon sesame oil
3 tablespoons peanut, safflower, or corn oil

Minced Seasonings
1½ teaspoons minced garlic
2 teaspoons minced gingerroot

Broccoli Sauce
2 tablespoons rice wine
1 teaspoon salt
1 teaspoon sesame oil

Mock Crabmeat Sauce
½ cup water or mushroom-soaking liquid
1½ tablespoons rice wine
½ teaspoon salt
½ teaspoon sugar
¼ teaspoon freshly ground white pepper
2 egg whites, lightly beaten

Thickener
1½ teaspoons cornstarch
1 tablespoon water

1 tablespoon minced carrot

3 tablespoons peanut,
  safflower, or corn oil
1 teaspoon minced garlic
1 pound fresh spinach,
  trimmed and cleaned

Spinach Seasonings
¾ teaspoon salt
1 tablespoon rice wine
1 teaspoon sesame oil

Minced Seasonings
1 tablespoon minced
  scallions
2 teaspoons minced
  gingerroot

2 10-ounce cans abalone
  mushrooms, drained and
  briefly blanched

Oyster Sauce
2 tablespoons soy sauce
1 tablespoon oyster sauce
1 teaspoon sugar
1 teaspoon sesame oil
½ cup water
1½ teaspoons cornstarch
¼ teaspoon black pepper

MOCK ABALONE IN OYSTER SAUCE

HAO YOU SU BAO YU　　蠔油素鮑魚

One can hardly discern the difference between the abalone mushrooms and real abalone in this flavorful meatless platter. If abalone mushrooms are unavailable, substitute straw or button mushrooms.

1　Heat a wok, add 1 tablespoon of oil, and heat until smoking. Add the minced garlic and the spinach. Toss lightly over high heat for 30 seconds; then add the **spinach seasonings**. Toss lightly and continue cooking until the spinach is barely limp. Arrange the spinach around the outer edge of a platter.
2　Reheat the wok, add the remaining 2 tablespoons of oil, and heat until very hot. Add the **minced seasonings** and stir-fry for about 10 seconds, until fragrant. Add the abalone mushrooms and stir-fry for about 1 minute, until heated through. Add the **oyster sauce**. Toss lightly over high heat and cook until the sauce has thickened. Spoon the mixture into the center of the platter and serve immediately.

VEGETARIAN LION'S HEAD

SU SHI ZI TOU 素 獅 子 頭

Lion's head, the classic eastern casserole, is a filling meal-in-one dish with its meatballs, cabbage, and broth. This tasty vegetarian variation is a trifle more subtle than the hearty original. Although Chinese cabbage is available year-round, it is at its best in late summer and early fall.

1 Place two bean curd cakes in the center of a linen dishtowel, gather the edges together, and twist to squeeze out as much moisture as possible. Place the bean curd in a bowl and repeat for the remaining cakes. Using a fork, mash the bean curd until smooth. Add the mushrooms, carrots, water chestnuts, and the **bean curd seasonings**. Stir vigorously in one direction until the ingredients are thoroughly combined. Add the eggs and stir to combine. Add the cornstarch and stir briefly to combine. Set the mixture aside.

2 Remove four of the outer cabbage leaves, rinse them lightly, and set aside. Cut the remaining cabbage into 2-inch squares, discarding the stem and keeping the harder pieces separate from the leafy ones.

3 Heat a wok, add 2 tablespoons of oil, and heat until very hot. Add the harder cabbage pieces and toss lightly over high heat for about 1½ minutes. Add the leafy pieces and continue stir-frying over high heat for about 1 minute. Add the **soup base** and heat the mixture until boiling. Cook for about 5 minutes and transfer the mixture to an earthenware casserole or a Dutch oven. Clean the wok.

4 Reheat the wok, add the remaining 2 tablespoons of oil, and heat until very hot. Shape the bean curd mixture into four oval-shaped balls and dip them in the **lion's head coating**. Carefully lower the coated balls into the hot oil and fry on both sides over high heat until golden. Arrange the balls on top of the cabbage in the casserole. Arrange the four whole cabbage leaves on top and cover the casserole.

5 Preheat the oven to 375°. Bake the casserole for 1 hour. Remove from the oven and serve.

4 cakes bean curd
½ cup minced (softened) Chinese black mushrooms
1 cup finely shredded carrots
¾ cup water chestnuts, plunged briefly into boiling water, refreshed in cold water, and minced

Bean Curd Seasonings
1½ tablespoons soy sauce
1 teaspoon salt
1 tablespoon rice wine
¼ teaspoon black pepper
2 teaspoons sesame oil
1 tablespoon minced scallions
2 teaspoons minced gingerroot

3 eggs, lightly beaten
½ cup cornstarch
1 pound Chinese cabbage (Napa)
4 tablespoons peanut, safflower, or corn oil

Soup Base
4 cups water
2 tablespoons rice wine
½ teaspoon salt

Lion's Head Coating
1 tablespoon soy sauce
1 tablespoon cornstarch
1½ tablespoons water

287

8 cups peanut, safflower, or
   corn oil
2 cups 1-inch lengths
   Chinese garlic chives,
   scallion greens, or leeks
3 cups fresh bean sprouts
½ teaspoon salt
2 tablespoons rice wine

Minced Seasonings
1 tablespoon minced
   gingerroot
1 tablespoon minced garlic

¾ cup finely shredded
   (softened) Chinese black
   mushrooms
2 cups finely shredded
   Chinese cabbage (Napa)
1½ cups finely shredded
   carrots

VEGETARIAN SPRING ROLLS

SU CHUN JUAN　素春捲

The pungent seasonings of Chinese black mushrooms and Chinese garlic chives give these rolls a pronounced flavor. Serve the fried rolls with duck sauce or a sweet-and-sour sauce for dipping.

1 Heat a wok, add 1 tablespoon of oil, and heat until very hot. Add the Chinese garlic chives and stir-fry for about 1 minute over high heat. Add the bean sprouts, salt, and 1 tablespoon rice wine; continue stir-frying over high heat for 1 minute, until the bean sprouts are slightly limp. Place the mixture in a colander and let it drain for 10 minutes; toss occasionally.

2 Heat a wok, add 2 tablespoons of oil, and heat until very hot. Add the **minced seasonings** and stir-fry for about 10 seconds, until fragrant. Add the black mushroom shreds, and stir-fry for another 10 seconds. Add the cabbage and carrot shreds. Stir-fry for about 30 seconds and add the remaining tablespoon of rice wine. Stir-fry for another minute over high heat and add the **spring roll sauce**. Toss lightly over high heat until the sauce has thickened. Spread the mixture out on a tray and let it cool for 15 minutes. Combine it with with the bean sprout–Chinese garlic chives mixture. Clean the wok.

3 Separate the spring roll wrappers and place them on a counter. Place 2 heaping tablespoons of the stir-fried mixture on one wrap-

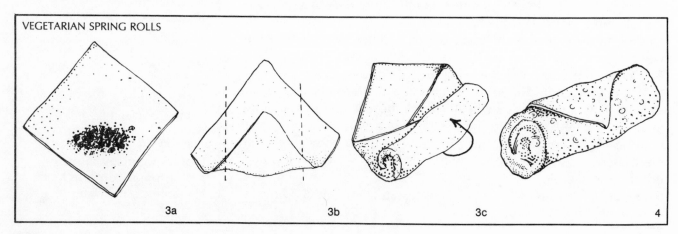

VEGETARIAN SPRING ROLLS

3a　　　3b　　　3c　　　4

per toward the edge of the wrapper closest to you (a). Spread the filling out evenly over the wrapper to within 2 inches of each end. Spread some of the **adhesive** on the opposite end. Gather in the sides (b) and roll up the wrapper to enclose the filling (c). Press to secure. Repeat for the remaining wrappers and filling.

4   Reheat the wok, add the remaining oil, and heat the oil to 375°. Add half the spring rolls and deep-fry, turning constantly over high heat for about 5 minutes, until golden brown. Remove with a handled strainer, and drain on absorbent paper. Reheat the oil and deep-fry the remaining spring rolls in the same manner. Arrange the spring rolls on a platter and serve immediately with duck sauce or sweet-and-sour sauce.

Spring Roll Sauce

3 tablespoons soy sauce
1 tablespoon water
1½ teaspoons cornstarch
1 teaspoon sesame oil

20 Shanghai spring roll (or
   lumpia) wrappers

Adhesive

1 egg yolk
2 tablespoons flour
3 tablespoons water

---

20 bean milk sheets

Bean Milk Seasonings

1 cup mushroom-soaking
 liquid (from mushrooms
 below)
1½ cups water
4 tablespoons soy sauce
3 tablespoons sugar
2 tablespoons sesame oil
1 tablespoon rice wine
1 teaspoon salt

1 ounce bean threads
¼ cup finely shredded
 (softened) Chinese black
 mushrooms
1 cup peanut, safflower, or
 corn oil

MOCK GOOSE

SU ER

An interesting facet of Chinese vegetarian cooking is its repertory of mock meat dishes. These platters, which often use soybean products such as bean curd and bean milk sheets, seek to imitate various kinds of meats, poultry, and seafood. They may not be carbon copies in taste to their originals, but their flavors are bound to please. Here is one example.

1   Soften the bean milk sheets in hot water for 5 minutes. Drain thoroughly and pat dry. Place the **bean milk seasonings** in a saucepan and heat until boiling, stirring constantly to dissolve the sugar. Soften the bean threads for 10 minutes in hot water. Drain and cut them into 5-inch lengths.

2   Place a bean milk sheet on a tray and generously brush it with the hot seasoning mixture. Place another sheet on top and brush again. Arrange four more sheets on top of one another, adding the seasoning mixture each time, and lay half the black mushroom shreds and half the bean threads in a lengthwise strip in the center to within an inch of each end. Sprinkle a tablespoon of the seasoning mixture on top. Place a bean milk sheet on top to cover the bean threads and black mushrooms, sprinkle some of the seasoning mixture on top, and add three more bean milk sheets, brushing each layer with the seasoning mixture. Fold in the sides and the ends of the bean milk sheets to create a loaf approximately 3 inches wide and 12 inches long. Use the remaining bean milk sheets, seasoning mixture, mushrooms, and bean threads to make another loaf. Wrap each loaf in cheesecloth or muslin and place the loaves on a lightly greased heat-proof plate. Put the plate in a steamer tray.

3   Fill a wok with water level with the bottom edge of the steamer tray and heat until boiling. Place the steamer tray over the boiling water, cover, and steam for 20 minutes over high heat. Remove the plate from the steamer tray and let the loaves cool to room temperature.

4   Heat a wok, add the oil, and heat the oil to 375°. Add one steamed loaf and fry for about 3½ minutes over high heat until both

sides are golden brown. Remove with a handled strainer, and drain on absorbent paper. Fry the remaining loaf in the same manner. Cut the loaves into 1-inch slices and arrange on a platter. Serve immediately.

VEGETARIAN EIGHT TREASURES

SU BA BAO

In the original stir-fried platter on which this vegetarian dish is based, pork cubes are one of the eight treasures. One hardly misses the pork in this spicy meatless version.

1   Place the bean curd between two paper towels and place a light weight on top. (This will compress the cake and remove excess water.) Let it sit for 1 hour. Drain the bean curd and cut it into ½-inch dice.
2   Heat a wok, add 2 tablespoons of oil, and heat until very hot. Add the bean curd, cucumber, carrot, water chestnuts, and peas; toss lightly over high heat, stirring constantly until the ingredients are hot, about 1½ minutes. Remove and set aside. Clean the wok.
3   Reheat the wok, add the remaining tablespoon of oil, and heat until very hot. Add the chili paste and stir-fry for about 10 seconds, until fragrant. Add the **sweet bean sauce** and cook until the sauce begins to thicken. Add all the cooked vegetables and the peanuts. Toss lightly and transfer the mixture to a platter. Serve immediately.

SIX SERVINGS

2 cakes bean curd
3 tablespoons peanut, safflower, or corn oil
¾ cup ½-inch-diced cucumber, cooked in boiling water until just tender
¾ cup ½-inch-diced carrot, cooked in boiling water until just tender
¾ cup ½-inch-diced water chestnuts, plunged briefly into boiling water and drained
¾ cup green peas, cooked in boiling water until just tender
2 teaspoons chili paste

Sweet Bean Sauce
2 tablespoons sweet bean sauce
3 tablespoons soy sauce
1½ tablespoons sugar
1 tablespoon rice wine
1½ tablespoons water

¾ cup dry-roasted unsalted peanuts

1 teaspoon active dry yeast
1 cup warm water
2 cups gluten flour or
    all-purpose flour

WHEAT GLUTEN

MIAN JIN 麥面 筋

Wheat gluten is an ingredient that plays a major role in Chinese vegetarian cookery. Its spongy texture and mild flavor make it extremely versatile; it may be steamed, stir-fried, deep-fried, or braised. Wheat gluten is easily made, as demonstrated here, or it may be purchased dried, frozen, or in cans at most Chinese grocery stores. Wheat gluten will keep for up to a week when refrigerated, or it may be frozen.

1   Dissolve the yeast in the warm water. Place the flour in a bowl. Add the yeast mixture and mix to a rough dough. Turn the dough out onto a lightly floured surface and knead vigorously for about 5 minutes until smooth and elastic. Place the dough in a lightly greased bowl, cover with a damp towel, and let rise for 2 hours in a warm place free from drafts.
2   Punch down the dough and knead lightly on a floured surface for 1 minute. Rinse the dough in running water, squeezing it repeatedly like a sponge. Continue rinsing and squeezing until the water runs clear. The dough should feel very spongy and be free of all starch. This is now the wheat gluten. Tear the gluten into 1-inch-square pieces, arrange the pieces on a lightly greased plate, and place the plate in a steamer tray.
3   Fill a wok with water level with the bottom edge of the steamer tray and heat until boiling. Place the steamer tray over the boiling water, cover, and steam for 10 minutes over high heat. Remove the wheat gluten and use as directed.

MOCK SWEET-AND-SOUR PORK

SU TANG SU ROU 素糖醋肉

Chinese vegetarian cooks are fond of recreating classic dishes using mock meat products. The fried wheat gluten and walnuts are intended to replace the cubes of pork found in the traditional version of this dish. The resulting vegetarian rendition is quite delicious.

1   Place the **sugar syrup** in a saucepan. Heat the mixture until the sugar has dissolved. Add the walnuts and heat until boiling. Reduce the heat to medium-low and cook for 20 minutes. Remove the walnuts with a slotted spoon and drain thoroughly. Discard the syrup.

2   Heat a wok, add the oil, and heat to 375°. Add the walnuts and deep-fry over high heat, stirring constantly until golden brown. Remove with a handled strainer, and drain. Reheat the oil. Add the wheat gluten pieces and deep-fry over high heat for about 5 minutes, stirring constantly until golden brown. Remove with a handled strainer, and drain. Remove the oil from the wok, reserving 1 tablespoon.

3   Reheat the wok, add the tablespoon of oil, and heat until very hot. Add the **minced seasonings** and stir-fry for about 10 seconds over high heat. Add the pineapple chunks and the pickled carrots. Toss lightly for about 1 minute and add the **sweet-and-sour sauce**. Continue mixing until the sauce has thickened and add the fried walnuts and wheat gluten. Toss lightly to coat with the sauce. Transfer the mixture to a platter, and serve immediately.

SIX SERVINGS

Sugar Syrup
½ cup sugar
2 cups water

2 cups walnut halves
6 cups peanut, safflower, or corn oil
½ recipe wheat gluten (page 292)

Minced Seasonings
1 tablespoon minced scallions
2 teaspoons minced gingerroot

1 cup pineapple chunks, drained
1 cup pickled carrots (page 223), drained

Sweet-and-Sour Sauce
⅔ cup water
¼ cup ketchup
3 tablespoons clear rice vinegar
3 tablespoons sugar
2 teaspoons soy sauce
1 teaspoon salt
½ teaspoon sesame oil
2 teaspoons cornstarch

10 dried Chinese black
mushrooms
2 10-ounce cans oyster
mushrooms, plunged
briefly into boiling water,
refreshed, and drained
4 cups peanut, safflower, or
corn oil

Minced Seasonings
1 tablespoon minced
scallions
2 teaspoons minced
gingerroot

1 cup fresh button
mushrooms, quartered

Sauce Base
1 cup dried-mushroom-
soaking liquid
2 cups water
2 tablespoons soy sauce
1 tablespoon rice wine
2 teaspoons sugar
½ teaspoon salt
1½ teaspoons Chinese black
vinegar

Thickener
2 tablespoons cornstarch
¼ cup water

2 cups snow peas, ends
snapped and veiny strings
removed
1 teaspoon sesame oil
12 sizzling rice cakes (page
36)

ASSORTED VEGETABLES OVER SIZZLING RICE

SHI JIN GUO BA 　　十件鍋巴

Oyster mushrooms have recently been introduced to the United States from Taiwan. Although they are canned, their flavor is quite delicate and, some claim, reminiscent of oysters — hence the name. Their distinctive shape and texture add a special touch to any dish, including this one.

1   Soften the dried black mushrooms in at least 1 cup of hot water for 20 minutes. Remove and discard the stems and cut the caps in half. Retain 1 cup of the liquid. Cut the oyster mushrooms into quarters.
2   Heat a wok or a casserole, add 2 tablespoons of oil, and heat until very hot. Add the **minced seasonings** and stir-fry over high heat for about 10 seconds, until fragrant. Add the fresh mushrooms and stir-fry for about 1 minute, stirring constantly. Add the black mushrooms and the oyster mushrooms. Toss lightly over high heat for 30 seconds and add the **sauce base** (including the black mushroom-soaking liquid). Heat the mixture until boiling and slowly add the **thickener**, stirring constantly to prevent lumps. When the sauce has thickened, add the snow peas and the sesame oil. Toss lightly and turn the heat to low.
3   Heat a wok, add the remaining oil, and heat the oil to 400°. Add half the rice cakes and deep-fry, turning constantly, until the cakes are puffed and golden. Remove with a handled strainer, and place in the bottom of a deep serving dish or bowl. Deep-fry the remaining rice cakes in the same manner. Pour the vegetable mixture over the rice cakes to create the sizzling sound. Serve immediately.

SOUPS 湯類

Although my Chinese surrogate mother, Huang Su Huei, is a superb cook and has her own established cooking school in Taipei and three best-selling cookbooks to her credit, she rarely planned dinner parties in her home. Instead, she would entertain guests and family in the noted restaurants of the city and we would feast on regional specialties from all parts of China. When asked for an explanation of why we never entertained at home, she curtly replied, "Too much trouble."

Her father's sixtieth birthday (an auspicious event in the Chinese culture), however, was another matter. She decided to prepare a banquet herself in her home. Invitations were dispatched to the many relatives, and the serious planning began. After witnessing the extensive preparations involved, I easily understood why such dinner parties were not planned more frequently: "Too much trouble."

Plotting the menu, so it seemed, was the most painstaking chore; consideration was given to the seasonal products available and, more important, to the food preferences of her father, her husband, the children, me, and the other guests (in that order). Foods traditionally reserved for such an event also had to be considered. Since noodles and steamed peach buns, both symbolizing longevity, are traditionally served on birthdays, they automatically became part of the menu. As soon as the other dishes were selected, calls were made to the chicken lady, directing her to set aside plenty of chicken feet for the stock, and to the butcher, informing him of the date of the meal and indicating the type of meat and bones required.

The house was cleaned from top to bottom and the best china and linens were made ready. A few days before the dinner, Huang Su Huei and I journeyed to the best market in the city, selecting only the plumpest chickens, the choicest meat, and freshest-looking vegetables.

The actual cooking for the party began with the preparation of the stock. This brew, made from chicken feet, pork bones, and trimmings, was the base for all the banquet's soups and sauces. My Chinese mother strongly maintained that the key to a superb dish was a superb stock (this same maxim was repeated to me by French

STEAMED CHICKEN IN YUNNAN POT

295

chefs when I later trained in France), and she insisted on making the stocks herself.

The procedure was not overly complicated, but her actions were deliberate and meticulous: First, the bones were blanched in boiling water to clean them. They were then cracked at the joints to allow the marrow and flavors to be released. If a richer stock was required, pork loin would be added after it had been blanched and scored, so that its flavors would emerge in the cooking. The bones (and meat) were then put in a big pot; water, scallions, gingerroot, and Shaohsing (rice wine) were added; and the pot was set on the stove to boil. Once the liquid reached a boil, the heat was adjusted so that the broth would simmer and yield a clear stock. (Vigorous boiling results in a cloudy stock, referred to as a "cream stock.") After six hours of gentle simmering, the pot was emptied and the fragrant liquid was strained through a fine-meshed sieve (and treated like liquid gold); the bones and meat, depleted of flavor, were discarded.

Since my Chinese mother was such an avid fan of soups, it was not unusual for her to plan two or three soup courses in a banquet menu. For her, as well as for most Chinese, soups are a vital part of any meal, be it a twelve-course banquet or a simple family dinner. Whereas soups seem to play a rather restricted role in Western cuisine, in China they have a much broader calling. During a multi-course banquet, light savory and sweet soups are served as entremets to cleanse the palate and to signify the end of a series of courses. In a family-style meal, soup is served along with the other dishes to provide nourishment and to function as a beverage. The Chinese credit soups with aiding digestion and improving circulation, so they are often served toward the end of a full meal.

Soups have been present in the Chinese diet since ancient times. The earliest form of this dish, and one that is still popular today, is *keng*, a stewlike concoction made with meat, fish, and vegetables. It was not unusual for this dish to be served at the beginning of a sumptuous banquet or with rice and millet as an everyday meal. During the Sung dynasty (960 to 1279), streets in the prosperous eastern city of Kaifeng were lined with small eateries that specialized in soups of all kinds. The universal appeal of these soups was obvious: They were nourishing, inexpensive, and delicious.

Some soups have been used for centuries to treat certain ailments.

STUFFED SHRIMP AND
CUCUMBER SOUP

In ancient China, a broth made from bamboo leaves dotted with early morning dew was believed to cure tuberculosis. Stocks simmered with assorted Chinese herbs were administered for a number of maladies. Even today, chicken soup, flavored with gingerroot in southern China and sesame oil in Taiwan, is prescribed daily for a month after childbirth to restore the body's energy.

As the regional chefs utilized the products of their provinces, delicious and unusual concoctions were added to the repertory of Chinese soups. Eastern chefs excelled at preparing soups with fish and seafood garnishes. Fujianese chefs in particular gained renown for their clear and delicate broths. The Cantonese distinguished themselves with flavorful stocks, often adding such exotic ingredients as snake, turtle, and frogs' legs as garnishes. Soups from Sichuan, Hunan, and Yunnan, the western provinces, were particularly varied, featuring both robust and refined seasonings. And northern chefs, who drew their expertise from all parts of China, contributed a broad range of masterpieces.

Chinese soups may be divided into two categories: light and heavy. Light soups are characterized by a clear broth with the addition of assorted garnishes of meat, fish, seafood, and vegetables. Soups of this type are cooked briefly so that the ingredients maintain their original textures. Steamed soups, also included in this category, are made by putting the ingredients in a covered heat-proof container and then steaming gently. The resulting broth is unusually clear and delicate.

Heavy soups are thickened with cornstarch or a flour-and-oil roux and garnished with meat, seafood, fish, and vegetables. Included in this group are soupy stews, made by putting the ingredients in a heat-proof casserole and simmering slowly so that the flavors marry.

In addition to their culinary significance, soups have on occasion provided inspiration for eloquent prose. Li Yü, a famous poet and essayist of the Ch'ing dynasty, articulated his devotion to soup in the following manner:

> As long as there is rice there should be soup. The relationship between soup and rice is like that between water and a boat. When a boat is stranded on a sandy bank only water can wash it back to the river; rice goes down better with soup. I would go so far as to say that it would be better to go without all main dishes than to have no soup.

STUFFED CHRYSANTHEMUM
FLOWER SOUP

RICH PORK BROTH AND HOMEMADE CHICKEN BROTH

To my mind, taking the time to make a good, flavorful stock from scratch is a necessity in soup making and desirable for general purposes. These two stocks are the ones used most frequently in Chinese dishes. The chicken broth, with its delicate flavor, may be used in any soup, whereas the pork broth is usually reserved for thicker, heartier soups or stews. In preparing either of the stocks, the following points should be considered:

1   The bones should be cracked and broken with the blunt edge of a cleaver or by the butcher, to allow the marrow and rich flavors to be released into the liquid.
2   The bones and meat should be blanched briefly in boiling water to clean them, so that the resulting broth will be as clear as possible.
3   Chicken feet make an excellent broth, as they contain natural gelatin and a great deal of flavor. If you can find them, use 3 pounds of feet in place of the roasting chicken or fowl called for in the recipe. If these are unobtainable, use a fryer or backs and necks.
4   In making the pork broth, 1-inch pieces of pork shoulder may be added to further enrich the broth.
5   Once the water and bones reach a boil, reduce the heat and simmer the mixture slowly, uncovered, so that the broth will not become cloudy. Skim the liquid repeatedly to remove any impurities.

RICH PORK BROTH

NONG GAO TANG　濃高湯

1   Using the blunt edge of a heavy knife or cleaver, chop the pork and chicken bones into 2-inch pieces. Blanch the bones for 1 minute in boiling water. Rinse them in cold water and drain thoroughly.
2   Place the pork and chicken bones, water, rice wine, gingerroot, and scallions in a soup pot. Heat until the liquid is boiling. Reduce the heat to low and simmer, uncovered, for 1½ hours. Periodically skim any impurities from the surface. Strain the broth through cheesecloth, removing and discarding the bones and seasonings. The broth will keep, refrigerated in an airtight container, for up to one week. It may also be frozen.

SIX CUPS

2½ pounds pork bones
1½ pounds chicken backs
　and necks
10 cups water
⅓ cup rice wine
3 slices gingerroot, smashed
　with the flat side of a
　cleaver
3 scallions, smashed with the
　flat side of a cleaver

CHINESE CHICKEN BROTH

CHING TANG　清湯

1   Using a heavy cleaver or a chef's knife, cut the chicken, through the bones, into 2-inch pieces. Blanch them in boiling water for 1 minute. Rinse them in cold water and drain thoroughly.
2   Place the chicken pieces, water, rice wine, and gingerroot in a soup pot. Heat until the liquid is boiling. Reduce the heat to low and simmer, uncovered, for 1½ hours. Periodically skim any impurities from the surface. Strain the broth through cheesecloth, removing the chicken pieces and reserving them for another use. The broth will keep, refrigerated in an airtight container, for up to one week. It may also be frozen.

SIX CUPS

1 whole roasting chicken or
　small fowl, about 3 pounds
10 cups water
⅓ cup rice wine
3 slices gingerroot, smashed
　with the flat side of a
　cleaver

1 pound boneless center-cut pork loin

Pork Marinade
1 tablespoon soy sauce
1 tablespoon rice wine
1 teaspoon sesame oil
1 teaspoon cornstarch

2 ounces bean threads
1 English ("gourmet seedless") cucumber
2 tablespoons peanut, safflower, or corn oil
6 cups chicken broth
1½ teaspoons salt
¼ cup Sichuan preserved mustard greens, rinsed and cut into paper-thin slices 1½ inches long and 1 inch wide
2 teaspoons soy sauce
1 teaspoon sesame oil
2 tablespoons minced scallion greens

SHREDDED PORK AND MUSTARD GREEN SOUP

ZHA CAI ROU SI TANG　　榨菜肉絲湯

On many a raw winter evening in Taiwan I quelled the gnawing pains of homesickness and hunger with a steaming bowl of shredded pork and mustard green soup at Earl's Noodle Stand on Hsin Yi Road. Even today, the smell of the fragrant broth summons vivid memories of Earl standing guard behind his trusty cash register. This is my version of that soup.

1　Remove any fat or gristle from the pork loin and discard. Cut the meat, across the grain, into slices ⅛ inch thick. Cut the slices into pieces 1½ inches long and 1 inch wide. Place the slices in a bowl, add the **pork marinade,** toss lightly, and let marinate for 20 minutes.
2　Soften the bean threads for 10 minutes in hot water to cover. Drain, and cut them into 6-inch lengths. Cut the cucumber in half lengthwise. Remove the seeds and cut each half crosswise into three sections. Cut the sections lengthwise into paper-thin slices.
3　Heat a wok, add the oil, and heat until very hot. Add the pork slices and stir-fry over high heat, stirring constantly until the color changes. Remove the pork slices, and drain.
4　Pour the chicken broth into a soup pot. Add the salt and heat until boiling. Add the bean threads, mustard green slices, and cucumber slices. Cook for about 3 minutes over high heat, skimming any impurities from the surface, and add the pork slices, soy sauce, and sesame oil. Toss lightly to blend, and transfer the soup to a tureen or bowl. Sprinkle the top with the minced scallion greens and serve immediately.

BEAN SPROUT AND SPARERIB SOUP

YA CAI PAI GU TANG 芽菜排骨湯

SIX SERVINGS

1 pound spareribs
1½ tablespoons peanut, safflower, or corn oil
1 tablespoon minced scallions
1 medium-sized tomato, peeled, seeded, and diced
1 tablespoon soy sauce

Soup Base
6 cups chicken broth
3 tablespoons rice wine
3 slices gingerroot, smashed with the flat side of a cleaver
1 teaspoon salt

½ pound soybean sprouts, rinsed lightly and drained

One might assume from the mild and delicate flavor of this soup that it is from eastern or northern China. Surprisingly enough, it is from Sichuan province, in the west. My Sichuanese teacher was fond of serving this dish after several fiery entrées; its soothing broth and pleasing textures refresh the palate after the spicy seasonings.

1   Direct the butcher to cut the spareribs crosswise into thirds so that they are 1½ to 2 inches long. Separate the ribs, cutting between the bones. Blanch the ribs in boiling water for 1 minute. Rinse in cold water and drain thoroughly.

2   Heat a wok, add the oil, and heat until very hot. Add the minced scallions and stir-fry for about 10 seconds, until fragrant. Add the diced tomato and stir-fry for 1 minute, stirring constantly over high heat. Add the soy sauce, toss lightly, cook for about 15 seconds, and remove the mixture.

3   Place the **soup base** in a large pot and heat until boiling. Add the spareribs and heat until boiling. Reduce the heat to low and simmer, uncovered, for 30 minutes, skimming the mixture occasionally to remove impurities. Remove and discard the gingerroot. Add the tomato mixture and the bean sprouts. Continue cooking for 20 minutes, skimming occasionally. Taste for seasoning, and adjust if necessary. Transfer the soup to a tureen and serve immediately.

1 pound medium-sized raw
shrimp, shelled
½ ounce pork fat, chopped
to a smooth paste

Shrimp Paste Seasonings
1 egg white, lightly beaten
1 teaspoon salt
1 tablespoon rice wine
1 teaspoon minced
gingerroot
1 teaspoon minced scallions
3 tablespoons cornstarch

Soup Base

6 cups chicken broth
2 tablespoons rice wine
1 teaspoon salt

¼ pound snow peas, ends
snapped and veiny strings
removed

Thickener
2 tablespoons cornstarch
¼ cup water

1 teaspoon sesame oil
2 tablespoons minced
Chinese ham, Smithfield
ham, or prosciutto

SHRIMP BALL SOUP

CHUAN WAN QIU

Few soups compare in delicacy and beauty to this one. With its fluffy, pink shrimp balls, crisp snow peas, and subtly seasoned broth, it will surely impress even the most sophisticated gourmet.

1   Devein the shrimp, rinse lightly, and drain thoroughly. Place the shrimp in a linen dishtowel and squeeze out as much moisture as possible. Mince the shrimp to a paste with two cleavers, or with a food processor fitted with the steel blade. Place the shrimp paste in a mixing bowl, add the pork fat and **shrimp paste seasonings,** and stir vigorously in one direction to blend the ingredients. Lightly throw the mixture against the inside of the bowl to combine evenly. Refrigerate the shrimp paste for 1 hour; then shape it into 1-inch balls.
2   Heat a large pot, add the **soup base,** and heat until boiling. Add the shrimp balls and heat the mixture until boiling. Lower the heat to medium and cook for about 3 minutes, or until the balls rise to the surface. Skim the soup to remove impurities. Turn up the heat to high and add the snow peas and the **thickener,** stirring constantly to prevent lumps. When the soup has thickened, add the sesame oil, toss lightly, and transfer the soup to a tureen. Sprinkle the minced ham over the soup, and serve immediately.

VEGETABLE BEEF SOUP

LUO SONG TANG　羅宋湯

While vegetable beef soup cannot be counted as a bona fide classic in Chinese cuisine, it has become popular all over China. A Chinese friend of mine whose family hails from Peking remembers this as a childhood favorite. The Chinese title gives a hint to the dish's origin: *Luo song* is a slang expression for "Russian-style."

1　Remove any fat or gristle from the beef and discard. Blanch the meat in boiling water for 1 minute. Rinse in cold water, and drain thoroughly.

2　Place the beef cubes in a heavy pot and add the **soup base.** Heat the mixture until the liquid is boiling and reduce the heat to low. Simmer, uncovered, for 1½ hours, skimming occasionally to remove any impurities, until the beef is tender. Discard the gingerroot and scallions.

3　Heat a large soup pot or casserole, add the oil, and heat until very hot. Add the onion and the tomatoes. Stir-fry for about 1 minute, until the onion is soft and transparent. Add the soy sauce and stir-fry for about 30 seconds. Add the cabbage, potatoes, and carrots. Toss lightly over high heat for about 1 minute, and add the cooked beef and broth. Heat the mixture until boiling and reduce the heat to low. Skim any impurities from the surface. Cook, uncovered, for 1 hour. Add the **soup seasonings,** toss lightly to blend, and transfer the mixture to a tureen. Serve immediately.

SIX SERVINGS

1½ pounds chuck or stewing beef, cut into 1½-inch cubes

Soup Base
8 cups water
2 tablespoons rice wine
3 scallions, smashed with the flat side of a cleaver
3 slices gingerroot, smashed with the flat side of a cleaver

1 tablespoon peanut, safflower, or corn oil
½ cup diced onion
2 medium-sized tomatoes, peeled, seeded, and diced
1 tablespoon soy sauce
3 cups Chinese cabbage (Napa), stem sections removed and leaves cut into 2-inch squares
2 medium-sized potatoes, peeled and diced
2 carrots, peeled and diced

Soup Seasonings
1 teaspoon salt
¼ teaspoon freshly ground black pepper
1 teaspoon sesame oil

1 carcass from Peking duck
2 ounces bean threads

Soup Base
2 slices gingerroot, smashed
  with the flat side of a
  cleaver
2 scallions, smashed with the
  flat side of a cleaver
8 cups water
3 tablespoons rice wine

4 cups Chinese cabbage
  (Napa), stem sections
  removed and leaves cut
  into 2-inch squares

Soup Seasonings
1 teaspoon salt
½ teaspoon freshly ground
  black pepper
1 teaspoon sesame oil

DUCK SOUP WITH CABBAGE AND BEAN THREADS

BAI CAI YA TANG 　　　　白菜鸭湯

Waste is akin to blasphemy in the Chinese culture. The carcass of a Peking duck, for example, although stripped of its meat and skin, is never discarded. Instead it is thrown into a pot of water with seasonings, cabbage, and bean threads and cooked at a ferocious pace. This dish is then served as the last course of a traditional Peking duck dinner. For those who don't happen to have the carcass of a Peking duck on hand, any cooked duck or turkey carcass will do nicely.

1   Using a heavy knife or a cleaver, cut the duck carcass, through the bones, into 2-inch pieces. Soften the bean threads for 10 minutes in hot water to cover. Drain, and cut them into 6-inch lengths.
2   Place the duck carcass pieces in a heavy pot. Add the **soup base** and heat until boiling. Reduce the heat to medium-low and cook the soup for 45 minutes, uncovered. Skim any grease from the surface. Add the cabbage and the bean threads. Cook for 30 minutes longer and add the **soup seasonings.** Toss lightly to combine, and transfer the soup to a tureen. Serve immediately.

SPINACH AND MEATBALL SOUP

BO CAI ROU WAN TANG　菠菜肉丸湯

SIX SERVINGS

I first sampled this soup a number of years ago in a Peking restaurant in Taipei. One of my Chinese teachers, a true gourmet, had decided that it was time to introduce me properly to authentic northern cuisine. He invited me to lunch and ordered some of his favorites. This soup was one of his selections, and I have been especially fond of it ever since.

1　Lightly chop the meat until fluffy and place it in a mixing bowl. Add the **meat seasonings** to the ground meat. Stir vigorously in one direction to mix the ingredients. Lightly throw the mixture against the inside of the bowl to combine evenly. Shape the mixture into 1-inch balls. Soften the bean threads for 10 minutes in hot water to cover. Drain, and cut them into 6-inch lengths.

2　Place the **soup base** in a large pot and heat until boiling. Add the meatballs to the broth and heat until boiling. Cook for about 10 minutes over medium heat, skimming any impurities from the surface. Add the bean threads and cook for another 5 minutes. Add the spinach and cook for about 1 minute. Transfer the soup to a tureen and serve immediately.

¾ pound ground beef, preferably chuck

Meat Seasonings
1 tablespoon soy sauce
1 tablespoon rice wine
1½ teaspoons sesame oil
½ teaspoon salt
1½ tablespoons cornstarch
1 tablespoon minced scallions
1½ teaspoons minced gingerroot

2 ounces bean threads

Soup Base
6 cups chicken broth
1 teaspoon salt
¼ teaspoon freshly ground white pepper
½ teaspoon sesame oil

½ pound fresh spinach, trimmed and cleaned

305

1 whole frying chicken,
    about 3 pounds
8 dried Chinese black
    mushrooms
4 paper-thin slices (about 2
    ounces) Chinese ham,
    Smithfield ham, or
    prosciutto

Soup Base
4 cups boiling water
¼ cup rice wine
½ teaspoon salt
½ teaspoon sugar
3 slices gingerroot, smashed
    with the flat side of a
    cleaver
3 scallions, smashed with the
    flat side of a cleaver

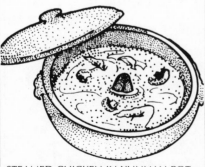

STEAMED CHICKEN IN YUNNAN POT

STEAMED CHICKEN IN YUNNAN POT

CHI GUO TANG 汽鍋湯

Apart from its spherical shape and unusual glaze, from outward appearances there seems to be little to distinguish a Yunnan pot from any other casserole. The truly distinctive feature is the cone-shaped chimney in the center of the vessel; it sprays the ingredients with a fine mist of steam, making them tender and juicy. Chicken, squab, and a variety of meats and vegetables may be cooked in this unusual pot. Yunnan pots may be purchased at any well-equipped Chinese grocery store.

1   Using a heavy knife or a cleaver, cut the chicken, through the bones, into 2-inch pieces. Blanch them in boiling water for 1 minute. Rinse in cold water and drain thoroughly. Soften the dried mushrooms for 20 minutes in hot water to cover. Remove and discard the stems. If the caps are large, cut them in half. Cut the ham slices into 2-inch squares.
2   Arrange the chicken pieces, mushrooms, and ham in the bottom of a Yunnan pot 9 inches in diameter. Pour the **soup base** on top. Cover the pot and place it in a steamer tray.
3   Fill a wok with water level with the bottom edge of the steamer tray and heat until boiling. Place the steamer tray over the boiling water, cover, and steam for 1½ hours over high heat. Check the water level in the wok after 1 hour and add more boiling water if necessary. Remove the pot, skim any fat from the surface, and discard the gingeroot and scallions. Serve the soup directly from the pot.

CRABMEAT AND CORN SOUP

XIE ROU YU MI TANG　蟹肉玉米湯

Most Americans are familiar with the classic Cantonese corn soup because it appears on the menus of many American Cantonese restaurants. In this flavorful variation of the classic, the minced chicken breast of the original recipe is replaced by lump crabmeat. With the creamed corn, the overall effect is a memorable combination of flavors and colors.

1　Pick over the crabmeat, discarding any pieces of shell or cartilage. If the crabmeat has been frozen, squeeze out any excess water. Shred the crabmeat, using your fingers. Place the crabmeat in a bowl, add the **crabmeat marinade,** toss lightly, and let marinate for 20 minutes. Beat the egg whites with the tablespoon of water until frothy.

2　Place the **soup base** in a large pot. Heat until boiling and add the creamed corn. Heat again until boiling and add the **thickener,** stirring constantly to prevent lumps. Add the crabmeat and simmer for 30 seconds. Turn off the heat and slowly add the egg whites in a thin stream around the edge of the pot. Stir once or twice, add the sesame oil, toss lightly, and transfer the soup to a tureen. Serve immediately.

SIX SERVINGS

¾ pound fresh crabmeat or defrosted frozen crabmeat

Crabmeat Marinade

1 tablespoon rice wine
1 teaspoon minced gingerroot
½ teaspoon salt

2 egg whites, lightly beaten
1 tablespoon water

Soup Base

6 cups chicken broth
2 tablespoons rice wine
1 teaspoon salt

1½ 17-ounce cans creamed corn

Thickener

2½ tablespoons cornstarch
¼ cup water

1 teaspoon sesame oil

STUFFED SHRIMP AND CUCUMBER SOUP

XIA GUA TANG　蝦瓜湯

Chefs from Fujian are known for their clear soups and delicate broths, which often contain fish and seafood garnishes, since this eastern province borders the sea. This soup, with its delicate flavor and attractive appearance, illustrates well the refinement of this regional cuisine.

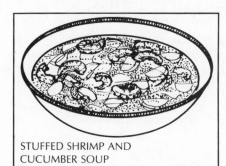

STUFFED SHRIMP AND CUCUMBER SOUP

1¼ pounds medium-sized
raw shrimp, shelled

Shrimp Marinade

1 tablespoon rice wine
2 slices gingerroot, smashed
with the flat side of a
cleaver
2 scallions, smashed with the
flat side of a cleaver
½ teaspoon salt

Shrimp Paste Seasonings

1 teaspoon pork fat, minced
to a smooth paste
10 water chestnuts, plunged
briefly into boiling water,
refreshed, and chopped to
a coarse paste
1 teaspoon minced
gingerroot
½ teaspoon salt
½ egg white, lightly beaten
1½ tablespoons cornstarch

2 English ("gourmet
seedless") cucumbers
2 tablespoons cornstarch

Soup Base

6 cups chicken broth
2 tablespoons rice wine
1 teaspoon salt
¼ teaspoon freshly ground
white pepper
1 teaspoon sesame oil

1 tablespoon minced scallion
greens

1   Rinse the shrimp lightly and drain thoroughly. Place the shrimp in a linen dishtowel and squeeze out as much moisture as possible. Refrigerate the shrimp for 1 hour. Divide the shrimp into a ¾-pound portion and a ½-pound portion. Set the ½-pound portion aside. Deeply score the remaining shrimp down the back to within ¼ inch of each end, removing the vein and creating a pocket. Place the shrimp in a bowl. Pinch the gingerroot and scallions in the **shrimp marinade** repeatedly for several minutes to impart their flavors. Add the marinade to the shrimp, toss lightly, and let marinate for 20 minutes. Discard the scallions and gingerroot.

2   Devein the remaining ½ pound of shrimp. Using two cleavers or a food processor fitted with the steel blade, mince the shrimp to a smooth paste. Place the shrimp paste in a mixing bowl, add the **shrimp paste seasonings,** and stir vigorously in one direction. Lightly throw the mixture against the inside of the bowl to combine evenly. Refrigerate the shrimp paste for 30 minutes.

3   Cut the cucumbers in half lengthwise, remove the seeds, and cut each half crosswise into three sections. Roll-cut each section into 1-inch pieces.

4   Lightly dust the pocket of one whole shrimp with cornstarch and stuff the cavity with a heaping tablespoon of shrimp paste. Using the underside of a spoon dipped in water, smooth the surface of the shrimp paste. Repeat for each shrimp. Arrange the shrimp, stuffed side up, on a greased heat-proof plate, and put the plate in a steamer tray.

5   Fill a wok with water level with the bottom edge of the steamer tray and heat until boiling. Place the steamer tray over the boiling water, cover, and steam for 6 minutes over high heat. Remove the plate from the steamer tray.

6   Pour the **soup base** into a pot and heat until boiling. Add the cucumber pieces and cook for about 2 minutes, until the cucumber is just tender. Skim the surface to remove any impurities. Add the stuffed shrimp and cook for 1 minute. Transfer the soup to a tureen, garnish with the scallion greens, and serve immediately.

STEAMED CHINESE CABBAGE CASSEROLE

GAN BEI DUN BAI CAI　　干貝燉白菜

The Chinese culinary term *dun* refers to the process of steaming in a closed receptacle. In this case the cabbage, black mushrooms, ham, and shrimp are placed in a heavy pot and broth is added. The pot is then covered and placed in a steamer, where the mixture gently cooks. In this manner, the delicate flavors of the ingredients are allowed to mingle and the resulting broth is clear and light.

1   Cut the cabbage head crosswise in half. Cut away and discard the stem. Cut the cabbage head halves lengthwise into strips about 2 inches wide, but don't separate the leaves. Rinse the dried shrimp and soften for 1 hour in hot water to cover. Drain and mince. Soften the black mushrooms for 20 minutes in hot water to cover. Remove and discard the stems. Cut the caps into matchstick-size shreds. Cut the ham into matchstick-size shreds.

2   In the bottom of a heavy heat-proof bowl or casserole, arrange the cabbage strips, cut edges up, tightly packed to line the bottom. Sprinkle the shredded ham and mushrooms and the minced shrimp on top. Combine the **soup seasonings** and the boiling chicken broth and pour the mixture over the cabbage. Cover the bowl tightly and place it in a steamer tray.

3   Fill a wok with water level with the bottom edge of the steamer tray and heat until boiling. Place the steamer tray over the boiling water, cover, and steam for 1 hour over high heat. Remove the bowl, skim any fat from the surface, discard the gingerroot and scallions, and serve immediately.

SIX SERVINGS

1 large head Chinese cabbage (Napa), about 2 pounds
1 teaspoon dried shrimp
6 dried Chinese black mushrooms
4 paper-thin slices (about 2 ounces) Chinese ham, Smithfield ham, or prosciutto

Soup Seasonings
4 scallions, smashed with the flat side of a cleaver
3 slices gingerroot, smashed with the flat side of a cleaver
2 tablespoons rice wine
1 teaspoon salt
1½ teaspoons sesame oil

4 cups boiling chicken broth

309

1 whole roasting chicken, 3½
to 4 pounds

Soup Base
6 cups water
¼ cup rice wine
3 slices gingerroot, smashed
with the flat side of a
cleaver
3 scallions, smashed with the
flat side of a cleaver
¾ teaspoon salt

½ cup canned Chinese
pickled cucumbers
¼ cup brine from pickled
cucumbers

CHICKEN AND PICKLED CUCUMBER SOUP

HUA GUA DUN JI   花瓜燉雞

In this simple yet classic soup, the tender chicken and delicately seasoned broth contrast beautifully with the crisp pickled cucumbers. This is one soup that should be served in the traditional Chinese manner — toward the end of the meal. The soothing broth aids digestion and refreshes the palate.

1   Remove the fat from the cavity and neck of the chicken. Rinse the chicken lightly, and using a heavy knife or a cleaver, cut it through the bones into 2-inch pieces. Blanch the pieces in boiling water for 1 minute. Rinse in cold water and drain thoroughly. Place the chicken pieces and the **soup base** in a heavy, heat-proof bowl or a pot. Place it in a steamer tray.
2   Fill a wok with water level with the bottom edge of the steamer tray and heat until boiling. Place the steamer tray over the boiling water, cover, and steam for 1½ hours over high heat. (Check the water level after 1 hour and add more boiling water to the wok if necessary.) Uncover the pot and skim any grease and impurities from the surface. Add the pickled cucumber and the brine, cover, and steam for another 10 minutes. Transfer the soup to a tureen and serve immediately.

4 cups Chinese cabbage
(Napa), stem sections
removed and leaves cut
into 2-inch squares
2 tablespoons peanut,
safflower, or corn oil

EIGHT-TREASURE MIXED SOUP POT

SHA GUO DOU FU   砂鍋豆腐

A vessel of considerable importance in the preparation of Chinese soups and casseroles is a sandy pot, commonly referred to as a *sha guo*. This pot is made from a mixture of sand and clay, which is then fired at a very high temperature so that it can withstand direct heat. The pot also conducts heat evenly and efficiently. Bean curd and fish heads are both often cooked in this kind of pot. If a sandy pot is unavailable, substitute any heavy casserole or a Dutch oven.

1   Separate the harder cabbage pieces from the leafier ones. Heat a wok, add the oil, and heat until very hot. Add the smashed garlic and stir-fry for about 5 seconds, until fragrant. Add the harder cabbage pieces and toss lightly over high heat, adding the tablespoon of rice wine. Stir-fry for about 1 minute and add the leafier pieces. Stir-fry for about 1 minute more and add the **soup base.** Heat the mixture until boiling, reduce the heat to low, and cook, uncovered, for about 30 minutes. Transfer the cabbage and liquid to a sandy pot, a heavy casserole, or a Dutch oven.

2   Remove any fat or gristle from the pork loin and discard. Cut the meat, across the grain, into slices about ⅛ inch thick, and cut the slices into 2-inch squares. Place the meat in a bowl, add the **pork marinade,** toss lightly, and let marinate for 20 minutes. Soften the bean threads for 15 minutes in hot water to cover. Drain, and cut them into 6-inch lengths. Soften the dried mushrooms for 20 minutes in hot water to cover. Remove and discard the stems. Cut the bean curd into 1-inch dice.

3   Devein and rinse the shrimp. Pat dry and place in a bowl. Pinch the gingerroot slices in the **shrimp marinade** to impart the flavor to the rice wine. Discard the gingerroot and add the marinade to the shrimp. Toss lightly and let marinate for 20 minutes.

4   Arrange the meat slices, bean curd, black mushrooms, bean threads, and carrots separately, each in its own spot, over the cabbage, leaving a place in the center for the shrimp. Cover the pot, and cook for 20 minutes over medium heat. Uncover, arrange the shrimp on top of the cabbage, and sprinkle the scallion greens over all. Cover, and cook for another 5 minutes. Serve directly from the pot.

---

2 cloves garlic, smashed with the flat side of a cleaver
1 tablespoon rice wine

Soup Base

6 cups chicken broth
2 tablespoons rice wine
1 teaspoon salt

½ pound boneless center-cut pork loin

Pork Marinade

1 teaspoon soy sauce
1 teaspoon rice wine
½ teaspoon sesame oil
1 teaspoon cornstarch

1 ounce bean threads
6 dried Chinese black mushrooms
2 cakes bean curd, about 3 inches square and 1 inch thick
½ pound medium-sized raw shrimp, shelled

Shrimp Marinade

2 teaspoons rice wine
2 slices gingerroot, smashed with the flat side of a cleaver
½ teaspoon salt

2 carrots, roll-cut into 1-inch pieces
¼ cup scallion greens diagonally cut into ¼-inch pieces

1½ pounds top sirloin of
beef, cut across the grain
into paper-thin slices

Meat Marinade
1½ tablespoons soy sauce
1 tablespoon rice wine
1 teaspoon sesame oil

1 pound Chinese cabbage
(Napa), stem removed and
leaves cut into 2-inch
squares
2 tablespoons peanut,
safflower, or corn oil
2 cloves garlic, smashed with
the flat side of a cleaver

Soup Base
2 tablespoons rice wine
6 cups chicken broth
1 teaspoon salt

2 ounces bean threads
2 cakes bean curd, about 3
inches square and 1 inch
thick
1 pound fresh button
mushrooms, rinsed,
drained, and stems
trimmed
½ pound fresh spinach,
cleaned and trimmed

MONGOLIAN BEEF FIRE POT

SHUAN NIU ROU   涮牛肉

Mongolian fire pot was introduced to Peking (and China) by the
northern people of Mongolia. It soon became universally popular
all over China and regional variations resulted. Eastern chefs developed a "ten varieties hot pot" with meat and seafood garnishes, and
the Cantonese created a "chrysanthemum fire pot," made with edible chrysanthemum petals. Today the traditional "rinsed lamb" fire
pot has inspired a "rinsed beef" rendition. This filling dish may be
served as a meal in itself. Here is my adapted version.

1   Place the meat slices in a bowl, add the **meat marinade,** toss
lightly, and arrange the slices attractively on a platter.
2   Separate the harder cabbage pieces from the leafier ones. Heat a
wok, add the oil, and heat until very hot. Add the garlic, stir-fry
briefly, and add the harder cabbage pieces. Stir-fry for about 1
minute over high heat, adding a tablespoon of the **soup base.** Add
the leafy cabbage pieces and stir-fry for another minute over high
heat. Add the remaining soup base and heat until boiling. Reduce
the heat to low and let simmer, uncovered, for 20 minutes.
3   Soften the bean threads for 10 minutes in hot water to cover.
Drain, and cut into 6-inch lengths. Cut the bean curd into 1-inch
dice. Arrange the mushrooms, bean curd, spinach, and bean

Dipping Sauce (Per Person)

2 tablespoons soy sauce
1 tablespoon rice wine
1 teaspoon Chinese black
vinegar
1 teaspoon sugar
½ teaspoon chili oil
(optional)
½ teaspoon fermented bean
curd (optional)

½ tablespoon minced
scallions
1 teaspoon minced
gingerroot
1 teaspoon minced garlic
1 egg, lightly beaten
(optional)

threads attractively on several platters. Place the platters containing the meat and vegetables on a table where a heated Mongolian fire pot has been set up. (If you do not have a Mongolian fire pot, use a pot and a hot plate, or an electric skillet, or an electric wok.) Put a bowl of **dipping sauce** at each diner's place.

4   Pour the stock into the fire pot and heat until boiling. Each diner takes a slice of meat, dips it into the hot stock until the meat is cooked, then dips the meat into the dipping sauce, and eats. The bean curd, mushrooms, bean threads, and spinach are placed in the stock a little at a time and cooked until done. The diners may help themselves to these ingredients, once again dipping in the sauce before eating. The bean curd, bean threads, and mushrooms should cook in 5 or 6 minutes, but the spinach should only take a minute. Once all the ingredients have been eaten, the flavorful soup is also consumed.

MONGOLIAN FIRE POT

STUFFED CHRYSANTHEMUM
FLOWER SOUP

½ pound ground pork
¼ pound raw shrimp, shelled

Egg Sheet Mixture
2 eggs, lightly beaten
2 teaspoons cornstarch
2 tablespoons water

1 teaspoon cornstarch

Chrysanthemum Garnishes
1 cup carrot (cooked for 1
    minute in boiling water),
    cut into matchstick-size
    shreds
1 cup dried Chinese black
    mushrooms, softened in
    hot water to cover, stems
    removed, and caps cut
    into matchstick-size shreds
1 cup cooked ham, cut into
    matchstick-size shreds
1 cup bamboo shoots,
    plunged briefly into
    boiling water and cut into
    matchstick-size shreds

STUFFED CHRYSANTHEMUM FLOWER SOUP

ZHU HUA GAN BEI   菊花干貝

The chrysanthemum (*zhu hua*) enjoys an important role in Chinese literature and culture. As a symbol of mid autumn and joviality, this flower is honored during the ninth month of the lunar calendar. It is said that the steamed mold floating in the delicate broth, with its colorful garnishes and egg sheet petals, evokes the image of a chrysanthemum in full bloom.

1   Lightly chop the ground pork until fluffy and place it in a mixing bowl. Slice three of the shrimp in half lengthwise along the back, removing the vein, and set aside. Devein the remaining shrimp, chop it to a paste, and add it to the ground pork.
2   Wipe the surface of a well-seasoned wok or a nonstick 10-inch frying pan with an oil-soaked paper towel. Heat the pan until a few drops of water sprinkled on the surface evaporate immediately. Add the **egg sheet mixture** and tilt the pan so that the egg forms a thin pancake about 10 inches in diameter. Place the pan back over the heat and cook until set and lightly golden. Carefully turn the pancake over and cook briefly on the other side. Remove and let cool. Place the egg sheet in a generously greased 8-inch heat-proof bowl; it should come partway up the side of the bowl. Sprinkle the surface of the egg sheet with the cornstarch.
3   Arrange the sliced shrimp, cut side up, in a circular design in the center of the egg sheet. Arrange half the **chrysanthemum garnishes** in four columns to cover the egg sheet and form a decorative pattern. Add the remaining chrysanthemum garnishes and the **meat seasonings** to the ground pork. Stir vigorously in one direction to combine evenly. Stuff the mixture into the bowl over the decorative pattern, being careful not to disturb the pattern. Smooth the surface with the underside of a spoon dipped in water. Place the bowl in a steamer tray.
4   Fill a wok with water level with the bottom edge of the steamer tray and heat until boiling. Place the steamer tray over the boiling

water, cover, and steam for 1 hour over high heat. Invert the bowl into a deep round soup bowl. Carefully make a cross in the egg sheet, starting in the center and cutting to within 2 inches of the edge. Gently fold back the egg sheet to reveal the garnish design.

5   Place the **soup base** in a pot and heat until boiling. Add the sesame oil. Slowly ladle the liquid around the steamed mold in the soup bowl. Serve immediately.

Meat Seasonings	Soup Base
2 tablespoons soy sauce	6 cups chicken broth
1 tablespoon rice wine	2 tablespoons rice wine
½ teaspoon salt	1 teaspoon salt
¼ teaspoon freshly ground black pepper	¼ teaspoon freshly ground white pepper
1½ teaspoons sesame oil	
2 tablespoons minced scallions	1 teaspoon sesame oil
2 teaspoons minced gingerroot	
1½ tablespoons cornstarch	

½ pound boneless center-cut
    pork loin

Pork Marinade

1 teaspoon soy sauce
1 teaspoon rice wine
½ teaspoon sesame oil
1 teaspoon cornstarch

6 dried Chinese black
    mushrooms
10 dried wood ears
2 cakes bean curd, 3 inches
    square and 1 inch thick

Soup Base

6 cups rich pork broth (page
    299) or chicken broth
2 tablespoons rice wine
1 teaspoon salt
½ teaspoon sugar

Thickener

3½ tablespoons cornstarch
6 tablespoons water

Soup Seasonings

3 tablespoons soy sauce
3 tablespoons clear rice
    vinegar
1½ teaspoons sesame oil
1 teaspoon freshly ground
    black pepper
2 tablespoons minced
    scallions
2 tablespoons minced
    gingerroot

2 eggs, lightly beaten

HOT AND SOUR SOUP

SUAN LA TANG 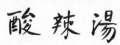 酸辣湯

Although hot and sour soup has become (at least to my mind) a too-familiar selection on Sichuan and Peking restaurant menus, its popularity continues. Perhaps it is the unique blending of flavors and textures that appeals to the American palate. Here is my version of this classic.

1   Remove any fat or gristle from the pork loin and discard. Cut the meat, across the grain, into slices ¼ inch thick. Cut the slices into matchstick-size shreds. Place the shreds in a bowl, add the **pork marinade,** toss lightly, and let marinate for 10 minutes. Soften the dried mushrooms for 20 minutes in hot water to cover. Remove and discard the stems. Cut the caps into matchstick-size shreds. Soften the wood ears for 20 minutes in hot water to cover. Cut away and discard the hard, bitter nib on the underside of the wood ears and cut the wood ears into matchstick-size shreds. Cut the bean curd into thin slices and then into matchstick-size shreds.
2   Place the **soup base** in a large pot and heat until boiling. Add several tablespoons of the hot broth to the pork shreds and stir to separate; then add the pork shreds to the pot. Heat until boiling and cook until the pork shreds change color, about 1 minute. Skim any impurities from the surface of the soup. Add the shredded mushrooms, wood ears, and bean curd. Heat the mixture until boiling and slowly add the **thickener,** stirring constantly to prevent lumps. Continue to skim the surface to remove impurities. When the soup has thickened, add the **soup seasonings.** Stir to blend, and taste for seasoning. If the soup is not spicy enough, add more vinegar and minced gingerroot. Remove the soup from the heat. Add the eggs, slowly pouring in a thin stream. Stir the soup once in a circular motion. Transfer the soup to a tureen and serve immediately.

SWEETS 甜點

On the fifteenth day of the eighth month of the lunar calendar, when the moon is reputed to be at its maximum brightness, Chinese the world over gather to celebrate the birthday of the moon. Some honor this holiday, called the Moon Festival or Mid-Autumn Festival, by exchanging gifts with relatives, friends, and business associates. Others present offerings to departed spirits and burn incense to "heaven and earth." And everyone eats moon cakes — often while gazing at the moon.

The Chinese bakeries, all of which manufacture these holiday cakes, start their preparations for this festival weeks in advance. The usual confections that line the shelves are cleaned off and pyramid-shaped mountains of numerous varieties of moon cakes replace them. A scarlet paper banner on each pile proclaims the name of the cakes in bold, black Chinese characters: Red bean paste, lotus seed paste, and eight-treasure moon cakes are just a few; the selection is extraordinary. The cakes may be moon-shaped or molded into the form of a rabbit, fish, pagoda, or horse and rider. While most are simply brushed with an egg glaze, producing a golden crust, it is not uncommon to find red, green, and brown food coloring used — and, in rare instances, gold leaf. Some cakes contain a salty duck egg yolk in the center, which provides a savory contrast to the sweet filling. Savory moon cakes filled with pork and vegetables are also available. As with other foods, there are regional versions of moon cakes, with various fillings and crusts.

Aside from their taste appeal, moon cakes are especially popular because of their influential role in Chinese history; they were instrumental in delivering the Chinese from Mongolian rule during the latter part of the Yüan dynasty (1271 to 1368). Concealed within the cakes, messages and plans for an uprising were passed from household to household. As a result of the rebellion, the Mongolian rulers were successfully overthrown, and the event marked the beginning of the Ming dynasty (1368 to 1644).

Like moon cakes, a number of other pastries and cakes play a prominent role in the Chinese diet and culture. Along with fruits,

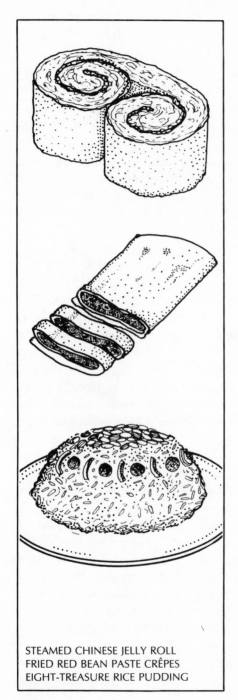

STEAMED CHINESE JELLY ROLL
FRIED RED BEAN PASTE CRÊPES
EIGHT-TREASURE RICE PUDDING

these foods constitute the varied and extensive category of Chinese sweets. Many confections are traditional holiday specialties, prepared in observance of age-old festivals and customs: Longevity peach buns are served on birthdays; red and white stuffed sweet rice balls are prepared for the Chinese New Year, and sweet *zong zi*, glutinous rice dumplings wrapped in bamboo leaves, are reserved for the Dragon Boat Festival. Unlike Western ones, Chinese cakes and pastries are not necessarily served as desserts; most commonly, they are served with tea as snacks, and as entremets during a traditional Chinese banquet. Because their flavor and texture is usually quite different from those of the dishes that precede them, they serve to refresh the palate. Fruits — by themselves or in soups, sweet salads, and other preparations — are served more often as desserts.

It appears that the concept of cakes was introduced to ancient China from the West; yet once the Chinese chefs had mastered the foreign techniques, they applied them using local products to create a diverse repertory. As in Western pastries, flour and eggs are the basic ingredients in many Chinese sweets. But unlike Western confections, lard rather than butter or margarine is the usual shortening, and rice and vegetables are common ingredients. Pastes made from red beans, lotus seeds, dates, or sesame seeds form typical fillings. Various nuts (walnuts, almonds, and peanuts) and seeds (olive kernels, apricot kernels, sesame seeds, and watermelon seeds) are also important.

The earliest Chinese cakes were made with honey and maltose, a malt sugar made from barley. The process of refining sugar cane was introduced from India during the seventh century, and it was later that the Chinese were able to produce the fine powdered sugar — they called it sugar frost — that is used today.

Cakes and pastries became very popular in ancient China, and remain so to this day. Crullers, rice cakes, and deep-fried puff pastries dusted with sugar are made in much the same manner today as they were ages ago. So are milk cakes and sweetmeats eaten in observance of the Festival of the Dead and sweet cakes prepared for the Buddhist holidays.

Whereas most Westerners prefer sweet cakes and pastries for dessert, the Chinese, as mentioned above, are partial to ending their meals with fruit.

A wealth of fruits was available in different parts of China as early as the T'ang dynasty (618 to 907). Peaches and grapes, introduced from central Asia, flourished in the north, as did jujubes, crab apples, grapes, quinces, loquats, pears, and plums. Tangerines, kumquats, and oranges thrived in the warmer, western provinces. The "Canton" orange, grown in Sichuan and Hubei, was a particularly popular strain. Later, this variety was introduced to Europe, where it spawned Seville, Valencia, and navel oranges. Canton and the southern provinces produced lychees, longans, rambutans, and bananas. These fruits were consumed fresh, candied in honey and sugar, or preserved by drying. Some were used in savory dishes, but most were served at the end of a meal, demonstrating their early importance in the Chinese diet as a dessert.

MOON CAKE

Most fruits also retain a symbolic role and are used as offerings in Chinese ritual and worship. The apple signifies harmony and peace. The orange symbolizes abundant happiness and prosperity. The peach is emblematic of marriage and immortality, and the plum of winter and longevity.

The recipes in this chapter represent a sampling of traditional and contemporary sweets.

6 cups water
2 cups sugar
1 tablespoon shredded
  orange peel
1 cup fermented wine rice
  (see below), with liquid
4 mandarin or navel oranges,
  peeled and sectioned

Fermented Wine Rice

1 cup glutinous (sweet) rice
1 wine yeast ball

SWEET ORANGE TEA

ZHU GENG

Sweet teas — or *gengs*, as they are referred to in Chinese — form a category of dishes that are served as snacks or as sweet entremets during a banquet. They are designed to refresh the palate and soothe the stomach. In addition to the orange rendition below, they are made with almonds, walnuts, dates, sesame seeds, or lotus seeds. Wine yeast balls (*jiu niang*), which are used in this recipe to make the fermented wine rice, are available (individually wrapped in packages) at Chinese grocery stores.

1   Combine 2 cups of water, 1 cup of sugar, and the shredded orange peel in a saucepan. Heat until boiling and reduce the heat to medium-low. Cook, uncovered, for 5 minutes; the mixture should now be a light syrup.
2   Place the fermented rice wine, 4 cups of water, and 1 cup of sugar in a saucepan and heat slowly, stirring occasionally, until the sugar has dissolved. Add the orange sections and the sugar syrup and continue cooking until the mixture is heated through. Pour the mixture into a serving bowl and serve immediately.

FERMENTED WINE RICE

1   Rinse the rice under cold running water until the water runs clear. Place the rice in a bowl with cold water to cover, and let it soak for 6 hours. Line a steamer tray with moistened cheesecloth or muslin, and spread the soaked rice evenly in the tray.
2   Fill a wok with water level with the bottom edge of the steamer tray, and heat until boiling. Place the steamer tray over the boiling water, cover, and steam over high heat for 30 minutes. Transfer the rice to a colander and rinse under cold running water until the water runs clear.
3   Place the rice in a 4-cup earthenware crock. Mash the wine yeast ball with the flat side of a cleaver; measure ¾ teaspoon of it, and stir it into the rice. Form a well in the center and let the rice

stand — tightly covered, in a warm, dark place — for 2 days. Transfer the fermented wine rice to a glass jar; there should be 2 cups of rice and one cup of liquid. It will keep indefinitely in the refrigerator.

STEAMED PEARS IN HONEY

MI ZHI LI ZI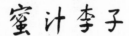

SIX SERVINGS

6 nearly ripe Anjou or Bosc pears
6 tablespoons honey
1 cup dried jujubes (Chinese dates)

In ancient China, the sweetest pears were reputed to be grown in the northern province of Shanxi. There the trees thrived in the moderate climate and fertile soil. Jujubes, also known as Chinese dates, flourished in this area too. This recipe, popular for centuries, combines the flavors of these two fruits.

1   Soften the jujubes for 1 hour in hot water to cover, changing the water twice. Drain the jujubes and remove the pits. Cut the jujubes crosswise into thin strips.
2   Cut a thin slice off the bottom of each pear so that it will stand upright. Cut a piece about 1 inch deep off the top of each pear and set aside. Using a fruit corer or a sharp paring knife, remove the core of each pear, being careful not to cut through to the bottom.
3   Arrange the pears upright on a heat-proof plate. Spoon a tablespoon of honey into each cavity and add some of the sliced jujubes to each one. Place the reserved tops on the pears, and, if necessary, fasten them securely with toothpicks. Place the plate in a steamer tray.
4   Fill a wok with water level with the bottom edge of the steamer tray and heat until boiling. Place the steamer tray over the boiling water, cover, and steam over high heat for 30 minutes, or until the pears are tender when pierced with a knife. Serve the pears hot or cold.

SIX SERVINGS

1 ounce dried silver ears

Steaming Liquid
4 cups water
4 slices gingerroot, smashed with the flat side of a cleaver
2 tablespoons rice wine

3 15-ounce cans loquats in syrup

SILVER EARS WITH FRUIT

SHUI GUO BAI MU ER 水果白木耳

Silver ears, or white wood ears, are a dried delicacy reserved for special sweet and savory dishes and soups. Similar to black wood ears, they are relished for their resilient texture and nutritious nature. Lychees, kumquats, pineapple, or any fresh fruit poached in syrup may be used in this soup. Serve it as a refreshing snack or as a light dessert.

1   Rinse the silver ears in warm water to remove any dirt and place them in a bowl with hot water to cover. Let soften for 1 hour. Drain the silver ears, and cut away any hard edges.
2   Place the softened silver ears in a heat-proof bowl, and add the **steaming liquid**. Place the bowl in a steamer tray.
3   Fill a wok with water level with the bottom edge of the steamer tray and heat until boiling. Place the steamer tray over the boiling water, cover, and steam for 1 hour over high heat. Remove the silver ears and let them cool. Discard the steaming liquid. Place the silver ears in a bowl, add the loquats in syrup, and toss lightly to mix. Refrigerate for at least 1 hour before serving.

SIX SERVINGS

CANDIED APPLE FRITTERS

BA SI PING GUO 拔絲蘋果

Snacking is very much a part of the daily routine in modern China. Concessions offering candy, fruits, and nuts are everywhere for the enjoyment of natives and tourists alike. In Peking, caramelized crab apples are among the snacks available, and in restaurants candied apple fritters, a more formal dish, are served frequently as a dessert. In the south, where tropical fruits thrive, an equally delicious variation using bananas is common.

1 Peel and core the apples. Rub the apples with a cut lemon half to prevent them from turning brown. Grease a large platter with peanut, vegetable, or corn oil. Prepare a bowl of ice water, into which the caramelized apples will be dipped.

2 Place the flour and cornstarch in a mixing bowl. Slowly add the eggs and beat vigorously with a whisk to combine evenly. Add the 1¼ cups ice water, whisking again to prevent lumps from forming. Refrigerate this batter for 20 minutes.

3 Cut each apple in half and cut each half into four wedges. Add the apple pieces to the batter and stir to coat the pieces.

4 Heat a wok, add the oil, and heat the oil to 350°. Slide half the apple slices into the hot oil and turn them over, removing any drips of batter from the oil. Deep-fry the slices for about 1½ minutes, turning constantly until pale golden. Remove with a handled strainer, and drain. Reheat the oil, add the remaining apple slices, and deep-fry them in the same manner. Reheat the oil to 425°.

5 Place the 1½ cups sugar and the ½ cup water in another wok or a saucepan. Heat slowly until the sugar has dissolved, stirring occasionally; once the sugar has dissolved, however, do not stir. Continue cooking the mixture over medium heat, occasionally brushing down the sides of the pan with a brush dipped in water (this will prevent crystals from forming). When the mixture has turned a light golden color (310°) and a chopstick dipped in the caramel leaves a thin string, turn the heat to the lowest setting.

6 Quickly deep-fry all the apples a second time in the hot oil until they are golden brown and crisp. Remove the apples with a slotted spoon and place them in the caramel. Working quickly, sprinkle the sesame seeds on the apples and carefully toss the apples so that they are evenly coated with the caramel. Transfer the apples to the greased platter and serve immediately. Before eating, dip the apple slices in the ice water to harden the caramel.

VARIATION: CANDIED BANANA FRITTERS (*BA SI XIANG JIAO*)
Use six just-ripe bananas roll-cut into 1½-inch pieces in place of the apple slices. Proceed in the same manner as above.

---

4 medium-sized Delicious or Granny Smith apples
1 lemon
1 cup all-purpose flour
½ cup cornstarch
2 eggs, lightly beaten
1¼ cups ice water
8 cups peanut, safflower, or corn oil
1½ cups sugar
½ cup water
2 tablespoons untoasted sesame seeds

2½ tablespoons unflavored
   gelatin
3 cups water
¼ cup sugar
½ tablespoon almond extract
½ cup sweetened condensed
   milk
1 15-ounce can lychees in
   syrup
1 15-ounce can loquats in
   syrup
2 cups fresh fruit of choice,
   cut into balls or 1-inch
   squares
3 tablespoons kirsch
   (optional)

ALMOND BEAN CURD

XIN REN DOU FU 杏仁豆腐

During the hot and humid summers in eastern, western, and south-ern China, cold fruit salads and sweet soups garnished with fruit are popular snacks. Pineapple, mangoes, and papayas — in addition to lychees and loquats — are traditionally served in this classic salad. The milky white squares of almond curd are said to bear a resem-blance to bean curd; hence the title.

1   Soften the gelatin in ½ cup of the water. Heat the mixture slightly, stirring constantly to dissolve the gelatin. Place the sugar, almond extract, and condensed milk in a mixing bowl and stir to blend. Slowly add the remaining 2½ cups of water, stirring to dis-solve the sugar. Add the dissolved gelatin and stir again. Pour the mixture into a chilled 9-inch round or square pan. Place the pan in the refrigerator and let it chill for at least 4 hours, or until firmly set.
2   In a large bowl, combine the lychees and loquats in syrup with the fresh fruit. Add the kirsch, toss lightly, and let macerate for 1 hour in the refrigerator. Cut the almond curd into 1½-inch dia-mond-shaped pieces and carefully fold them into the fruit. Serve immediately.

2 cups dried jujubes
   (Chinese dates)
4 cups water

WALNUT JUJUBE SOUP

HE TAO LAO    合 桃 酪

Rich nut creams such as the one below have been prepared by the Chinese since the T'ang dynasty. These sweet soups are served as snacks, desserts, or as entremets in a formal banquet.

1   Soften the jujubes for 1 hour in hot water to cover, changing the water twice. Drain the jujubes and remove the pits. In a blender or a food processor fitted with the steel blade, purée the jujubes to a

paste, adding ½ cup water. Add the walnuts and cream of rice and blend until smooth, adding 1 cup of water. Transfer the mixture to a saucepan and add the remaining 2½ cups water, stirring to blend. Add the sugar and heat slowly over low heat, stirring constantly until the mixture is hot and slightly thick. Add the vanilla extract, stir to blend, and transfer the mixture to a tureen. Serve immediately.

¾ cup shelled walnuts
3 tablespoons cream of rice
5 tablespoons sugar
2 teaspoons vanilla extract

STEAMED BREAD PUDDING

PU DING

After reading the list of ingredients, one suspects that this is not a traditional Chinese recipe. The Chinese title *pu ding*, a direct transliteration from the English, further strengthens this theory. Origin aside, this steamed pudding is guaranteed to please even the most discriminating palate; it was a favorite of my Chinese sister and brothers, who often devoured it for breakfast.

1   Place the bread slices in a bowl and add hot water to cover. Let sit for 10 minutes. Drain the bread in a fine-meshed sieve. Squeeze the bread in your hands to remove as much water as possible. Place the softened bread in a bowl, and using a fork, mash it to a paste. Add the sugar, eggs, melted shortening, and vanilla extract, stirring well after each addition. Generously grease a 1½-quart ring mold with melted butter and pour the pudding mixture into the mold. Cover the mold securely with a piece of aluminum foil and place it in a steamer tray.
2   Fill a wok with water level with the bottom edge of the steamer tray and heat until boiling. Place the steamer tray over the boiling water and steam the pudding for 1 hour over high heat. Remove the mold and run a knife between the pudding and the mold. Unmold the pudding onto a platter.
3   Place the **orange sauce** in a saucepan and heat slowly until thick, stirring constantly. Pour the sauce over the pudding and serve.

SIX SERVINGS

18 slices white sandwich
  bread, crusts removed
1¼ cups sugar
6 eggs, lightly beaten
6 tablespoons melted
  shortening or butter
2 teaspoons vanilla extract

Orange Sauce
1½ cups freshly squeezed
  orange juice
¼ cup sugar
2 tablespoons Grand Marnier
1½ tablespoons cornstarch

1 cup all-purpose flour
1 teaspoon ground
  cinnamon
1 teaspoon salt
1 cup ice water
2 eggs, lightly beaten
1 teaspoon vanilla extract
1 tablespoon melted lard or
  butter

Adhesive
2 tablespoons all-purpose
  flour
¼ cup water

1½ cups red bean paste,
  homemade (see next page)
  or canned
2 cups peanut, safflower, or
  corn oil

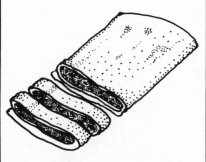

FRIED RED BEAN PASTE CRÊPES

326

FRIED RED BEAN PASTE CRÊPES

DOU SHA GUO BING　　豆沙窩餅

Red bean paste, a filling used in many Chinese sweets, is available in cans in most Chinese grocery stores. I much prefer to make it myself, however, because the flavor is far better. While Westerners unfamiliar with this condiment may be slightly skeptical, they will find that its taste is sweet and pleasantly rich. Azuki beans, the small reddish-brown beans used to make the paste, are available (packaged in plastic bags) in most Oriental markets.

1　Place the flour, cinnamon, and salt in a mixing bowl. Slowly add the water, beating vigorously to prevent lumps from forming. Add the eggs and continue beating until the mixture is well blended. Add the vanilla extract and mix again. Cover the batter and refrigerate for 30 minutes. Blend in the melted lard or butter.
2　Heat a wok or a well-seasoned 10-inch skillet and brush with melted lard or butter. The pan is hot enough when a few drops of water sprinkled onto the surface evaporate immediately. Pour about one fourth of the batter into the pan and tilt the pan so that a thin, round 10-inch pancake is formed. Cook over medium heat until the crêpe is set and lightly golden. Remove it from the pan and let it cool with the uncooked side up. Make three more crêpes in the same manner. Stir the **adhesive** until it is a smooth paste.
3　Spread one fourth of the red bean paste in a strip 2 inches wide in the center of the uncooked side of one crêpe. The paste should come to within 1 inch of each end. Spread a bit of the adhesive on the edge of the crêpe furthest from you. Fold in the sides of the crêpe, then the edge closest to you, and finally the opposite end, to enclose the bean paste. The filled crêpe should now be a rectangle 6 inches long and 4 inches wide. Repeat for the remaining crêpes.
4　Reheat the wok, add the oil, and heat the oil to 375°. Slide two of the crêpes into the wok seam side up, and fry them on both sides over high heat until golden brown, about 2½ minutes. Remove with a handled strainer, and drain on absorbent paper. Deep-fry the remaining crêpes in the same manner. Cut the crêpes into 1-inch slices, arrange on a platter, and serve.

RED BEAN PASTE
DOU SHA

Red Bean Paste
½ pound azuki beans
¾ cup sugar
¾ cup lard or butter
2 teaspoons vanilla extract

1 Rinse the beans and discard any discolored ones. Place the beans in a bowl, add water to cover, and let the beans soak for 12 hours. Discard any that float to the surface. Drain the beans and place them in a pot with 3 cups of water. Cook over high heat until the water boils, reduce the heat to medium-low, and cook, uncovered, for 1½ hours, or until the beans are very soft and the mixture is almost dry.

2 Transfer the beans to a blender or a food processor fitted with the steel blade and chop to a smooth purée. Return the mixture to a saucepan, add the sugar and the lard or butter, and cook, stirring constantly over medium heat, until the mixture is very thick and comes away from the sides of the pan, about 20 minutes. Remove from the heat and add the vanilla extract. Let cool. Makes 3 cups.

4 eggs, at room temperature
⅔ cup sugar
2 teaspoons vanilla extract
2 teaspoons minced
    blanched orange or lemon
    peel
1 cup sifted all-purpose flour
½ teaspoon salt
¼ cup confectioners' sugar
1 cup peach preserves

STEAMED CHINESE JELLY ROLL

STEAMED CHINESE JELLY ROLL

RU YI FENG JUAN   如意鳳捲

Spongecake, a sweet relished by the Cantonese for its ethereal texture and delicate flavor, is often garnished with a number of sweet and savory toppings. In this recipe the spongecakes, after they are spread with peach preserves, are rolled into a shape that resembles the Chinese symbol for happiness.

1   Line two 12-inch bamboo steamer trays with parchment paper.
2   Break the eggs into a mixing bowl and beat vigorously until they are light and frothy. Add the sugar and continue beating (if you are using an electric beater, use the highest setting) until the mixture is thick and forms a ribbon, about 5 minutes. Add the vanilla extract and the orange or lemon peel. Lightly fold in the flour and salt. Spread half the batter evenly in a thin layer in each of the two lined steamer trays. Lightly tap the steamer trays against a hard surface to knock out any air bubbles.
3   Fill a wok with water level with the bottom edge of a steamer tray and heat until boiling. Place one of the trays over the boiling water and cover. Steam for 7 minutes over high heat, until the cake is light and springy. Turn the cake out onto a linen dishtowel that has been dusted with confectioners' sugar. Peel away the parchment paper and cover the cake with another dishtowel. Steam the other cake for 7 minutes over high heat and repeat the process with the towel. When the cakes are cool, spread the peach preserves over the cakes on the side that was toward the parchment. Roll up one of the cakes in toward the middle, so that the two rolls meet at the center. Repeat for the second cake. Wrap the cakes in a towel and let sit for 1 hour. Arrange the rolled cakes on a platter, seam sides down. Sprinkle the tops with confectioners' sugar, cut the cakes into 1-inch slices, and serve.

STEAMED CHINESE CAKE

MA LA GAO　馬 拉 糕

One is sure to find *ma la gao* on any Cantonese *dim sum* tray. Though most traditional recipes use only brown sugar as a seasoning, I prefer to add orange peel and vanilla extract for extra flavor.

1　Sift together the flour, baking powder, baking soda, and salt. Generously grease a 7-inch tube pan, making certain that it is thoroughly coated.

2　Break the eggs into a mixing bowl and beat vigorously until light and lemon-colored, about 5 minutes. Add the brown sugar and continue beating for another 3 minutes. Add the milk, vanilla extract, orange peel, and orange juice, mixing well after each addition. Alternately fold in the dry ingredients and the melted butter. Pour the batter into the greased pan, and place the pan in a steamer tray.

3　Fill a wok with water level with the bottom edge of the steamer tray and heat until boiling. Place the steamer tray over the boiling water, cover, and steam for 1 hour over high heat. (Check the water level in the wok after ½ hour. Add more boiling water if necessary.) The cake should be light and springy to the touch. Remove the pan from the steamer tray, and let the cake cool. Unmold the cake onto a platter, slice it, and serve.

SIX SERVINGS

2¼ cups all-purpose flour
2 teaspoons baking powder
½ teaspoon baking soda
1 teaspoon salt
6 eggs
1½ cups light brown sugar, tightly packed
1 cup milk
2 teaspoons vanilla extract
2 tablespoons minced blanched orange peel
Juice of 1 orange
8 tablespoons lard or butter, melted and cooled

3 cups all-purpose flour
½ tablespoon baking powder
4 eggs, lightly beaten
6 cups peanut, safflower, or
    corn oil

Caramel
1 cup sugar
½ cup honey
½ cup water
¼ teaspoon clear rice vinegar
    (optional)

1 cup raisins

FRIED NOODLES IN CARAMEL

SHA JI MA 沙其馬

These squares are often sold in Chinese grocery stores, wrapped in plastic. To my mind, the flavor of the homemade variety is infinitely better. Three tablespoons of sesame seeds may be sprinkled on top of the squares as a garnish.

1   Place the flour and baking powder in a mixing bowl and stir to combine. Add the beaten eggs and mix to form a rough dough. Turn the dough out onto a lightly floured surface and knead for about 5 minutes, until smooth. Cover the dough with a towel and let it rest for 30 minutes. Cut the dough in two. Using a rolling pin, roll out each half to a large rectangle about ⅙ inch thick. Cut the rectangle lengthwise into 2-inch strips. Cut the strips crosswise into matchstick-size shreds. Dust the shreds with flour to prevent them from sticking together. Lightly grease an 8-by-12-inch lasagna pan.
2   Heat a wok, add the oil, and heat the oil to 375°. Add a third of the shreds and deep-fry, stirring constantly until puffed and golden brown, about 5 minutes. Remove with a handled strainer, and drain on absorbent paper. Reheat the oil and deep-fry the remaining shreds in the same manner, reheating the oil between batches.
3   Place the **caramel** ingredients in a heavy wok or saucepan and slowly cook over low heat, stirring until the sugar has dissolved. Turn up the heat to medium and continue cooking, occasionally swirling the mixture in the pan, until it is a light caramel, about 310° on a candy thermometer. Add the fried noodles and the raisins. Toss so that the noodles will be coated evenly with the caramel and the raisins will be evenly distributed. Pour the mixture into the greased lasagna pan, and using the flat side of a cleaver, press the noodles into a compact rectangle. Let the mixture cool and cut it into twenty squares. Arrange them on a platter and serve.

DEEP-FRIED SESAME PUFFS

KAI KOU XIAO　　閧 口 笑

TWENTY PUFFS

2¼ cups all-purpose flour
1 teaspoon baking powder
½ teaspoon salt
4 tablespoons lard or butter
¾ cup sugar
2 eggs, lightly beaten
1 tablespoon minced
　　blanched lemon peel
1 cup untoasted sesame
　　seeds
6 cups peanut, safflower, or
　　corn oil

The literal translation of the title of this recipe is "open-mouth laughs." When these dough balls are deep-fried to a golden brown, a large crack appears in the surface of each one, creating the image of an open mouth. These amusing snacks are delightful with tea.

1　Sift together the flour, baking powder, and salt. Cream the lard or butter and the sugar for about 5 minutes, until light and lemon-colored. Add the eggs and mix to blend. Add the lemon peel and slowly mix in the sifted dry ingredients. Mix to a rough dough and turn out onto a lightly floured surface. Briefly knead to a smooth dough and form the dough into a snakelike roll. Cut the roll into twenty pieces.
2　Roll each piece into a ball and roll each ball in the sesame seeds so that the outside is completely coated.
3　Heat a wok, add the oil, and heat the oil to 350°. Add half the balls and deep-fry over medium heat, stirring constantly until the balls begin to expand and crack. Turn the heat to high and continue frying until golden brown. Remove with a handled strainer, and drain on absorbent paper. Reheat the oil, and deep-fry the remaining balls in the same manner. Arrange the sesame balls on a platter and serve immediately.

TWENTY-FOUR FILLED
COOKIES

Crust
4 cups all-purpose flour
1 tablespoon baking powder
¾ cup dried milk powder
1 teaspoon salt
3 eggs
1¼ cups sugar
¾ cup lard or butter, melted
   and cooled to room
   temperature
1 teaspoon vanilla extract

Filling
1 pound pitted chopped
   dates
½ cup lard or butter
1½ teaspoons ground
   cinnamon
2 teaspoons freshly
   squeezed lemon juice

Glaze
1 egg, lightly beaten
1 tablespoon water

½ cup pine nuts

DATE-FILLED CRISPS

ZAO NI BING 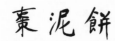 棗泥餅

Dates are a popular fruit in China and are used in sweet pastries and soups. Puréed to a smooth paste and flavored with lard and sugar, they form the filling for numerous steamed buns and pastries. Traditionally, the olive kernel, an oval seed that is the innermost pit of the black canarium, is used as a garnish in this recipe, but since it is not widely available in the United States, I have substituted pine nuts.

1   To make the **crust**, sift together the flour, baking powder, dried milk powder, and salt. Break the eggs into a mixing bowl, add the sugar, and beat vigorously until a ribbon is formed, about 5 minutes. Add the melted shortening, vanilla extract, and the sifted dry ingredients to the egg mixture, folding after each addition. Mix to a rough dough, turn out onto a lightly floured surface, and knead briefly to a smooth dough. Form the dough into a long snakelike roll and cut it into twenty-four pieces.
2   To make the **filling**, place the dates in a saucepan with 4 cups of hot water. Heat until boiling and reduce the heat to low. Let the mixture simmer for about 15 minutes, stirring occasionally, until the water has evaporated. Continue cooking and stirring until the paste is thick and sticky. Add the lard or butter and continue cooking, stirring constantly until the mixture comes away from the sides of the pan. Remove from the heat and add the cinnamon and lemon juice. Stir to blend, and let cool. Divide into twenty-four portions.
3   Press each dough piece into a 3-inch circle with the edges thinner and the center thicker. Place a portion of the filling in the center of one circle and gather up the edges of the dough to enclose the filling. Pinch the edges to seal. Roll the filled dough into a ball and flatten it to a 2½-inch round. Make the remaining cookies in the same manner. Arrange the cookies on two lightly greased baking sheets, spacing them about 1 inch apart. Brush the surface of each cookie with the **glaze** and sprinkle a few pine nuts in the center.
4   Preheat the oven to 375°. Bake the cookies for about 30 minutes, until golden brown. Cool and serve.

MOON CAKES

YUE BING 月餅

Although moon cakes are made with both sweet and savory fillings, the sweet variety seems to be more popular and more readily available in the United States. The eight-treasure moon cake, with its fillings of dried fruits and assorted sweetmeats, is especially relished by the Chinese. Here is my adapted version of this classic festival food. A special mold (available through the Whip and Spoon, 161 Commercial Street, P.O. Box 567, Portland, Maine 04101, or the Chinese Grocer, 209 Post Street, San Francisco, California 94108) is generally used to shape the cakes, but one may shape them by hand and simply inscribe a design on top.

1   To make the **crust** sift together the flour, baking powder, dried milk powder, and salt. Break the eggs into a mixing bowl, add the sugar, and beat vigorously until a ribbon is formed, about 5 minutes. Add the melted shortening, vanilla extract, and the sifted dry ingredients to the egg mixture, folding after each addition. Mix to a rough dough, turn out onto a lightly floured surface, and knead briefly to a smooth dough. Form the dough into a long snakelike roll and cut it into twenty-four pieces.

2   Assemble the **filling** and stir to combine evenly. Divide the filling into twenty-four portions.

3   Preheat the oven to 375° and lightly grease two baking sheets. Using your fingers, press each dough piece into a 3-inch circle with the edges thinner and the center thicker. Place a portion of filling in the center, gather up the edges of the dough circle to enclose the filling, and pinch the edges to seal. Roll the cake into a ball and flatten it to a 3-inch round. Carve a decorative design on top, or press the cake, seam side up, into a lightly floured moon cake press and invert it onto the baking sheet. Arrange the cakes about 1 inch apart on the baking sheets. Brush the surface with the **glaze**. Bake the cakes for about 30 minutes, until golden brown. Cool and serve.

TWENTY-FOUR MOON CAKES

Crust

4 cups all-purpose flour
1 tablespoon baking powder
¾ cup dried milk powder
1 teaspoon salt
3 eggs
1¼ cups sugar
¾ cup shortening or butter, melted and cooled to room temperature
1½ teaspoons vanilla extract

Filling

1 cup chopped pitted dates
½ cup sweetened flaked coconut
1 cup coarsely chopped walnuts or pecans
1 cup apricot preserves
½ cup raisins

Glaze

1 egg, lightly beaten
2 tablespoons water

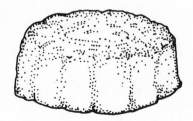

MOON CAKE

Crust
1 cup all-purpose flour
1 cup cake flour
½ cup lard or butter, cut into
    tablespoon-size pieces
1 egg, lightly beaten
¼ cup sugar
2 to 4 tablespoons ice water

Filling
¾ cup sugar
3 egg yolks
2 whole eggs
1 cup half-and-half
½ cup heavy cream
2 teaspoons vanilla extract

CUSTARD TARTLETS

DAN TA

The number of *dim sum* dishes prepared by the Cantonese is impressive. Sweet and savory pastries, dumplings, breads, and noodles all are included in this extensive category of snacks. There is no finer example of *dim sum* than the sweet tartlets below, and their flaky crust and creamy custard filling make them a superb snack with tea. In the traditional recipe, lard is used in the crust and the custard is made simply with egg yolks and water. This is my adapted version.

1   To make the **crust**, sift together the two flours and place them in a bowl. Add the lard or butter and cut it into the flour until the mixture resembles cornmeal. Add the egg and sugar. Stir to combine, and slowly add the ice water. Mix to a rough dough and turn out onto a lightly floured surface. Mix the dough briefly until somewhat smooth. Cover with plastic wrap and refrigerate for 1 hour.
2   To make the **filling**, place the sugar, egg yolks, and eggs in a mixing bowl. Whisk lightly until the sugar is dissolved. Add the half-and-half, cream, and vanilla extract and mix well.
3   Form the dough into a long snakelike roll about 2 inches in diameter, and cut it into twenty-four pieces. Using your fingers, press each piece into a 3-inch circle and fit it into a 2½-inch tartlet tin. Refrigerate the crusts for 30 minutes. Arrange the tartlets on a baking sheet and fill each shell with the custard mixture.
4   Preheat the oven to 325°. Bake the tartlets in the lower third of the oven for 30 minutes, or until a needle inserted into the custard comes out clean. Let the tartlets cool for 10 minutes; then remove them from their tins and place on a cake rack to cool further. Serve at room temperature.

WALNUT COOKIES

HE TAO BING 合桃餅

Like almonds, walnuts appear in both sweet and savory dishes. First introduced from the West during the T'ang dynasty, they are particularly popular in the south, where these cookies originated. The crisp wafers are excellent with tea.

1   Sift together the flour, salt, and baking soda. In a bowl, cream the lard, shortening, and brown sugar until light, about 5 minutes. Add the eggs and mix until they are evenly incorporated. Add the dry ingredients and the vanilla extract. Using a wooden spoon, mix to a smooth dough.
2   Drop the dough, by heaping tablespoonfuls, onto a greased cookie sheet. Dip your thumb in flour, and make an indentation in the center of each cookie. Brush the cookies with the **glaze** and place a walnut half in each indentation.
3   Preheat the oven to 350°. Bake the cookies for 10 to 12 minutes, until puffed and golden brown. Cool and serve.

ABOUT THIRTY COOKIES

2¼ cups all-purpose flour
1 teaspoon salt
1 teaspoon baking soda
½ cup lard
½ cup shortening
1 cup light brown sugar, tightly packed
2 eggs, lightly beaten
1½ teaspoons vanilla extract

Glaze
1 egg, lightly beaten
1 tablespoon water

30 walnut halves

2 cups glutinous (sweet) rice

Rice Seasonings

2 tablespoons lard or butter
3 tablespoons sugar
1 teaspoon vanilla extract

4 slices candied orange peel
5 maraschino cherries, cut in
   half
¼ cup raisins
1¼ cups red bean paste,
   homemade (page 327) or
   canned

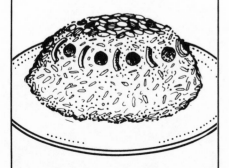

EIGHT-TREASURE RICE PUDDING

EIGHT-TREASURE RICE PUDDING

BA BAO FAN

This sweet pudding is one of the better-known confections in the repertory of Chinese sweet dishes. It is generally served at a banquet or a formal dinner for the Chinese New Year, a wedding, or any other festive occasion. The traditional sweet garnishes include red and black dates, red and green papaya shreds, preserved kumquats, and lotus seeds. I have adapted the standard recipe to use fruits that are readily available.

1   Rinse the rice in cold running water until the water runs clear. Place the rice in a bowl, add cold water to cover, and let sit for about 2 hours. Drain the rice and place it in a saucepan with 2 cups of water. Cook over high heat until the water boils, reduce the heat to low, cover, and cook for 20 minutes, until craters appear in the surface of the rice. Remove from the heat and let sit, covered, for 10 minutes. Add the **rice seasonings** and mix to blend evenly.
2   Lightly grease a heat-proof bowl that is 7 inches in diameter and 3 inches high. Cut the candied orange peel into small triangles. Arrange the raisins in the center of the bowl and alternately place the candied orange peel and the maraschino cherry halves around the raisins in a decorative pattern. Spread half the glutinous rice in the bottom of the bowl, being careful not to dislodge the decorative pattern. Pat the rice down firmly and make a depression in the middle. Add the red bean paste and spread it evenly over the rice. Pack the remaining rice on top, spreading it evenly. Smooth the surface of the rice with the underside of a spoon dipped in water. Place the bowl in a steamer tray.
3   Fill a wok with water level with the bottom edge of the steamer tray and heat until boiling. Place the steamer tray over the boiling water, cover, and steam for 1 hour over high heat. (Check the water level after ½ hour and add additional boiling water if necessary.) Remove the rice pudding, invert it onto a platter, and serve immediately. To reheat, steam for 15 minutes over high heat.

METRIC
CONVERSIONS

INDEX

METRIC CONVERSIONS

GENERAL CONVERSIONS

	AMERICAN	BRITISH	METRIC
WEIGHT	1 ounce	1 ounce	28.4 grams
	1 pound	1 pound	454 grams

	AMERICAN	BRITISH	METRIC
VOLUME	1 U.S. teaspoon	1 U.K. level teaspoon	5 milliliters
	1 U.S. tablespoon (3 teaspoons)	1 U.K. dessertspoon	15 milliliters
	1 U.S. cup (16 tablespoons)	⅚ breakfast cup (8 fluid ounces)	236 milliliters (about ¼ liter)
	1 U.S. quart (4 cups)	⅚ Imperial quart	1 scant liter
	1 U.S. gallon (4 quarts)	⅚ Imperial gallon	3¾ liters

	AMERICAN	BRITISH	METRIC
LENGTH	1 inch	1 inch	2½ centimeters (25 millimeters)
	12 inches (1 foot)	12 inches (1 foot)	30 centimeters

Note: All conversions are approximate. They have been rounded off to the nearest convenient measure.

SELECTED MEASUREMENTS

	AMERICAN (SPOONS AND CUPS)	BRITISH (OUNCES AND POUNDS)	METRIC
FLOUR (*All-purpose, unsifted*)	1 teaspoon	⅛ ounce	3 grams
	1 tablespoon	⅓ ounce	9 grams
	1 cup	4¼ ounces	120 grams
	3⅔ cups	1 pound	454 grams
HERBS (*Fresh, chopped*)	1 tablespoon	½ ounce	15 grams
MEATS (*Cooked and finely chopped*)	1 cup	8 ounces	225 grams
RICE (*Raw*)	1 cup	7½ ounces	215 grams
SEASONINGS: scallions, garlic, gingerroot (*Chopped, sliced, or minced*)	1 tablespoon	⅓ ounce	9 grams
	1 cup	5 ounces	140 grams
SPINACH AND LEAFY VEGETABLES (*Fresh, cooked*)	1¼ pounds, raw = 1 cup, cooked (squeezed dry, chopped)	1¼ pounds, raw	550 grams, raw
SUGAR (*Regular granulated or superfine granulated*)	1 teaspoon	⅙ ounce	5 grams
	1 tablespoon	½ ounce	15 grams
	1 cup	6½ ounces	185 grams
VEGETABLES (*Raw—chopped fine, such as carrots or celery*)	1 cup	8 ounces	225 grams

A Note to the User: All conversions are approximate. The weights have been rounded off to the nearest useful measure. Weights and measures of specific ingredients may vary with altitude, humidity, variations in method of preparation, etc.

OVEN TEMPERATURES

FAHRENHEIT	CENTIGRADE	BRITISH REGULO SETTING	FRENCH SETTING
212°F	100°C		1
225°F	107°C	¼	2
250°F	121°C	½	3
275°F	135°C	1	3
300°F	149°C	2	4
325°F	163°C	3	4
350°F	177°C	4	4
375°F	191°C	5	5
400°F	204°C	6	5
425°F	218°C	7	6
450°F	232°C	8	6
475°F	246°C	8	6
500°F	260°C	9	7
525°F	274°C	9	8
550°F	288°C	9	9

INDEX

Carol Wood's design for this book was
inspired by a geometrical grid system of
modular blocks used in classic Oriental
design. Ms. Wood works as a multi-
media art director and graphic designer
and currently lives in Los Angeles.